Nietzsche's Epic of the Soul

Nietzsche's Epic of the Soul

Thus Spoke Zarathustra

T. K. Seung

LEXINGTON BOOKS
Lanham • Boulder • New York • Toronto • Oxford

LEXINGTON BOOKS

A division of Rowman & Littlefield Publishers, Inc.
A wholly owned subsidiary of The Rowman & Littlefield Publishing Group, Inc.
4501 Forbes Boulevard, Suite 200
Lanham, MD 20706

PO Box 317
Oxford
OX2 9RU, UK

British Library Cataloguing in Publication Information Available

Library of Congress Cataloging-in-Publication Data

Seung, T. K., 1930–
  Nietzsche's epic of the soul : Thus spoke Zarathustra / T. K. Seung.
    p. cm.
  Includes bibliographical references (p.   ) and index.
  ISBN 0-7391-1129-9 (cloth : alk. paper)—ISBN 0-7391-1130-2 (pbk. : alk. paper)
  1. Nietzsche, Friedrich Wilhelm, 1844–1900. Also sprach Zarathustra. 2. Superman
(Philosophical concept) 3. Philosophy. I. Title.
B3313.A44S48 2005
193—dc22   2005006553

Printed in the United States of America

For my lovely grandchild

Elyssa Naeun Kim

Contents

Preface

Thus Spoke Zarathustra is Nietzsche's most enigmatic work. It has posed enormous difficulties for interpretation. We cannot even be sure what kind of book it is supposed to be. On the surface, it looks like a collection of speeches or aphorisms. But it has been called a tragedy, a comedy, and even a parody. For any given literary work, the recognition of its genre provides the basic framework for its interpretation. But such recognition does not come easily for Nietzsche's masterpiece. This is what Robert Pippin calls the basic problem of how to read *Zarathustra*. This problem becomes immensely magnified when we try to see the thematic connection of various sections. Their succession appears to be as arbitrary and as accidental as the succession of notes in serial music. Pippin says that there is "nothing close to a standard reading of the work's intention, form, development, resolution, or lack of resolution." This gloomy view is resoundingly seconded by Alexander Nehamas, according to whom the single most serious problem with *Zarathustra* is "the fact that the book resists a unified reading, concealing its general structure and strategy, its overall point." He goes on to say, "Despite some efforts to read *Zarathustra* as a coherent whole, most of Nietzsche's readers still only dip into the book here and there, dazzled by its brilliant parts and passing over the rest in silence." This is surely not a satisfactory response to what Nietzsche regarded as his most profound gift to humankind. In this book, I propose to remedy this situation by disclosing the thematic unity of Nietzsche's mysterious work.

By and large, this work has been read as a collection of philosophical speeches that Zarathustra gives for the edification of his audience. But it is impossible to find a coherent development of philosophical ideas in the sequence of those speeches. Such a development is mercilessly disrupted by the frequent intrusion of those sections that contain no philosophical ideas. The most notable example is Part IV of *Thus Spoke Zarathustra*. It reads like a burlesque. Many commentators try to cope with this anomaly by severing it from the first three Parts and treating it as an unwelcome and embarrassing addition. Even those who do not outright disown Part IV regard the first three Parts as *Zarathustra* proper and the last Part as a comic relief from the serious discussion in the first three Parts. The sequence of these two segments is supposedly modeled after the sequence of high tragedy and humorous satyr play in the ancient Greek theater. They have tried to justify this interpretive measure on the ground that Part IV was privately circulated after the official publication of the first three Parts.

Unfortunately, the severance of Part IV does not solve the problem. Even Part III contains too many sections extraneous for the exposition of philosophical ideas. Its last section, "The Seven Seals", presents no philosophical aphorisms. It is a song of seven stanzas, each of which ends by expressing Zarathustra's ardent love for Eternity. The preceding section, "The Other Dancing Song", is equally extraneous to philosophical exposition. It records Zarathustra's game of love with Life. These two sections of Part III are concerned with his existential problem rather than any philosophical message. So are the two sections before "The Other Dancing Song". "The Convalescent" chronicles Zarathustra's seven-day ordeal with a monster from the abyss, and "On the Great Longing" describes the deep melancholy of his soul and foretells her future redeemer. Thus the last four sections of Part III recount a sequence of momentous events that overtake him as an existential subject. But his existential agony is not contained completely within these last four sections of Part III. It is already poignantly expressed in the three songs, "The Night Song", "The Dancing Song", and "The Tomb Song" of Part II. Even if all these existential passages are excised, there is still one more remaining problem. Zarathustra's philosophical message is internally incoherent. In Part I, he advocates the creative will. But the ground of creativity is eradicated by his vision of eternal recurrence in Part III, which reduces all human beings to helpless puppets. Whatever they do will be the repetition of what they have done countless times in the previous revolutions of the eternal ring.

There is no way to secure the thematic coherence of *Zarathustra* by reading it as a collection of philosophical speeches. Those speeches are so perplexing and so incoherent that many sensible but cautious scholars have wisely kept themselves away from this thicket of confusing ideas and conflicting themes. But I dare propose a new way to unravel this thematic tangle. This is to focus on the work's existential overtone and read it as a poem that features Zarathustra as a tragic hero. Nietzsche had this in mind in his reference to *Thus Spoke Zarathustra* as a tragedy in *The Gay Science* 342. But it is not like the Greek tragedy, which brings about the devastating destruction of a tragic hero. Nietzsche's work is a tragedy in the same sense as Goethe's *Faust* is. When Goethe calls this play a tragedy, he only means that it is concerned with a serious theme rather than a lighthearted one. This is the meaning Nietzsche gives to the word "tragedy" in his discussion on the alternation of the age of comedy with the age of tragedy in the opening section of *The Gay Science*. The tragic hero Zarathustra is redeemed just as Goethe's hero Faust is saved by the end of the play. Hence it is less misleading to call these two works epics rather than tragedies. So I want to classify Nietzsche's long poem as an epic. This is the framework for my poetic interpretation of *Zarathustra*.

My project is to establish and articulate the epic unity of Nietzsche's poem. My first step is to identify and elucidate the main thematic ideas of the book. I have identified two such ideas: the concept of a sovereign individual and the concept of a deterministic universe. By "the sovereign individual" I mean an individual who recognizes no authority higher than his or her own. This is the watershed between modern and pre-modern political philosophy. In ancient Greece and medieval Europe, it was not the individuals, but the state or the community that was assumed to have sovereignty. But modern political philosophy began with the premise that sovereignty belongs only to the individuals as their inalienable right and that the state is formed by the consent of these sovereign individuals. Implicitly or explicitly, all contractarians—Hobbes, Locke, Rousseau, Hume, and Kant—have accepted the sovereignty of individuals as the basic premise for their theories of the state. In *Thus Spoke Zarathustra*, individual sovereignty covers a much broader scope than the political arena. It commands all phases of human existence. It is the sort of sovereignty that used to be attributed only to God and never to any human beings. Such a sovereign individual is called the superman because he or she transcends the limits of humanity.

I have traced the genesis of this ideal. It originated with the followers of Martin Luther during the Reformation and became secularized in the hand of Herder. Goethe's portrayal of Faust was his poetic rendition of this superhuman ideal, and Richard Wagner gave his own version in the superhero Siegfried of *The Ring of the Nibelung*. Shelley's *Prometheus Unbound* was still another poetic rendition of the superhuman hero, who dares to replace the old God and take over the new world. The defiant Prometheus was a favorite theme among the Romantic poets, beginning with Goethe's poem "Prometheus". In his initial plan for *Thus Spoke Zarathustra* shortly after his inspiration from the rock of Surlei, Nietzsche also thought of installing Prometheus as his superhuman hero. Alongside this literary line of development, the superhuman ideal was also elaborated by the Young Hegelians, especially Ludwig Feuerbach, Bruno Bauer, and Max Stirner. The long tradition of striving for the superhuman ideal evolved in the confluence of philosophy and literature, or rather in the vortex of Faustian ethos. In short, the superman was not Nietzsche's invention, although it has been received as such by many. What is new with him is his attempt to situate the Faustian hero in the ring of eternal recurrence.

The eternal recurrence has been the most controversial topic in Nietzsche scholarship that has brought forth an endless series of disputes and commentaries. But I will show that this strange notion may be no more than a poetic device for elucidating the agony of individuals caught in the iron mesh of a deterministic universe. The concept of a deterministic universe is a legacy of modern science from Galileo and Newton to Laplace and Einstein. It goes against the notion of a sovereign individual who wants to impose his will on the world. In a deterministic universe, all human beings are only puppets; all their actions are predetermined by the causal mechanism. Such a helpless condition and predicament of human beings are dramatically portrayed by the metaphor of eternal recurrence. In the ring of eternal recurrence, everything is predetermined for eternity. Such a deterministic universe and its resultant agony are already stated in "On Redemption" of Part II, well before the official announcement of eternal recurrence in "On the Vision and the Riddle" of Part III. A deterministic universe is like an eternal ring because it has no open future of new possibilities.

A deterministic universe, whether it is Newtonian or Einsteinian, can be viewed from two perspectives. From the temporal perspective, it is subject to change. From the eternal perspective, however, it contains no change because everything in it can be viewed as eternally present. Likewise, the eternal recurrence can be viewed from two perspectives. When it is viewed from the eternal perspective, it is called the eternal ring or the well of eternity and the word "recurrence" is not even mentioned. That is the way the eternal ring is described in "The Drunken Song" of Part IV. Nothing occurs or recurs in the eternal perspective; the concept of occurrence or recurrence belongs to the temporal perspective. In "On the Vision and the Riddle", the eternal recurrence is described in the imagery of temporality such as the gateway and the time lines. I have stressed these two perspectives for understanding the thematic function of eternal recurrence in *Thus Spoke Zarathustra*. These two perspectives can be captured in the poetic metaphor of eternal recurrence. A great number of commentators have pointed out the absurdity of taking the doctrine of eternal recurrence in its literal sense. If it is indeed naïve and ludicrous to take it literally, the only sensible alternative may well be to take it metaphorically. This is my reason for reading the eternal recurrence as a poetic metaphor for the deterministic and eternal universe.

The dual perspective of nature was an important legacy from Spinoza. In his metaphysics, the ultimate reality can be viewed from the temporal or the eternal perspective. It is called God when it is viewed from the eternal perspective. It is called Nature when it is viewed from the temporal perspective. Spinoza is the father of modern European naturalism: Nature is the all-embracing reality, the infinite substance, whose existence is eternal and necessary. This conception of Nature goes against the traditional theistic doctrine that its existence is contingent on God's creation. Nothing can be left outside the eternal reality of Nature. Such an absolutely self-embracing reality can best be described by the poetic image of an eternal ring. From the eternal perspective, everything is eternally present in Spinoza's universe, too, because it is deterministic. His metaphysics was the fountainhead of determinism for modern European philosophy. The problem of being trapped in the inexorable web of causal chains was again Spinoza's central concern. He wrestled with the difficult task of coping with the sorrow and joy of human existence embedded in the deterministic universe. But he was not a pessimist. On the contrary, he advocated the mystery of intellectual intuition, by which human sufferings could be turned into active joys and become intellectual love of God or Nature. He located the suffering of finite creatures in their alienation from the infinite substance, Mother Nature. By intellectual intuition, he believed, we can gain a direct vision of the infinite substance as a system of divine ideas that can secure our perfect union with Mother Nature and thereby transform the woe of alienation into the joy of reconciliation. All these ideas of Spinoza became the basic materials for the composition of Nietzsche's *Zarathustra*. No wonder, Nietzsche confessed to Overbeck that he was amazed to find a wonderful precursor for many of his thoughts in Spinoza.

These two thematic ideas of *Zarathustra*, namely, the sovereign individual and the deterministic universe, are the two central ideas that have governed the development of modern European culture. As long as these two ideas are kept apart from each other, there is no problem. But they generate an intractable problem when they are placed together. How can the individual be a creative master in the deterministic world? This problem originated in medieval Christian theology as the problem of free will against predestination. Before his fall, did Adam have free will? Did God know what choice Adam would make before his fall? Most medieval theologians from Augustine to Aquinas had no choice but to give affirmative answers to these two questions. They had to give the affirmative answer to the first question because they believed that Adam had free will before his fall. They had to give the same affirmative answer to the second question because they believed in divine omniscience. But the second affirmative answer entails that whatever Adam will do is predetermined, which goes against his presumed freedom of choice. This was the most critical issue for medieval Christianity, which the theologians had to consign to their religious mystery because they could not resolve it. But it was taken out of the mystery chest for an open debate by such audacious figures as Erasmus (for free will) and Luther (for predestination), when the Europeans gained a heightened consciousness of their individual power and dignity during the Renaissance and the Reformation.

In modern Europe, this theological problem was reformulated in terms of natural science. Given that everything in the world is determined by the causal laws of nature, how is the autonomous will possible? In this secular version, the problem of free will and determinism became much more stringent and pervasive than in its medieval version. Whereas the latter had restricted the scope of dispute to the religious matters of salvation, the former expanded it to all other phases of human life. In this expanded version, the problem of free will became the biggest stumbling block for all major philosophers of modern Europe from Leibniz and Spinoza to Hegel and Schopenhauer. Whereas these philosophers have tried to settle this problem theoretically, Nietzsche turns it into an existential problem to be resolved by his epic hero Zarathustra. As a metaphysical problem, as Kant says, the conflict between free will and determinism may indeed be impossible to resolve. In the existential domain, however, we can still act on the postulate of freedom or determinism, that is, the assumption that our actions are free or that they are causally determined. Though the ideas of freedom and determinism are metaphysically intractable, they may be not only practically useful but also existentially indispensable. For these metaphysical ideas are the essential features of human existence. Nietzsche employs the existential dialectic of those ideas for mapping out Zarathustra's epic journey. This is the premise for my epic reading of Nietzsche's philosophical poem.

The conventional interpretation of *Zarathustra* may be called the tripartite reading: Only the first three Parts are assumed to be important for its thematic development and the last Part is regarded as a gratuitous addition. But I advocate a quadripartite reading: All four Parts are equally indispensable. The last Part is especially important because it provides the denouement of the suspense that has been built up in the first three Parts. In the tripartite reading, there is a long tradition of exalting the ending of Part III, "The Seven Seals", as the real coda of Nietzsche's entire poem. R. J. Hollingdale says that the glowing conclusion of Part III is the book's true climax. Laurence Lampert believes that Zarathustra concludes his marriage with Eternity and achieves happiness in "The Seven Seals" of Part III. But these readings willfully and wishfully go against the text. The alleged marriage never takes place in "The Seven Seals". Each of the seven stanzas in this section ends by repeating the same passionate expression of love: "For I love you, O Eternity!" But this passionate expression cannot be the celebration of Zarathustra's love fulfilled. If it were, Eternity should be there with him for the celebration. But Eternity is nowhere in sight to respond to Zarathustra's passionate call. In "The Seven Seals", he is still desperately seeking the fulfillment of his love. I textually demonstrate that the seven stanzas are meant to explain why his love is perpetually frustrated in the temporal world.

"The Seven Seals" only restates the agony of unfulfilled love and longing that Zarathustra experienced in "On the Great Longing" of Part III. For this reason, Heidegger locates the climax of the book in "On the Great Longing" rather than in "The Seven Seals". Because his passionate longing is perpetually frustrated, as we will see later in this book, Zarathustra reorients his love from the temporal to the eternal mode in the next section, "The Other Dancing Song" of Part IV. This reorientation of his love is meticulously marked by concluding this section with Zarathustra's roundelay, the prophecy of Life that his love will be fulfilled in the eternal domain. The roundelay ends with the line: "But all joy wants Eternity." This is the first time Eternity is mentioned as the object of joy and love in the whole book. Seven times in "The Seven Seals", the same love and longing for Eternity will be expressed by the phrase "For I love you, O Eternity!" To the end of Part III, however, Eternity will remain as the object of aspiration rather than possession. In "The

Seven Seals", Zarathustra's frustrated love is exposed like an open wound, and he is moaning and panting over its bleeding. There is no way to bind this open wound and heal it without writing Part IV.

There is still another reason for writing Part IV. The central crisis of the book is not resolved, either, by the end of Part III. What is the nature of this crisis? When and where does the central crisis take place? It takes place when Zarathustra is clobbered by his most abysmal thought, a monster summoned from the abyss, in "The Convalescent" of Part III. He is so stricken that he cannot eat or drink for seven days. Who is this monster? It is as monstrous as the ancient monsters such as centaurs and satyrs. This monster is the combination of an animal and a human being, namely, a snake and a dwarf, the spirit of gravity. The dwarf and the snake are the interchangeable symbols of chthonic forces emanating from Life at the center of the earth. In one singular instance, these two symbols are fused into one image of a monster that clobbers Zarathustra in "The Convalescent". The meaning of these chthonic symbols is most critical for understanding the central theme of the whole book because this work is, above all, a relentless probe into the secret of Life and her will to power. Only for those who can recognize the critical function of those symbols, I dare say, the plotline of *Thus Spoke Zarathustra* will begin to unfold itself. For those chthonic symbols generate the power that propels the thematic progression of the entire work.

The dwarf is the small man, whose eternal recurrence gives Zarathustra "the great disgust with man" in "The Convalescent". His disgust is not restricted to any particular type of man called the small man in distinction from the great man, but extends to all human beings whether they are the smallest or the greatest. This is why his disgust is called "the great disgust with man" without any qualification. Every human being is an ugly dwarf. In that case, Zarathustra is also one of these repulsive creatures. He now realizes that the ugly dwarf is his earthly animal self, that is, his ultimate self. This self-recognition is the knowledge that chokes him. He feels revulsion not simply at the eternal recurrence or even at the eternal recurrence of the small man, but at the recognition of his own dwarfism, that is, the realization that he is only one of the countless dwarfs helplessly chained to the iron ring of eternal recurrence. This is the abysmal thought that precipitates the central crisis of the book. This is the crisis of his self-recognition. He crumbles under the shattering impact of his own newly revealed self-identity just as Oedipus Rex did on the recognition of his own identity as the killer of his own father and the husband of his mother.

Though the central crisis explodes in "The Convalescent", it does not originate there. It has been steadily building up ever since Zarathustra's terrifying discourse on the causal determination of human will in "On Redemption" of Part II. When the central crisis finally explodes in "The Convalescent", it demolishes the leonine will that Zarathustra brandished as a Faustian hero in the preceding section, "On Old and New Tablets". The decisive blow is delivered by the monster from the abyss, who embodies the overwhelming power of Mother Nature. Paradoxically, this tragic event also leads to Zarathustra's redemption. When he is crushed as the Faustian superman, he is reborn as the Spinozan superman. The notion of the superman is confusing because the Nietzsche deploys two diametrically opposed models in his epic. The Faustian superman asserts his autonomous will against the whole world; the Spinozan superman accepts cosmic necessity as his own will. The former bravely struggles to transcend all human limits; the latter wisely accepts those limits as essential features of his own being. The Spinozan superman recognizes that the autonomous will is only an illusion and that the true freedom lies in the union of human will and cosmic necessity. The Faustian superman is a Promethean lion, who is determined to shatter everything opposed to his will. But the Spinozan superman is like a child of innocence, who has no will of its own. "The Convalescent" marks the transformation of a Faustian hero into a Spinozan superhero. This transformation is Zarathustra's overcoming his old self for the sake of his new self. This is the most critical phase in his project of self-overcoming. It corresponds to the metamorphosis of a lion to a child, the final stage in his enigmatic scheme of three metamorphoses.

The Faustian superman is the individual self; the Spinozan superman is the cosmic self. But they are not two separate entities. They are two different ways of understanding one and the same self. The individual self is our normal conception of the self. It is perceived as the agent of action and the master of its autonomous will. As such an agent and master, the individual self faces the world and acts on it. The cosmic self is the cosmic conception of the self. It is understood not as an independent agent, but as a dependent component in the constitution of the whole world. Everything that happens to and in the self is determined by all the things that take place in the world. The cosmic self is a physical link in the cosmic chain of causation and interdependence. Such a physical link is the physical or animal self. Consider the consciousness of yourself as an individual. It is causally determined by your brain state, which is in turn determined by the condition of your body, which is in turn determined by the state of the solar system, which is in turn determined by the state of the cosmos. Such a cosmically determined self cannot set its desires and feelings against the world. Even its will should be understood as an extension of cosmic necessity. Hence a cosmic self is coextensive with the whole universe, and its recognition is much more elusive than the recognition of an individual self. For this reason, it takes so much trouble and so much time before Zarathustra can see through the misleading picture of his individual self and recognize his cosmic self.

When Zarathustra gains the Spinozan wisdom and recognizes his cosmic self in "The Convalescent", he claims to have achieved his redemption. But his redemption is far from perfect. His cosmic self, which he calls his soul, is still suffering from mysterious melancholy in the next section, "On the Great Longing". Although he can intellectually accept cosmic necessity, he cannot emotionally be enchanted with it. Likewise, he can accept his earthly animal self as his cosmic self, but there is no way for him to be in love with this repulsive creature. His cosmic self can be as oppressive and hideous as the natural forces that govern the world. For this reason, his helpless soul is still depressed by melancholy even after his redemption. Consequently, he desperately seeks a way to love his dwarfish earthly self in the last three sections of Part III. His strange game of love with Life in "The Other Dancing Song" of Part III portrays his earnest struggle to love his own earthly animal self. After all, this ugly animal self is an inseparable feature of Life, the personification of Mother Nature. Because Zarathustra cannot directly express his love for this ugly dwarfish self, he projects it to the mysterious domain of Life. His love of Life is his love of the dwarf, his cosmic self, in disguise. But he realizes that his love is doomed to perpetual frustration. Thus the last three sections of Part III record the agony of his perpetually frustrated love and longing. Out of this agony and frustration, Zarathustra resolves to reorient his love from the temporal to the eternal world. This is how the central crisis is linked to the problem of his unfulfilled love.

Finally in "The Drunken Song" of Part IV, he resolves the central crisis by fulfilling his long frustrated love in a mystical union with Life. This mystical event is prepared by his interaction with the higher men, which I interpret as a psychodrama for the purgation of his soul. This event is analogous to the purgation of sins in Dante's Purgatory in preparation for the flight of redeemed souls to the Empyrean. The mystical denouement of Nietzsche's epic is his appropriation of Spinoza's naturemysticism and his notion of intellectual intuition. The morning after the mystical event, Zarathustra emerges with his new radiant power like the rising sun in "The Sign". He has finally achieved a harmonious union of his individual self with his cosmic self by transforming the war between the two into love. This is his Dionysian love, the loving union between the individual and the cosmic self, because the cosmic self is Dionysian. This loving union empowers Zarathustra with Dionysian dynamism and activism because he can draw the inexhaustible power from his Dionysian self. In this regard, his mystical experience flows in the opposite direction to that of the traditional mystical experience. Whereas the latter withdraws from the turbulent world into the quiet inner peace, the former breaks out from the quiet mystical communion into the world of dynamic activities. Such a dynamic transformation is fully displayed when Zarathustra emerges as the hero of Dionysian dynamism in "The Sign" after his mystical intoxication in "The Drunken Song".

The Dionysian union of the individual self with the cosmic self is strikingly similar to the Zen Buddhist union of the individual mind with the Buddha mind and the Taoist union with the flow of Tao. But the ultimate union can never be secured by the individual will because its exertion can only intensify the rift between the individual and the cosmic self. For this reason, the Taoist sages and the Zen masters have long taught the way of *wu-wei*, the way of inaction. Instead of acting as an individual self, one should be infused with the power of the cosmic self. This infusion is the mystery of Mother Nature that transcends the power of all individuals. For Zarathustra, this mysterious infusion spells out the mystical coda of his epic journey, which is played out as quietly as the sound of a midnight bell in the last two sections of Part IV. Thus the thematic resolution of Nietzsche's epic is not given until the end of Part IV, although this Part has usually been dismissed as an absurd burlesque. In his letter of February 12, 1885 to Carl von Gersdorff, Nietzsche refers to Part IV as "a sort of sublime finale." In chapters 5 and 6 of this book, I show that Part IV is not a low comedy that it has usually been taken to be, but a sublime finale that it was designed to be by its author. This is the ultimate outcome of my interpretation.

In my interpretation, the struggle of human will against cosmic necessity is the central theme of *Thus Spoke Zarathustra*. Its four Parts lay out the four successive stages in the development of this momentous theme. Part I paints an uplifting picture of the Faustian superman and his autonomous creative will. This picture is as vibrant as the radiant sun and as a soaring eagle in the sky. Part II exposes the brutal agony of human suffering under the crushing weight of cosmic necessity. Zarathustra is terrified by his own talk on this brutal agony in "On Redemption" of Part II. Parts I and II lay out the two protagonists, human will and cosmic necessity. The two protagonists can also be described as the Faustian individual self and the Spinozan cosmic self. The conflict between these two selves is painted as Zarathustra's battle against the dwarf, his archenemy. Part III stages the ensuing battle between the two protagonists until they clash in an open conflict. This is Zarathustra's seven-day ordeal and his convalescence in "The Convalescent". Unfortunately, even the natural health he regains with the help of his animals is not sufficient for his existential need. It cannot fulfill his passionate longing for the bliss of love. His unfulfilled love is finally fulfilled in his mystical union with Eternity in "The Drunken Song" of Part IV, where his individual will is fused with the cosmic necessity of the whole universe. This is the plotline for my unified reading of Nietzsche's complicated work.

This plotline develops dialectically. Zarathustra nurtures his individual self by the assertion of his autonomous will and recognizes his cosmic self by its power over his individual self. This is the dialectical interplay between the Faustian theme of an individual self and the Spinozan theme of a cosmic self. The interplay of these existential themes constitutes the Nietzschean existential dialectic. But it cannot be resolved in a Hegelian synthesis because there is no third term that can reconcile the individual and the cosmic self. Nor can it be resolved by the Kierkegaardian decision of Either/Or, because the two protagonists are equally ineliminable and irrepressible. Even when Zarathustra's Faustian self is crushed by his Spinozan self in "The Convalescent", the former keeps coming back again and again in the remainder of Part III and in Part IV. The same is also true of his cosmic self; there is no way to eliminate cosmic necessity. Hence there is no way to resolve the conflict of the individual with the cosmic self. Their conflict is as interminable as the process of life itself. This interminable conflict is the ultimate problem for all human beings, who try to secure their selfhood in the turbulent world of Mother Nature. Zarathustra's heroic struggle to work out this formidable problem is Nietzsche's master plan for his great epic.

This master plan is spelt out in great details in the six chapters of this book, but the heart of my interpretation lies in chapters 4 and 6. Chapter 4 delineates the central crisis in Zarathustra's epic career, which develops in the last four sections of Part III. Chapter 6 articulates the resolution of this crisis, which unfolds in the last four sections of Part IV. This crisis is Zarathustra's central problem in coping with his own self and the world. In Nietzsche's philosophy, all existential problems have their roots in the matrix of self-relation. On this point, he is not a whit different from Kierkegaard. But this coincidence is not accidental. Both of them had grown up under the formative influence of the Lutheran Church. The primacy of self-relation motivates Nietzsche's repeated exhortation for the avoidance of others (the herd, the neighbor, and even the friend) and for the return to one's own self in solitude. But Zarathustra can find his real self only through a long detour of the whole world. This is his epic journey of discovering the identity of his ultimate self. In this regard, his epic struggle drastically diverges from the traditional mold, in which the hero confronts his enemies and obstacles outside himself. The Homeric heroes, Achilles and Odysseus, are the classical examples. Though they wage their courageous battles against external foes, they never face the problem of mastering their own selves, a far more formidable task than that of mastering others. This awesome task of self-mastery is Zarathustra's epic mission. His struggle against external forces eventually turns out to be his struggle against his own cosmic self. Therefore, his epic journey is the battle of self-relation.

The epic of self-relation is Nietzsche's daunting invention. Nobody has ever attempted such an inventive task before or after his *Zarathustra*. Especially unique is the nature of Nietzsche's epic hero. He is so unique that he does not fit the traditional mold of an epic hero. Sometimes he even behaves like an anti-hero. But he is too awesome to fit that model because he has the power and courage to wrestle with his cosmic self, which is embodied in the whole world. Hence it is hard to classify the Nietzschean hero by using standard labels. In chapter 6, I explore this problem by examining Nietzsche's work as a psychological epic and placing it in the long tradition of Christian epics such as Dante's *Divina Commedia,* Milton's *Paradise Lost,* and Bunyan's *Pilgrim's Progress.* These works chronicle the spiritual progress of Christian souls in a psychological landscape, and their epic journeys are sustained by the invisible power of God. Nietzsche has constructed his epic of the soul by naturalizing the Christian God. Zarathustra's epic journey is sustained by the visible power of Mother Nature; it is a secular offshoot of the long venerable tradition of Christian sacred epics. In this secular form, as we will see, Nietzsche's psychological epic reads more like the Zen fable of ox-herding on enlightenment and redemption than the Christian psychological epics. The Zen fable recounts the enormous difficulty of finding the true self just as Nietzsche's psychological epic does. Both of them are concerned with the problem of self-alienation and self-reconciliation.

Thus I have carved out a highly religious reading of Nietzsche's *Zarathustra* and this outcome is still amazing even to my own self. At the outset of my project, nothing could have been further from my mind than religious concern. Like most Nietzscheans, I was solely concerned with Nietzsche's message for the godless world. But the death of God was a religious problem and its resolution in his hand has turned out to be religious, too. A great number of Nietzscheans erroneously assume that their master has branded all religions, especially Christianity, as the gravest human decadence. Hence his ultimate aim is to eradicate Christianity from the earth altogether. But that would only lead to the secular culture that Zarathustra despises and reviles on his descent from his mountain cave. The crushing weight of secular culture has smothered all spiritual values. In "The Tomb Song" of Part II, he recalls his youthful wish that "All beings shall be divine to me" and "All days shall be holy to me." The pious Christians at least had their deep sense of piety and sanctity. The death of God is not the solution for his problem, but his most critical problem. By the end of the Prologue, he decides to launch a campaign to spiritualize the secular world by destroying old values and creating new ones. Thus he begins his epic battle for the redemption of the godless world. This epic battle is integrally linked to his heroic struggle with his own self. His spiritual campaign goes through the Faustian and the Spinozan phases, which are respectively governed by the Faustian and the Spinozan self. The agenda for the Faustian campaign is given in "On Old and New Tablets" of Part III; the agenda for the Spinozan campaign is given in "On the Higher Men" of Part IV. In these two long speeches, Zarathustra lays out his spiritual program. But he revamps the Faustian agenda in the Spinozan agenda, which is then realized in the birth of Dionysian faith.

The desecration of natural existence has not been engineered by the secular culture. Prior to the emergence of Christianity, the sanctity and eternity of Nature were assured by all primitive religions. Nothing could be more sacred than Mother Nature because she was believed to be the eternal source of all life. But Christianity degraded Nature by reducing her to a cluster of contingent material objects created by God and by relocating the ultimate source of sanctity from earth to heaven. But the death of God has completely dissolved the sense of sanctity and divinity and left Nature even more degraded than ever before because there is no one left to intervene in the molestation and exploitation of her resources in the secular world. Spinoza tried to restore the sanctity and divinity of Nature by transferring all divine attributes from the Christian God to her and by exalting her as the only Divinity. But he does not advocate religious rituals for the adoration of Mother Nature. This is the vital element missing from his scheme of restoration. Zarathustra secures this vital element by instituting a nature-religion. If Mother Nature is really divine, we should express our reverence to her through rituals and display our sense of gratitude in festivals. To have such rituals and festivals for Mother Nature is to have a nature-religion. Such a natural religion is instituted by Zarathustra's consecration of the Ass Festival in Part IV.

By the power of natural devotion, he can foster deep reverence for Mother Nature and all her creation, including his own natural existence. Thus he can cultivate his spiritual integrity and prevent the deterioration of his values to cheap secularism. He tries to achieve such a positive development not by abolishing Christianity, but by converting it from an anti-natural religion to a natural one in the Ass Festival. This natural religion is the religion of Dionysus, which is represented by the Ass-God in the Ass Festival. This startling outcome explains Nietzsche's lifelong involvement with the god of Dionysus. He began his career by plunging into the mystery of Dionysus in *The Birth of Tragedy* and expressed his allegiance to the same god time and again. At the end of *Beyond Good and Evil*, he poses himself as "the last disciple and initiate of the god Dionysus." At the end of *Twilight of the Idols*, he celebrates the Dionysian eternal life and calls himself the last disciple of the philosopher Dionysus. In the last note for *The Will to Power*, he pits the cult of Dionysus against the cult of the Crucified. He has indeed denounced those religions that negate natural life. But he has also stressed the need for a new religion of affirmation to replace the old religions of negation, as it has been pointed out by such perceptive scholars as Nishitani Keiji and Laurence Lampert. The cult of Dionysus is such an affirmative religion.

This new religion of nature is the religion above all religions. It is not the simpleminded reversion to the primitive worship of natural spirits. Nor is it a dogmatic repudiation of the anti-natural religions. On the contrary, it fully realizes the original love and reverence for Mother Nature that was expressed as the superstitious worship of local deities in primitive religions and that was misdirected toward the supernatural beings by the anti-natural religions. This new religion is for the worship of Mother Nature as the cosmic principle of Life and the goddess of all creation. This is the ultimate outcome for Zarathustra's campaign for the spiritualization of secular culture. He has found the secret power to sanctify our natural existence and redeem it from the degradation of secular humanism. Nikolai Berdyaev calls it the religious renaissance that moves the new humanity out of godless humanism to divine humanism.

In one of his letters, Nietzsche says that *Thus Spoke Zarathustra* was conceived as the fifth Gospel. In fact, many passages in this work read like the Christian Gospels in its style of exposition. But the fifth Gospel is not meant to be a mere addition to the four Gospels. It is the Gospel for the nature-religion of Dionysus. Its function is to announce a new religion to replace the religion of the New Testament just as the latter replaced the religion of the Old Testament. Nietzsche's allegiance to the god of Dionysus is not only philosophical but religious. But his avowal of the Dionysian allegiance has rarely been taken as anything more than a rhetorical flourish. It is about time to take it as a pious expression of his religious reverence for Dionysus. But the ultimate source of Nietzsche's new Gospel is not only the Greek mystery cult, but also Spinoza's natural philosophy. In ancient Greece, Dionysus was only one of the many deities. But Zarathustra's Dionysus is Mother Nature, whom Spinoza exalts as the only Divinity. This Spinozan conception of Nature and God is the direct source of inspiration for Nietzsche's nature-religion and for his composition of its Gospel. Hence *Thus Spoke Zarathustra* is a special epic that also serves as a gospel at the same time. This gospel and epic is addressed to all those who are struggling, in despair and yet with courage, to restore the sanctity and dignity of their precarious selfhood under the crushing weight of secular culture.

In the course of planning and writing this book, I have received gracious help from many friends and scholars. Although I cannot name all of them, I want to express my gratitude to some of them. My project began with the inspiration from Joan Stambaugh's effort to find a few elusive mystical passages in *Thus Spoke Zarathustra*. Because this courageous approach went against the mainstream of Nietzsche scholarship, she designated the mystical Nietzsche as the other Nietzsche. In this book, I have tried to reveal her other Nietzsche as really the central Nietzsche in *Zarathustra* by firmly linking his mysticism to Spinoza's pantheism. Chul Bum Lee went over every draft of my manuscript. Kathleen Higgins read the first draft of my manuscript and commented almost on every page. She drew my attention to the importance of Carl Jung's work on *Thus Spoke Zarathustra*. I consulted her before anyone else on almost every textual problem in this work. Greg Whitlock also read the first draft and sent me many incisive comments. He opened my eyes to the critical influence of Ludwig Feuerbach on Nietzsche and Wagner. I had frequent talks with Edwin Allaire on Spinoza. In the summer of 2003, Sharon Vaughan read through the second draft of the manuscript and gave me many useful comments for the third draft. For my discussion of Nietzsche's view on nature-religion, I relied on my frequent talks with Aloysius Martinich and his unpublished lecture notes. On medieval theology, I consulted Ernest Kaulbach. On the Old and the New Testaments, Michael White was my patient guide. Martha Newman acquainted me with the historical background of the Ass Festival. Walter Wetzels resolved my numerous questions on German language and literature. On Hinduism and Buddhism, I had frequent discussions with Stephen Phillips. On Greek religion and philosophy, I relied on a formidable array of instructors: David Armstrong, Erwin Cook, John Kroll, Alexander Mourelatos, and Paul Woodruff. Thomas Denton guided me on many stylistic questions. I am finally grateful to our departmental Chair Nicholas Asher and Richard Lariviere, the dean of our college, for the Dean's Fellowship of The University of Texas at Austin, which allowed me to write the first draft of this book without any distraction during the fall semester of 2002.

Abbreviations

A *Anti-Christ* in *Twilight of the Idols* and *The Anti-Christ* (London: Penguin, 1968). Translated by R. J. Hollingdale.

BGE *Beyond Good and Evil* (Cambridge: University Press, 2002). Translated by Judith Norman.

BT *The Birth of Tragedy and Other Writings* (Cambridge, University Press, 1999). Translated by Ronald Speirs.

D *Daybreak* (Cambridge: University Press, 1997). Translated by R. J. Hollingdale.

EH *Ecce Homo* (London: Penguin Books, 1979). Translated by R. J. Hollingdale.

GS *The Gay Science* (Cambridge: University Press, 2001). Translated by Josephine Nauchhoff.

GM *On the Genealogy of Morals* (Oxford: University Press, 1996). Translated by Douglas Smith.

HH *Human, All Too Human: A Book for Free Spirits* (Cambridge: University Press, 1986). Translated by R. J. Hollingdale.

TI *Twilight of the Idols* in *Twilight of the Idols* and *The Anti-Christ* (London: Penguin, 1968). Translated by R. J. Hollingdale.

WP *The Will to Power* (New York: Random House, 1967). Translated by Walter Kaufmann and R. J. Hollingdale.

Z *Thus Spoke Zarathustra: A Book for All and None* (New York: Penguin Books, 1978). Translated by Walter Kaufmann. The direct quotations from this edition are indicated by the reference notes, which begin with Z and show the page number, e.g., (Z, 24). Occasionally, I refer to two other English translations. R. J. Hollingdale's (London: Penguin Books, 1969). Thomas Common's (New York: Random House, 1905?). The latter is an unusually literal translation of the original text.

CHAPTER ONE

The Superman

(Prologue and Part I)

In the Prologue, Zarathustra descends from his mountain cave to distribute his wisdom, which he has gathered like the honey of a bee for ten years. On his way down to the human world, he meets an old hermit, who had seen Zarathustra on his way up to the mountain ten years ago. Recognizing Zarathustra after all those years, the old hermit says, "At that time you carried your ashes to the mountains; would you now carry your fire into the valleys?" (Z, 10). Prior to his ascent to the mountain, Zarathustra's fire must have gone out and he must have rekindled the fire during the past ten years in the cave. The old hermit seems to detect the rekindled fire in Zarathustra's new appearance: His eyes are pure, his mouth hides no disgust, and he walks like a dancer. The hermit says that Zarathustra has become a child and an awakened one and assumes that the awakened one is now on his way to wake up the sleepers (Prol. 2). The hermit warns Zarathustra against going to the people, but the latter replies, "I love human beings." The hermit has already tried to love human beings only to find that they are not worthy of his love. He says that he now loves only God because love of human beings would kill him. In response, Zarathustra says that he is bringing them a gift. The hermit tells him to give them only alms. Zarathustra replies that his gift has nothing to do with alms. The hermit finally laughs at Zarathustra's stubbornness and advises him to live like himself, that is, like a bear among bears and a bird among birds and making songs in praise of God. Only then Zarathustra realizes that this old hermit has not yet heard anything of the great news that God is dead. The death of God is old news for Zarathustra. God was his old fire that had gone out more than ten years ago.

When Zarathustra reaches the next town, many people are gathered in the market place to watch a tightrope walker, who is scheduled to perform later. He makes three speeches to the market crowd. The first speech is on the superman, the second one on man, and the last one on the last man. He opens the first speech by saying, "*I teach you the superman.*" He tells his audience that man is only a bridge from beasts to the superman. This is the theme of his second speech. Human beings should never be content with merely being human because to be a human being is not much better than a worm or an ape. Hence they should move beyond humanity. This is to overcome man by rising above the limits of humanity and create something superhuman. That is the meaning of 'the superman'. He is not exhorting the crowd to live up to some lofty human ideals and achieve human perfection. He is hoisting a superhuman ideal for their aspiration. He tries to justify the superhuman ideal by invoking a cosmic principle of creative evolution: "All things so far have created something beyond themselves" (Z, 12). All species of animals, whether worms, apes, or humans, are meant to be not the end points, but only the transitory passages to ever higher and higher beings. This cosmic principle of evolution is not Darwinian. The Darwinian evolution does not move from the lower to the higher forms of life because there is no such distinction in the forms of life. It is no more than a process of mutation, which produces just another form of life, neither better nor worse than the previous one. And it takes place by accident, not by any aspiration. But Zarathustra does not advocate such an accidental view of evolution. He takes it as a matter of the will. He tells his audience, "Let your will say: the superman shall be the meaning of the earth" (Prol. 3). This is the message he wants to give to humankind, who are moving from theistic to post-theistic culture. In the old theistic culture, God gave meaning to the earthly existence. Now that God is dead, he says, man must become the superman and create the new meaning of the earth.

The superhuman ideal directly leads to Zarathustra's contempt of modern humanity, whose condition he denounces as "poverty and filth and wretched contentment." His contempt culminates in his derision of the last man. This is the theme of his third and final speech. The last man is the ideal that captivates the secular culture of modern humanity. The last man is the counter-ideal to the superman. The former is projected as the ultimate end of human progress; the latter is conceived as the ultimate end of superhuman achievement. Whereas the superhuman ideal demands the strenuous struggle to overcome the limits of humanity, the human ideal dictates the creation of happiness and comfort for human beings. Trapped in their nest of modern comfort, the market crowd shows no sign of spiritual vitality to break out of the limits of humanity. Zarathustra tries to wake them out of their spiritual slumber by ridiculing the last man and exhorting them to aspire for the superman. Their secular culture is disgusting to him because he is holding up his superhuman standard against them. In that regard, he shares a common ground with the hermit, the lone relic from the old religious ethos. He still worships God. But God is dead for both Zarathustra and the townsfolk; they represent the secular ethos. The townsfolk are relatively happy in their secular natural life. But Zarathustra finds their happiness disgusting. On this point, he shares the hermit's sensibility. Neither of them can stand the secular ethos because they have their own superhuman ideals. The hermit, Zarathustra, and the people in the market place represent three different spiritual conditions.

Spiritual Aspiration (Prol. 3)

What is strange about Zarathustra is his allegiance to the superhuman standard even after the death of God. There is nothing unusual for the hermit to hold on to his superhuman ideal because it is his Christian legacy. But why has the superhuman ideal not been abandoned by the atheist Zarathustra? His strange position may be explained by Ludwig Feuerbach's philosophy of religion. According to him, human beings created the concept of God by projecting their ideal of perfection in intelligence, will, and love (*The Essence of Christianity*, 3, 29). There is one systematic method for this projective creation: it moves from the limited to the unlimited. Whereas intelligence, will, and love are limited as human attributes, they become unlimited when they are projected as divine attributes. He says, "The divine being is nothing else than the human being, or, rather, the human nature purified, freed from the limits of the individual man, made objective—*i.e.*, contemplated and revered as another, a distinct being" (*The Essence of Christianity*, 14). He uses the prefix '*über*' to express the move beyond the limits of humanity.[1] His two favorite *über*-words are 'superhuman' (*übermenschlich*) and 'supernatural' (*übernatürlich*).

To be religious is to believe in the objective reality of God thus created and projected by human beings. From this follows Feuerbach's famous remark, "Religion is the dream of the human mind" (*The Essence of Christianity*, xxxix). But this dream expresses the essence of humanity, its ultimate aspiration. Human beings project their ideal of perfection to the divine world because they cannot realize it in their own world. Hence Feuerbach regards religion as "the childlike condition of humanity" (*The Essence of Christianity*, 13). When human beings come of age and awake from their religious dream, he says, they will recognize their God as the projection of their own ideal. Their ideal of perfection was alienated from them when it was projected to the almighty God, before whom they stood as abject objects. They can overcome this alienation by appropriating the concept of divine perfection for their own perfection. Man first transfers his essence to the external world and makes it alien to himself, and then brings it back to himself and appropriates it as his own essence. This detour of alienation and appropriation is the road map for the spiritual development of humanity. Without such a detour, humanity would have remained in the condition of beasts.

---

1. Greg Whitlock pays special attention to Feuerbach's use of *über*-concepts and its relation to the concept of the superman (*Returning to Sils-Maria*, 112, n. 75). He counts twenty-four occurrences of *übermenschlich* and its cognates in *The Essence of Christianity*, sixty-five occurrences in all his published works, and twenty-eight occurrences in his unpublished work, "Der Gottesbegriff als Gattungswesen des Menschen" (Whitlock's e-mail of August 26, 2002).

Whereas the process of alienation separates God and man, the process of appropriation brings them together. Feuerbach looks upon the Incarnation as the first bold attempt for this process of appropriation and reconciliation. If the Incarnation is taken literally as the event of God becoming a man, it is a miracle that can never take place in the real world. But there is nothing miraculous in it if it is taken as the human appropriation of divine attributes. Feuerbach says, "But the incarnate God is only the apparent manifestation of deified man; for the descent of God to man is necessarily preceded by the exaltation of man to God" (*The Essence of Christianity*, 50). To appropriate the divine attribute is to deify man and exalt him to the divine level. The descent of God to man and the ascent of man to God are two ways of describing the same process of appropriating the alienated divine attribute. But this revolutionary idea of God and man was beyond the comprehension of the medieval Christians, and the Incarnation was taken to be a great mystery. Thus, Feuerbach says, medieval Catholicism became the height of religious alienation in the history of Christianity. On his account, the Protestant Reformation was the beginning of the religious movement to overcome the alienation of medieval Christianity.

Feuerbach's philosophy of religion was an adaptation of Hegel's philosophy. In his *Phenomenology of the Spirit,* Hegel introduced the doctrine of alienation and appropriation to account for the emergence and decline of religion. According to him, the Christian God was only an alienation of the Absolute Spirit from humanity in medieval Christianity, and the alienated God has been appropriated as the essence of humanity in modern Europe. This doctrine inspired not only Feuerbach, but also many other Hegelians. In his *Life of Jesus,* David Strauss says that the central idea of Christianity is the union of God and man and that this revolutionary idea repudiates the Judaic alienation of spirit from man. He also says that the Gospels are the poetic renderings of human desire to transcend the finitude of humanity. In his later writings, he claims that the old religious ideals have now become realizable in this world thanks to two developments: the moral and political enlightenment and the triumph of science and industrial technology. He believes that the spirit of

Christianity is to realize the divine ideals not in one human being, Jesus Christ, but in all human beings. This is his Hegelian interpretation of Christianity, which dictates the conversion of theism to humanism and the realization of divine ideals as human ideals.

Strauss was not so radical as the left-wing Young Hegelians such as Feuerbach, Bruno Bauer, and Max Stirner. Whereas the latter flatly denies the existence of God, the former still accepts it. Strauss can talk about the union of God and man because he still believes in God. He only objects to the alienation of God from man and insists on their unity. For the left-wing Young Hegelians, however, there can be no such unity because they deny the existence of God. Whereas Strauss reads the Gospels as mythological descriptions of God, Bruno Bauer and Max Stirner take them as artistic fabrications. Many conservative Hegelians believed that Hegel's philosophy saved religion, because they could cite many passages from their master to the effect that religion as well as philosophy was an expression of the Absolute Spirit. This conservative understanding of Hegel was only a pious self-deception, so argued Bruno Bauer in *The Trumpet of the Last Judgement against Hegel the Atheist and Antichrist: An Ultimatum.* As the title of this book indicates, Bauer exposes Hegel not only as an atheist but also as an Anti-Christ. This is the common ground for the left-wing Young Hegelians. In their view, Hegel teaches that the concept of God is only a human projection to be annulled when human beings achieve their mature self-consciousness. Hence Bauer says that the radical Hegelians "have only torn away the thin veil which briefly concealed the thought of the master and revealed—shamelessly enough—the system in its nakedness" (*The Trumpet of the Last Judgement*, 95). Their master has already pronounced the death of God. But they take it as a most joyful event in opening up the possibility of overcoming the human alienation and realizing divine ideals in the secular world.

There are two ways to secularization. The natural way is to disown the Christian legacy and dismiss all Christian ideals as illusions. This is the way of critical rejection, which makes a clean break with the religious tradition. This type of response usually belongs to atheism that is based on natural science. The Young Hegelians refused to follow the natural way because they did not want to resign themselves to the limits of humanity and disown its limitless aspiration. Bauer quotes their master's pronouncement that human beings lying in the trench of finiteness are only oxen (*The Trumpet of the Last Judgement*, 125). Feuerbach also wants to preserve the infinite aspiration of humanity as a valuable legacy of Christianity. This is the way of constructive retention. He believes that Christian ideals should not be discarded because they express the very essence of all human beings, namely, the aspiration to overcome the limitations of humanity. The essence of humanity is never fixed once and for all because it is potentially infinite (*The Essence of Christianity*, 2). Because of its potential infinitude, the human species is engaged in a perpetual struggle to go beyond its limitations. This is Zarathustra's superhuman ideal of perpetual self-overcoming.

The way of critical rejection was typically French; the way of constructive retention was uniquely German. The champions of the French Enlightenment only tried to get rid of God and find happiness as enlightened natural human beings. But this simple-minded atheism was not good enough for the Germans largely because they had been bred in the Lutheran tradition. Max Stirner says,

> At the entrance of the modern time stands the 'God-man'. At its exit will only the God in the God-man evaporate? And can the God-man really die if only the God in him dies? They did not think of this question, and thought they were finished when in our days they brought to a victorious end the work of the Enlightenment, the vanquishing of God: they did not notice that man has killed God in order to become now—"*sole* God on high." (*The Ego and Its Own*, 139)

Unlike the Frenchmen of the Enlightenment, the Germans could not be content with merely getting rid of God and becoming simple human beings. For the Germans, the death of God should not be a destructive event, but a constructive stage for the birth of man as the real God. Without this constructive outcome, the long travail of Christianity would turn out to be a terrible waste of almost two millennia. This uniquely German

movement came as a Lutheran legacy of Christianity. The ideal of deify-
ing humanity had been an essential feature of medieval Christianity. For
the medieval Christians, this ideal was expressed in the mystery of transubstantiation: humanity will be transformed to divinity just as the bread
and wine of the Eucharist are transformed to the flesh and blood of Jesus
Christ. But they believed that this ideal could not be realized in this
world. Radicalizing this traditional belief, Martin Luther taught his followers that the transformation of humanity could take place in this world.
This was his ideal of God-man. The Incarnation is not to be restricted to
one miraculous event. On the contrary, it is meant to be a universal
model for the life of all Christians. Stirner takes this Lutheran ideal as the
starting point of modern ethos. In his view, the ultimate aim of modern
European secularization is not simply to get rid of God from the God-
man, but transform man into "sole God on high."

During the Reformation, many followers of Martin Luther tried to
live up to the God-man ideal. In this superhuman endeavor, they were inspired by Christ's own words. He had taught his followers to seek divine
perfection. This was the central point of his sermon on the mountain
(Matt. 5:1-7:29). Against the common moral code that we should love
our neighbor and hate our enemy, Christ teaches his followers to love
their enemy. This is dictated by the ideal of divine perfection, which far
exceeds the ideal of human perfection embodied in human laws. The followers of Martin Luther were so zealous in pursuit of their superhuman
ideal that their admirers and detractors invented a new word 'superman'
(*Übermensch*). Some admirers described them as a new breed of human
beings, a true human, a superman, or as a being of God and of Christ.
Others ridiculed them by saying that they "walk all in the spirit and are
supermen and superhuman angels or have become angelic and all spirit,
so that they must not perform any more human labor" (Jacob and
Wilhelm Grimm, *Deutsches Wörterbuch,* 23:27). So 'superman' emerged
as a word of awe and ridicule for the zealous followers of Martin Luther.

Centuries later, Herder gave the word 'superman' its first secular
meaning as "the original genius" and Goethe used it to refer to his magician hero Dr. Faust. The idea of attributing superhuman power to a magi-

cian goes back to the Renaissance magic. In *The Tragedie of Doctor Faustus*, Christopher Marlowe says, "A sound Magitian is a Demi-god." In Goethe's work, Faust may not be a demi-god, but he tries to become one. In the opening scene, he despairs over the limitation of human sciences. Although he has mastered the four medieval sciences of philosophy, jurisprudence, medicine, and theology, Faust realizes that he is no more than a poor fool (*Faust* 354-59). He turns to magic to go beyond the reach of these human sciences. This is his first attempt to rise above the limits of humanity. He wants to gain an intuitive knowledge of what holds together the whole world by directly perceiving its innermost workings. This is the sort of knowledge that is supposedly accessible only to God. When Faust opens the magic book and beholds the sign of the macrocosmos, he feels like a god. When he conjures up the Earth Spirit, she appears in the flashing of a red flame and scares him. In jeering at the cowering Faust, she refers to him as superman (*Faust* 490). In spite of this humiliation, he will strive to become a superman to the end of the play by transcending the limits of humanity.

The Young Hegelians (Prol. 3)

By the time the Young Hegelians took over the superhuman ideal, they proposed many ambitious projects for its realization and contentiously argued against one another. Feuerbach argued for the superhuman perfection of humanity. When he talks about the essence of man, he means the essence of human species rather than of any individual. Hence he considers human perfection in social terms. He says, "The essence of man is contained only in the community and unity of man with man" (*Principles of the Philosophy of the Future*, 71). He claims to derive this collective ideal from the concept of God as the Holy Trinity, whose union he regards as the secret of communal and social life (*Principles of the Philosophy of the Future,* 72). His collective ideal was further developed by Marx and Engels. Bruno Bauer proposed the rational state as his ideal, faithfully adhering to Hegel's theory of the state. He was following not only Hegel but also Thomas Hobbes, who had deified the secular state well before Hegel, by calling the great Leviathan the mortal god (*Leviathan* 2.17.13). This mortal god has the power of redeeming humanity from the brutal state of nature.

While all these Young Hegelians were taking collectivist approaches for the realization of the superhuman ideal, Max Stirner alone took the individualist approach.[2] He holds that the individual is the ultimate reality and that every individual is unique. Everyone should become the owner of his or her unique self (*The Ego and Its Own,* 318). For Stirner, God is not a community but an individual, who cares only for himself, thinks only of himself, and satisfies only himself (*The Ego and Its Own,* 5). Since God is an unlimited sovereign, the humanization of divine attributes dictates that every individual should have an unlimited sovereignty over himself. To be such a sovereign is to own oneself and to be "an almighty ego" (*The Ego and Its Own,* 149). But most individuals are owned by others. One becomes a student or a teacher not in the way one wants to be, but in the way it is dictated by others. This is to be owned by others. As a unique individual, Stirner says, "I am my species, am without norm, without law, without model, and the like" (*The Ego and Its Own,* 163). He candidly admits that he can make little out of his unique self, but that does not change the importance of his unique self. He says that "this little is everything, and is better than what I allow to be made out of me by the might of others, by the training of custom, religion, the laws, the state" (*The Ego and Its Own,* 163). But the individuals cannot appeal to anyone else for the protection of their ownness or sovereignty. They have to rely on their own power. Hence one's ownness is coextensive with one's power (*The Ego and Its Own,* 166, 187, 227, 318). Such is also the case with the almighty God.

The Young Hegelians' naturalistic humanism is different from the standard atheistic version. The former is governed by superhuman ideals, and the latter by mere human ideals. The latter is known as secular hu-

---

2. Nietzsche was not directly acquainted with Stirner's writings. The remarkable affinity of their ideas is discussed by R. W. K. Paterson (*The Nihilistic Egoist*, chap. 7) and by Keiji Nishitani (*The Self-Overcoming of Nihilism*, chap. 6).

manism. But the former is so rare that it has gained no clear label. I propose to call it secular superhumanism or superhuman naturalism. In his announcement of the superman, Zarathustra is advocating his version of secular superhumanism. Just like the Young Hegelians, he retains the superhuman ideal for human perfection in the secular world. The road to becoming the superman, which is supposed to be a long process of perpetual self-overcoming, is an adaptation of Feuerbach's idea that the human species is engaged in the perpetual struggle to overcome its limitations. Zarathustra's call for fidelity to the earth also follows Feuerbach's teaching that there is no other reality except the natural world. In his attempt to humanize the divine, Feuerbach modifies Hegel's speculative idealism by stressing the importance of empirical research and the natural world. For this reason, he is sometimes mistaken for a materialist. But he does not believe in the primacy of matter over spirit or the dualism of mind and matter. He faithfully adheres to the Hegelian monism: the unity of mind and matter. But he differs with Hegel on the ultimate source of all things. For Hegel, it is Logic, the matrix of Concepts and Ideas; for Feuerbach, it is Nature. But his Nature is not dead matter, but living spirit in its potency.

Zarathustra of the Prologue is a Young Hegelian, for whom the death of God transforms the ideal of divine perfection to the ideal of human perfection, and heaven is replaced by earth as the arena for the realization of this ideal. God is dethroned as the king of heaven; man is enthroned as the king of earth. With this transposition of man to God, Zarathustra has created the superman, thereby rekindling the fire that has gone out with the death of God. The notion of superhuman (*übermenschlich*), which was chiefly adjectival in Feuerbach's use, becomes a noun, the superman (*Übermensch*), for Zarathustra. But his superhuman ideal is different from Feuerbach's. The former is a superhuman individual; the latter is a superhuman society. Zarathustra's ideal is highly individualistic because he detests all collective social orders. In this regard, he is closer to Max Stirner than to any other Hegelians. For Stirner, collective entities such as humanity and the state are the new idols that alienate human beings from their true selves as much as the old God did

(*The Ego and Its Own,* 34-40, 89-103). Instead of being enslaved to the collective entities, the individual should become an absolute sovereign. To be such a sovereign is to be like God and that may be Zarathustra's ideal of becoming the superman. This supports Peter Berkowitz's claim that Zarathustra's ultimate goal is self-deification (*Nietzsche,* 207-10).

As a human version of divine perfection, the concept of superhuman individual has already been operating much more pervasively in modern European culture than the human version of divine social order. Its first manifestation was the ideal of the Renaissance man, who strove to shape his destiny with his own will. This ideal was the foundation for the formation and development of the Faustian ethos from Marlowe's to Goethe's *Faust*, that is, the notion of the Faustian hero, who struggles and strives to overcome all human limitations. The Faustian hero dares to reshape the whole world in his own image just like God. Zarathustra's notion of superman is closely linked to Goethe as well as to the Young Hegelians. For this reason, his aspiration diverges from the normal run of secular humanism or atheism. Most humanistic atheists would simply reject the otherworldly ideals, whether of God or angels, and return humanity to the natural condition, much like the condition of the people Zarathustra encounters in the market place. Whereas he says that the superman shall be the meaning of the earth, they would say that man shall be the meaning of the earth. Human beings should seek human perfection and human happiness by satisfying their natural needs and desires like other animals. There is no guarantee that they will succeed in this endeavor. On the contrary, they are more likely to become victims of natural disasters and misery. However, if they are fortunate enough to achieve some measure of natural happiness, most secular humanists will feel happy for them.

The Secular Ethos (Prol. 4-10)

Zarathustra feels nothing but contempt for the happiness of the townsfolk and calls it their wretched contentment. He compares his contempt of these people with the old Christian contempt. With the Christians, the soul looked contemptuously upon the body; with today's people, the body should say, "Is not your soul poverty and filth and wretched contentment?" (Z, 13). He exhorts his audience to have the greatest contempt for their reason, virtue, justice, pity, and even their meanness. What is the cause for this great contempt? Their reason, virtue, justice, and pity are the standard elements of human ethics or the pillars of secular ethos. Their existence has become all-too-human. Their secular comfort has put to sleep the burning ambition that has driven humanity for the perpetual spiritual evolution. To wake them up from their spiritual slumber, Zarathustra shouts for lightning and frenzy. The superman is this lightning that should kindle frenzy in these sluggish people. But the people in the market place have no idea of what he is talking about. Taking the talk of lightning and frenzy as his cue, the tightrope walker begins his performance. Zarathustra decides to exploit this event as an allegory for the evolution of humanity toward the superman. He says that man is a rope over an abyss between the beast and the superman and that it is an extremely hazardous journey to cross over the abyss.

Zarathustra regards humanity only as a bridge on the hazardous journey to the superman (Prol. 4). That is to say, humanity should be only a means and never be an end in itself. This is a degrading view of humanity, namely, human life is not worth living for its own sake. The medieval Christians took a similar degrading view of human life because their existence was full of misery. They could justify their earthly existence only as a bridge to happiness in the kingdom of heaven. But the people in the market place are situated differently. Their existence is not racked with famine and starvation, disease and torture. On the contrary, they are content with their existence because they have the comfort of modern material progress. In this regard, Zarathustra's mission is different from the traditional religious mission of Gotama Buddha or Jesus Christ. Their redemptive missions were on the hermit's mind, when he advised Zarathustra to lighten the burden of the people. To alleviate their suffering is surely to lighten their burden. But to do so is only to give alms and that is not Zarathustra's mission. His mission is to awaken the people to his superhuman ideal and make them realize that their present happiness is only a wretched contentment.

Zarathustra behaves like a Christian missionary, who walks into a fairly prosperous community and shouts that their happiness and prosperity are contemptible in comparison with the supernatural glory and happiness they can have in the kingdom of God. In fact, this is what the Christian missionaries did when they came to China in the seventeenth century. The Chinese were completely baffled by the Christian supernatural aspiration, because they could see no point in seeking anything beyond virtue and happiness of the natural world. Zarathustra cannot make any better headway with his audience than the Christian missionaries could with the Chinese folk. They feel no need at all for the superhuman ideal. He may now realize what the hermit meant by saying that human beings were too imperfect and that love of them would kill him. The hermit must have been repelled not from human beings as such, but from their secular culture and its shallowness. Anyone who still has the sense of superhuman sanctity like the hermit or Zarathustra is bound to be disgusted with the people wallowing in the cheap happiness of secular culture. The hermit's and Zarathustra's sense of sanctity is a theistic legacy, but this legacy is completely obliterated by the secular culture in the market place. He tries to move his audience by his praise of those willing to sacrifice themselves for the superhuman ideal. But he gets nowhere. As his last resort, he ridicules the last man, the quintessence of secular culture. He describes the last man as the most contemptible creature to arrive on the surface of the earth.

Zarathustra says, "'What is love? What is creation? What is longing? What is a star?' thus asks the last man, and he blinks" (Z, 17). He blinks because it is hard for him to wake out of his spiritual slumber. He is too sleepy to grasp what Zarathustra is talking about, that is, what it means to love, to create, to have a longing, and to shoot for a star. So he is ridiculed by Zarathustra. But that is unfair to the last man. In his own secular existence, he knows what it means to love, to create, to have a longing, and to shoot for a star. But the last man is despicable to Zarathustra because he has no idea of doing these things on the superhuman level. By the superhuman standard, the last man has become too small. But the last men say, "We have invented happiness" (Z, 17). This statement galls Zarathustra more than anything else because he takes their happiness as the most despicable feature of secular culture.

The last men secure their happiness by using science and technology to construct a utopia much like The Brave New World. They say that man is clever and knows everything. By their knack of science and engineering, they make everything agreeable, even their dreams and death. They can even transform their work into a form of entertainment. They have developed an efficient health-care system. They allow no one to become rich or poor because wealth and poverty requires too much exertion. They love their neighbors and rub against one another for warmth. There is no shepherd, but one herd. Everybody wants the same; everybody is the same as everybody else. Whoever feels differently goes voluntarily to a madhouse. They are living in an egalitarian society, whose members are hardly distinguishable from one another. This is the sort of society that David Strauss may have dreamed of when he said that the old religious ideals have now become realizable in this world thanks to two developments: the moral and political enlightenment and the triumph of science and industrial technology. Just as Nietzsche condemns him as a cultural philistine in "David Strauss, the Confessor and the Writer", Zarathustra is now jeering at the last man's secular culture.

A while ago, we noted two ways to secularization: secular humanism and secular superhumanism. Zarathustra's talk in the market place is the confrontation of a secular superhumanist with the people of secular humanism or bourgeois ethos. If he cannot win over the people to his superhuman ideal, the entire movement of secularization will go to the dogs. This is a terrifying prospect for him. It is not easy for us to appreciate his distress over the profanity of secularization, because we are the children of secular culture. But the nineteenth century Europeans had a different sensibility. In *The Communist Manifesto,* even such adamant atheists as Marx and Engels lament over the fact that all that is holy is profaned by the bourgeoisie. In "The Tomb Song" of Part II, we will find Zarathustra lamenting over the loss of his youthful dream that "All be-

ings shall be divine to me" and "All days shall be holy to me." But this
dream has been shattered under the crushing weight of secular culture.
The last men take special pride in their invention of happiness. In the age
of great religions, people expected to achieve happiness only in the other
world because they could not get it in this world. If the last men can indeed invent happiness on earth, they can claim to have overcome the religious alienation by realizing the old religious ideals in this world as
David Strauss said. In Zarathustra's view, however, they have only degraded the lofty ideal that human beings have developed through their
long spiritual struggle. In retaliation, he ridicules the last men by trivial-
izing their achievements: They make everything too small and hop
around like fleas and beetles.

This vicious attack has been taken by some commentators as a well-
deserved critique of the trivialization of human existence under the industrial capitalism. But the critique is a grossly unfair assessment of
modern secular culture. Marx and Engels rendered a far more balanced
verdict on the bourgeois culture in *The Communist Manifesto*: "It has accomplished wonders far surpassing Egyptian pyramids, Roman aque-
ducts, and Gothic cathedrals; it has conducted expeditions that put in the
shade all former Exoduses of nations and crusades." Zarathustra's treatment of the last man is too cavalier, if he stands for the secular humanist.
Carl Jung says that the last man is a very ordinary and quite reasonable
individual, who leads a life of moderation and avoids the vice of excess.
In his view, Zarathustra is cursing a fairly normal human being for no
good reason (*Nietzsche's* Zarathustra, 110). Robert Pippin voices a similar response to Zarathustra's contempt of the last man. In his view, the
community of the last men stands on "the paradigmatic bourgeois virtues—peace, security, and the rational, efficient satisfaction of (one's
rather narrowly defined) interests." He says that Zarathustra's denuncia-
tion of this bourgeois culture is "more than a little controversial" (*Modernism as a Philosophical Problem*, 89). Hence Zarathustra's denuncia-
tion is never taken seriously by his audience. They can find nothing
amiss with the last man and his happiness. On the contrary, they are eager to be turned into the last men. With this response, Zarathustra finally

realizes the impossibility of communicating with his audience. He suspects the worst of them and says, "But they think I am cold and I jeer and make dreadful jests" (*Z*, 18). He may have been earnest in his preaching, but he clearly jeered at the lowly form of their existence. His suspicion turns into paranoia; he detects hatred in their laughter. That is a gross distortion on his part because their laughter is harmless. They just look upon him as a strange jester, whose talk of the superman makes no sense.

Many commentators have blamed Zarathustra's failure of communication either on his ineptitude in sizing up the audience correctly or on the deficiency of the audience to appreciate his lofty ideal. Both views may be true. But I propose to consider another question: What right does he have to deride the secular existence of normal human beings? What is really wrong with the townsfolk and their secular ethos? There appears to be nothing wrong with them until they are subjected to his superhuman ideal. He may say that human life is always contemptible, whether it is happy or unhappy, and that it can have value never in its own right, but only as a means to transcend the limits of the lowly humanity. But that is a highly degrading view of human life. His teaching that the superman should be the meaning of the earth presupposes his conviction that man is too despicable to be its meaning. This debasing view of humanity is dictated by his superhuman ideal, which he can justify only by taking Feuerbach's stand that the superhuman aspiration is the essence of humanity. But this stand may be another illusion about the essence of humanity. Although it may be impossible for us to be free from the notion of perfecting ourselves, it may be only an illusion to strive for superhuman perfection. Is Zarathustra not being victimized by his old God even after his death, insofar as his superhuman ideal is a secular manifestation of his old God? This is the vexing question raised by the Prologue.

In the market place, where the crowd is snugly nestled in the secular culture, to float the superhuman ideal appears to be as dangerous as walking the tightrope. In fact, the tightrope walker loses his balance during his performance and falls off the rope to the ground, when the jester jumps over him from behind. This may be the omen of what is going to happen to Zarathustra's risky venture. Hence he feels empathy with the dying man. He realizes that his project of transcending humanity is as hazardous as the stunt of walking over the tightrope. As a preacher, he is almost as dead as the tightrope walker. There is no way for him to move the people because they are happy in their secular life. He knows that they are beyond his reach. After burying the dead man, he spends the dark night in desperation. When he wakes up the next morning, he gains a new truth and insight. He no longer wants to be the shepherd for the herd. They neither need nor deserve his attention. He will enlist new companions by luring them away from the herd and make them his fellow creators. They will break up the old table of values and create new values. The values he wants to break up are the values of secular culture. His hatred of the last man is his holy hatred, as Nikolai Berdyaev says (*The Meaning of the Creative Act,* 82). Zarathustra cannot condone the despicable last man to be the ultimate end of the godless world. He is determined to imbue the secular culture with new spiritual values. This is his ambitious campaign for the spiritualization of secular culture.

When Zarathustra formulates this new plan in his heart, the sun stands high at noon. He can see his eagle with his serpent soaring through the sky. The eagle stands for his pride and the serpent for his wisdom. He would like to be wise through and through like his serpent, but he knows that is impossible. He asks his pride to go along with his wisdom, but that may not always be possible, either, because his wisdom may leave him one day. In that case, he will let his pride fly with his folly. Carl Jung says that the eagle represents the spirit and the serpent the body (*Nietzsche's* Zarathustra, 18). The eagle flies in the air; the serpent crawls on the ground. These two motions represent the spirit and the body. Jung symbolically identifies the serpent not only with the body, but also with the earth. The body belongs to the earth and the serpent crawls on the ground. He says that the serpent stands for the terrestrial or chthonic forces (*Nietzsche's* Zarathustra, 18, 227). Heinrich Zimmer has a similar view of the serpent. He says that the serpent represents the life-force of the earth (*Myths and Symbols in Indian Art and Civilization,* 74). In that case, the serpent represents the earthly force that drives the secular culture in the market place. Human beings cannot be any different from other species of animals as long as they are governed by earthly forces. The great religions tried to endow humanity with spiritual values that cannot be gained by mere brutes. But those spiritual values have been dissolved with the death of God. Zarathustra is now proposing the superman as his scheme of spiritualization for the godless world. This new scheme is symbolized by the flight of the eagle with the serpent coiled around its neck. Without this flight, the serpent will be stuck to the earth forever just like the market crowd. Hence its flight with the eagle can be taken as the symbol for his campaign to spiritualize human existence in the natural world.

Three Stages of Spiritual Development (Part I.1-5)

In "On the Three Metamorphoses", Zarathustra describes the three stages of spiritual development for humanity. These three stages constitute the road map for the campaign of spiritualization that was formulated in the Prologue. The spirit first becomes a camel, the strong reverent spirit, who bears heavy loads. Then it becomes a lion, which conquers his freedom and becomes his own master. The lion seeks out and fights his last master, the dragon, whose name is 'Thou shalt'. The mightiest of all dragons declare that all values have long been created and there shall be no more 'I will'. It stands for what Stanley Rosen calls the dead weight of tradition (*The Mask of Enlightenment*, 80). The lion slays the dragon and asserts 'I will'. It is the spirit of defiance and independence. But the lion lacks the power to create new values. It can say a sacred No, but not a sacred Yes. The lion can provide freedom as the precondition for creation, but not the power of creation itself. That power belongs to the child. The transformation of lion to child is the final metamorphosis. Zarathustra describes the child as "innocence and forgetting, a new beginning, a game, a self-propelled wheel, a first movement, a sacred Yes" (Z, 27). With a clean slate of innocence, the spirit can create its own values.

The three metamorphoses produce three types of will. The will of a camel is obedient and reverent; it is dependent on its master. The will of a lion is defiant and independent, but it is not completely its own. It is defined by its defiance and opposition to its master. The will of a child alone is truly its own because it stands on its relation to itself rather than to some other agents. Because it is self-contained, it is called a self-propelled wheel. Only in this self-contained state, the spirit gains the power of creation. The assertion that the will of a child alone can create new values has baffled some commentators. A child seems to have no will of its own in any meaningful form, especially in comparison with the will of a lion or even a camel. For this reason, Peter Berkowitz claims to see an ominous defect in Zarathustra's image of the child-creator (*Nietzsche*, 158). Stanley Rosen says that the child cannot mark the ultimate end of human spiritual development (*The Mask of Enlightenment*, 83). But we cannot deal with these objections until we can see the development of Zarathustra's spiritual campaign.

In "On the Teachers of Virtue", Zarathustra goes to hear a sage, who praises sleep as the ultimate end and bliss of human life. The sage says that sleeping well is no mean art because it requires the service of all virtues and disciplines. After hearing this lecture, Zarathustra laughs and says that the wisdom of the sage is to stay awake in order to sleep well and that the sage and many other teachers of virtue know no better meaning of life. The sage's teaching reflects a highly pessimistic view of life. But who is this sage? Werner Dannhauser cites Socrates and his praise of dreamless sleep in the *Apology* (*Nietzsche's View of Socrates*, 253). Contemplating his probable death sentence, Socrates says that death must be a marvelous gain if it is only a dreamless sleep and that few days of our life, even the happiest ones, are better than a night of good sleep. This negative view of life had a long tradition in ancient Greece. According to Solon, two young men wanted to take their mother to a great festival for the goddess Hera at Argos, but their oxen did not come home from the field in time to carry her in a cart to the festival. So they took the place of oxen and pulled their mother's cart five miles to the festival. The whole assembly of worshippers witnessed this deed of extraordinary devotion and praised the two young men. Overjoyed at their praise, the mother besought the goddess to bestow her highest blessing on her two sons. In consequence of this prayer, the two youths fell asleep in the temple and never woke up. This incident is supposed to show how much peaceful sleep is better than life (Herodotus, *The Persian Wars*, 17).

The same grim view of life was contained in Silenus's counsel to King Midas, which is cited in *The Birth of Tragedy* 3: The best thing for humans is not to be born and the second best is to die soon. Socrates is expressing the wisdom of Silenus in his praise of dreamless sleep. But he had never sat on a professorial chair. He praised sleep not to his students, but to the members of the Athenian Assembly, who were presiding over his trial. Hence he does not fit Zarathustra's description of a sage lecturing to his students from a professorial chair. The description makes a better fit with a Stoic sage of ancient Greece. The word 'sage' was a favorite term with the Stoics. The Stoic sage was supposed to be free of all passions. The Stoics advocated *apatheia* (tranquility) as the highest state of happiness, and this highest state is hardly distinguishable from dreamless sleep. Although it is called happiness, it is not an ecstatic bliss. It is the state of being free of all passions and sufferings. Zeno of Citium, the founder of Stoicism, says that the *prokopton* (the progress maker) in philosophy can judge his progress in virtue by the calming of his dreams, like the coming of an absolute calm over a stormy sea (*Plutarch's Moralia* 1:441). For him, the quality of sleep is the best measure for the quality of virtue and happiness. The calmest sleep manifests the highest level of virtue. So the Stoic sage of tranquility and his doctrine of virtue come closest to the sage's lecture under Zarathustra's description.

Assuming that the sage is a Stoic of antiquity, why does Zarathustra talk about his lecture on virtue right after "On the Three Metamorphoses"? What is the connection between Sections 1 and 2 of Part I? I propose that the dreamless sleep of a Stoic sage should be taken as the original condition of humanity prior to its spiritual development in the three stages of the camel, the lion, and the child. That condition should be natural rather than spiritual. The sage's praise of sleep is given in the context of natural life; he says nothing about life after death. This is in perfect accord with the Stoic philosophy, which admits nothing beyond the natural world. In that regard, the sage's teaching is categorically different from the religious worldview presented in the following section, "On the Afterworldly". But some commentators construe "the teachers of virtue" as religious teachers. Robert Gooding-Williams take them as Platonic-Christian teachers who advocate their ascetic ideal (*Zarathustra's Dionysian Modernism,* 128). Greg Whitlock reads their teaching as a parody of Christian virtues (*Returning to Sils-Maria,* 64). But the religious teaching in general belongs to "On the Afterworldly", which initiates the course of spiritual development. The sage's talk on sleep and happiness is given in the context of natural life in this world: Peaceful sleep is the highest happiness that can be achieved in natural life.

"On the Afterwordly" describes the first step in the spiritual development of humanity. This is the revolutionary step of creating the other world beyond the natural world. This revolutionary step produced the great religions, which imposed the divine commandments on human beings. This is the metamorphosis of humanity to a camel. Prior to this event, human beings had thought of nothing beyond their natural existence. But their natural life was so full of misery and anxiety that their ultimate concern was to minimize the pain of their existence. Under such circumstances, dreamless sleep was perhaps the best they could hope for. This was the Stoic resignation. To be sure, this is not a correct description of Greek philosophy as a whole. Before the emergence of Stoicism, Plato and Aristotle had advocated highly active ethical and political programs. With the decline of ancient Greek states, their optimism began to be overshadowed by the pessimism of the Stoics and Epicureans. But the Stoics could not think of finding their redemption in the other world because their materialism did not permit any other world beyond the natural one. To project the other world as a solution for the problem of suffering in this world was the next step after the Stoic resignation in the history of spiritual evolution. Likewise in Zarathustra's teaching, the Stoic teaching precedes the afterworldly religion. To project the other world is to wake out of sleep in this world and begin the journey of spiritual development beyond natural existence.

By identifying the preacher of dreamless sleep as a Stoic sage, I am creating a highly implausible picture of Zarathustra as a poetic character.

In the market place of the Prologue, he is preaching to a nineteenth century audience, and then he is attending a Stoic lecture of the Hellenistic age. He appears to have a life that spans more than two thousand years. That is highly implausible. Most readers would rather take Zarathustra as a denizen of nineteenth century Europe because he is Nietzsche's mouthpiece. In that case, we had better assume that the sage is someone occupying a professorial chair in nineteenth century Europe and lecturing on the Stoic doctrine of virtue. On this assumption, Harold Alderman says that the sage advocates the conventional wisdom of Stoicism that life is without sense (*Nietzsche's Gift,* 44). But it is not credible to take the sage as a professorial figure, who attracted a large flock of students by advocating Stoicism in nineteenth century Europe. So it is better to place the sage in the Hellenistic Europe and expand the scope of Zarathustra's life. Since he is a poetic character, who was supposedly born over two thousand years ago, we can imagine his career spanning the last two thousand years. In "On the Teachers of Virtue", he indeed covers a long time span. This section opens with him attending the Stoic lecture on virtue, but ends with his comment on nineteenth century Europe: "Today too there may still be a few like this preacher of virtue, and not all so honest; but their time is up" (*Z,* 30).

To take Zarathustra not merely as a denizen of nineteenth century Europe, but as someone whose life spans the entire history of European culture provides an important historical perspective to his narration. If he is taken to be only a denizen of nineteenth century Europe, he will have a limited range of interaction with others. All the people he meets and all the events he witnesses will be confined to nineteenth century Europe. On the other hand, if he is given a much longer life span, he will function as an Olympian surveyor of the entire European history. This is to ascribe a telescopic view to Zarathustra, which appears to have been the author's own intention. In comparing *Zarathustra* with *Beyond Good and Evil,* Nietzsche says that the former is far more farsighted than the latter, which is "constrained to focus sharply on what is close at hand, the age, what is *around us*" (*Ecce Homo,* "Beyond Good and Evil 2"). Zarathustra's telescopic perspective is best stated in the first line of "On the

Thousand and One Goal": "Zarathustra saw many lands and many peoples." The many peoples he saw range over his native Persians, the ancient Greeks, and the modern individuals. His telescopic perspective cannot be confined to any particular age or culture.

In "On the Afterworldly", Zarathustra talks about the afterworldly religions. He once thought that the world was the dream of a suffering and tortured god. By creating the world, the god wanted to look away from his suffering and lose himself in the joy of intoxication. This is the theory Nietzsche entertained in *The Birth of Tragedy* ("An Attempt at Self-Criticism", 5): "The world as the release and redemption (*Erlösung*) of god, *achieved* at each and every moment, as the eternally changing, eternally new vision of the most suffering of all, the being most full of oppositions and contradictions, able to redeem and release itself only in *semblance (Schein)*." Now Zarathustra realizes that this suffering god was a man-made ghost he invented to cope with his own problem of suffering. This is an adaptation of Feuerbach's theory that human beings create the gods. On Zarathustra's theory, they created the gods for their redemption from suffering. The sick and the decaying despised their bodies and the earth and invented the heavenly realm for their escape. But there is no other world beyond this world of bodies. In "On the Despisers of the Body", Zarathustra expands the notion of body: "in your body he [the self] dwells; he is your body" (Z, 34). The self is your body. The creative self is the creative body. This is the identity thesis of self and body. It is derived from Feuerbach's naturalism: "I am a real sensuous being and, indeed, the body in its totality is my ego, my essence itself" (*Principles of the Philosophy of the Future*, 54). When the self cannot create beyond itself, Zarathustra says, it gets angry and becomes a despiser of the body and then creates the other world. The body is the ultimate source of all human creation.

"On Enjoying and Suffering the Passions" is a continuation of the same theme because the passions belong to the body. Zarathustra says, "Once you suffered passions and called them evil. But now you have only your virtues left: they grew out of your passions" (Z, 36). When we suffer from our passions, they are called devils. But they become angels when they are turned into virtues. Zarathustra says, "Once you had wild dogs in your cellar, but in the end they turned into birds and lovely singers" (*Z*, 37). Passions have to be sublimated. Even after their sublimation, passions and virtues alike are difficult forces to control. They are jealous of each other and each of them wants to be the master of others. Every human being is a battlefield of passions and virtues. Zarathustra says that many have gone into the desert and even taken their lives because they got weary of the battling passions. This battle of passions explains the sage's teaching on good sleep as the ultimate bliss. He told his disciples to send the virtues to sleep to avoid their conflict. The problem of unruly passions also explains the projection of the other world. When the will is frustrated and defeated by those passions, it becomes weary of this world and longs for the other world. Zarathustra's teaching is to have no more than one virtue and to make this one virtue uniquely one's own.

The Internal Mastery (Part I.6-10)

"On the Pale Criminal" is well known for its difficulty of interpretation. Stanley Rosen calls this section the most difficult section of *Zarathustra* and gives an elaborate interpretation that runs thirteen pages. He sums up his complicated exegesis in two points: (1) the production of disciples is a flat contradiction of the doctrine of the superman and (2) the prophet must perish in order to enter the promised land (*The Mask of Enlightenment*, 98). Laurence Lampert says that this section deals with criminal justice (*Nietzsche's Teaching*, 43). Greg Whitlock says that the pale criminal represents a lion, which fails to become a child and reverts to a camel (*Returning to Sils-Maria*, 73). Robert Gooding-Williams says that the pale criminal is the victim of a Christian-Platonic reason and morality (*Zarathustra's Dionysian Modernism*, 133). Alan White construes this section as a battle between the pale criminal's soul and body (*Within Nietzsche's Labyrinth*, 77-80). The divergence of these conflicting views clearly show that it is hard to determine the central theme of this section.

This section discusses the battle of passions. Since this was the theme of the preceding section, I propose, it is further developed in this section. In the preceding section, Zarathustra said that every human being is a battlefield of unruly passions, which he called the wild dogs. The pale criminal is a victim of those wild dogs. He became a criminal because he could not control his passions. His crime involved two acts, a murder and a robbery, and his motive has become an important point of dispute. The judge says that he killed in order to rob. But Zarathustra says that the judge did not fathom the criminal's soul deep enough to understand his true motive. According to him, the murder was the primary motive: the criminal was driven by his uncontrollable impulse to kill. Since this impulse makes no sense to his poor reason, he commits the robbery to make his behavior appear rational. He followed his poor reason because he did not want to be ashamed of his madness. This is the madness before the crime, that is, the sheer madness to kill. But his deed has produced another madness, the lead of guilt upon his soul. This is the madness after the crime.

After naming the criminal's madness before and after the crime, Zarathustra raises the momentous question, "What is this man?" He gives two descriptions of this man. First, he is a heap of diseases, "which, through his spirit, reach out into the world: there they want to catch their prey" (Z, 39). Second, he is a ball of wild snakes, "which rarely enjoy rest from each other: so they go forth singly and seek prey in the world" (Z, 39). "A ball of wild snakes" stands for a bundle of unruly passions, which can rarely enjoy peace because they are engaged in a perpetual fight against one another. This perpetual fight in the soul was introduced as the battle of wild dogs in the previous section. This violent battle drives the passions to seek their prey outside in the world. This was the madness before the criminal deed. It is the healthy madness of strong passions. But the "poor reason" tries to control the wild passions with rational constraints and arguments. This rational enterprise produces guilt by defining right and wrong, and the resulting guilt turns his passions into a heap of diseases. Hence the man can be described as a ball of snakes and as a heap of diseases.

Under either of the two descriptions, it is the poor body that suffers because it has to house those battling passions. Zarathustra says that the poor soul of the criminal interpreted the suffering of his body as murderous lust and greed for the bliss of knife. He believes that the perpetual strife of passions in the body is the ultimate sickness for producing all sins and crimes in every age, although sins and crimes may take on different forms in different ages. In the olden days, the sick became heretics or witches; in our days, they become robbers or murderers. This is the cultural difference. In our totally secularized world, violent passions cannot be expressed in the religious crimes of heresy and witchcraft. Zarathustra is giving a pathological account of crimes, and his pathology is based on physiology. Because of his pathological view of crimes, he says that a criminal should be called sick but not a scoundrel, a fool but not a sinner. The sick want to inflict suffering on others because they suffer from their own passions. Because they are driven to find an outlet for their warring passions, they seek their prey in the world. This is Zarathustra's criminal pathology.

His pathology is meant not only for the criminals, but for all human beings. Even the pale criminal knows this. Hence he has no respect either for himself or for any other human being. He says, "My ego is to me the great contempt of man" (Z, 38). Zarathustra says that even the judge would be just another filthy and poisonous worm if he were to disclose what is going on in his thought. But the vitality of primitive passions and instincts is exactly what is required for generating the strong and creative will and eventually breeding the superman. For this reason, Zarathustra links the pale criminal's death to the superman. It is not sufficient for the judges to be reconciled with their killing of the criminal. He says, "May their sorrow be love for the superman." The sorrow over the death of the criminal can be seen from two different perspectives. His death is a sad event because it is the misfortune of another human being, or it is another failure of transforming the warring passions into a creative will for the superman. The former perspective is not important for Zarathustra because no human beings can be the meaning of the earth. For this reason, it is not sufficient for the judges to be reconciled with the death of the criminal. He is taking the latter perspective because only the superman can justify human existence.

The creative will, however, cannot be formed by simply letting primitive instincts run wild. They have to be overcome by sublimation, as Zarathustra taught in the preceding section. Even the eyes of the criminal say, "My ego is something that shall be overcome" (Z, 37). He can see the need to overcome himself because he feels contempt for his present self as a member of humanity. The sense of contempt is the necessary step for self-overcoming. So he adds, "my ego is to me the great contempt of man." Zarathustra says that the pale criminal's judgment on himself is his highest moment because it indicates his noble desire to overcome his base self. Zarathustra urges him not to let the sublime return to his baseness. There is no redemption for those who relapse to their baseness by abandoning their aspiration. The moment of sublime contempt in the heart of the pale criminal is what links him to the hope for overcoming humanity and advancing toward the superman.

Zarathustra notes that his pathological account of crimes is not palatable to the ears of the good people because the sickness of the criminals is not their evil. In his view, the madness of the pale criminal is much more honorable than their wretched contentment. "The wretched contentment" is the expression he used in describing the spiritual condition of the last man, whose pristine passions and instincts have been totally denatured and domesticated. In contrast, the criminal's madness attests to the vitality of his untamed passions and instincts. So Zarathustra says, "Indeed, I wish they [the good people] had a madness of which they might perish like this pale criminal" (Z, 39). The life of wild instincts is indeed a perilous path as demonstrated by the fate of the pale criminal, but Zarathustra regards it as the path of truth, loyalty, and justice because it is true, loyal, and just to one's own instincts. Unlike the pale criminal, the good people are already dead because they have been untrue to their natural instincts. But he warns that his respect for the criminal and his pathological view of crimes should not be taken as a crutch or an excuse for criminal behavior.

"On Reading and Writing" paints the condition of Zarathustra as a man of healthy passions and instincts. Whereas the pale criminal could not control the blood of his passions, Zarathustra has mastered it. He feels his elevation above the other mortals: "I no longer feel as you do: this cloud which I see beneath me, this blackness and gravity at which I laugh—this is your thundercloud" (Z, 40). "This blackness and gravity" is the misery of suffering from warring passions, the affliction of most people. Since he has conquered this misery, he can laugh at all tragedies in plays and real life. But for those who cannot do this, "Life is hard to bear" (Z, 41). In his view, they are only butterflies and soap bubbles, who are victimized by the spirit of gravity. The phrase "the spirit of gravity" is introduced for the first time without any explanation. Given its context, it appears to mean a sense of being oppressed by the burden of life ("Life is hard to bear"). The spirit of gravity is what he just called "this blackness and gravity." He wants to kill the spirit of gravity by mastering the art of flying and dancing. With its mastery, he says, "Now I am light, now I fly, now I see myself beneath myself, now a god dances through me" (Z, 41). He has gained the power of levitation to fly over the spirit of gravity. If this is truly his feeling, he appears to have succeeded in the Feuerbachian project of humanizing the divine attributes and attaining the superhuman status. As we will see later, the spirit of gravity is the basic limitation of humanity that must be overcome before the advent of the superman.

The thematic relation of the two sections, "On the Pale Criminal" and "On Reading and Writing", can be illuminated by "The criminal and what is related to him" in *Twilight of the Idols* (Expeditions 45). Nietzsche says that a strong human being becomes a sick criminal under unfavorable conditions. He degenerates because the oppressive society does not allow his strongest instinct to come into its own. Such a degenerate soul feels and is treated like a social outcast, who becomes paler than the others. Nietzsche says, "It is society, our tame, mediocre, gelded society, in which a human being raised in nature, who comes from the mountains or from adventures of the sea, necessarily degenerates into a criminal." But the strong individuals do not always suffocate and degen-

erate under social pressure. Nietzshe acknowledges the exceptional individuals, who are stronger than their societies. He cites the Corsican Napoleon as the most famous example. No wonder, he calls Napoleon the
superman (*GM* I.16). For the same reason, as we already noted,
Zarathustra also feels like a superman.

In "On the Tree on the Mountain", Zarathustra runs into a young
admirer, who wants to emulate him for climbing and flying high. But the
young man is still stumbling. The higher he climbs, the more weary he
becomes. Above all, his envy of Zarathustra is killing him. Zarathustra
counsels him that like a tree a human being can reach the height by sending the roots downward into the dark and deep evil, that is, into one's
deep passions and instinctual forces. But the young man cannot secure
such a solid instinctual foundation for his flight because he has not
gained the mastery of his passions. Zarathustra tells him that he is not yet
free and that he is still searching for his freedom. Unfortunately, the
search is hazardous. He says to the young man, "You aspire to the free
heights, your soul thirsts for the stars. But your wicked instincts, too,
thirst for freedom. Your wild dogs want freedom; they bark with joy in
their cellar when your spirit plans to open all prisons" (Z, 43). In "On the
Pale Criminal", the primitive instincts and passions were called wild
snakes. In "On Enjoying and Suffering the Passions", they were called
wild dogs. These wild dogs are now barking for their freedom in the
heart of this timid young man. The snakes and wild dogs, which represent the untamed primitive instincts, constitute the spirit of gravity. The
timid young man is now terrified and enslaved by those wild beasts.
Zarathustra tells him that such an enslaved soul has the danger of becoming clever and deceitful. He further advises the young man, "Do not
throw away the hero in your soul! Hold holy your highest hope!" (Z, 44).

For Zarathustra, "the highest hope" is not a casual expression. In the
Prologue, he used it to refer to the superman. From that we may gather
that to gain the mastery over one's passions and to overcome the spirit of
gravity are the requisite steps for becoming the superman. These superhuman requirements are the basic themes that run through the three con-
secutive sections of "On the Pale Criminal", "On Reading and Writing",

and "On the Tree on the Mountain". These three sections are addressed to the enormous difficulty of converting primitive instincts to a creative will. The first one shows the danger of letting loose the wild instincts, while the last one shows the fear of doing so. The criminal is too bold; the young man is too timid. Either of these two cases is a failure. But the middle section shows the success in this difficult conversion. Zarathustra urges the young man to maintain his sense of nobility by holding on to his love and hope. A noble person has the will to create something new and a new virtue, whereas the good people want to preserve the old. Zarathustra warns the young man against the danger facing a noble soul. It is not the danger of becoming one of the good, but that of turning into a churl, a mocker, and a destroyer through frustration and despair. This danger arises when the noble ones lose their highest hope. He says that he saw it happen. They slandered all high hopes and lived impudently for brief pleasures, barely casting their goals beyond the day. "Spirit too is lust," they said. Then the wings of their spirit broke. Once they thought of becoming heroes, but they are now voluptuaries. The sense of nobility can be sustained only by the highest hope. Without its support, a noble soul can be easily degraded because it is only a ball of snakes.

This story of spiritual degradation is continued in the next section, "On the Preachers of Death". The preachers of death say terrible things against life: "Life is only suffering," "Thou shalt kill thyself," or "Let us step aside and beget no children." They preach the renunciation of life because they have become weary of it. Why have they become weary of life? Zarathustra's answer to this question is: "There are terrible ones who carry around within themselves the beast of prey and have no choice but lust or self-laceration. And even their lust is still self-laceration" (Z, 45). Our primitive instincts, which have been compared to wild snakes and dogs, are now called the beast of prey. Zarathustra has already shown various ways of coping with this beast. The first one was the way of violence shown by the pale criminal. The second is the way of fear and anxiety shown by the timid young man. The third is the way of voluptuaries, which can gratify the passions without running the risk of violent crimes. He is now showing the fourth way, the way of self-laceration, which is taken by those who turn the savage beasts against themselves. They are the ascetics. St. Augustine tried to seek happiness by living voluptuously in his youth. When he became disillusioned with his hedonistic pursuit, he became hateful of his passions and turned against them. The way of self-laceration is not limited to the saints. As Zarathustra points out, there is a secular version, which is to get lost in furious works and restless activities, or to seek diversion in what is fast, new, and strange. These are the clever tricks to wear out the unruly wild dogs.

With "On the Preachers of Death", we are back to the theme of "On the Teachers of Virtue". The Stoic sage taught that dreamless sleep is the highest bliss attainable for human beings. The preachers of death are saying that death is better than life if death is no more than dreamless sleep. Both of them are seeking their way out of human misery. Zarathustra has tried to account for human misery on the premise that the soul is the body that houses a ball of snakes. He has scrutinized many different ways of coping with this ball of snakes: the way of violence, the way of fear and anxiety, the way of hedonistic indulgence, the way of self-laceration, and the way of diversion through work and entertainment. The last one is perhaps most common in our age, and the wretched contentment of the people in the market place may belong to it. They were in the market place to seek entertainment in something new and strange, and they would try to lose themselves in their works when they went to their work. None of these methods appear to make any better sense than the Stoic way of sleep without dreams. Although all of them have been invented to cope with the turmoil and torment of their passions in this world, they only degrade human existence. They may be called the ways of self-degradation.

What then is the right way to cope with wild passions? This question was on Zarathustra's mind in "Reading and Writing". He claimed to have risen above the tragic dimension of human life and to have conquered the spirit of gravity. He has mastered the art of dancing and flying like a god. He has won the war against the instinctual passions to the envy of the young man. But he does not tell you how he has done it. This is the most baffling feature of his talk. At any rate, his mastery over the ball of snakes shows what it is like to have a life truly worth living and perhaps what it is like to be a superman. But those who have not won the victory over their passions have to continue their war, and Zarathustra gives his advice to them on this warfare in "On War and Warriors". If one gains the sort of mastery over one's passions that Zarathustra advocates, one can become what he calls a saint of knowledge. If one cannot become such a saint, he says, one has to be a warrior. A saint ranks higher than a warrior. The former has won the battle, whereas the latter is still engaged in it. The relation between a saint of knowledge and a warrior is like the relation of a stoic sage (*sophos*) and a philosopher (*philosophos*). Whereas the sage has gained wisdom, the philosopher is only in love with it, that is, he is still struggling to achieve it. Zarathustra is talking to the warriors, who are still suffering from "the hatred and envy of their hearts" just like the young man in "On the Tree on the Mountainside".

All his remarks indicate that Zarathustra is talking about the war against passions. When he says that it is not the good cause that hallows war and that it is the good war that hallows any cause, he sounds like a typical warmonger and he has been roundly condemned as such. But he stresses the nature of war rather than its cause because the cause is already well known to anyone, who has followed his discourse in the preceding sections. It is the mastery of passions. Lest his readers forget it, he restates it a few lines later, "Your love of life shall be love of your highest hope; and your highest hope shall be the highest thought of life" (*Z*, 48). He says that this highest thought of life is the idea that man is something that shall be overcome and that this thought is his command to the warriors. To overcome man is to master the snakes and the wild dogs in his heart. He is talking to those who can fight this war only in obedience to his command because they have not become saints of knowledge by gaining complete mastery of their passions.

To be deviled by passions is the most common fate for human beings. Therefore, to gain the mastery of passions is to overcome (*überwinden*) man and to transcend the limits of humanity. This is to become the superman (*Übermensch*). Zarathustra has been articulating the notion of the superman in the last few sections. It looks similar to the Stoic ideal of self-mastery and self-sufficiency. The Stoics called it the ideal of *autarcheia*, which can indeed make human beings like gods. But there is one important difference between Zarathustra's and the Stoic ideals. For their mastery over passions, the Stoics resorted to a highly ascetic and repressive discipline. That is the way of self-laceration: it is to turn the passions against oneself. This is not to enjoy them, but to enslave them. To enjoy the passions without repression is Zarathustra's goal of self-mastery in "On Enjoying and Sufferng the Passions". That alone is truly to be like the gods.

Zarathustra is again talking like Max Stirner, who says that all of us can easily despair over the difficulty of controlling our natural instincts. He says that every human being is an "abyss of lawless and unregulated impulses, desires, wishes, passions, a chaos without light or guiding star!"(*The Ego and Its Own*, 56). This is no different from Zarathustra's view of it as a ball of wild snakes or a bunch of wild dogs. As a right way to cope with the chaotic impulses, Stirner counsels against not only the holy man's religious renunciation of sensuality, but also the enslavement to appetites (*The Ego and Its Own*, 56-57). To be the master of oneself, one should own one's appetites instead of being owned by them. This is Stirner's ideal of self-ownership and becoming an almighty God-like ego. God owns everything, and is never owned by anything. Zarathustra is advocating the same ideal of divine ownership and mastery for human beings.

The Way of Solitude (Part I.11-14)

Zarathustra's war sermon continues in the next section, "On the New Idol". Talking to those who have vanquished the old god, he says, "You have grown weary with fighting, and now your weariness still serves the new idol" (Z, 49). The new idol is the state, which has become an escape and refuge for those weary of fighting the war against their own passions. He calls the state the coldest of all cold monsters. The state disguises itself as the people: "I, the state, am the people" (Z, 48). But that is a lie.

Zarathustra says that the people (or folk) is the creator of its own unique values. It invents its own language of customs and rights. This idea is a legacy of Herder and Schlegel, who claimed the people or folk as the creator of cultural values. By the middle of the nineteenth century, this idea had become an important element in German culture. The people was taken as the creator of myths by David Strauss (*Life of Jesus*, 81-86) and as the creator of art by Richard Wagner (*The Art-Work of the Future*, 73-82, 204-5; *Opera and Drama*, 155). Zarathustra says that the state creates nothing but lies and that it produces only the confusion of values. The state is also the surrogate for the old God. It makes the same promise that God used to make: "I will give you everything if you adore me." It makes the same demand that God used to make, the hellish sacrifice from all its followers. It has invented a death for many and glorified death as life, thereby rendering a great service to all preachers of death.

The state is now providing the same service that used to be provided by the old God—the refuge for those exhausted in their fight against their unruly passions. So Zarathustra says that the state is for the superfluous. In his condemnation of the state, he sounds like Max Stirner, who designated the state as the surrogate of the old God and the greatest enemy of the individual (*The Ego and Its Own*, 89-105). Stirner says that every state is despotism whether the despot is one or many (*The Ego and Its Own*, 175). But he does not recommend a political revolution to overthrow the state because such a revolution would create another social institution for the oppression of individuals. He recommends rebellion as the only remedy against the state power, presumably the rebellion of individuals that involves no organization. It appears that Zarathustra does not even trust the rebellion of individuals. His only viable recourse is to flee to one's solitude for the sake of freedom. He says that there are still many places on the earth, where great souls can be free. This is a surprise move on his part. Given his sermon on war and warriors in the previous section, you would expect him to issue a call to fight against the state. But he does not. This is in support of my claim that he was only talking about the war against passions in that sermon.

Freedom is the only important cause for Zarathustra. In the previous sections, he talked about internal freedom, the freedom from passions. In this section, he is stressing external freedom, the freedom from the state. A truly sovereign self should be enslaved neither to internal passions nor to external authorities. Zarathustra extends the sermon of solitude from the state to the market place in "On the Flies of the Market Place". He says that solitude ceases where the market place begins. In the market place, you are dazed by the noise of great men and stung all over by the stings of small men. But they do not know what greatness means. For them, it is to put on a big show and make a loud noise. To be a great man is to be a great actor. The market place recognizes only the showmen. But they have no conception of greatness because their business is to entertain the small creatures, the flies of the market place. Zarathustra says that the true greatness lies in creating new values, which takes place far from the market place. He says, "Around the inventors of new values the world revolves: invisibly it revolves. But around the actors revolve the people and fame: that is 'the way of the world'" (Z, 52). Again he does not issue a call to fight against the market place, but only repeats the same advice: "Flee into your solitude!" At least in this case, he admits the futility of fighting against the people in the market place because there are too many of them, and warns his audience against the danger of being crushed under the pressure of the numerous small and miserable creatures.

In "On Chastity", Zarathustra shifts his attention to the war against sexuality. He begins this section by contrasting life in the forest with life in the cities. Life in the forest is life in solitude. In the cities, he says, "there too many are in heat" (Z, 54). He is envious of the innocent sensuality of animals and wishes human beings were as innocent of their sexual impulses as those animals. He believes that human sensuality becomes a bitch in cities and that the bitch of sensuality destroys solitude. This section is against the city as much as the previous sections were against the state and the market place. The city corrupts our sexual passions and disrupts our solitude. Zarathustra recognizes the virtue of chastity as a way to cope with sensuality. But this virtue is almost a vice in many who abstain from sex because they are still haunted by the bitch of sensuality. He counsels not the killing of sensual desires, but their innocence. Since it is godlike to enjoy the innocence of sensuality, it should be regarded as an essential feature of the superman. Zarathustra says that those whose sensuality is innocent do not even know what chastity is. Chastity is human, but innocence is divine. The virtue of chastity involves restraint and repression, but the state of innocence does not. The latter alone belongs to true freedom. In this regard, Zarathustra's ideal of freedom and self-mastery is far beyond the Stoic ideal and truly superhuman.

Just as the bond of sexual relation can endanger solitude, so does the bond of friendship. In "On the Friend", Zarathustra talks about the danger of friendship for solitude. For the hermit seeking solitude, he says, the friend is the third person, who can come between his I and his me. The third person is "the cork that prevents the conversation of the two from sinking into the depths" (Z, 56). Because "there are too many depths for all hermits," he says, "they long for a friend and his height." They use friends to avoid their depths. Therefore, Zarathustra says, our longing for a friend is our betrayer. Whatever one wants to see in one's friend is the projection of what one wants to see but cannot find in oneself. Hence one should never trust or rely on one's friend. Friendship is the pitfall for those who cannot stand on their own. The best way to avoid this pitfall is to be capable of being an enemy to a friend. Zarathustra says, "In a friend one should have one's best enemy." Instead of seeking the height in one's friend, one should offer it for him to surpass, thereby becoming an arrow and a longing for the superman. Therefore one should never expose one's naked self to a friend because a naked self is too ugly to serve as a model for anyone's emulation. Zarathustra says, "You cannot groom yourself too beautifully for your friend" (Z, 56). Even compassion for a friend should conceal itself under a hard shell.

This is a strange notion of friendship, which turns upside down our normal conception of friendship. Zarathustra's counsel not to trust or rely on our friends goes against our normal understanding that they can be trusted and relied on even when nobody else can be. His idea of concealing oneself by ornament to a friend clearly violates the sense of candor and trust one expects between friends. Carl Jung says that Zarathustra is trying to create a fantastical friend by laying down strange conditions, which can never be fulfilled by any human being (*Nietzsche's* Zarathustra, 627). But the fantastical conception of friendship is unavoidable for a hermit, who is seeking complete self-sufficiency in solitude. Zarathustra not only mentions the hermit at the beginning of the section, but also refers to solitude in its middle, "Are you pure air and solitude and bread and medicine for your friend?" (*Z*, 57). The hermit in solitude wants to be a self-sufficient human being. This is the Stoic ideal of self-sufficiency. This ideal has two dimensions, internal and external. Internally, it requires the mastery over one's passions; externally, it requires independence from others. For the external dimension of self-sufficiency, Zarathustra has argued for solitude in the last four sections. Friendship in its normal conception can be a dangerous pitfall for anyone seeking such a complete self-sufficiency, because the normal friendship has been designed for the simple reason that such a total self-sufficiency is impossible.

Since the ideal of total self-sufficiency is not possible for human beings, it has long been regarded as a divine attribute. Zarathustra's ideal of a self-sufficient hermit is another instance of humanizing the ideal of divine perfection for the advent of the superman. The ideal of self-sufficiency is equivalent to Stirner's ideal of self-ownership. To own oneself is to depend on no one else; to depend on others is to be owned by others. Stirner seldom talks about friendship or having friends. But he talks about the danger of love. In ancient Greece, love (*philos*) was another name for friendship. He says that every love is either selfish or unselfish (*The Ego and Its Own*, 259-62). The selfish love is the love of possession. You possess or try to possess what you love, thereby securing your ownship or mastery of what you love. Unselfish love serves the opposite function; it is to be owned by what one loves. Stirner takes family love as a salient example. If one loves one's family, one surrenders one's autonomy to it. Likewise, he says, romantic or religious love equally destroys individual autonomy (*The Ego and Its Own*, 260). He cannot tolerate unselfish love because it is detrimental to the absolute sovereignty of an almighty ego. For the same reason, neither can Zarathustra tolerate normal friendship. The ideal of absolute individual sovereignty is a legacy from the Lutheran tradition. Martin Luther already humanized this ideal in his conception of a Christian, who must stand alone before God. This was a radical break with the medieval Christianity, which stressed the communal bond of human beings in the Mystical Body of Christ. The medieval Christians assumed that nobody was self-sufficient enough to stand alone before God. But the Protestants were so preoccupied with their individual autonomy that they were determined to protect it even against the bond of fellowship and mutual reliance.

The Protestant ethos sets apart Zarathustra's ideal of individual autonomy from the Stoic ideal of *autarcheia*. Unlike Protestant individuals, the Stoics regarded friendship as an indispensable condition for their autonomy and well-being. In their view, friendship does not endanger or compromise the ideal of self-sufficiency (Glenn Lesses, "Austere Friends: The Stoics and Friendship"). To rely on a friend is not really to rely on others because a friend is an extension of oneself. Therefore the power of self-sufficiency is expanded and reinforced by friendship. Moreover, the Stoic friendship is not limited to a few personal friends, but extends to all wise men. A Stoic sage is united with his fellows by the bond of friendship because all wise persons are friends to each other. In the ideal Stoic world, even the state will wither away (A. A. Long, *Hellenistic Philosophy*, 205). In his *De res publica,* Cicero goes one step further and holds that an ideal state is a society of friendship. In his celebrated treatise on friendship, he says that virtue can never reach its greatest height without friendship and that a good friend is the best support of all. Even the Epicureans, who were hedonistic egoists, did not falter on the question of friendship. They commended friendship zealously although it may not have been compatible with their ideal of self-sufficiency and invulnerability. They believed that friendship was choice-worthy not merely for its benefit but as an end in itself (Phillip Mitsis, *Epicurus' Ethical Theory*, 98-128).

This classical conception of friendship was radically changed in the modern West, and this change is reflected in European literary tradition. The deep bond of friendship was a popular theme for medieval literature from *The Song of Roland* (the friendship of Roland and Oliver) to *Don Quixote de la Mancha* (the friendship of Don Quixote and Sancho Panza). Even Dante's relation with his three guides during his journey in the afterworld reflects the deep sense of medieval friendship, and he talks about the enduring influence that Cicero's treatise on friendship had on his own life (*Convivio* I.12; II.12). It is instructive to compare Dante's friendship with his three guides in his *Commedia* with Christian's relation to his companions in Bunyan's *Pilgrim's Progress*. Christian begins his pilgrimage by abandoning his own family against their plea not to leave them. In the course of his journey, he never forms an enduring friendship with anyone except Faithful and Hopeful, the two figures representing his own self. In general, the Puritans avoided relying on others in their approach to God. Hence they experienced such deep spiritual isolation from one another that they were called separated brethren. Their spiritual isolation is well documented by Max Weber in *The Protestant Ethic and the Spirit of Capitalism*. According to him, English Puritan literature is full of warnings against placing trust in the friendship of men. He says, "Even the gentle Baxter advises profound suspicion even of one's closest friend, and Bailey goes so far as to recommend trusting no one and saying nothing compromising to anyone: God alone should have our confidence" (*The Protestant Ethic and the Spirit of Capitalism*, 74).

The medieval sense of friendship was continuous with the ancient friendship of Achilles and Patroclus, and Damon and Pythias. But that sort of deep friendship started to disappear in modern European literature, beginning with Boccaccio's *Decameron*. For all the impressive variety of its one hundred stories, this Renaissance masterpiece contains not a single heart-warming story of friendly trust and devotion. The protagonists and the antagonists alike are so fearfully jealous of their own autonomy that they are incapable of deep friendships. You may say that the Boccaccian ethos is sickly and that the Boccaccian individuals are monsters.

They may be monsters by your human standard, but they are becoming like God by their own superhuman standard.

The Way of Creation (Part I.15-17)

So far Zarathustra has talked about the internal and external conditions for autonomy and self-sufficiency. But these conditions are not the ultimate ends. They provide the basis for the creation of new values, which was mentioned briefly in "On the Flies of the Market Place". In "On the Thousand and One Goals", Zarathustra returns to the creation of values and declares that the will to power is the creator of values. He has seen many lands and many peoples, but found no greater powers than good and evil. No people can live without esteeming, without formulating their own tablets of good and evil. They are the tablets of their self-overcoming, the records of their will to overcome their greatest difficulties. Since these difficulties are different for different peoples, each of them has to devise its own unique system of values. Zarathustra highlights the unique character of each value-system by citing the tablets of good and evil created by the Greeks, the Persians, the Jews, and the Romans. By devising these unique tablets of value, he says, they created the meaning of their existence. He then gives an unusual account of creation: "To esteem is to create" (Z, 59). In general, to create means to create a new object. But to esteem may not require the creation of a new object because it is possible to esteem an existing object. He says that esteeming itself is the most estimable treasure among all esteemed things, because value is created only by esteeming. The creation of value is different from the creation of objects. This is his unique view of values.

Zarathustra may appear to announce the radical thesis that values are created by human beings, that is, they have no independent existence. But he says that to create values is to esteem them. Let us consider the problem of passions. To esteem them is to create their values. For another example, to appreciate water is to create its value. We may drink water day after day without appreciating its value. Then water may have no value for us because we do not esteem it. But that is not to say that water is valueless. We come to esteem water when it becomes hard to obtain. Zarathustra stresses the great difficulties that generated the ancient tablets of the good. He says, "Praiseworthy is whatever seems difficult to a people; whatever seems indispensable and difficult is called good" (Z, 58). This is a reflection of Spinoza's wisdom: "All noble things are as difficult as they are rare" (*Ethics,* pt. 5, prop. 42). This is not to say that the great difficulties create the great values. On the contrary, the great values come to be esteemed through the great difficulties that are encountered by the will to power. So it may be said that the will to power creates values by overcoming difficulties.

In the ancient world, Zarathustra says, the creators were the peoples. In the modern age, however, the creators are the individuals. In fact, the individual is the most recent creation. In "On the New Idol", he said that every people creates its own values. We noted that he was echoing Herder's and Schlegel's view of the people as the agent of creation. Now he is introducing the individual as the creator of values. This transformation has taken place with the emergence of Protestant individualism. In their nostalgic talk of the people, Herder and Schlegel were still thinking about the pre-modern Germanic tribes. Zarathustra describes the transformation of the old communal ethos into the new individual ethos: "The delight in the herd is more ancient than the delight in the ego; and as long as the good conscience is identified with the herd, only the bad conscience says: I" (Z, 60).

This is a loaded description of the old and the new ethos. Zarathustra uses the pejorative word 'herd' in describing the communal ethos ("the delight in the herd"). In the communal ethos, he says, the good conscience was identified with the herd. But 'herd' is a bad word for 'community'. The tribal people would have agreed that the good conscience is identified with the community, but they would have been horrified to have their community referred to as a herd. In the old communal ethos, Zarathustra says, only the bad conscience said: I. That is a correct statement. In a communal culture, it is a serious crime to assert one's individuality against the community. But the old age of communal values has been replaced by the new age of individual values. This cultural transformation can best be illustrated by Martin Luther's stand against the Catholic Church. By the standard of the old ethos, his stand against the Church was the sin of defying the authority of the community. By the standard of the new ethos, however, it was the virtue of creating new values. Whereas the old communal ethos created one thousand goals for one thousand peoples, Zarathustra says, the new individual ethos will create one universal goal. He is now calling for that one goal: "Only the yoke for the thousand necks is still lacking: the one goal is lacking" (*Z*, 60). What is this one final yoke? It is the eternal recurrence, the yoke for the superman. This point will become clearer in Part III.

In "On Love of the Neighbor", Zarathustra again comes back to the relation of self to others. He says that one's love of a neighbor is often an escape from oneself. It is the question of 'You' and 'I'. He says, "The 'You' is older than the 'I'; the 'You' has been consecrated, but not yet the 'I': so man crowds toward the neighbor" (*Z*, 86). In the preceding section, he said that the creator of values was the people in the olden days and that the individual is the most recent creation. He also said that the delight in the herd is more ancient than the delight in the ego and that the good conscience is identified with the herd and the bad conscience with the individual. Since the individual has to take a big risk in asserting his I, he is tempted to take his refuge in the herd. His neighbors are his nearest herd. Zarathustra says that the individual not only wants to lose himself in his neighbor, but also would like to make a virtue out of it, namely, the virtue of neighborly love. But this dubious virtue only indicates that such an individual is suffering from a sickly love of himself. Without a healthy self-love, Zarathustra says, one can turn his solitude into a prison. Love of the neighbor can be the escape hatch from this prison. When one cannot endure oneself, he says, one seeks relief in one's neighbor. Instead of the nearest (the neighbor), he contends, one should love the farthest, that is, the superman. Since the superman is not here yet, he advises his audience to love him by creating friends in anticipation of him.

To create friends is a novel proposal. In "On the Friend", he never talked about creating friends. But how can you create friends? For those who cannot stand their neighbors, Zarathustra recommends the following formula of creating friends: "then you would have to create your friend and his overflowing heart out of yourself" (Z, 61). This enigmatic formula is supposed to create a fantastic friend, "in whom the world stands completed, a bowl of goodness—the creating friend who always has a completed world to give away" (Z, 62). This friend is so fantastic that Laurence Lampert identifies him as Zarathustra, that is, he is recommending himself as the creative friend (*Nietzsche's Teaching*, 65). But this reading cannot be textually justified. If the fantastic friend is meant to be Zarathustra, he and his overflowing heart cannot be created "out of yourself." It may be better to take the enigmatic formula as Zarathustra's oracular way of saying that you should become a friend to yourself. The friend you can create out of yourself cannot be anyone but yourself. That is the only kind of friend you can love and trust without jeopardizing your sovereignty. With such a friend, you will be spared all the anxiety about friendship voiced in "On the Friend". But you can be such a perfect friend to yourself only by becoming a self-sufficient individual who has his own complete world. Your own world is the only world you can give away to yourself. Living in your own complete world, you would have no need to run to your neighbor under any circumstances. This is the ultimate outcome of radical individualism: A sovereign individual can find a true friend only in himself if he has his own complete world.

This form of radical individualism is perhaps best exemplified by Richard Wagner's *Tristan and Isolde*. In the love duet, the two lovers sing together the enigmatic phrase, "then I myself am the world." This passage is startling because it appears in their description of the ecstatic union of two lovers, which they long to experience in the world of night (the noumenal world of cosmic unity) when the world of day (the phenomenal world of individuation) fades away. The enigmatic phrase may indicate the complete harmony between 'I' and 'my world' in the ecstatic union. Even so, you would expect them to say 'we' rather than 'I'. But they want to say that each 'I' is his or her own world. Michael Tanner says that such a world is a world of fantasy (*Wagner,* 152). That may be true. Their notion of the individual world is in line with Schopenhauer's theory of individuation, which governs the entire opera. The word 'and' in "Tristan and Isolde" becomes a critical problem for the two lovers not only in their duet but also throughout the entire opera. Since the two lovers cannot live together, they express their wish to die together. Even this wish, however, is destined to be denied in the Schopenhauerian world of individuation. On the lonely shore, the dying Tristan is anxiously waiting for Isolde's arrival by ship. When she finally arrives and rushes toward Tristan, calling his name, he totters toward her only to slip from her embrace to the ground and leaves her all to her lonely stricken self. She feels betrayed because they had vowed to die together. Now she pours out her lamentation: "Awake once again. Hear my cry! Isolde is calling; she has come faithfully to die with Tristan!" She can be united with him only in the love-death, where the individuals are absorbed into the cosmic unity of the all-encompassing Will. In the domain of individuation, every individual is trapped in his or her own world.

By the end of "On Love of the Neighbor", Zarathustra has almost perfected the superhuman ideal in the image of a totally self-sufficient individual, who can give a complete world to himself. This ideal image sets the stage for his discourse in the next section, "On the Way of the Creator". He opens the section with two questions: "Is it your wish, my brother, to go into solitude? Is it your wish to seek the way to yourself?" (*Z*, 62). It is easy to lose oneself in the herd, he says, because it is comfortable to share a common conscience with the herd. You can recover your self from the herd only by taking a solitary way to your self. Only then, Zarathustra say, you can be a first moment and a self-propelled wheel. These are the metaphors he used to describe the child as the last stage of the three metamorphoses. The child is the one who can be the master of one's own being. Zarathustra says that this truly creative agent is not one of the lustful and ambitious. He talked about their corruption in "On Chastity". Now he says that they are only bellows that inflate with emptiness. He characterizes the creative agent in terms of freedom and distinguishes two kinds of freedom ("free from what?" and "free for what?"). This distinction amounts to the difference between the lion's freedom and the child's freedom. The lion's freedom is the freedom from servitude, which is not sufficient for the creation of values. Zarathustra says, "There are some who threw away their last value when they threw away their servitude" (Z, 63). The child's freedom is the freedom for its own sovereignty. This is the freedom of a creator, who is not only free from others, but also free to give himself his own good and evil. Just like the old God, he is the sole authority for his law from its legislation to its execution. This is the lonely self-creator.

Zarathustra compares the lonely creator to "a star thrown out into the void and into the icy void of solitude" (Z, 63). He talks about the spiritual crisis that will come upon such a solitary existence: You will cry, "I am alone!" And you will even say, "All is false!" This is the crisis of value, which will eventually haunt every lonely creator of values. Since the solitary individual cannot appeal to any authority in his creation of values other than his own judgment, he can never find any ground for their justification. Hence he may well have to admit, "All is false!" But that is not the end of his difficulties. He will be hated and slandered by the good and the just for his defiant stand. But they are not the worst enemy for the solitary one. He says, "But the worst enemy you can encounter will always be you, yourself; you lie in wait for yourself in caves and woods" (Z, 64). This idea clearly sets him apart from Max Stirner, who was chiefly concerned with the danger of having one's sovereignty and creativity abrogated by others. For Zarathustra, however, that is not the greatest danger for the lonely individual. The weight of an old self is the greatest obstacle to the creation of a new self. There is no single fixed self for any individual. Every individual is a Heraclitean flux, which perpetually creates a new self by destroying an old one. In the domain of self-creation, the relation of an old self to a new one is more critical than the relation of oneself to others. The creation of a new self requires the destruction of an old self. At the end of this section, Zarathustra says, "I love him who wants to create over and beyond himself and thus perishes" (Z, 65).

Just before this concluding statement, Zarathustra discusses the problem of self-creation in terms of self-relation in three paragraphs, each of which begins with the two words, 'Lonely one'. In the first paragraph, he says, "Lonely one, you are going the way to yourself. And your way leads past yourself and your seven devils" (*Z*, 64). Your seven devils are the seven unruly passions of your old self that have to be conquered by the new self. In "On Enjoying and Suffering the Passions" he said that our passions are called devils when we suffer from them and that they are called angels when they are turned into virtues. The way to your new self leads past your old self because the new self has to surpass the old one. To go against your old self is to be "a heretic to yourself." To destroy an old self for a new one is "to consume yourself in your own flame." In the second paragraph, he says, "Lonely one, you are going the way of the creator: you would create a god for yourself out of your seven devils" (*Z*, 64f). The seven unruly passions repressed by the old self will be made into a god when they are sublimated by the new self.

The second paragraph involves a dramatic reversal in the process of self-creation. The first paragraph simply talks about passing and destroying the old self and its seven devils, but the second paragraph talks about the creation of a god out of those seven devils. The devils that make up the old self are not to be condemned and discarded, but be redeemed and transformed into a god. By this process, the old self is born as a new child. The doctrine of self-creation has become popular among the followers of Nietzsche. But it is open for two interpretations. To create oneself may mean to invent oneself (self-invention) or to esteem oneself (self-appreciation). In "On the Thousand and One Goals", Zarathustra said that to create was to esteem. As we already noted, the idea of creation usually implies the idea of invention. But to esteem something is not to invent it. By esteeming the passions, we may redeem them, thereby transforming them from devils to a god. The tablets of value created by different peoples may be their inventions or the records of their appreciation and redemption. By applying these two ideas of creation, we may define self-creation as self-invention or self-appreciation. The idea of self-invention is to invent a new self to replace the old one. The idea of self-appreciation is to create a new self by esteeming or redeeming the old one. The idea of self-invention is contained in the first paragraph, and the idea of self-appreciation in the second paragraph. The conflict of these two ideas in the notion of self-creation will be one of the most critical issues in Parts II, III, and IV.

The idea of self-creation is Zarathustra's program of creating the superman by transforming a human being to a god. In the third paragraph, he highlights self-love as the engine for self-creation. He concludes his sermon by his final benediction on the lonely creator. Now his sermon on the creative will is almost complete. It is built on his previous sermons on the mastery of passions and on solitude. They lay the ground for the sovereign individual, who can perpetually consume himself for the creation of an ever new self. This task of self-creation is the expression of self-love. The remaining five sections of Part I are only incidental remarks that follow his final elaboration on the creative will in "On the Way of the Creator". Let us briefly pause and consider the general plan of Part I. It began with the road map of spiritual development from the camel through the lion to the child in the first section. We noted that the state of sleep without dreams praised in "On the Teachers of Virtue" was the original state prior to the development of these three stages. We also noted that the final stage, the state of a child, is reached in "On the Way of the Creator". The journey from the original to the final state takes up fifteen sections of Part I.

The fifteen sections can be divided into three segments. The eight sections from section 3 through section 10 are chiefly concerned with the mastery of passions. Every human being is a bundle of warring passions or a ball of snakes. Hence the mastery of these passions is the first step for becoming the superman. The next four sections (11-14) are about protecting one's integrity from external forces by fleeing to solitude. These two groups of eight and four sections depict the metamorphosis of a camel to a lion. The last three sections (15-17) are devoted to the creation of values. Section 15 introduces the will to power, the most important idea for the creation of values. When the will to power becomes creative, it creates a new self. But this creative self can be recovered only

in solitude. Furthermore, the awesome task of creating oneself is to redeem and transform the self harboring the seven devils into a god. The
seven devils are none other than the ball of snakes. As long as you hate
and despise this devilish self, Zarathustra says, it is your worst enemy.
You can love your devilish self only by turning it into your best friend.
Now we can understand his statement that "you would have to create
your friend and his overflowing heart out of yourself." By "out of yourself," he meant "out of your devilish self." We can now describe the
process of self-creation as the process of transforming a devil into a god,
your worst enemy into your best friend, and your self-hatred into your
self-love. This is the fabulous task of realizing the superman. This superhuman task belongs to the metamorphosis of a lion to a child. This is the
ultimate end for Zarathustra's ambitious campaign of spiritualization that
was launched at the end of the Prologue. This is his grand strategy for
redeeming the secular culture of The Motley Cow by the power of his
new superhuman ideal.

His spiritual campaign began not in the first section of Part I, but in
the Prologue. When he was descending from his mountain cave to the
market crowd, the hermit described him as the awakened one and advised him not to go to the sleepers. Zarathustra regarded the natural existence of the market crowd as no better than sleep and tried to wake them
up with the lightning of the superman. But they only blinked in response
to his lightning message. Their secular culture is worse than the state of
dreamless sleep that the Stoic sages were seeking. Today's market crowd
live under the illusion of shaping the destiny of their existence. That is
why they claim to have invented happiness. The ancient Stoics were too
wise to have such illusion about their own existence. Zarathustra called
the invented happiness of the market crowd their wretched contentment.
They do not even know the difference between happiness and contentment. The satisfaction of natural desires is contentment and that may be
the ultimate end of natural existence. But to take it as the ultimate end of
human existence is to degrade our divine aspiration for limitless perfection. Hence his spiritual campaign is to wake up humankind from the
sleep of secular culture and rekindle their divine aspiration.

Zarathustra's Farewell (Part I.18-22)

The four sections of Part I, which follow "On the Way of the Creator", are incidental observations. They lead up to Zarathustra's farewell in the final section. In "On Little Old and Young Women", he tells a woman, "Let the radiance of a star shine through your love! Let your hope be: May I give birth to the superman!" (Z, 66). His preaching on the creative will is presumably addressed only to men and not to women. But women can still play an important role by pregnancy. They can give birth to the superman. "On the Adder's Bite" shows Zarathustra's immunity to the adder's poison. He says to the adder, "When has a dragon ever died of the poison of a snake?" He is not afraid of the adder's bite any more than a dragon would be. The adder is an ordinary snake; the dragon is an extraordinary beast. Both of them represent the primitive instincts and passions, as we will see more clearly later. The dragon may stand for the self-mastery of Zarathustra, whose passions have been sublimated or whose devils have become gods, while the adder may stand for the small man, whose passions are still unruly. In "On Child and Marriage", he again stresses that human reproduction should be a bridge to the superman. Marriage and reproduction should be governed by the principle of self-overcoming and be dedicated to the production of the superman. "On Free Death" teaches the right way to die, which is to die at the right time. One should not live too long and become superfluous.

By the end of "On Free Death", Zarathustra abruptly brings his preaching to bear upon on his own mission: "Verily, Zarathustra had a goal; he threw his ball: now you, my friends, are the heirs of my goal; to you I throw my golden ball" (Z, 74). The time for his exit has arrived by the end of Part I, "On the Gift-Giving Virtue". That should be the time for his free death. The golden ball is no longer in his hand; it has been passed to his heirs. After his farewell speech, he starts leaving the town called The Motley Cow and his disciples accompany him to a crossroad. When he is about to leave them for his lonely walk ahead, they present a farewell gift, a staff with a golden handle, on which a serpent coils around the sun. This gift incites him to give a speech on the nature of the

gift-giving virtue. He says that beautiful gold always gives itself. Therefore it is the image of the highest virtue, the gift-giving virtue. He distinguishes two types of selfishness, sickly and healthy. The sickly selfishness is greedy and grabby ("Everything for me"). The healthy selfishness
never grabs anything for its own sake, but only to give it as a gift. He assigns the sickly selfishness to the sick body. The healthy and the sickly
selfishness are commonly regarded as matters of the spirit, but he says
that such matters are only the images of the body. The spiritual degeneration is the bodily degeneration. When the body is elevated and resur-
rected, it produces the healthy spirit, which can become the lover and
benefactor of all things. Such a spirit has a heart that flows broad and full
like a river. It is the gift-giving virtue, which is represented by the sun on
the farewell gift from his disciples.

The sun and its abundant radiation is a venerable symbol of God and
his limitless gifts that goes back to Plato's analogy of the Good to the sun
in Book 6 of the *Republic*. Elaborating on this Platonic metaphor, Plotinus says that the cosmic Soul gives life to the material world like the sun
shining its brilliance upon a cloud (*Enneads* V.1.2). He again uses the
same Platonic metaphor in saying that the emanation of Intelligence from
the One may be compared to the brilliant light encircling the sun and
ceaselessly generated from that unchanging substance (*Enneads* V.1.6).
Pseudo Dionysius Areopagite uses the same metaphor in comparing God
to the sun, whose limitless light renews, nourishes, and flourishes all the
sensible beings (*The Divine Names* 4.8). Scotus Erigena restates Pseudo
Dionysius' teaching by comparing the power of God to the inexhaustible
ray of the sun and to a river that flows from a limitless source (*On the
Division of Nature*, bk. 2, ch. 32; bk. 3, ch. 4). Bonaventure reaffirms this
Christian conception of God by calling Christ's love of the world the radiant heat of the Eternal Sun (*The Tree of Life,* Prol. 3). He also compares Christ's love to the eternal sweet Stream from the Fountain invisible to all mortal eyes (*The Tree of Life* III. 47)

Zarathustra is now using the metaphor of not only the sun, but also
the stream. But he is using these metaphors to describe the power of not
God, but of man. Any human being who can be so described is like God.

He is the superman, who has transcended the limits of humanity. His power is limitless like the radiant sun and the eternal stream. His love of others is really his love of himself. Hence his gift to others is really a gift to himself. A strong, healthy self has a much broader boundary of self-hood than a weak, sickly self. Those who are normally regarded as others by the weak self are accepted as the extension of oneself by the strong self. This is clearly a mark of transcending the normal limits of being a human self. When Zarathustra set out on his journey, he took the sun for his model. Now we can see that this model expressed his ambition to elevate man to the position of God. He is now urging his followers to be like God in being independent and self-sufficient and in freely giving and caring for others out of abundant self-love. On the farewell staff, the sun is connected to the serpent. In the Garden of Eden, the serpent was the malicious creature to lure Adam and Eve to their perdition out of envy. On the farewell staff, however, the serpent stands for the natural force that generates the sun and its radiance. Thus the symbolism of the fare-well staff redeems the natural force from the Christian damnation and re-stores its sanctity and generosity. The union of the sun and the serpent on the staff represents the unity of God and the earth. This symbol portrays Spinoza's conception of Mother Nature as the supreme deity and reality.

Changing his voice, Zarathustra now urges his disciples to remain faithful to the earth and continue to be creative fighters. He warns against the hundred ways the human spirit has been misled to make mistakes, which still live in our body. He says, "Indeed, an experiment was man" (Z, 77). The human history has been a series of experiments to find out the destiny of humanity. He then says, "Still we fight step by step with the giant: accident" (Z, 77). This is his first mention of the giant called accident. Since this giant is beyond anyone's control and will, it poses the enormous threat against the creative will that he has preached in Part I. Although he mentions it casually, it will haunt him relentless and mer-cilessly for the remainder of his career. Changing the tone of his voice once more, Zarathustra tells his disciples that they have to walk their own lonely ways. They should cease to be mere followers and believers. But he promises to return when they have all denied him. In fact, he promises two returns. He will make the first return to seek his lost disciples when they have denied him, and the second return to celebrate the great noon when man stands in the middle of his way between the beast and the superman. On that great occasion, he will get together with his disciples to celebrate the advent of the superman. With this prophecy for his second and third coming, Zarathustra finally leaves his disciples for his solitude. This is the end of Part I.

His mission appears to be completed. He has rekindled a new fire from his old ashes and dispensed it as the new meaning of the earth for humanity. This is his ideal of the superman. But this ideal is a Christian legacy. It began with the creation of God by the projection of human aspirations. But this projection was the alienation of human ideals from human beings. The re-appropriation of the alienated ideals has taken a long series of spiritual movements. First, Jesus Christ exhorted his followers to seek divine perfection. Second, the medieval Church expressed this aspiration for divine perfection in the sacrament of transubstantiation: As wine is turned into Christ's blood, humanity will be transformed into divinity. Third, Luther and his followers brought it closer to the earth in their doctrine of Incarnation, that is, their God-man ideal. Fourth, Herder and Goethe removed the superhuman ideal from Christianity and secularized it. Fifth, then the Young Hegelians completely naturalized it. But the naturalization of Christianity has produced The Motley Cow. It is important to note the function of The Motley Cow in Zarathustra's epic journey. It represents the secular culture after the death of God. He cannot take The Motley Cow as the terminal point of naturalization. He has to find a way to spiritualize the secular culture. So he launched his campaign of spiritualization. The secular culture of The Motley Cow is the ultimate target for this campaign, and its ultimate ideal is the superman, who can transcend the limits of humanity by securing a complete mastery over passions and an absolute autonomy from others. This Faustian ideal of radical individualism will be sorely tested in Part II.

CHAPTER TWO

The Suffering Soul

(Part II)

In "The Child and the Mirror", Zarathustra is back in his mountain cave and waiting like a sower, who has scattered his seed. This is what you would expect from the conclusion of Part I, where he sowed the seed of his superhuman ideal. But he says that he still has much to give. During months and years of solitude after his return, his wisdom has grown and caused him pain with its fullness. He has become impatient because he cannot dispense his new wisdom. But that is not the motive for his second mission. He decides to go on the second mission in response to a horrible dream, in which a child brings a mirror and tells him to look at his mirror image. In the mirror, he finds not himself, but a devil's mask and sneer (*eines Teufels Fratze und Hohnlachen*). The German word *Fratze* is usually translated as 'grimace' in the English editions of *Zarathustra*. But it can also be translated as 'mask'. We will see that 'mask' will make better sense when we get to "The Soothsayer". In his interpretation of this mirror image, he says, "Verily, all-too-well do I understand the sign and the admonition of the dream: my *teaching* is in danger; weeds pose as wheat" (*Z*, 83). The devil's mask is a baffling imagery. He does not explain why the devil's mask signifies danger for his teaching. This is the way he opens his game of masks, a game of concealment and dissemblance, which will be sustained to the end of Part II.

Because of his enemies, Zarathustra says, his disciples have become ashamed of his teaching. So he laments, "I have lost my friends; the hour has come to seek my lost ones" (*Z*, 83). The loss of his disciples to his enemies may appear to fulfill the requirement for his second mission that he laid out at the end of his first mission. But the fulfillment of this requirement is highly suspect for the following reason. He had expected that his disciples would deny him when they grew up and became independent. By outgrowing his teaching, they would eventually deny it. But that is not what is happening to them, according to his interpretation of the mirror image. His disciples are now ashamed of his teaching because they are deceived by his enemies' distortion of it. Instead of becoming independent, they have been duped by his enemies. He gives no indication that they are even denying his teaching or rebelling against him. In all likelihood, they have not become independent enough to do either. The presumed present condition of his disciples is completely different from what he had predicted for his second coming. Their growth has become sickly and abortive instead of being healthy and fruitful as he had hoped. This unfortunate development may reflect the danger of accidents that worried him at the end of Part I. So he sets out on his second mission as a victim of accidents with a voice of suffering. He says, "From silent mountains and thunderstorms of suffering my soul rushes into the valleys" (Z, 84). He is talking about the pain and suffering of his own soul. This voice of suffering is his new voice.

The problem of suffering was Nietzsche's overriding concern in *The Birth of Tragedy*, and the redemption from suffering was the central theme of that book. But his view on suffering and tragedy was not retained by Zarathustra of Part I. In "On the Afterworldly", he said, "I overcame myself, the sufferer; I carried my own ashes to the mountains; I invented a brighter flame for myself. And behold, then this ghost *fled* from me" (Z, 31). He wrote off his previous concern with suffering and the afterworld as a momentary delusion. In Part I, he never treated suffering as an important problem. To be sure, he talked about it in "On Enjoying and Suffering the Passions". But the passions can be the objects of joy although they can be the source of suffering for those weak souls like the pale criminal. In "On Reading and Writing", Zarathustra boasted of his courage to laugh at all tragic dramas and real tragedies in life. He contemptuously dismissed those who say, "Life is hard to bear." He called them butterflies and soap bubbles. In "On the Preachers of Death", he disdained those who say, "Life is only suffering" or "Life is refuted." He said that they only refuted themselves, because they were talking about not life in general but only their own miserable existence. The problem of suffering was not worthy of his attention because it was the problem of the weaklings. So he stood disdainfully above the problem of suffering in Part I.

All of a sudden in Part II, Zarathustra launches his second mission as a man of suffering and wants to speak from his own thunderstorms of suffering. This change in his mood is reflected in the different tones of the two missions. His first teaching mission was prepared by the ten years he had spent enjoying his spirit and solitude and partaking in the quiet happiness of the sun. Then he set out to give his wisdom and message like the happy radiation of the sun. His teaching was going to flow out of his overflowing love and wisdom. This voice of exuberant elation in the first teaching mission gives way to the voice of grief and suffering in his second teaching mission, which is motivated by his anger and revenge against the enemies who have supposedly distorted his teaching. His motive for his second teaching mission is diametrically opposed to the lofty motive of his first teaching mission. With this lofty motive, he wanted "to go under" like the sun to the people. In his second teaching mission, he really goes under in the emotional sense. He stoops to the lowly motive of revenge, although he may try to disguise it as the noble motive of a brave warrior.

In Part II, Zarathustra starts out as a suffering warrior, who is eager to get on his wildest horse and hurl his spear against his enemies. His spear will be the torrent of new speech that has come to him. He attributes the new speech to his new wisdom: "My wild wisdom became pregnant on lonely mountains; on rough stones she gave birth to her young, her youngest" (Z, 85). Evidently, the lioness of his wisdom became pregnant and bore a young cub on the mountains after his return from his first teaching mission. The speech from this young cub is not going to be gentle like the shepherds' flutes. It will blow like storms and hit like lightning bolts. Thus Zarathustra threatens his enemies with the proclamation of a bruising battle: "But let my enemies believe that *the evil one* rages over their heads" (*Z*, 85). The sneering devil he saw in the mirror may indicate "*the evil one.*" In that case, the mirror image may be the portent for his future fight against his enemies. But he does not say who his enemies are. He only says that he is determined to fight till he finds the Blessed Isles. This impending battle will be the central theme of Part II.

Suffering and Redemption (Part II.2-8)

In the next section, Zarathustra arrives on the Blessed Isles and begins his new teaching mission. But his new teaching sounds like his old teaching. He talks about God and the superman, two familiar topics from his old teaching. Instead of creating God, he tells his audience, they should create the superman. He expands the notion of creation by extending it to the creation of the world. This is something new. In "On Love of the Neighbor", he talked about a creative friend, who has a completed world. But he never talked about the creation of that world. Now he tells his audience to create their own worlds to realize "your reason, your image, your will, your love" (*Z*, 86). He then links his theme of creation to the two worlds of permanence and impermanence. He brands as a poetic fiction the permanent world along with God. The real world is impermanent; it is the world of time and becoming. Just like the perfect God, the permanent world leaves no room for creation. Therefore, we should praise the impermanence of the real world. This is Zarathustra's teaching.

Now he advances an enigmatic claim, "Creation—that is the great redemption from suffering and makes life easy to bear." Again the theme of creation is old and familiar, but the redemption from suffering is something new. This new idea naturally follows the theme of suffering introduced in the opening section of Part II. In Part I, he advocated the creative will in preparation for the advent of the superman. Now he baldly announces creation as the great redemption from suffering. This is a big change on his part for two reasons. First, he is assigning a new function to creativity. Second, the redemption from suffering has now become his new concern. The big change, however, can easily escape our notice because what he says after this bald announcement is still compatible with what he had taught in Part I. He says, "But that the creator may be, suffering is needed and much change" (Z, 87). He calls suffering the birth-pang of a creator. This is the instrumental view of suffering. Insofar as suffering functions as the means or instrument for creativity, it is not evil but good. We should seek it instead of avoiding it. But there are sufferings that do not serve instrumental functions, for example, the crippling diseases that can turn human beings into vegetables. They are evil, pure and simple. What is the redemption from this type of suffering? This is the tough question that will occupy his attention to the very end of his career.

Zarathustra locates the problem of suffering in feeling: "All feeling suffers in me and is in prison." This is the passive dimension of human existence. To suffer means to be passive, which is the meaning of the Greek word *pathe* (suffering). Our feeling is always passive; it indicates what is done to us. In Part I, Zarathustra was chiefly concerned with the active dimension of human existence, because he wanted to stress the creative will. He is now recognizing the passive dimension of human existence for the first time. Although feeling is the source of suffering and imprisonment, he holds, the will has the power to liberate the imprisoned feeling. The distinction between the active willing and the passive feeling creates an enormously difficult problem. The distinction presupposes that the will is completely insulated from feelings and passions. This is the standard notion of the autonomous will that is best exemplified by Kant's theory of rational will. Now suppose that the separation of the will from desires and passions is a huge metaphysical error as Nietzsche has repeatedly said. Then the will cannot be the liberator, while feeling is a prisoner. But Zarathustra cannot easily discard the liberating power of the will because it has been the most essential feature of his superhuman ideal. What is the real relation between the liberating will and the imprisoned feeling? This will be the central question for Part II.

After stressing the role of the will as the liberator from suffering, Zarathustra again talks about its creative function and its joy in begetting and becoming. His powerful will is going to be the hammer that will perfect the image of man buried deep in the ugliest stone. Thus the conclusion of "Upon the Blessed Isles" seems only to restate and reaffirm the theme of creation from his earlier teaching. But it will be overshadowed by the theme of suffering and redemption in the remainder of Part II. There is a subtle dialectical development in his thought. He becomes aware of his passivity in his attempt to assert his active will, because it runs into the obstacles of resistance. These obstacles are what he meant by "the giant of accident" in the last section of Part I. The more deeply we get involved in the active dimension of our existence, the more keenly we feel its passive dimension or our vulnerability to suffering. Thus, the problem of the creative will inevitably leads to the problem of suffering. This dialectical development between the active will and the passive feeling may have led to the birth of Zarathustra's new wisdom, which was conceived and delivered as a young cub after his return to his cave from his first teaching mission. In that case, his new wisdom is an essential complement to his old wisdom. In his old wisdom, he completely disregarded the passive dimension of human existence because he was so obsessed with its active dimension. Hence the resulting superhuman ideal turned out to be too divine and too unreal. It deals with only one half of human existence. The function of his new wisdom may well be to recognize and redress this grave deficiency and imbalance.

The next section ("On the Pitying") is obviously connected to the problem of suffering. The German title for this section, *von den Mitleidigen,* is derived from *Mitleiden* (to suffer with someone), which is in turn derived from *Leiden* (suffer). 'Compassion' is a better English word to convey the sense of *Mitleiden* than 'pity', because the English prefix 'com' is equivalent to the German prefix *mit*. Compassion is an important concept in Schopenhauer's philosophy of suffering. Although we all suffer from the illusion of individuation in the phenomenal world, he said, we can in our compassion feel the misery of others as our own, transcending the boundary of our selfish egos and experiencing the cosmic unity of all beings in the noumenal world. For him, compassion is the only ultimate ground for true morality. Zarathustra is going against this doctrine in repudiating the feeling of pity and compassion. To be sure, he recognizes suffering as a serious problem, but he is rejecting Schopenhauer's resolution, because compassion makes the sufferer shameful and even vengeful, thereby further aggravating his suffering. He is not against helping friends in need. He says, "if you have a suffering friend, be a resting place for his suffering" (Z, 90).

The theme of suffering and pity is further developed in "On Priests". The spirit of priests is drowned in their pity. That is another adverse effect of pity and another wrong way to cope with the problem of suffering. Although some priests are the heroes of suffering, Zarathustra says, many of them have not only suffered too much, but also want to make others suffer by enslaving them to the fetters of their Redeemer. They preach repentance, the life of corpses, with their song of muffled melancholy. Nevertheless, he is respectful of the priests. He says, "Yet my blood is related to theirs, and I want to know that my blood is honored even in theirs" (Z, 91). When some priests pass by him, he feels compassion for them even against his own preaching. This attitude of kinship and respect toward the priests was completely different from the contemptuous attitude he had taken toward the preachers of death in Part I. Whereas he had distanced himself from those preachers, he is now recognizing his kinship with the priests. But the latter are hardly distinguishable from the former. Just as the priests want to make others suffer, so the preachers of death would make life insufferable for their neighbors. In this section, he shows himself prone to suffering through his kinship and compassion, whereas he appeared to be above suffering altogether in Part I. This is again the difference between Part I and Part II.

There is one more new element in Zarathustra's response to the priests. This is his concern with redemption. This point may become clear by comparing "On Priests" with "On the Afterworldly" of Part I. The problem of suffering is the common feature of these two sections. The afterworlds are created out of suffering; the priests are the heroes of suffering. In "On Priests", Zarathustra uses the noun 'redeemer' seven times and the verb 'redeem' three times. In "On the Afterworldly", he never used these two words and made the disparaging use of one related word 'redemptive' ("redemptive drops of blood"). "On the Preachers of Death" of Part I contains not a single word related to redemption. In "On the Afterworld", Zarathustra confidently assumes that the healthy body is the simple solution for all sufferings. But he has evidently lost this confidence. He now says that redemption is beyond the reach of any human beings, the greatest and the smallest alike, and that it will be possible only with the superman. For the first time, he is connecting the superman to the problem of suffering and redemption. In Part I, there was no need for him to make this connection because he never accepted suffering as a serious problem. He taught the ideal of superman as the new meaning for the godless world and the creative will as the bridge to that highest hope. Now he is so concerned with the problem of suffering and redemption that he appears to have forgotten his old carefree spirit of creativity.

In "On the Virtuous", Zarathustra considers one more method of redemption beside the priestly way. That is the way of virtue. The Stoics thought that virtue was the only defense against suffering from passions. Although one can have no control over what lies outside the soul, they believed, one can control what lies in the soul. The control and mastery over the internal world can be gained by developing the four cardinal virtues of wisdom, courage, justice, and self-control. With these virtues, one can achieve *apatheia*, a complete immunity to all sufferings and passions. If *apatheia* is possible, it should be the redemption from suffering. Because of the implicit reference to the Stoics, "On the Virtuous" has a close link to "On the Teachers of Virtue" of Part I. The titles of these two sections share the common reference to virtue, the primary concern of the Stoics. But the virtuous have their own problem. Zarathustra says, "They still want to be paid." They want to be paid for their virtue. This expectation of payment is degrading to virtue. One should not even say that virtue is its own reward because such a remark still associates virtue with the degrading notion of reward. Because virtue is what is dearest to one's heart, he says to his disciples, "your virtue is your self" (Z, 94). One should love one's virtue as a mother loves her child.

The notion of getting paid for virtue is wrong for another reason. There is no paymaster for virtue, Zarathustra says. The Stoics knew very well that virtue could not be an absolutely reliable protection against suffering. Even the most virtuous could not avoid suffering from misfortunes beyond their control. To cope with this sort of contingency, the Stoics advocated the providence of God, whom they called Zeus, Logos (or Reason), or the Soul of the World. This cosmic governor was supposed to assure the concordance between virtue and happiness, by properly rewarding the virtuous and punishing the wicked. In Zarathustra's words, this is to build the system of reward and punishment into the foundation of things. Kant is impressed with such a cosmic system of reward and punishment, but he is equally certain that it often fails in this world, where the wicked prosper at the expense of the virtuous. So he transposes the Stoic principle of reward and punishment to the other world. Since the moral system of reward and punishment is imperfect in this temporal world, he argues, there must be an eternal world, in which it will work perfectly and reward the virtuous with happiness commensurate with their virtue. This Kantian idea is the target of Zarathustra's criticism in his statement, "Do you want rewards for virtue, and heaven for earth, and the eternal for your today?" (*Z*, 93).

The cosmic system of reward and punishment is supposed to implement the principle of justice. In Zarathustra's view, this principle only expresses the sense of revenge and retribution, the most natural response to our suffering. But the sense of revenge only aggravates the original suffering. Here lies the irony of the Stoic doctrine of providence for reward and punishment. Although it is installed as the divine protection against suffering, it turns out to be the expression of revenge, the most invidious form of suffering. Since the divine protection against suffering is placed outside the soul, it goes against the Stoic ideal of virtue as the internal bulwark against suffering. The ideal of complete self-sufficiency is violated by the reliance on providence. The Stoic idea that virtue is one's own and depends on nothing outside oneself is the basic premise for Zarathustra's entire discourse in "On the Virtuous". Especially, it is the unmentioned premise for his critique of twelve prevalent views of virtue. Every one of them is not only defective but also comical because all of them alike make virtue dependent on something else, thereby destroying its independence.

I have tried to connect "On the Virtuous" to the problem of suffering and redemption, but you may object to my attempt because this problem is not even mentioned in this section. In fact, the two words 'suffering' and 'redemption' never appear in the whole section. I have relied on the implicit references to the Stoics and Kant. Lampert notes the reference to Kantian metaphysics of morals (*Nietzsche's Teaching*, 94). But the connection between Kant and the Stoics is not accidental. Kant's ethic is highly Stoic. Once these references are recognized, it looks fairly obvious that this section is addressed to the problem of suffering and redemption. On the other hand, if we do not connect it to this problem, then it will stand out as a strange digression that breaks up the thematic flow of Zarathustra's discourse. The problem of suffering and redemption has been the central theme since the opening of Part II. In the last three sections, Zarathustra has considered three ways of seeking redemption. The first one is to relieve the suffering of others by compassion. The next two are the ways of coping with one's own suffering, the priestly way and the Stoic way. The priestly way is to seek it in the other world; the Stoic way is to seek it in this world. There can be no other ways. If so, the present section should be read not as a senseless digression but as a sensible progression in the thematic development.

Each of the first five sections of Part II can be read as an independent unit. So there are two ways of reading *Zarathustra*. One of them is the monadic approach. This is to read each section as a self-contained unit. The other is the connectionist approach. This is to establish the thematic connection between the succeeding sections, although such connection is not even mentioned by the author. The meaning that emerges by such connections may be called the sequential meaning. I will try to illustrate it by one simple example: "I ate too much. I became sick. I could not go to work." Each of these three sentences is grammatically independent, that is, there are no grammatical connectives that link them with one another. But there are two ways of reading these three sentences. If they are taken monadically, their sequence has no significance. But their sequence has important meaning in the connectionist approach, which can be unpacked by restating them as "Because I ate too much, I became sick. Therefore, I could not go to work." The sequence of sentences performs the same function as the grammatical connectives. This is what I mean by "sequential meaning."

Zarathustra urges his disciples to dissociate virtue from the sense of justice and revenge and love their virtue for its own sake. But he does not say that virtue is the redemption from suffering, or that his disciples should seek redemption in their self-sufficiency. On the contrary, he seems to recognize the impossibility of realizing self-sufficiency in the next section, "On the Rabble". In "On Priests" and "On the Virtuous", he talked about our passions and virtues, over which it is plausible to secure our independence and self-sufficiency. In "On the Rabble", he shifts his attention to our relation with others, which is detrimental to our independence and self-sufficiency. These are the two dimensions of suffering and redemption. The first one is the relation to our internal world, and the second one is our relation to the external world. So far Zarathustra considered the first dimension, and he will consider the second dimension in the next few sections.

In "On the Rabble", Zarathustra locates the external source of suffering in the rabble. He says, "Life is a well of joy; but where the rabble drinks too, all wells are poisoned" (Z, 96). He describes the rabble's poisonous way as follows. They poison the holy water with their lust and call their dirty dreams pleasure. When their damp hearts come near the fire, they smother the flame. In their hands, the fruit trees grow mawkish and wither at the top. Some people get so disgusted with them that they even turn away from life. Others would rather go into the desert and share the thirst with the beasts of prey than share the same cistern with them. But the poisonous rabble is powerful and the politics has degenerated to the filthy game of haggling with them. For Zarathustra, the rabble makes life far more difficult to bear than even death and torture. You may feel that his complaint is rather strange. How can one suffer from the rabble? He is complaining about the social and cultural domination by the rabble. One can surely feel suffocated and nauseated under their domination. That is suffering from the rabble. Therefore, Zarathustra is seized with nausea with the filthy rabble. But he can do nothing but close his eyes and hold his nose because they are so powerful. He is right again. There is little one can do against the rabble and their domination.

Zarathustra says, "How did I redeem myself from nausea?" (Z, 98). This question again expresses his concern with the problem of redemption. He says that he has overcome his nausea by flying to the highest spheres beyond the reach of the rabble and finding the fountain of pleasure there. This is the way of solitude he advocated for coping with the flies in the market place in Part I. Now he says that he can only live with his hope for the future because the present age is completely taken over by the rabble. If so, he cannot easily dismiss the problem of rabble. In fact, the same problem continues to plague him in the next section ("On the Tarantulas") where he extends his attack to the egalitarians, the agents of revenge. Their sense of revenge comes from their repressed envy against the powerful. Their vengeful sense of justice demands equality. But Zarathustra says that men can never be equal because the basic principle of life dictates inequality. Life is a perpetual struggle for power and more power, which leads to greater and greater inequality. It strives to "build itself up into the heights with pillars and steps" (Z, 101). The demand for equality goes against this basic drive of life. Since life is the theater of war for the will to power, the weak are bound to suffer under the power of the strong. The envy of the strong and the revenge against them are the natural forms of suffering for the weak. These two forms of suffering produce the tarantulas, who disguise their envy and revenge as the demand of justice and equality.

Zarathustra is finally bitten by a tarantula. This incident makes a strong contrast with the adder's bite in Part I, which he took as a testimony to his power. He said then that the bite could not hurt a dragon. But he does not feel safe against the tarantula. He is so scared of being sucked into the tarantula's whirlpool of revenge that he asks to be tied to a pillar. This is his candid admission that he is unsure of his own power to cope with the violent sense of revenge. He is as candid as he was in admitting his susceptibility to compassion in "On Priests". But the sense of revenge is far more ravaging than the sense of compassion, and he screams for the redemption from revenge: "For *that man be delivered from revenge*, that is for me the bridge to the highest hope, and a rainbow after long storms" (Z, 99). The highest hope is the superman. Here again he connects the role of the superman to the problem of redemption, which he now describes as the deliverance from revenge.

In "On the Famous Wise Men", he extends his attack to those intellectuals, who have served the people as their advocates and ideologues. Since the ordinary people are not intelligent or learned enough to advocate egalitarianism, they have to depend on the service of intellectuals. Therefore, the attack on the rabble naturally leads to the attack on the famous wise men. They claim to be the servants of the people, but they have sold their souls for comfort and honor. But their real master is not the people, but those in power. In order to get along smoothly with the people, the powerful harness a famous wise man like a little ass in front of their horses and cover him with a lion's skin. But the harnessed wise man has no spirit but only a revering will. Zarathustra says that the true spirit belongs to the free spirits. Whereas the famous wise men dwell comfortably in cities, the free spirits suffer in deserts for the sake of truth and freedom. They have the lion-will and disdain the happiness of slaves. They are hounded out by the people because they are hateful to them. The free spirits are the polar opposite to the famous wise men. Zarathustra gives a long eulogy on spirit, its happiness, its spark, its pride, and even its modesty. Finally he flaunts this spirit in his own wisdom. But he never mentions the problem of suffering and redemption in this section. It appears that his sense of suffering is completely vanquished by his new spirit of exuberant power. But this powerful spirit will be completely shaken by his renewed sense of suffering in the next section.

Dark Night of the Soul (Part II.9-11)

In "The Night Song", Zarathustra is finally alone in the stillness of night. But he keenly feels something "unstilled" and "unstillable" in himself.

This is his craving for love and it arises from his role as light. He says that he is light, but wishes that he were night. Since his loneliness stems from the fact that he is girt with light, he envies the dark night that can suck at the breast of light. If he had such a pleasure of the dark night, he would bless even the little sparkling stars for their gifts of light because then he would never feel lonely. But his situation is not so fortunate. He says, "But I live in my own light; I drink back into myself the flames that break out of me" (*Z*, 106). He is so self-contained in his own light that he can never know the happiness of those who receive his gifts. Then he talks about the cleft between giving and receiving. Because he cannot cross this cleft, he feels the malice to hurt and rob the recipients of his gifts. His malice finally turns into revenge, which kills his joy of giving. He says, "Such revenge my fullness plots: such spite wells up out of my loneliness. My happiness in giving dies in giving; my virtue tired of itself in its overflow" (*Z*, 106). He is tired of his gift-giving virtue, which was celebrated as the greatest virtue at the end of Part I. It can no longer generate the delight of giving, but only the despair of loneliness and the malice and vengeance against the receivers. What has happened to Zarathustra? What has turned his greatest virtue and delight into this misery?

When Zarathustra set out on his first teaching mission, he took the sun for his model. In the last section of Part I, he took the sun as the symbol of his gift-giving virtue. The great star radiates its gift out of its overflowing abundance. It is the symbol of self-sufficiency and independence. These attributes were supposed to be the prerogatives of God, the infinite being, who needs nothing outside himself. Although the concept of self-sufficiency was the classical ideal for a perfect sage, no one thought that a mortal could ever come close to realizing it. But Zarathustra has not only flaunted this ideal as his own, but also urged it upon his disciples by asking them to go their own way of solitude. But the ideal of self-sufficiency excludes dependence on others. The sun radiates immense benefits for others, but never expects any return. If it were to expect anything in return, it would become dependent on others and cease to be self-sufficient. Hence the medieval theologians preached that God was never affected by the response of his creatures to his love. Zarathustra has tried to live up to the divine ideal of not being affected by the responses of his recipients. This self-contained posture is portrayed in his statement: "But I live in my own light; I drink back into myself the flames that break out of me." But he has forgotten what he said to the sun at the outset of his epic journey: "You great star, what would your happiness be had you not those for whom you shine?" (Z, 9). Even the happiness of the sun depends on the response of its beneficiaries.

Zarathustra's divine posture of self-sufficiency has broken down because it suppresses the most basic need of finite human beings, that is, the need to be connected with others. This suppressed need is that "something unstilled, unstillable" in him, which he identifies as "a craving for love." He now realizes the impossibility of overcoming this obstacle in his mighty struggle to transcend the limits of humanity. He was already dimly aware of this obstacle in his first salutation to the sun: "You great star, what would your happiness be had you not those for whom you shine?" (Z, 9). Even the sun cannot be totally self-contained and self-sufficient for its happiness. For Zarathustra, the gift-giving virtue of the sun has now turned into his dreadful loneliness and his vengeful wretchedness. In "On the Way of the Creator" of Part I, he told his disciples that the way to solitude was "the way of your affliction." He now wishes to be night rather than light, a receiver rather than a giver, because night can have the experience of sucking at the breasts of light. Total independence is one thing, but total isolation is another. So he wants to know whether he is touching the souls of his recipients. But he cannot cross the cleft that separates them from him. Thus he comes to recognize his dependence on others, which provokes his sense of revenge against his recipients. As we noted in the case of the rabble and the tarantulas, the sense of dependence on others and the weakness against them generate the sense of revenge. The others do not have to be merciless predators or exploiters.

This is not the first time Zarathustra experiences the sense of revenge. He experienced it when he was bitten by a tarantula. But he is now tortured by the revenge out of his own abundance. His is the revenge of a giver rather than a receiver. The tarantula's is the revenge of a receiver.

The revenge of a giver is the second wave of revenge for Zarathustra. It is far more devastating than the first wave and forces him to reverse his former valuation of light and darkness. In his new valuation, light becomes cold and night becomes warm. The suns and stars are no longer the objects of his admiration and emulation. They are no more than the objects of motion that follow their inexorable will. In praise of the warmth of night, he says, "Oh, it is only you, you dark ones, you nocturnal ones, who create warmth out of that which shines. It is only you who drink milk and refreshment out of the udders of light" (*Z*, 107). This is his paean to the mighty power of night, mightier than the power of the sun and day. Unfortunately, however, he cannot escape the predicament of the sun: he feels nothing but ice all around him. Although night has come, he must still be light. In "The Night Song", he reveals his own suffering for the first time. In Part I, he stayed above suffering and sought solitude as the best insulation from the slings and arrows of the world. But he warned his disciples about the danger of solitude, "But the time will come when solitude will make you weary, when your pride will double up, and your courage gnash its teeth. And you will cry, 'I am alone!'" (*Z*, 63). His prophecy is now being fulfilled in his own case.

Zarathustra has insulated himself and his love from the receivers in order to maintain his position of self-sufficiency and independence. He now finds that this tactic of emotional insulation completely stifles his own need of being loved. Thus he comes to recognize his own dire need for love and connection with other human beings. This is a dramatic change in his outlook on life. He now recognizes the bitter truth that it is impossible to live up to the ideal of total self-sufficiency. Every human being has to depend on some other human beings, and this universal dependence inevitably leads to the sense of suffering and revenge. He ends "The Night Song" by recognizing the boundless matrix of his existence: "Night has come; now all fountains speak more loudly. And my soul too is a fountain" (*Z*, 107). Night is the fountain of all fountains. It is the symbol of Nature unbounded. The fountain of all fountains was a popular medieval metaphor for describing God's inexhaustible life-giving power. Scotus Erigena says that the Divine Goodness is the ultimate source for the river of life and wisdom that flows to all creatures (*On the Division of Nature,* bk. 3, ch. 4). Bonaventure compares God to the eternally gushing fountain that nourishes all living things (*The Tree of Life,* Prol. 3). Zarathustra has naturalized this Christian metaphor and made it into the symbol of Mother Nature. Moreover, he now sees his own soul as one of many fountains flowing out of the ultimate fountain of Nature. That ultimate fountain will appear as Life in "The Dancing Song". As a dependent fountain, Zarathustra can only suffocate himself by pursuing his ideal of total self-sufficiency and self-isolation. That is why he now feels an unquenchable craving for love and says, "Night has come; now all the songs of lovers awaken. And my soul too is the song of a lover" (Z, 105). He will indeed sing his song of love for the fountain of all fountains in the next section.

One evening, Zarathustra runs into a group of girls dancing in a forest. He does not join the dance, but offers to sing for their dance. In this song, he recounts his first encounter with his lady of love, Life. He felt that he was sinking into the unfathomable Life, when he was recently looking into her eyes. Why was he sinking? The answer to this question is given in the prelude to the song, in which Zarathustra offers to sing a mocking song on the spirit of gravity, his supreme and most powerful enemy. It was the spirit of gravity (heaviness) that was weighing him down in the ocean of life. That was indeed the condition of his life in "The Night Song". In the darkness of night, he was deeply depressed by existential problems spawned by the spirit of gravity. That is the sort of feeling one would experience in getting drowned in a deep ocean, which can be as dark as it is in the middle of night. But Life saved him by pulling him out with a golden fishing rod. This pathetic picture of Zarathustra in his helpless condition makes a dramatic contrast with the mighty picture of his sun-like radiance in Part I. Instead of flying across the sky, he was sinking into the unfathomable ocean only to meet the indignity of being saved by Life's fishing rod. When she fished him out of deep water, he was not even asking for help. She came to his aid like the radiant sun with her golden fishing rod. This is a dramatic role reversal. His role has changed from active to passive, from giving to receiving, from independence to dependence.

Zarathustra's heroic posture and his fuss over his predicament are only big jokes for Life. She even mocks at his description of her as unfathomable. She says, "Thus runs the speech of all fish; what *they* do not fathom is unfathomable" (Z, 108). She understands herself as only changeable and wild. Perhaps, that is why she is unfathomable to men because they can deal only with the stable and the tame. She goes on to say that men are trying to impose their own virtues on her even when they call her profound, faithful, eternal, and mysterious. Because they cannot transcend their narrow perspective and appreciate her in her own right, she appears to be unfathomable to them. Throughout the conversation, she treats him like a little child. After all, he is only a small fish saved by her fishing rod. He now recognizes his own helplessness in understanding the "unfathomable" Life and becomes skeptical about his vaunted wisdom. Evidently, his relation with Wisdom has been severely strained by his memorable encounter with Life. When he approaches Wisdom for a secret talk, she says in anger and jealousy that he wants and loves Life. Caught in this triangular relation, he admits that he deeply loves only Life, most of all when he hates her. But he is still well disposed toward Wisdom because she resembles Life.

This is the gist of the song he sang about his encounter with Life. At the outset, he offered to sing for the dancing girls a dancing and mocking song on the spirit of gravity. But the tone of his song is far from mocking. He is overwhelmed by the spirit of gravity not only during his encounter with Life, but even after his song. When the girls are gone after their dance, he hears a series of ringing questions, "Why? What for? By what? Whither? Where? How? Is it not folly still to be alive?" (Z, 110). These are indeed depressing questions. He says that they are asked by the evening. Why does the evening ask these questions? What does the evening stand for? I suppose it stands for Life. While Life is associated with night and evening, Wisdom has been associated with day and the sun. Whereas we have known Wisdom from the beginning of his teaching mission, we meet Life for the first time in "The Dancing Song". The series of ringing questions are the tough questions about Life, which have tormented him lately. But the spirit of gravity is the source of these questions. By spawning these troublesome questions, the spirit of gravity makes our life unbearable. To indicate the subtle link between the ringing existential questions and the spirit of gravity, Zarathustra names the spirit of gravity as his archenemy in the prelude to the song and then pours out those questions after the song.

In "The Dancing Song", Wisdom gets demoted to the second fiddle. Up to this point, she has been the only fiddle for Zarathustra's performance in the dispensation of his accumulated wisdom. Life has now become his prima donna and Wisdom her handmaid. This is perhaps the most important reversal of roles in his career because these two ladies represent two different modalities of human existence. Wisdom represents the way of knowledge, the cognitive mode of existence. Life represents the way of feeling and desire, the affective mode of existence. Life is associated with night and its darkness; Wisdom is associated with day and its light. The cognitive mode of existence is cerebral; the affective mode is visceral. Life has her own wisdom. It is the wisdom of night, whereas Wisdom is the wisdom of day. The wisdom of day is on the surface of consciousness; the wisdom of night is submerged under consciousness. Under the aegis of Wisdom, Zarathustra conducted his mission primarily as a cognitive task. In the course of this largely cerebral enterprise, he got entangled with the difficult visceral problems of feeling such as the whirling sense of revenge, the ravaging sense of isolation, and the irrepressible craving for love. The aegis of Wisdom or her cognitive way was totally helpless against these overwhelming emotions. In this desperate situation, Life came to his rescue and this was his visceral experience.

The shift of allegiance from Wisdom to Life brings about radical changes to Zarathustra. It was much easier for him to maintain the posture of self-sufficiency in his consort with Wisdom. After all, his wisdom is in his possession; it is his virtue under his command. But he cannot maintain this commanding posture over Life, who has saved him with her fishing rod. He is a helpless suppliant, who needs her care and support. This difference in posture is represented by the difference between light and darkness, day and night, which are associated with the difference between Wisdom and Life. With Wisdom, Zarathustra feels that he is with the sun, or rather he radiates like the sun. With Life, on the other hand, he feels that he is with night. The world of light is the theater of action, but the world of darkness is not conducive for action. It is hard to be in command of the world of darkness. Light is the requisite condition for taking the commanding control of the theater of action. In the world of night, Zarathustra becomes a receiver rather than a giver. He is a humble suppliant rather than an overbearing commander. This radical change in his posture from a commander to a suppliant introduces a comic element. For the dramatic deflation of a pretentious posture always provokes big laughter.

"The Dancing Song" introduces a heavy dose of comedy and irony for the first time in the book. The first shot of this heavy dose is given by Zarathustra's own recounting of how he was saved from deep waters by a fishing rod. There is nothing so comical in the entire book as this episode. He is only a small fish drowning in the sea of life. Prior to this moment of humiliation, he had tried to play the heroic role of saving the whole world from the death of God and its consequent catastrophe. When he tries to describe Life with big words such as 'unfathomable', 'profound', 'eternal', 'faithful', 'mysterious', Life brushes them aside with her mocking laughter. These big words are carried over from the day of his heroic posture, and their dismissal in her mocking laughter further heightens the comic character of his deflated stature. To be sure, he talked about laughter as the best way to kill the spirit of gravity in "On Reading and Writing" of Part I. But this talk was more cerebral than visceral because he had yet to encounter the spirit of gravity as a visceral experience. Laughter was only in his talk, not in his deed. In "The Dancing Song", at least for the audience, laughter has become real.

The difference between the two worlds of light and darkness also brings about different orientations toward oneself and others. The world of light highlights one's relations with others. The sun shines not for itself but for others and light is an essential medium for getting in touch with others. In the world of darkness, however, one is more inclined to be in touch with oneself. Even in our meditations, we close our eyes to immerse ourselves in the world of darkness. Under the aegis of Wisdom, Zarathustra was chiefly concerned with teaching and enlightening others under the blessing of sunlight. But he comes to face himself and recognizes his own problems in the darkness of night. He ends "The Night Song" by four lines, each of which begins with "Night has come." Two of these lines talk about 'I' and the other two about 'my soul'. This turn toward himself marks the irrevocable change in Zarathustra's existential orientation. Now he has to heal himself before healing others. The physician has turned out to be a patient in critical condition. Only through his own existential travail does he come to see as the problem with himself what initially appears to be the problem with others. For example, he initially diagnosed the problem of revenge as the sickness of tarantulas, but eventually recognized it as his own. He has supposedly got it by the tarantula's sting, but that again shows a lack of self-knowledge. External agents cannot transmit the sense of revenge like a contagious disease. They can only activate the sickness of revenge if it is already in its dormant stage. If Zarathustra's revenge became active and rampant by the tarantula's sting, he had harbored it all along well before he was bitten. The same is true of the nausea he feels with the rabble. He would not be so distressed by nausea unless it was deeply rooted in his own person. Although this sort of self-recognition is not attained yet, he is definitely turning his attention to himself.

"The Tomb Song" is also a song of suffering, but its tone is different from that of "The Night Song". In "The Tomb Song", Zarathustra carries an evergreen wreath of life to the tombs of his youth and tries to redeem the dreams and ideals of his youth buried in those tombs. When he gets to the tombs, he pours out his vindictive accusations against his enemies, who killed the ideals and dreams of his youth. When he was waiting for happy omens from the birds, they led a revolting monster of an owl to frighten away his birds. When he tried to renounce nausea, they changed those close to him into putrid boils. They galled his best honey and dispatched the most impudent beggars to his charity. When he wanted to have the best dance in his life, they persuaded his singer to strike up a horrible dismal tune. His enemies are depicted as the cruel agents of boundless malice. For all their obstructions and interference, he vows, there is still his indomitable will. He concludes his song by hailing his will as the shatterer of all tombs and the champion of all resurrections. He is determined to shatter the tombs of his youth and resurrect all his buried dreams.

For the first time, he is bitterly blaming his enemies for his troubles. Just compare his laments in this song with those in "The Night Song", in which he could not even think of any enemies who can do terrible things to him. The description of his enemies shows not only how malicious they were, but also how vulnerable he was. The exposure of his vulnerability hardly goes well with his former heroic posture. If he had been self-sufficient and powerful, they could not have done all those terrible things. Even if they had done so, he would not be moaning over them. But he is blaming all his misfortunes on his enemies. The whirlwind of revenge has now taken over his entire existence. This was inconceivable for the Zarathustra of Part I, who descended from his mountain with his superhuman ideal. He then preached, "Injustice and filth they throw after the lonely one: but my brother, if you would be a star, you must not shine less for them because of that" (Z, 64). After the crushing experience of being picked up by Life's fishing rod, he no longer pretends to rise above the suffering of frail mortals probably because he has recognized his own frailty. That surely explains not only that he is a victim of revenge, but also that he does not even try to hide it from others. By resolutely brushing aside all his former pretenses and heroic postures, he is now accepting his mortal self in all its frailty. This is a phenomenal development in his existential stance.

What torments him most is not only his hatred of the enemies, but also his despair over the lost dreams and ideals. The dearest of these dreams and ideals was his wish, "All beings shall be divine to me" and "All days shall be holy to me" (Z, 111). Evidently in his youth, he had an ardent longing to see all things as divine and holy. But the death of God has extinguished the sense of divinity and sanctity, thereby producing the secular culture. Revolting against its degrading values, he launched his ambitious campaign to spiritualize the secular culture in the Prologue. Now he realizes that the sense of divinity and sanctity has been dissolved in his own life. What appeared to be the problem of others in Part I has turned out to be his own in Part II. The lost dreams of his youth are still his dearest possessions. He wants to redeem them with the evergreen wreath of life. Without their redemption, his life would be as cheap as the secular culture. When he introduced his notion of redemption in "Upon the Blessed Isles", he described it as the liberation of feeling from the prison of its suffering. Since the prison of suffering was situated in the present, his project of redemption appeared to be focused on the present. But he now finds that the present suffering contains the despair over the lost dreams of the past. For the first time in his career, he recognizes the need to redeem the past rather than the future.

By its nature, the will is oriented toward the future and has no control over the past. But Zarathustra cannot extricate himself from the past because the dead dreams and ideals of his past are still embroiled in the present prison of his suffering. He regards his will as the trustworthy custodian of his old dreams and as their redeemer. In that case, his indomitable will should take care of the past as well as the future. This is an incredible extension of the domain of will. In Part I, his will had nothing to do with the past because it was only concerned with the future and the advent of the superman. Now, however, he wants to redeem the past. But what does it mean to redeem the past? He will not face this strange question until "On Redemption". For the moment, his salutation to his will ("Hail to thee, my will!") at the end of "The Tomb Song" turns into his further exposition on the will to power in "On Self-Overcoming".

Life: The Will to Power (Part II.12-17)

The discourse in "On Self-Overcoming" goes through two stages. First, Zarathustra talks to "the wisest" and then he recounts his lesson from Life on the will to power. The wisest are supposedly working for the truth. But he tells them that their will to truth is their will to power in disguise. When he introduced the will to power for the first time in "On the Thousand and One Goal" of Part I, he lauded its power of creating values. Now he extends its power to the domain of truth by reducing the will to truth to the will to power. Truth is created by the will to power. This is contrary to the normal view, that is, truth is discovered rather than created. Since the domain of truth is coextensive with the whole universe, the creation of truth amounts to the creation of the universe. For the creation of the universe, the wisest want "to make all things thinkable" in spite of its doubt that it is really so. Everything shall yield and bend to this demand of the will to power, which creates the world in its own image. But the mere creation of the world is not good enough for the wisest. Zarathustra says, "You still want to create the world before which you can kneel: that is your ultimate hope and intoxication" (*Z*, 113). This is the very idea behind his campaign of spiritualization. But this is an impossible dream. Whatever you can create only manifests your power and there is no reason for you to feel any reverence for your own power. The sovereign will, which can create its own world, may never know any reverence. Max Stirner says that nothing is holy to a sovereign individual (*The Ego and Its Own*, 165). A Chinese proverb says, "One who carves the Buddha never worships him." Our world that has done away with the gods is destined to be profane; the profanity of The Motley Cow is the inevitable outcome of secularization. But such a profane world is too disgusting and too despicable for Zarathustra. So he will relentlessly wage his war against it. Thus the problem of profanity and sanctity is a mystery that will haunt our epic hero to the end of his long journey.

In "On the Thousand and One Goal" of Part I, Zarathustra gave the impression that the will to power belongs to the people, who create values. But he now makes the distinction between the wisest and the unwise. The unwise are the people who follow the values created by the wisest. The wisest can create truth because their will is dominant and assertive. The unwise are the people who follow the values thus created because their will is weak and submissive. Thus, the talk on truth leads not only to the will to power, but also to the distinction between the strong and the weak. This is the basic truth of life that he has learned by his extensive observations on all living things. He elaborates on this truth by three principles of all life. First, whatever lives, obeys. Second, he who cannot obey himself is commanded. Third, commanding is harder than obeying because commanding takes many experiments and hazards. Everyone wants to be master and commander even at the risk of life. But the weak cannot overpower the strong. Therefore the weaker is persuaded to serve the stronger by their own will to power. But even the weak assert their own mastery if they meet someone even weaker. No one would renounce the pleasure of ruling over someone. When the weak cannot openly attain mastery, they will steal the power from the strong by worming themselves into their hearts. Whether one conquers the weaker or submits to the stronger, one expresses the will to power. Even when people make sacrifices or cast amorous glances, they are manifesting the same will to power. The will to life or survival is not the ultimate principle of existence. Even life is sacrificed by the will to power. But the will to power involves great hazard because it is the chancy game of dice to the death even for the strongest.

This is the gist of Zarathustra's talk to the wisest. He tells them that he has learned this ultimate truth about all living beings by crawling in the very heart of life. Then he relates his secret talk with Life about her will to power. Life says to him in confidence, "I am *that which must overcome itself*" (Z, 115). The will to power manifests itself as the basic force of Life to overcome itself perpetually. The will to power for Life is different from the will to power that Zarathustra attributed to the individuals. The former is the cosmic will to power; the latter is the individual will to power. He has never talked about the cosmic will to power before. Even the will to power he attributes to ancient peoples in "On the Thousand and One Goal" is not cosmic but localized in some groups of people. So is the will to power for the wisest. Life explains the relation of their individual will to power to hers: "And you too, lover of knowledge, are only a path and footprint of my will; verily my will to power walks also on the heels of your will to truth" (Z, 115). The individuals and the groups of individuals are the agents for her will to power. Probably to

stress the impersonal character of her cosmic will to power, Life is referred to as "It" in this discourse, whereas Life was personified as a
woman in "The Dancing Song". The cosmic will to power cannot operate
the same way as the individual will to power. The perpetual struggle between the contending parties, which is unavoidable for the individual
will to power, is unnecessary for the cosmic will to power because there
can be no power to contest it. Therefore, Life must contest and struggle
against itself. Life makes this point: "Whatever I create and however
much I love it—soon I must oppose it and my love; thus my will wills it"
(Z, 115).

The game of Life as a perpetual struggle of its will to power to overcome itself is a poetic image of Spinoza's conception of Nature. On his
theory, Nature and God are the same. This is also true of Zarathustra's
world, in which Life is Nature or God. Spinoza says, "The power of God
is His essence itself" (*Ethics,* pt. 1, prop. 34). He says that the divine essence is best realized in the knowledge of God. For Life, however, the
best realization of the divine essence is not the highest level of knowledge, but the fullest display of power. Life says that the love of knowledge is only a path and footprint of the will to power. This is the nineteenth century version of Spinozism. Since Spinoza's seventeenth
century, the primary concern of Europe shifted from knowledge to power.
But this was not as big a shift as it may sound. Even in the seventeenth
century, knowledge in general was pursued not for its own sake, but for
the sake of power as demonstrated by Francis Bacon's *The Advancement
of Learning.* He and other scientists shared this view of science with the
alchemists and magicians of the Renaissance.

The nineteenth century version of Spinozism was Goethe's Romantic
version, which inspired many German intellectuals from Schelling and
Hegel to Wagner and Nietzsche. Goethe interpreted the infinite power of
Nature as the infinite creative activity of life. This conception of Nature
and her power is the basis for Zarathustra's conception of Life and her
will to power. For this reason, Rose Pfeffer says that Nietzsche's notion
of the will to power is derived from Spinoza through Goethe's mediation
and reformulation (*Nietzsche,* 158-63). She also notes that Nietzsche

himself was not fully aware of the historical background of his own idea. In fact, he criticizes Spinoza for the view that the function of power is limited to its self-preservation (*WP* 688). But she attributes this critique to his misreading of Spinoza, whose conception of power includes not only the element of self-preservation, but also the elements of growth and expansion. She points out, "Nietzsche did not take into consideration that Spinoza's *conatus* contains three elements: conservation (*suum esse conservare*); the striving for perfection (*id omne, quod hominem ad majorem perfectionem—ducit, appetat*); the striving for heightening of power (*quod nostrum agenda potentiam auget*)." By putting all these three elements together, she says, Goethe formulated his notion of will to power, which is exemplified in his view of Nature and Faust's perpetual striving (*Nietzsche,* 163). This reformulation of Spinoza's doctrine by Goethe laid the ground for Zarathustra's conception of Life and her will to power.

The game of power is the breeding ground for all the feelings of revenge and suffering. The ultimate agent for this game is not the contending individual wills, but Life and her cosmic will to power. In Life's perpetual struggle to overcome itself, every individual is only an instrumental agent. In "On the Thousand and One Goals", Zarathustra attributed the creation of values to the individual will to power. Now he attributes it to Life and its cosmic will to power. By clarifying this link between the individual and the cosmic creator of values, he claims to have solved the riddle in the heart of the wisest. He says that all values are transitory because they are constantly created and destroyed in the perpetual process of Life's self-overcoming. He compares the violent act of creation to the breaking of an eggshell for the creation of a new chicken. One should never be distressed over the destruction of the past, but joyfully accept it as the sign of new creation. If this is the truth about Life, it should provide consolation for Zarathustra's painful mourning over his broken dreams. He should look upon those dead dreams of his youth as the broken eggshells for the creation of new values. This is the creative approach to life. There is no point in pining over the lost dreams of the past, if the creation of new ideals always requires the destruction of old

dreams. His suffering belongs to the painful process of Life and her perpetual struggle to overcome herself by destroying old values and creating
new ones.

The present section began with the will to truth. The reduction of the
will to truth to the will to power may give the impression that the power
of the will alone counts in the creation of truth. This view will be cri-
tiqued in the next section, "On Those Who Are Sublime". Zarathustra
ridicules the sportive monsters called the sublime. He describes one of
them as follows. With a swelled chest, the sublime one stands there in
torn garments, decked out with ugly truths, the spoil of his hunting. He
was hunting in the woods of knowledge and came home from a fight
with savage beasts. But he looks terribly repulsive because he is himself
a savage beast. Zarathustra says that he must discard his heroic will and
become the will-less one. Only then can he become beautiful. To be
powerful is not enough. Zarathustra says, "But just for the hero the *beautiful* is the most difficult thing" (Z, 118). He adds that no violent will can
attain the beautiful by exertion. These remarks should be taken as his refinement on his discourse on the will to power, which may have given
the impression that power is everything and that the heroic will is the
best. But power is not everything; it should become beautiful. Likewise,
the heroic will is not the best; the will-less one is better.

Who is the sublime one? He is one of the wisest, to whom Zarathustra addressed his discourse on the will to power in the last section. The
sublime one was hunting in the woods of knowledge. The wisest are
probably the Stoic sages. The sublime one is called "an ascetic of the
spirit." The critique of the sublime one is readily applicable to the Stoic
ideal of self-mastery Zarathustra has advocated in the past. His ridicule
of the sublime one is highly self-reflective. He shows it by the opening
sentence of this section: "Still is the bottom of my sea: who would guess
that it harbors sportive monsters?" (Z, 116). The important phrase is "my
sea": the sublime monsters are at "the bottom of my sea." This is to say
that they are his own monsters. The combative posture of the sublime
one is hardly distinguishable from that of the warrior he praised in "On
War and Warriors" of Part I. But he now finds it repulsive as a matter of

taste. The combative posture of a tiger is no longer sufficient for him. In describing the battle of the sublime one, he says, "He subdued monsters, solved riddles: but he must still redeem his own monsters and riddles, changing them into heavenly children" (*Z,* 118). This passage is also self-reflexive. In the last section, he claimed to have solved the riddle in the heart of the wisest. But that does not mean that he has redeemed his own monsters. That explains why the sublime one is tense and ugly. He is still engaged in a fierce battle with his monsters and repressing them with his heroic will. Only by changing those monsters into heavenly children, he can "stand with relaxed muscles and unharnessed will." Only then can he become gracious and beautiful. But this is the most difficult task for the sublime one, according to Zarathustra.

In his critique of the sublime ones, he is reviewing and revising the Stoic ideal that he had advocated for the mastery of passions. He is now convinced that power alone is not enough because it is ugly. But he is still contemptuous of the weaklings and respectful for the sublime ones. He expects nothing from the weaklings because they are powerless and hopeless. But he expects a lot from the sublime ones because they are powerful and capable of great things. But they have to become gracious and beautiful. If they do, Zarathustra assures them, their souls will shudder with godlike desires. He says, "this is the soul's secret: only when the hero has abandoned her, she is approached in a dream by the superhero." So far, the soul of the sublime one has been an object of conquest by a combative hero, but she will be courted by a superhero when this hero transforms his violent aggressive posture into a beautiful and gracious one. With his power and beauty, the superhero can fulfill the superhuman ideal of becoming a god. This section demonstrates the importance of knowing the right way to approach one's soul in the project of self-overcoming. Power alone is not sufficient for this project. One can only become a monster by exerting one's power without proper knowledge.

Zarathustra has shown what is wrong with the will of the sublime, but he is still contemptuous of the weaklings. While the sublime ones have nothing but power in their will, the weakling have no power in their own will. In the next few sections, he will critique the will of the weak lest their will be mistaken for the will of a child, which he set up as a model for the sublime to emulate. His first target is the cultured people in "On the Land of Education (*Bildung*)". The German word *Bildung* means not only education but also culture, and R. J. Hollingdale translates the title of this section as "The Land of Culture". The people in the land of culture accumulate many different cultures and make themselves into a glittering patchwork. This mixture of cultures makes it impossible to have beliefs, which leads to sterility, the opposite of creativity. They have no culture of their own; they have only the "paintings of all that men have ever believed' (*Z*, 120). The cultured people are the opposite of the sublime ones. In the previous section, Zarathustra compared the sublime ones with the weaklings. In the present section, he calls the cultured people the little females. Whereas the sublime ones are too strong and too stiff, the cultured people are too weak and too effeminate. Their weakness arises from their lack of faith. In their land of patchworks of beliefs, Zarathustra feels totally homeless. This feeling of alienation is the opposite of the uneasy kinship he felt with the sublime ones. Neither the strong sublime ones, nor the weak cultured people can gain the right knowledge and belief for self-overcoming.

Kaufmann's translation of "*Von der unbefleckten Erkenntnis*" as "On Immaculate Perception" is not literal. The literal translation is "On Spotless Knowledge". Although this section is addressed to the problem of knowledge, it is hard to determine what sort of knowledge is under discussion. Laurence Lampert says that it refers to the objective spirit of modern science (*Nietzsche's Teaching*, 124). Stanley Rosen links it to the Platonic intuition of the eternal Forms (*The Mask of Enlightenment*, 162). Greg Whitlock suggests a richer association by linking it to Kant's notion of disinterested aesthetic experience, Schopenhauer's ethics of the will-less contemplation of beautiful Ideas, and Wagner's ascetic music after his conversion to Christianity. These three were the three stages in the development of Kant's aesthetic ideas, which in turn emerged as the revival of Platonic Forms. Whitlock believes that his interpretation is supported by the original title of this section, "On the Contemplatives" (*Returning to Sils-Maria*, 158-60). Schopenhauer advocates the contemplation of Platonic Forms as a way out of suffering in the phenomenal world. Whitlock's interpretation can be further supported by the pervasive sexual imagery of this section. Although such imagery cannot be found in Kant's aesthetics, it is central in Schopenhauer's ethics and aesthetics and Wagner's music. It is also central in the Platonic ascent to the eternal Forms because it is claimed to be the ascent of *eros* (sexual love) in the *Symposium*. For these reasons, I am inclined to take the theme of this section to be primarily Schopenhauer's Platonic ethics and aesthetics.

Whitlock's Schopenhauerian interpretation can be linked to Lampert's interpretation. The objective spirit of modern science is the central theme in Kant's theory of knowledge. Kant secures its objectivity by pure intuition and pure concepts in his epistemology and by the disinterested perception of the beautiful in his aesthetics. Because his notion of purity means freedom from empirical content, it is interchangeable with his notion of disinterest, the freedom from empirical interests.[1] The Kantian notion of disinterest inspired Schopenhauer and the later Wagner because it appeared to give the human beings the power to rise above the grubby world of empirical interests. Lampert's interpretation of "immaculate perception" as the objective spirit of modern science has the advantage of connecting this section to the previous section on two levels. First, the culture of no belief or disbelief has often been lauded for its unbiased objective spirit. Second, this culture is the product of modern science, whose spirit of objective inquiry has destroyed the traditional beliefs. But the spirit of objective inquiry is as sterile as the skepticism of the cultured people. Whatever 'spotless knowledge' means, it is called 'contemplation', which is supposed to be the pure mirror for the reflection of reality. This pure mirror is without the will, that is, desires and passions, which Zarathustra calls the will to love and die. But spotless knowledge should not be mistaken for the innocence of a will-less child.

In "On Scholars", Zarathustra extends his discourse on knowledge to the scholars, who are professionally devoted to the acquisition of knowl-

---

1. Nietzsche calls Kant's conception of knowledge "disinterested contemplation" and repudiates it in favor of his perspectivism, the view that knowledge is always governed by our interests which constitute our perspectives (*GM* III.12).

edge. In this section, his self-reflection becomes more pronounced. It opens with a self-reflective note: "Zarathustra is no longer a scholar." A sheep makes this statement after eating his ivy wreath, thereby setting up a comic tone for his satiric picture of scholars. Sitting in the cool shade, they want to be mere spectators and gape at the thoughts of others. The posture of spectators is in line with the spirit of immaculate perception and that of the cultured people. Though they pose as wise men, their wisdom has the odor of swamps and they croak like frogs. Their intellectual condition is like the stagnant swamps: they keep repeating their tiresome stories and rehashing the same old ideas. Their pedantic spirit loves to complicate every problem by threading and knotting them with their fingers. They work like clockworks, which grind everything small and reduce it to white dust. They are vengeful against each other like spiders waiting for their prey. And they play with loaded dice. This is why Zarathustra had to leave the society of scholars. He says that he walks over their heads with his thoughts.

In "On Poets", he brings his discourse on knowledge and belief to bear upon the poets. His charges against the poets are merciless. They are blatant liars. They pretend to have special secret access to knowledge. They flaunt their tender sentiments as special inspirations from nature. The most serious charge against them is their shallowness. Their thoughts never penetrate deep enough to touch the bottom. For Zarathustra, the deep reality is the world of bodies, the physical world, while the spiritual world is a poetic fiction. This point was already asserted in "On the Despisers of the Body" of Part I. It is reaffirmed in the opening of this section, where he starts talking about the relation of the body and the spirit. Since he has come to know the body better, he says, the spirit appears to be only a parable. The poets cannot speak the truth, he says, because they know nothing about the physical reality. But they cover up their ignorance by making up parables about unreality such as the gods and the supermen. The German word *Dichter* (poet) means someone who makes up things, because the verb *dichten* means 'make'. The poetic parables are fictions. Instead of going deep into the physical world, poets have fabricated the dubious things above heaven and above clouds. This comes right out of Ludwig Feuerbach's theory of poetic creation. According to him, the world of religion is the world of feeling and imagination, where the poets spin out fictions about supernatural beings (*The Essence of Christianity*, 9-11, 208). The same charge is made by other Young Hegelians, David Strauss, Bruno Bauer, and Max Stirner. In the spirit of these Young Hegelians, Richard Wagner says, "God and gods, are the first creations of man's poetic force" (*Opera and Drama,* 153).

Zarathustra says that the poets, old and new, are too shallow to dive into deep reality. To cover up their shallowness, they muddy the waters, from which they pull up only salted slime. Because they are shallow and empty, they are the victims of their own vanity. The poet is the peacock of peacocks, who craves for spectators. He has to show off his dubious finery in front of an adulating audience, even when the audience is no better than a bunch of buffaloes. What is remarkable about these charges against the poets is his refusal to hold himself above them. Admitting that he is one of the poets, he delivers these charges in the name of "we the poets" ("we do lie too much", "we also know too little", and "we are bad learners"). He does not exempt his superman from his ridicule. He admits that his superhuman hero is as fictitious as the old God. Here again he becomes highly self-reflective and self-critical. But he concludes his talk by noting that some poets have become highly critical of themselves. He can already see the emergence of their penitent spirit.

Descent to the Abyss (Part II.18-19)

Who are the poets of penitence? Zarathustra is one of them. He is talking about his own penitence. His own poetry has been as shallow as any other poetry. His heroic ideal of superman is not deeper than any other poetic ideals. They do not even scratch the surface of true reality. He is willing to amend his shallowness and deepen his poetic insight by descending into the physical world. For all his harsh critique of poets, he repudiates only shallow poetry. He wants a truly deep poetry, deep enough to plumb the abyss of reality. He can have such poetry only by descending to the abyss. So we can distinguish the poetry of descent from the poetry of ascent. The latter has created only superficial illusions about the gods and the supermen. The former will produce hard truths about the earthly heroes and heroines. Zarathustra has repeatedly stressed the abyss, the center of the earth, as the ground of all existence. Only the penitent poets, who descend to the abyss, can write the true poetry of our earthly existence. He will undertake such a journey to the underworld in "On Great Events". This journey is supposed to take place on an island, not far from the Blessed Isles, with a fire-spewing mountain, which the legend says is placed like a huge rock at the gate to the underworld.

During Zarathustra's stay on the Blessed Isles, the crew of a ship went for rabbit-hunting. They suddenly saw him flying toward the fire-spewing mountain and shouting, "It is time! It is high time!" The captain of the crew said that he was descending to hell. Indeed, he disappeared and the people said that the devil had taken him. But he came back on the fifth day and recounted his conversation with the fire hound, in which the relation of surface phenomena and deep reality comes back as his central theme. The following is his report. The earth has a skin, which has two diseases. One of them is man and the other is the fire hound, about which many lies have been told. To get to the bottom of this mystery, he went over to the fire-spewing mountain and saw the naked truth. So he is now well informed about the fire hound and all its devils. These devils stand for the nauseating rebels, who advocate social revolutions. He recounts his harangue against the fire hound, whose content turns out to be much like the charges he had made against the poets. Because the fire hound drinks copiously only from the surface of the sea, its salty eloquence is mendacious and superficial. His devils know how to bellow and darken with ashes, just like him. But all the bellowing and smoking of the fire hound and his devils is really hollow. Nothing really important takes place in their ostensibly big shows.

Zarathustra finally tells the fire hound that the greatest events take place not in the loudest but in the stillest hours. This is because the world revolves not around the inventors of new noise, but around the inventors of new values. This is the statement he made to denigrate the people of the market place in "On the Flies of the Market Place" of Part I. He now adds that the revolution of the world around new values is inaudible. That is why the greatest events take place in the stillest hours. All the talks on political and social issues constitute the noisiest poetry in the world, but they do not touch the really deep problems because the fire hound and his devils stay on the surface of the earth. They are only fussing over the diseases on its skin. This is Zarathustra's ultimate charge against the social reformers and revolutionaries. The fire hound is their collective symbol. He finally tells the fire hound that there is another fire hound, which really speaks out of the heart of the earth. This is the golden fire hound that exhales gold and golden rain rather than ashes, smoke, and slime. And laughter flutters out of this golden fire hound like colorful clouds. This golden fire hound takes the laughter and the gold from the heart of the earth. Zarathustra explains this extraordinary phenomenon by saying that the heart of the earth is of gold.

The golden heart of the earth is the abyss, the abode of Life. This is indicated by gold and laughter, two special attributes of Life. In "The Other Dancing Song", Zarathustra will see gold blinking in the eyes of Life. The laughter that the golden fire hound takes from the heart of the earth is the same laughter that came from Life in "The Dancing Song". Gold is the emblem of Life. The golden center of earth is the ultimate source of Nature's primal energy, even for the golden radiation of the sun. Zarathustra's report on the heart of the earth has a strong allusion to Empedocles. The former goes through the fire-spewing mountain for his trip to the underworld, just as the latter is said to have leapt into the crater of Etna. Both of them are the fire hounds of golden wisdom. On the basis of volcanic activity, Empedocles holds that many fires burn beneath the surface of the earth and that the sun is an offshoot of the subterranean fire. In his geological account, Zarathustra has changed Empedocles' fire into his gold. But his geological account should not be taken literally. "The heart of the earth" is his poetic metaphor for the rock bottom of the physical universe. Likewise, his descent to the underworld is a poetic metaphor for scientific reduction to reach the rock bottom of nature in the next section. Until then it suffices to note that both Empedocles' fire and Zarathustra's gold are the emblems of power and energy. The power of life will be the critical topic in the next section.

"The Soothsayer" opens with the Soothsayer's gloomy talk. The whole earth is cursed. The harvests are poisoned, the wells have dried up, and the soil cracks. The people have become too weary to die; they are walking and living in tombs. Moved by this speech, Zarathustra can neither eat nor drink for three days and then falls into a deep sleep and a nightmare, in which he turns his back on all life. He becomes a night watchman and a guardian of tombs upon the lonely mountain castle of death, where he sees the triumph of death over life in the musty vaults. Death permeates everything he sees and smells. When he tries to open the gate with his old rusty keys, the wings of the gate make horrible noise. Then three strokes strike at the gate like thunder and the vaults echo and howl three times. He goes to the gate and cries twice, "Alpa, who is carrying his ashes up the mountain?" Then he presses the key to lift the gate, but the gate does not budge an inch. But a roaring wind tears its wings apart and casts up a black coffin before him. Then the coffin bursts open and spews out a thousand peals of laughter, which mocks and throws him to the ground. This horrible moment wakes him out of his nightmare. But he does not know how to interpret this dream of Gothic horrors.

His most beloved disciple offers the following interpretation. Zarathustra is the roaring wind that tears open the gates of the castle of death. He is also the coffin full of mocking laughter. With the power of his laughter, he can frighten all the night watchmen and guardians of tombs. He will frighten and prostrate them with his laughter. This is the sign of his triumph over death. In support of his interpretation, the disciple refers to Zarathustra's earlier dream in "The Child with the Mirror". He says, "Verily, *this is what you dreamed of:* your enemies" (Z, 136). At the beginning of this chapter, we noted the baffling character of the devil's mask in the mirror image. The disciple is taking the sneering devil as an image of his master, who frightens and prostrates his enemies with his sneering laughter. Understandably, the disciple would like to see his teacher as the triumphant hero over death. But his interpretation completely distorts the dream. In the dream, Zarathustra did not frighten all the night watchmen and guardians of tombs. He was the frightened night watchman and guardian of tombs. Instead of triumphing over death, he was overcome by death. He did not produce the thousand peals of laughter; on the contrary, he was thrown to the ground by that laughter. The disciple has completely misinterpreted the dream because of his high hope for his teacher as the radiant prophet for the redemption of humanity. In response to this wishful interpretation, Zarathustra takes a long look at the disciple and shakes his head.

For our understanding of the dream, we should separate it from the Soothsayer's talk. The Soothsayer is usually taken as a Schopenhauerian pessimist. This is justified by his gloomy talk. But the nightmare does not depict a Schopenhauerian world. Death has smothered every spark of life in the castle of death. Nothing moves; even time is scarcely noticeable. Everything is shrouded in the odor of dusty eternity. This dead world is not a Schopenhauerian world, a cauldron of living and suffering, in which countless passions strive for satisfaction against one another. It is the world of the cosmic will and its perpetual struggle and suffering. But there is neither struggle nor suffering in the world of Zarathustra's castle of death, because it contains no living beings. It is devoid of all motions until the explosion of scornful laughter. This dead world is the polar opposite of the Schopenhauerian world. The castle of death, I propose, is the outcome of scientific reduction. It is the world of dead matter. In "On Poets", Zarathustra condemned poets for their shallowness because they did not plumb secrets of the physical world, and commended the penitent poets for their willingness to mend this mistake. Since he is one of the penitent poets as we noted, he should descend to the center of the earth and survey the ultimate nature of the physical world.

By the metaphor of descent, I propose, Zarathustra means the scientific reduction of the physical world. Scientific reduction is to reduce the phenomena (for example, consciousness) of a higher level to those (for example, the brain state) of a lower level. Hence it is a descent from a higher to a lower level. Throughout his teaching career, he has advocated naturalism or physicalism. In "On the Despisers of the Body" of Part I, he identified mind and body. But the identity of mind and body is not the same as the reduction of mind to body. On Feuerbach's identity theory, the body is as spiritual as it is physical. Nature is spirit materialized or matter spiritualized. Since every physical object is basically spiritual, it is alive, too. On the other hand, reductionism reduces all living things to dead matter. The living things are only the epiphenomena of dead matter. Life is only an illusion and a surface phenomenon. Scientific reduction kills not only God, but all living things. The whole world becomes a dungeon of death, which encounters Zarathustra in his nightmare. Nietzsche entertains this form of reductive materialism in *GS* 109, where he categorically repudiates the notion that the universe is a living organism and advocates the view that the living is only a form of what is dead. What then is the connection of this dead world to the Soothsayer's talk? Schopenhauer's pessimism in its original form is too spiritual for Zarathustra's physicalism. His nightmare is the physicalistic reinterpretation of Schopenhauer's pessimism. To put it another way, the problem of suffering and pessimism need not be the monopoly of Schopenhauerian idealism. It can also be generated by scientific naturalism when it becomes reductive and positivistic. This point is clearly noted by Nietzsche (*GS* 347).

Let us return to Zarathustra's nightmare. To his surprise, the castle of death pours out a torrential outburst of laughter, which expresses the irrepressible force of life. This outburst of laughter is mocking Zarathustra. Let us now consider how he has earned this treatment. At the most deadly moment of his dream, there are three strokes at the gate, and he goes to the gate and asks, "Alpa, who is carrying his ashes up the mountain?" This is a strange question because he knows that he is the one who carried the ashes to the mountain. But this passage may indicate the terrible feeling he had suffered when his fire was extinguished and turned into ashes. He must have felt as dismal and as desolate as he is feeling now, that is, the whole world is dead. But the presumed dungeon of death explodes with the force of life. This explosion has been prepared by Zarathustra's descent to the underworld in the preceding section. In his geological account of the hearth of the earth, we noted, he has changed

Empedocles' fire to his gold. We also noted that both fire and gold are emblems of the living force. Zarathustra also said that the golden fire hound takes not only gold but also laughter from the heart of the earth. The exploding laughter in the dungeon of death is the laughter from the heart of the earth. It is the explosion of life in what appears to be the dungeon of dead matter. The dungeon of death is the metaphor for the mechanistic view of the world. In *BGE* 36, Nietzsche says that the mechanistic view is the view from outside and that the worldview from inside is the will to power and nothing else. In the dungeon of death, Zarathustra is being initiated from the outside into the inside of the universe. The mechanism is the outside view that conceals the inside view. This distinction between the inside and the outside view is indicated by the peal of laughter that explodes from a thousand masks of children. A mask usually covers a face. It stands for an external view that conceals an internal state. Such concealment produces an illusion.

Zarathustra's nightmare was an illusion. He encounters the castle of death in the kingdom of night. This is quite a change from "The Night Song" and "The Dancing Song". In these two songs, night was the kingdom of life. In his nightmare, however, night has become the kingdom of death. But the night of death abruptly changes into the night of life at the critical moment of the nightmare. What has initially appeared to be the castle of death turns out to be Zarathustra's momentary pessimistic delusion induced by reductive materialism. The delusive character of his pessimism is further indicated by the fact that his dream is only a dream. Although the material world appears to be dead, it is charged with the irrepressible and inexhaustible forces of life. This point has already been made by Life in her secret instruction to Zarathustra in "On Self-Overcoming". We noted that Life's description of itself as the perpetual will to power was a poetic image of Spinoza's conception of Nature. According to the materialistic conception of Nature, matter has no power of its own. The material objects can move only when they are pushed by external forces. Hence they are not only powerless, but also lifeless because life requires power. This is why reductive materialism inevitably leads to the conception of a totally dead world. But Spinoza's Nature is neither powerless nor lifeless because power is its essence. The explosion of laughter reaffirms Zarathustra's faith in the will to power as the ultimate force of Nature and enables him to overcome the momentary pessimistic crisis in the castle of death. But the laughter is still a mocking laughter. It mocks not only his momentary fear that the whole world is dead, but also his ambitious mission to rekindle the dead fire of life. It takes an over-blown estimation of one's power to entertain such a mission. Just imagine a tiny human being trying to rekindle the dead fire of the whole world. That is indeed ludicrous.

It may be instructive to compare Zarathustra's dream of Gothic horror with another dream of horror, which Zarathustra had at the beginning of Part II. In the mirror held by a child, he saw a devil's mask (*Fratze*) and scornful laughter (*Hohnlachen*).[2] These two words *Fratze* and *Hohnlachen* appear again in the description of the later dream: "And out of a thousand masks (*Fratzen*) of children, angels, owls, fools, and child-sized butterflies laughed (*lachte*) and mocked (*höhnte*) and roared at me." *Fratze* becomes *Fratzen*, and the noun *Hohnlachen* is changed into two verbs *lachte* and *höhnte* in the description of the later dream. Another important change is the role of the child. Whereas the child holds the mirror for Zarathustra in the first dream, the masks of children mock and laugh at him in the second dream. To be sure, the masks of children are not children, but only masks for angels, owls, fools, and butterflies. But all of them are like children because they are creatures of natural innocence, who represent the power of nature. They laugh at Zarathustra and his pessimism. This is their mocking laughter.

Zarathustra's descent to the underworld resembles Faust's descent to the underworld of the Eternal Mothers, which Mephistopheles describes as the everlasting void containing only Nothing (*Faust* 6246-56). When Faust descends there, he finds it totally devoid of life. Although nothing

---

2. Kaufmann translates *Fratze* as "grimace" rather than "mask." Although the German word means both 'grimace' and 'mask', the latter makes better sense for these two dreams than the former. Hollingdale confuses the readers by his inconsistency. He translates the German word 'grimace' for the earlier dream and as 'mask' for the later dream.

lives there, the moving forms of life swarm around in the eternal mode
(*Faust* 6429-32). The eternal void is the matrix of all life, just as the
deathly valley in Zarathustra's dream is the fountain of all life. The dungeon of death is the abyss, the center of the earth and the source of Life.
The abyss is the bowel of the universe. It is the breeding ground of all
drives and passions. Their motions are so chaotic that their breeding
ground appears to be Nothing. Chaos and Nothing are hard to distinguish.
Hence Zarathustra mistook the ultimate abode of all life for the castle of
death. He now realizes that his nightmare was only a momentary delusion. For his atonement for this error, he invites the Soothsayer to a
hearty meal. He has repeatedly said that pessimism is produced by a
weary body. In that case, there can be no quicker remedy for his weariness than a hearty meal. Now that he has returned from the dream world,
he will visit the real world in "On Redemption", which opens with his
encounter with the cripples and beggars. They are the real victims of suffering in the real world. This transition from the dream world to the real
world is indicated by "the great bridge" he crosses before running into
the cripples and beggars in "On Redemption".

The Will and the Past (Part II.20)

As a representative of these victims of misfortune, a hunchback challenges Zarathustra to heal the cripples. But he declines the challenge. He
says that to take away the hump from the hunchback is to take away his
spirit and that to restore sight to the blind will make them to see too
many wicked things. Then he gives his story of the inverse cripples, who
are much worse than the ordinary cripples. Whereas an ordinary cripple
lacks something such as a leg or an arm, an inverse cripple has too much
of something. Someone has a huge ear, which overshadows his entire
body, and he is known as a great man although he is only a thin stalk that
barely supports his gigantic ear. The inverse cripples are far more hideous and pathetic than the normal cripples. After giving this flippant response to the hunchback's challenge, he turns to his disciples and begins

to talk in profound dismay on the crippled condition of humanity. All human beings are only fragments and dreadful accidents, which are scattered like the ruins of a battlefield. He finds this most unendurable. He would not know how to live unless he were a seer of that which must come: "A seer, a willer, a creator, a future himself and a bridge to the future—and alas, also as it were, a cripple at this bridge: all this is Zarathustra" (*Z*, 138-39).

His self-description is enigmatic. He starts out by projecting himself as a seer and a creator and then downgrades himself to one of the cripples at this bridge. They represent the crippled condition of humanity waiting for the redeemer. He is again connecting the superman to the problem of suffering and redemption. He gives three different formulas of redemption from the crippled condition of humanity. Here is the first one:

> I walk among men as among the fragments of the future—that future which I envisage. And it is my sole concern (*all mein Dichten und Trachten*[3]) that I compose into one and bring together what is fragment and riddle and dreadful accident. And how could I bear to be a man if a man were not also a poet (or creator) and a riddle-solver and a redeemer of accident.

The important word in this passage is 'accident' (*Zufall*). The accident is an event that happens against the will. For example, the traffic accident is an accident because it happens against someone's will. Therefore, an accident is opposed to the will. In the closing section of Part I, Zarathustra casually referred to the giant of accident and treated it in abstraction. Now he sees accidents everywhere. They shatter human beings to frag-

---

3. The phrase *all mein Dichten und Trachten* is an idiomatic expression, which means "my whole mind," or "all my thoughts and efforts." But the English translators try to save its literal meaning. Kaufmann translates it as "all my creating and striving." One meaning of *dichten* is to make or create. Thomas Common translates *mein Dichten* as "my poetization." Hollingdale translates *mein Dichten* as "my art." These translations are meant to be linked to Zarathustra's reference to man as a poet (*Dichter*). But Kaufmann reads *Dichter* as 'creator'.

ments, which lack unity. Redemption is to bring the fragments into a unified whole. Zarathustra first assigns this function to himself and then to any human being who can be a poet or creator. This is presumably the role of a true poet in contrast to that of a false one. Whereas the false poet plays with fables and fictions, the true poet works with reality. He is no longer a cripple waiting on the bridge for redemption because he is the true poet who can do it himself.

Instead of stopping with this glorious posture of himself, he gives another formula of redemption: "To redeem those who lived in the past and to transform every 'it was' into 'thus I willed it'—that alone should I call redemption" (Z, 139). This is the second formula of redemption, which locates the object of redemption in the past. The first formula does not even mention the past; it is situated in the present for the future. The fragments to be redeemed belong to the present for the future use ("I walk among men as among the fragments of the future—that future which I envisage"), and to redeem those fragments is to create something out of them by composing them into one. In the second formula, redemption is the transformation of the past. To redeem the past is to transform every "it was" into "thus I willed it." But "thus I willed it" also belongs to the past as much as "it was." Therefore, the second formula involves two aspects of the past, the past to be redeemed and the will of the past. The notion of transforming the past by the will of the past makes no sense because the will of the past can no longer be exercised in the present. The very idea of redeeming the past makes no sense, either, because the past cannot be called back and reshaped. Although this idea is truly strange, it has been foreshadowed by "The Tomb Song", in which Zarathustra mournfully talked about redeeming the dead dreams and ideals of his youth. As we noted, his concern was shifting from the lightning (the superman) of the future to the resurrection of the past.

How can the will work on the past and redeem it? Zarathustra tells his disciples that he has already taught them that the will is the liberator and joy-bringer. Indeed, he taught it "On the Blessed Isles". We raised the question of how his will can be a liberator if his feeling is a prisoner. He now admits that the will is also trapped in the prison of the past. Because the will is totally powerless against the past, he says, "It was" is called the will's gnashing of teeth and its loneliest agony. The will becomes angry against the past, because the past is the stone it cannot move. The will cannot will backward because it has no control over the past. Then, how can the will cope with the past? He says that it tries to redeem itself in a foolish way because every prisoner becomes a fool. The liberator becomes a malefactor, who wreaks revenge on time and the past. This folly acquires spirit, thereby becoming the spirit of revenge. In "On the Tarantulas", he talked about the sense of revenge, which cried out for redemption. Now he locates the ultimate source of revenge in the rage against the past and time. The tarantula's revenge is the repressed envy and anger of the weak against the strong. But the past is the ultimate cause that has produced the difference between the weak and the strong. Therefore, the ultimate object of revenge is the past.

The two formulas of redemption have two different orientations. The first formula is future-oriented; the second formula is past-oriented. These two formulas dictate two different forms of the will, the forward-looking will and the backward-looking will. By its nature, every will is future-oriented. The will works in the present for the future. In Part I, Zarathustra introduced and elaborated on the creative will as the agent working for the future and preparing for the advent of the superman. The first formula of redemption comes right out of his teaching in Part I. But the second formula arises from the theme of suffering and redemption he has been developing in Part II. With the novel notion of transforming the past, the will has to be reoriented from the future to the past. It has to work on the past rather than on the future. Since to transform the past is an impossible task, it only provokes revenge against the past that can never be undone. Zarathustra enumerates some of the crazy doctrines produced by this revenge against the past, for example, that suffering is a punishment, or that everything in time passes away and perishes as a punishment, or that all things are ordered morally according to justice and punishment.

All these crazy doctrines have been spun out of the spirit of revenge against the immovable stone of the past, which has given humanity the most profound occasion for reflection and spiritualization. In the last chapter, we noted that God was created by projecting the human aspirations for transcending the limits of humanity and that the ideal of superman was also created to transcend those limits. In Part II, Zarathustra has been existentially experiencing those limits through his sufferings. Now he realizes that the stone of the past is the ultimate source of all those limits. This is the most devastating limit of humanity. The struggle to overcome such an awesome obstacle leads to profound reflection. In that case, one can become a superman by devising a way to control the stone of the past better than those crazy doctrines. He says that he has tried to lead his disciples away from these crazy doctrines by his teaching:

> 'The will is a creator.' All 'it was' is a fragment, a riddle, a dreadful accident—until the creative will says to it, 'But thus I willed it.' Until the creative will says to it, 'But thus I will it; thus shall I will it.' (*Z*, 141)

The entire past (All 'it was') is now regarded as a dreadful accident that is opposed to the will. What can the will do about it? It can say (1) "thus I willed it," (2) "thus I will it," or (3) "thus I shall will it." (1) belongs to the second formula, which we noted was impossible for execution. Zarathustra now advocates (2) and (3). (2) describes the act of willing in the present. It is hard to determine whether (3) describes the act of willing in the present or in the future. The expression "I shall will it" may describe a present decision or as a prediction of a future decision. Since Zarathustra is talking about the act of willing rather than its prediction, I am inclined to take the expression as a decision of the present moment. So I am putting together (2) and (3) as two versions of a present decision. The act of willing is moved from the past in (1) to the present in (2) and (3). This is the third formula of redemption. Although the will cannot go back to the past and act in the past as it is required in the second formula, it can act in the present as it is required in the third formula. Hence the third formula remedies the fatal defect of the second formula.

With the third formula, the only thing needed for the redemption of the past is the power to will it. If you can will the past, you will be freed from the rage against it because the past can no longer stand against your will. But the idea of willing the past is not easy to understand. In our normal understanding, the will is situated in the present and works for the future. Because the past is beyond our control, we never think of using our will to work on the past or alter it. But Zarathustra is now recommending the past-oriented will, the idea of willing backward. This novel recommendation seems to defy our basic understanding of the will. Fully aware of this difficulty, he asks, "But has the will yet spoken thus? And when will that happen?" (Z, 141). Evidently, it has not yet happened, and perhaps nobody knows when and how it can ever happen, because nobody has even thought of it. He concludes his talk by adding to these two questions many more enigmatic ones. "How shall this be brought about? Who could teach him [the will] also to will backwards?" These are his final questions, which mark the strange ending of his strange talk. They may indicate that he does not really understand his own talk. He suddenly stops talking and looks extremely terrified.

He began this talk in dismay and now ends it in terror. With terrified eyes, he gazes upon his disciples. His eyes pierce their thoughts and the thoughts behind their thoughts. He is trying to penetrate the layers of unspoken thoughts in their minds. After this tense moment, he laughs and says that it is difficult to live among men because to maintain silence is so difficult especially for a babbler. He has surely been babbling about the things beyond his comprehension. His excuse for babbling may be good enough for his disciples, but not for the hunchback. He asks Zarathustra why he speaks otherwise to the cripples than to his disciples. Zarathustra has a quick answer: one should speak to hunchbacks in a hunchbacked way. The hunchback concedes this point, but comes back with another question, "But why does Zarathustra speak otherwise to his pupils than to himself?" This is a serious charge of concealment. We noted earlier that Zarathustra was engaged in a game of masks in Part II. His game of concealment is becoming ever murkier and trickier. Zarathustra makes no attempt to deny the hunchback's charge of concealment. That is the enigmatic ending of the whole discourse on the notion of willing backward as the redemption of the past.

Zarathustra's talk on redemption is truly mysterious. Let us go over it once more. The hunchback recognizes three stages in his discourse: (1) his talk with the cripples, (2) his talk with the disciples, and (3) his talk with himself. The cripples challenge him to heal their infirmities. This challenge reminds us of Christ's healing miracles, but Zarathustra responds to it by refusing to heal the cripples. Some commentators say that he is doing so because he is practicing his doctrine of pity (Lampert, *Nietzsche's Teaching,* 141; Whitlock, *Returning to Sils-Maria*, 169). But there is a simpler account of his refusal. He has repudiated the power of miracle healing along with God and the supernatural power. After refusing to heal the cripples, he talks about the inverse cripples only to conclude that all human beings are fragments and accidents. Then he locates the ultimate cause of these sufferings in the past and gives a long lecture on the redemption of the past. Although his talk began as a response to the hunchback's request for help, it seems to drift away completely from the suffering of the cripples. Because his talk is becoming so embarrassingly irrelevant for the original topic of discussion, the hunchback covers his face during his entire talk to hide his embarrassment.

Whereas the problem of suffering for the cripples is in the present, Zarathustra focuses his talk on the past. He is talking about how to redeem the past rather than the present. That is not only irrelevant for the cripples but also sounds highly scholastic. For this reason, the hunchback says that Zarathustra is just telling his pupils tales out of school. But these tales out of school are dictated by Zarathustra's determinism. All the fragments and accidents in the present flow from the past by the cosmic principle of causation. Every accident is an accident because it is produced by the past. Whatever is produced by the past is an accident because we have no control over the past. Whenever we have no control, we become subject to alien forces. That is the nature of suffering. Zarathustra is now attributing all our suffering to the past in particular and time in general. Whatever happens to us is determined by our past, over which we have no control. Furthermore, we have no control over our present and future either because they are determined by our past. This totally passive condition of our existence is the polar opposite to the totally active condition of the sovereign individual Zarathustra built up in Part I. The latter is now completely smothered by the former.

Let us now try to understand the three formulas of redemption. The first formula is to create something from the fragments by composing them into a meaningful whole. Let us call it the creation formula, which has been well elaborated by Alexander Nehamas. He says, "By creating, on the basis of the past, an acceptable future, we justify and redeem everything that made this future possible; and that is everything" (*Nietzsche*, 160). He assumes that redemption and justification are the same thing. But they are different. The scheme of justification operates in the context of means and ends: the ends can justify the means. This is what Nehamas has in mind, when he says, "In particular, the significance of the past lies in its relationship to the future. And since the future is yet to come, neither the significance of the past nor its nature is yet settled" (*Nietzsche*, 160-61). This is an instrumental view of the past and its redemption. Let us now compare it with the non-instrumental view. Suppose that you have done something terrible in the past, for example, you killed your brother to monopolize the inheritance from your parents. Now you earnestly wish to redeem this horrible past and use your terrible experience in reforming yourself and generously help millions of poor people. In that case, are you redeeming your terrible deed by this new creative act? You may say that there is no way to redeem your past murderous act by performing any later creative act, regardless the magnitude of its beneficence, because the instrumental use of the past is not its redemption.

The second formula is impossible to implement, as we noted earlier. There is no way to transform "it was" to "thus I willed it," if I did not will it already in the past. Zarathustra remedies this fatal defect of the second formula by changing its "thus I willed it" into "thus I will it" and "thus shall I will it" of the third formula. The third formula is to will the past, but there are two ways of doing it. You can will your past as it is or by transforming it. Of course, it is impossible to transform the past in reality because it is inalterably fixed for eternity. But we can transform the past in an artistic manner. This is the transformation formula that Nehamas advocates by taking Marcel Proust as his model (*Nietsche*, 167-69). In his *Remembrance of Things Past*, Proust recollects and recreates his past, but he does not use it to create a better future. He does not even look forward because his attention is on the past. This past-oriented reorganization may be called the method of re-creation or transformation in contrast to the future-oriented method of creation. But they are alike in using the past and not redeeming it. Although the method of transformation does not use the past for a future creation, it is still using the past for the creation of a beautiful picture. Therefore, to make a beautiful picture of the past is not the same as to redeem it.

Many doctrines of redemption that have been spun out by the sense of revenge against the past indeed employ the transformation formula. In *The City of God*, for example, Augustine rewrites the entire history of humankind for Christian redemption. This is a much more stupendous project than Marcel Proust's. Augustine wants to show that the perpetual suffering of humanity has not been senseless and accidental, but providential and beneficial. This is his way of transforming the past of humanity for its redemption. The transformation project for redemption has been used even in the secular domain. Many historians have tried to rewrite the histories of their nations, painting them in greater glories than they really were. But the past cannot be transformed, whatever revisions they may make about it. This is Zarathustra's immobile stone. Therefore the transformation formula is not faithful to his intention. The right way to understand the third formula is to will the past as it is. This is the acceptance formula, which will be endorsed by Zarathustra in Part III.

There appears to be nothing creative in accepting the past. But Zarathustra calls upon the creative will for this task. To accept the past is not creative in the normal sense. But we have already noted that Zarathustra's notion of creation is different from our normal understanding of creation. In "On the Thousand and One Goals" of Part I, he said, "To esteem is to create." The will to accept the past means to accept it willingly, which is to esteem it. In that case, the acceptance of the past is a creative act. Although he had propounded the creative will as the central theme of his teaching, he has now taken away the creative power in its normal sense from the will by making it the prisoner of the past. You may assume that the will is not a prisoner but a creative agent at least in the act of willing the past. But the act of willing the past is also determined by the past. If the will is the prisoner of the past, it should also be the prisoner of the present because the present is the product of the past. If it can have no control over the present, it can have no control over the future, either, because the future is determined by the present and the past. The will is so tightly imprisoned in the past, the present, and the future that it can have no freedom and no creative power in the normal sense. Many commentators have noted that Zarathustra's teaching on the creative will is crushed by the eternal recurrence. But it is already eliminated by the causal power of the past in "On the Redemption."

The creative will is generally understood to have the power and freedom in the present for the future. In this normal understanding of the will, it looks forward because it is future-oriented. This normal understanding is incompatible with Zarathustra's view. For him, the only way to gain control over the present and be creative for the future is to establish control over the past by willing it because the past determines the present and the future. So he tells his disciples to will the past. In this abnormal understanding of the will, it looks backward because it is past-oriented. The backward willing is so contrary to our normal understanding of the will that even Zarathustra may not know how to do it. So he says, "Who could teach the will also to will backwards?" So he has created a terrible collision between two conceptions of the will, one forward-looking and the other backward-looking. He has given a long discourse on redemption only to find himself in this terrible collision. But this collision did not pop up suddenly in the present discourse on redemption. On the contrary, it has been building up over the long period of his preaching and teaching. In Part I, he had preached on the importance of forward-looking will for the sake of the superman. Then in Part II, he gradually introduced and developed the notion of backward-willing in connection with the problem of suffering and redemption. In "On Redemption", he finally brings them to an open collision, in which the backward will completely overpowers the forward will.

The forward-looking will and the backward-looking will are not really two separate wills, but two different ways of looking at one and the same will. Robert Solomon regards these two ways as two perspectives (*Living with Nietzsche,* 181). The will looks forward in contemplating its future action. The will is the cause of its action. This is the forward-looking will. It is the will of foresight. But the same will can also be regarded as an effect of the past causes. This is the backward-looking will. It looks backward to its causes. It is the will of hindsight. The forward-looking will may feel free, but it may turn out to be determined when its causal conditions are examined retrospectively. The distinction between these two forms of will is roughly equivalent to Kant's distinction between the autonomous and the heteronomous will (*Critique of Pure Reason,* A448/B476-A451/B479). It is worth comparing these two distinctions for our better understanding of Zarathustra's notion of the twofold will. On Kant's theory, the will can never be free in the phenomenal world because everything in the phenomenal world is governed by the causal laws. Only in the world of noumena, Kant says, the will is free of causal determination because the noumena stand beyond the spatial and temporal framework of causation. But the will has to operate in the world of phenomena. So he makes the mystifying claim that the will is free from the noumenal perspective but unfree from the phenomenal perspective. He calls the free will the autonomous will and the unfree will the heteronomous will. This is Kant's doctrine of the twofold will.

Although Zarathustra does not accept the world of noumena, his view of the twofold will is much like Kant's twofold perspective on the will. The forward-looking will feels the freedom of choice and action just the way the Kantian autonomous will does in the noumenal perspective, because it is oblivious of its causal conditions. But the backward-looking will is conscious of its own necessity just the way the Kantian heteronomous will is in the phenomenal perspective, because its causal conditions cannot escape the hindsight. Since Zarathustra does not accept the noumenal world, he cannot follow Kant's tricky maneuver of deploying the dual perspective. He has only the phenomenal world, whose determinism eliminates the possibility of free will. This simple idea of determinism is the terrifying thought that erupted in his discourse on redemption. It completely destroys the foundation for Zarathustra's teaching on the creation of values and the superman. But he does not want to express his terrifying thought to the disciples because he has already driven himself into deep waters by his injudicious babbling. So he keeps it only in his inner speech with himself. Sensing this inner dialogue of terror, the hunchback asks, "But why does Zarathustra speak otherwise to his pupils than to himself?" Understandably, he declines to answer this question.

Zarathustra's terrifying thought cannot be a total surprise to him or his audience. In "On Self-Overcoming", he was instructed by Life on her will to power as the cosmic principle governing the entire physical world. She told him that the contending individual wills were not the ultimate agents for the perpetual game of power and that the individual wills were only the path and footprints of her will to power. In the world that is governed by her almighty will, the individual wills can never have their autonomy. In that case, the individual will can never have the power of redemption because it should be treated as just another accident. In "On Redemption", Zarathustra is only explicating Life's bald description of her awesome cosmic power in terms of causal determination. In "On Self-Overcoming", she told him that she was the will to power that sustained the whole world. He is now saying that the whole world is a network of causal determination. From these two propositions, we can deduce that the universal causal determination is the manifestation of Life's will to power. Therefore, the individual will is totally vanquished by Life's overflowing will to power.

You may object to this interpretation because Life is not even mentioned in "On Redemption". But I am providing a sequential meaning to this section. Let us trace the thematic sequence of the last four sections. In "On Poets", Zarathustra denounced the poets for their shallowness. He said that they knew nothing because they never descended to deep reality and that they were covering up their ignorance by creating poetic fictions such as the gods and the supermen and placing them above heaven and clouds. He then praised the penitent poets for their willingness to brush aside the dubious poetic fabrications and make the descent for real truth.

In "On Great Events", he made the descent to the abyss, presumably the ultimate fountain of Life, only to find the dungeon of death in his nightmare in "The Soothsayer". But he was mocked by the explosion of laughter and power in the dungeon of death, and then he ascended to the surface of the earth and confronted a group of cripples in "On Redemption". Given this sequence of events, his causal account can be taken as his explanation of the surface phenomena as the emanations of Life and her will to power from the abyss.

In Part II, Zarathustra functions as the advocate for the teaching of Life, whereas he was the advocate for his own teaching in Part I. He proclaimed and advocated the superman on his own authority. He was a teacher, pure and simple, in Part I, but he becomes a learner in Part II. He learns from Life and from his suffering which comes from Life. In "On Poets", he denounces the poets as bad learners. Instead of learning the truth, they proclaim their poetic fabrications. As an authoritative teacher, he was a purely active agent, who depended on no one else. As a patient learner and a penitent poet, he is a basically receptive agent, who has to depend on others. As an active agent, he was the hero of day. As a receptive agent, he has become a child of night. These two roles are indicated by the poetic images that mark his two missions. His first mission opened with his salutation to the sun, the symbol of overflowing virtue, and ended with the same symbol. His second mission opened with a nightmare, in which he was victimized by his powerful enemies, and will end with another nightmare in "The Stillest Hour". Nightmares and dreams in general are the emblems of the powers acting on the self. They never appeared in Part I, but begin to show up in Part II. This is because Zarathustra's mode of existence has changed from the active mode in Part I to the receptive mode in Part II.

The Collision of Two Wills (Part II.21-22)

Collision of the two wills is the keynote that opens "On Human Prudence": "Not the height but the precipice is terrible. That precipice where the glance plunges *down* and the hand reaches *up*. There the heart becomes giddy confronted with its double will. Alas, friends, can you guess what is my heart's double will?" (*Z*, 142). Zarathustra now describes the two wills as upward and downward. The upward-pulling will is his longing for the superman; the downward-pulling will is his attachment to humankind. The former draws him up to the height; the latter pulls him down to the depth. Although the twofold will pulls in opposite directions, he cannot abandon either side of its pull. He has to preserve both his longing for the superman and his attachment to humanity. To this end, he has devised four rules of human prudence. The first rule is not to be on guard even at the risk of getting deceived by every rogue. This is to gain the trust of the people. The second rule is to be friendly with the vain, thereby reinforcing his attachment to the people. The third rule is to preserve the ideal of the superman by banking his hope on evil people, who can produce great wonders. The fourth rule is to disguise himself as one of the vain and dignified to mingle with "the good and the just."

Of these four rules of prudence, only the third one is connected to the upward will, and the other three to the downward will. This is a surprising development for Zarathustra. He had disdainfully dismissed the good and the just, while he was solely concerned with the superman and the future. He is now giving the good and the just far greater attention than the superman. This radical change on his part appears to reflect the extraordinary awareness of the past that he has gained in "On Redemption". We can see this point by noting that the upward will is equivalent to the forward-looking will. When we plan for the future, we hope to make progress, that is, to advance to a higher level than our present position. The forward movement should be an ascent. By the same logic, the downward will is equivalent to the backward-looking will. Our past should be on a lower level than our present position, if we have made any progress on the past. Zarathustra is restating the difference between the forward-looking and the backward-looking will as the difference between the upward and the downward will. Because "the forward-looking will" and "the backward-looking will" are cumbersome expressions, let us replace them with "the autonomous will" and "the heteronomous will." The autonomous will looks forward; it is not aware of its causal past. But the heteronomous will looks backward; it is aware of its being determined by the events of the past.

If human beings are caught in the conflict between these two wills, one may think, they can resolve the conflict by relinquishing one of them. But Zarathustra says that it is impossible to relinquish either. You cannot dismiss the heteronomous will because we are trapped in it. Nor can you dismiss the autonomous will. Even if you subscribe to determinism and believe that your will is already determined by your past, you must still make your decisions as though you had free will. Although the past has determined your will, it does not tell you what you should do. Therefore, you cannot avoid the existential problem of making your decisions and exercising your will. The autonomous will is as irrepressible and as in-eliminable as the heteronomous will. Thus everyone is inevitably caught in the collision of the two wills. He is stressing this point not only in his talk, but also placing himself on a slope for this talk. In the first line of this section, he says, "Not the height: the slope (*Abhang*) is frightful."[4] Because he is standing on a slope, he is pulled upward and downward at the same time. But he does not want to relinquish either of the two wills. This is the poetic image for portraying his predicament of getting caught in the collision of the two wills.

In "The Stillest Hour", Zarathustra bids his second farewell to his disciples. This time, he is going away not on his own will, but under the stern command of an angry mistress. She has ordered him to return to his solitude. Her name is My Stillest Hour and he had a talk with her in his dream. He recounts the talk as follows. Speaking in a voiceless voice, she opens the talk by saying, "You know it, Zarathustra." This whisper makes him cry out for terror, drains the blood from his face, and renders him speechless. The voiceless voice talks again, "You know it, Zarathustra, but you do not say it!" And he defiantly replies, "Yes, I know it, but I

---

4. The German word *Abhang* is translated as 'precipice' by Walter Kaufmann, as 'abyss' by R. J. Hollingdale, and as 'declivity' by Thomas Common. But none of them can capture the poetic picture of standing on a slope and being pulled upward and downward at the same time.

do not want to say it." But it is never explained even to the end of their talk what it is that he knows and does not want to say. When she tells him not to hide in his defiance, he begs her to release him from this task because it is beyond his power. But she tells him to speak his word and break. He replies, "Alas, is it *my* word? Who am I? I await the worthier one; I am not worthy even of being broken by it" (*Z*, 146). Then she says that he is not humble enough to do it, and he protests by saying that the hide of his humility has born everything under the sun.

The voiceless voice tells him to command because what is needed most is someone to command great things. What is most unforgivable in him is that he has the power but does not want to rule. He defends himself by saying that he lacks the lion's commanding voice. She counters it by saying that it is the stillest words that bring on the storm. Now he says that he is ashamed, probably because that is exactly what he preached in "On Great Events". She finally gives him her final instruction. He must become like a child and act without shame, but he cannot do so because the pride of youth is still upon him. Whoever would become like a child must overcome his youth. After reflecting on this advice and trembling for a long time, he says, "I do not want to." He is now resisting his metamorphosis from a lion to a child. Then he is surrounded by laughter, which tears up his entrails. The voiceless voice makes its final statement: "O Zarathustra, your fruit is ripe, but you are not ripe for your fruit. Thus you must return to your solitude again; for you must yet become mellow" (*Z*, 147). Then it laughs again and vanishes. Everything around him becomes quiet with a twofold stillness. He lies on the ground and sweat pours from his limbs. This is a summary of the story Zarathustra tells his disciples to explain why he has to leave them and return to his solitude.

What is the mysterious "it" that Zarathustra does not want to speak? Walter Kaufmann identifies it with the doctrine of eternal recurrence (*Z*, 82). As Kathleen Higgins points out, this is not a convincing account because it stands on the assumption that the doctrine is already formulated in Zarathustra's mind (*Nietzsche's* Zarathustra, 140). But there is no such indication in the text. The unspeakable "it" is obviously the one thing that even the talkative Zarathustra could not bring himself to discuss in

"On Redemption", namely, the conflict of the twofold will and the horror of determinism. It was so terrifying that he had to stop talking. Even the hunchback suspected that he was holding it back from his audience. There may be one objection to this conjecture. In defense of his refusal to speak the unspeakable 'it', Zarathustra says, "Alas, is it *my* word?" (Z, 146). He questions his authorship of 'it'. If 'it' concerns his own frightful thought, he should not disown 'it' because it is obviously his word. But we have noted that his entire discourse on redemption was his exposition of the secret instruction he had received from Life. Therefore, 'it' is the message from Life. He is now being reprimanded for not completing the exposition by refusing to spell out its terrifying conclusion. This terrible task of completing the unfinished exposition will be undertaken in the vision of eternal recurrence in Part III. In that regard, 'it' is related to the eternal recurrence.

The conflict of the twofold will kept haunting him even in "On Human Prudence". "The twofold stillness," which surrounds him after his talk with the voiceless voice, is the textual pointer deliberately planted by the author for the referential identification of the unspoken 'it'. Except for this function, the expression "the twofold stillness" makes no sense at all. The two wills have been the two central themes of Zarathustra's speeches. The autonomous will was introduced and elaborated as the main theme of Part I. The notion of creation was the keynote for its development, which was retained in Part II. In "Upon the blessed Isles", he denounced the permanent world because it left no room for creativity and praised the impermanent world as the proper theater for the creators. To his bitter grief, he realized that there was no room for freedom even in the impermanent world because it was also causally governed by its past. Hence the will can never be free and autonomous. Thus the heteronomous will becomes his counter theme in his speeches on the problem of suffering and redemption in Part II. By the end of Part II, the theme and the counter theme came to the inevitable collision, which terrified Zarathustra and silenced his talking. This silence eventually led to the twofold silence in "The Stillest Hour". Hence it is called the twofold stillness because both the theme and the counter theme are now silenced.

These two themes have been delineated in Parts I and II, and their conflict will be developed and resolved in Parts III and IV. This is roughly the thematic plan for the composition of this work.

Though Zarathustra evaded the hunchback's probing questions, he cannot elude the awesome lady of "The Stillest Hour" because she has already placed him under her command. To remind him of this fact, she says, "You are the one who has forgotten how to obey." She commands him to be a commander, but he wants to be excused on the ground that he lacks the lion's voice. To his surprise, she tells him that he must become like a child rather than a lion before he can become a commander. She is telling him that he could not speak his terrifying thought because he was trying to behave like a lion. His pride has not allowed him to expose his terror on the twofold will to his disciples. But he cannot overcome his pride until he becomes a child. Until then, as the awesome lady says, he will not be ripe to pick his ripe fruit. This is the ironic ending of his second teaching mission, which he began by posing himself as the north wind for harvesting the ripe figs on the Blessed Isles. Now he must become a child for the harvest. For this final stage of self-perfection, he must leave his disciples and return to his solitude. This final stage was prophesied in the allegorical metamorphoses of the three animals. The camel has to become a lion, but the lion has to become a child.

Who is this voiceless lady called The Stillest Hour? She is the lady of night. She is Life. We have encountered her on three occasions. First, she was represented as night or rather the kingdom of silence and darkness in "The Night Song". The voiceless voice is the voice of her silence. Second, she appeared as the lady, who came to Zarathustra's rescue in "The Dancing Song". This episode explains why she now talks to him in "The Stillest Hours" not as a stranger, but as someone who has already secured her lordship over him. There is no other lady who fits this role except for Life. He became her liege when she saved him from drowning by fishing him out of deep waters with her golden fishing rod. Third, he encountered her mocking laughter in a thousandfold magnification when he descended to the abyss in "The Soothsayer". The voiceless voice leaves the same laughter behind her when she vanishes after her talk with

Zarathustra. His encounter with Life in "The Stillest Hour" should be understood as a continuation of his journey downward into deep reality, which he began in "On Great Events". In his nightmare of "The Soothsayer", he made the descent, but never came face to face with Life. He felt her power only indirectly through the thousandfold magnification of her mocking laughter. His encounter with the voiceless lady also takes place in a dream of descent to the abyss. At the onset of this dream, he feels the ground giving under him and becomes frightened down to his very toes. This time, his encounter is direct: he talks directly with her. This encounter may indicate that he has gained a deeper understanding of the ultimate nature of the physical world.

There is another textual ground for identifying the awesome lady as Life. In her talk with Zarathustra, she speaks eleven times. That is the same number as the number of lines that will be sung in the roundelay of "The Other Dancing Song" of Part III. The roundelay has twelve lines representing the twelve strokes at midnight, but the last line is left unsung. Claus-Artur Scheier says that the eleven speakings by The Stillest Hour correspond to the eleven lines of the roundelay and that the twelfth line is filled by silence in both cases (*Nietzsches Labyrinth*, 204-8). This is an astute observation, which helps us establish the identity of The Stillest Hour as Life. As we will see, the roundelay is Life's prophecy on the future of Zarathustra's love. In both cases, night and dream are the central media. The voiceless voice talks in a dream of night and the roundelay talks about the deep dream of midnight. The last line is left blank to indicate that the song has yet to be finished. When it is finally completed in "The Drunken Song" of Part IV, as we will see later, the twelfth line will be filled.

Zarathustra's encounter with the nameless lady resembles Goethe's encounter with his nameless lady, which is narrated in his poem "Dedication". One beautiful morning, while he is climbing a mountain, a godlike woman appears out of the mist and floats before him. In a soft voice of love, she says to him, "Do you not know me? Do you not recognize the one who often gave you healing balm when you were wounded sorest?" These are exactly the questions that the voiceless awesome lady can put to Zarathustra, if she is Life. In "The Dancing Song", she saved him from drowning with her golden fishing rod. But he does not reveal her name for the same reason that Goethe refuses to name his lady. Their relation with the ladies is not only private but also embarrassing. Although Goethe refuses to name his lady, he tells her that he knows her by many names. Zarathustra can say the same thing to Life. In "The Dancing Song", she told him that men had given her many different names such as 'profound', 'faithful', 'eternal', 'mysterious', and even 'unfathomable'. Goethe tells his lady that he has lost the many friends he had while wandering and that he now knows only her and no one else. Then she smiles and says, "Scarcely are you free from the crudest delusion, / Scarcely have you mastered the most childish will, / Yet you believe you are already good enough to be superman." Goethe is being chided for taking himself to be a superman even before mastering the most childish will. On the other hand, paradoxically, Zarathustra is being urged to become like a child to secure the commanding will. In spite of this difference, their common ground is their delusion about themselves. Goethe's delusion lies in his overestimation of his own power; Zarathustra's delusion lies in his erroneous belief that he should have the leonine will to control his destiny. Each of them is shown the way to becoming the superman by a nameless lady.

If the awesome lady is Life, why then is her identity not revealed? There are two sides for this game of concealment. On one side, Zarathustra refuses to name her; on the other side, the lady does not disclose her identity. There are two reasons for these two moves. She is the abyss that Zarathustra has reached by his descent. As we noted earlier, his descent to the underworld resembles Faust's descent to the underworld of the Eternal Mothers, which Mephistopheles describes as the everlasting void containing only Nothing. If she is the abyss, Nothing, she cannot be named or described. This is one of the two reasons. The other reason is the game of masks that Zarathustra has been playing in Part II. This game reaches its climax in his encounter with the voiceless voice. The awesome lady chastises him for concealing his terrifying thought just the way the hunchback complained. Zarathustra was concealing it not only to his disciples but even to himself. Life is responding in kind to his game of masks and refuses to reveal herself to him, because she has all along been the ultimate target for his game of concealment and dissemblance. As we noted earlier, even the immovable stone of the past only displays the awesome power of Life, Mother Nature. At the outset of this chapter, I said that Zarathustra initiated his game of masks in the first section of Part II. But even his performance in Part I may also have been a game of masks. In "On Poets", he said that the superman was one of the shallow fabrications by the poets. The superman was the centerpiece of his show in Part I. In that case, he did not begin his game of masks at the opening of Part II. He was then just beginning to recognize the nature of his tricky game for the first time.

Let us now consider the function of masks. Zarathustra hides himself behind his masks to protect his self-image. You can see this in his beloved disciple's interpretation of his nightmare in "The Soothsayer". He reveres Zarathustra as the master of life over death by taking him as the roaring wind that tears open the gates of the castle of death and as the coffin full of mocking laughter. This is the disciple's understanding of the master in accordance with his mask of superhuman mastery that has adorned his appearance. But this mask does not simply mislead others. It also misleads the master himself. It is this mask of self-sufficiency and super-mastery that has led to his devastating agony of isolation and loneliness in "The Night Song". Hence the mask alienates himself from others and even from himself. This is the most ravaging effect of masks. When his autonomous will is shattered under the crushing weight of the past, he cannot openly talk about his frightening discovery again because of his mask. An open confession of this discovery would expose what lies behind his superhuman mask. So he creates a mask of silence to protect his mask of mastery. As one lie leads to another lie, one mask dictates the fabrication of another mask.

In Part II, Zarathustra is so obsessed with his own mask that he can see nothing but masks wherever he looks. In "On Priests", he says that the humility of priests is only a mask for their vengefulness and that they have built their sweet-smelling caves called churches and their stairways of repentance to hide themselves. The so-called virtue is only a mask of the virtuous for the secrets of their heart, which are written in the filthy words of the cosmic paymaster: 'revenge', 'punishment', 'reward', and 'retribution' ("On the Virtuous"). The ideal of equality is only a mask for envy and revenge ("On the Tarantulas"). The famous wise men just wear the mask of wisdom and spirit ("On the Famous Wise Men"). The ugly combative posture of those who are sublime is their mask to hide the beast and monster still unconquered in their heart ("On Those Who Are Sublime"). The cultured people hide themselves behind their mask of patched cultures ("On the Land of Education"). The pursuit of immaculate knowledge is only a mask of purity for the lecherous heart ("On Immaculate Perception"). On this mask, Zarathustra says, "Behind a god's mask you hide from yourselves, in your 'purity'; your revolting worm has crawled into a god's mask" (*Z*, 123). The fire hound hides its shallowness behind the mask of big noises ("On Great Event"). Finally, the poets are the master mask-makers and mask-users. They not only wear the pompous mask of inspiration, but also create the masks of gods and the superman and hoist them above humanity. Thus the Part II is a long parade of glittering masks.

Even the castle of death is a mask that hides the exhaustible power of life ("The Soothsayer"). In this case, a mask appears to be generated by illusion and ignorance. But this is not an exception to the rule. Masks are always generated from illusion and ignorance and lead to deception and manipulation. Zarathustra's mask of the superman was generated from his illusion of human capacity and his ignorance of the world that governs his own will. As we have already noted, he opened Part II with a sense of suffering, whereas he had pretended to stand aloofly above it because of his superhuman mask in Part I. But the sense of suffering is an ominous threat to any superhuman posture. The superman should be absolutely immune to suffering because he is an absolute sovereign like God. Zarathustra betrayed his fear of threat to his superhuman mask when he read the devil's mask as the danger to his teaching in "The Child with the Mirror". Thus he begins to recognize his own mask and present a parade of masks in Part II. But this parade begins and ends with a child. It begins with a child presenting the devil's mask in the mirror and ends with the voiceless voice's command to Zarathustra to become like a child. Only by regaining the innocence of a child, he can outgrow his game of concealment and dissemblance and overcome the alienation he has brought upon himself by his devilish game. But he cannot fully regain his innocence until the end of Part IV. Up to that final moment, he will continue to intensify and magnify his game of masks. In Part III, it will become the game of sphinx, a game of riddles shrouded under the cover of silence. The continuous complication of his tricky game has been the chief obstacle to unraveling the thematic plot of his epic journey.

Let us now compare the ending of Part II with that of Part I. At the end of Part I, Zarathustra said farewell to his disciples like a radiant sun going over the horizon. He boasted of having given his disciples everything he had and flaunted his gift-giving virtue. This radiant mood cannot be found at the end of Part II. Instead of overflowing self-confidence and abundance, he now talks in fear and trembling. The aura of a radiant sun is replaced by the terrifying darkness of night and its chilly silence. He concludes his sad farewell with a lament, "Alas, my friends, I still could tell you something, I still could give you something. Why do I not give it? Am I stingy?" (*Z*, 147). He can no longer boast of his abundance and generosity. He is so overcome by his pain that no one knows how to comfort him. When night comes, he goes away all alone. In Part I, he came down from his mountain cave to teach others; in Part II, he came to understand his own existence, especially the mystery of human will. When he advocated the superman in Part I, his conception of human existence was one-dimensional. In Part II, he has learned that it has two dimensions. The two-dimensional view has led to his game of masks. The one-dimensional person wears no mask.

The will is not only projected to the future, but also determined by the past. It can look not only forward and upward, but also backward and downward. The forward-looking will is assumed to be autonomous and creative; the backward-looking will is known to be heteronomous and powerless. The autonomous will belongs to an individual; the heteronomous will belongs to Life, Mother Nature. Hence the former is overpowered by the latter. This frightful thought terrified Zarathustra in "On Redemption" and became the unspeakable "it" in "The Stillest Hour". The autonomous will becomes Faustian when it reaches the superhuman level. It is exemplified by the will of Goethe's Faust. The heteronomous will is Spinozan; it reflects Spinoza's teaching that our will is determined by cosmic necessity. In Part I, Zarathustra talked like a lion and flaunted his Faustian will for his campaign of spiritualization. But his Faustian will is shattered in Part II and his Faustian campaign has disintegrated. At this critical point, he is commanded by the voiceless voice of "The Stillest Hour" to become like a child. This is the final step in the ladder of spiritualization that was laid out in the allegory of three metamorphoses. His campaign of spiritualization must shift from the Faustian to the Spinozan mode. He conducted the Faustian campaign with his own Wisdom and taught others the scheme of three metamorphoses. In the Spinozan campaign, Life orders him to undergo the final metamorphosis for his own sake. Thus his spiritual campaign is redirected from others to his own existence, and Wisdom is replaced by Life in Part II. Wisdom vanishes altogether without any formal notice never to be seen again to the end of his spiritual campaign. Hence his encounter with Life turns out to be the most critical event in his epic journey.

CHAPTER THREE

The Twofold Will

(Part III.1-12)

The problem of the twofold will, which terrified Zarathustra by the end
of Part II, will be the central theme in Part III. John Richardson says that
Nietzsche understands the individual as a synthesis of conflicting wills
(*Nietzsche's System,* 45). By the word 'wills', Richardson means no
more than drives and instincts. But the twofold will stands on a higher
level than the individual drives and instincts. It can be understood only in
its relation to the world. Zarathustra undertakes their joint investigation
by becoming a wanderer in "The Wanderer" and reconsidering the problem of accidents, which broke wide open the problem of the twofold will
in Part II. Now he presents a different account of accidents.

> The time is gone when mere accidents could still happen to
> me; and what could still come to me now that was not mine al-
> ready? What returns, what finally comes home to me, is my
> own self and what of myself has long been in strange lands
> and scattered among all things and accidents. (*Z,* 152)

The accidents that appeared to be fragments scattered on the battlefield
in "On Redemption" of Part II are now seen as essential elements of his
own self. They are simply coming back to himself after being scattered
in strange lands. They were mistaken to be accidents because they were
assumed to belong to alien forces. In that case, no accidents can ever
happen to him. This is a fantastic view of the self. Just imagine that you
are hit by a terrorist bomb. If you accept this view, you have to say that

getting hit by the bomb is not an accident because it is an essential feature of your self. Since it came from the terrorists, you have to say that even the terrorists also belong to your self. Eventually you have to say that everything happening in the whole world is an essential feature of your self. Your selfhood becomes coextensive with the whole universe. This is Zarathustra's notion of his cosmic self.

He opened Part II with the image of himself as a sneering devil in the mirror, and this self-image foretold the central theme to be developed in the remainder of Part II, namely, the suffering and redemption of the self. But these two features of the self arise from its connection to accidents, and to understand this connection is to expand the concept of the self from the individual to the cosmic level. This will be the central theme of Part III and his ultimate task. He calls it his ultimate peak and his longest and hardest path. He says that peak and abyss (*Abgrund*) are now joined together. The word *Abgrund,* which is never used lightly in *Zarathustra,* means the groundless ground (*Grund*), namely, the ground that has no ultimate ground, the bottomless ground. In the last chapter, we talked about his descent to deep reality, but he is not going to reach any bedrock in his descent because the deep reality is the abyss (*Abgrund*), the bottomless ground. But the peaks arise from this bottomless ground. Just as the highest mountains come out of the sea, he says, "It is out of the deepest depth that the highest must come to its height" (*Z*, 154). The union of peak and abyss means the union of the upward and the downward motions, the ascent and the descent. These two motions were introduced in connection with the distinction between the upward and the downward will in "On Human Prudence" of Part II. In Part III, the metaphors of ascent and descent will be extensively used for describing the conflict of these two wills.

The notion of ascent and descent is a Platonic theme. Some commentators have said that Zarathustra's initial descent from his mountain cave is the reversal of Plato's allegory of the cave. Whereas the Platonic sage goes down to the cave, Zarathustra goes up to the cave. The location of the cave is reversed. Therefore the latter is the reversal of the former. But this is only a misleading appearance. Both of them ascend for their enlightenment and descend to dispense their wisdom to the people. Zarathustra's cave is located on a high mountain; Plato's cave is located underground. The former is the locus of wisdom; the latter is the locus of ignorance. Zarathustra's cave serves the same noetic function as the Platonic Heaven. He gains his wisdom in the cave high on the mountains just as the Platonic sage gains his wisdom in the Platonic Heaven of eternal Forms.

In Part II, however, Zarathustra did not gain his wisdom by ascending to a mountain cave. He gained it by descending to the underworld. He said that the penitent poets would gain their knowledge of reality by descending to the underworld. This is truly a reversal of the Platonic scheme. In this regard, Part II is differently constructed from Part I. As we have seen, Part II consists of a series of descending moves, which finally reaches the darkest and the lowest point in "The Stillest Hour". In Part III, Zarathustra reverses his descent and begins his ascent. But his ascent is said to be inseparable from his descent because the depth sustains the height. In "On the Tree on the Mountain" of Part I, Zarathustra counseled a young man that like a tree a human being can reach the height by sending the roots downward into the dark and deep evil, that is, into one's deep passions and instinctual forces. His talk of height and depth is psychological rather than geological. The inseparable connection between the height and the depth and between ascent and descent will be the central theme for Part III.

The Nature of the Universe (Part III.2)

In "On the Vision and the Riddle", Zarathustra relates his vision of the eternal recurrence to sailors on a ship. In the deadly pallor of dusk, he was climbing a gloomy mountain, presumably the highest peak he mentioned in the previous section. On his shoulder, he is carrying a dwarf, the spirit of gravity. He taunts Zarathustra by calling him "you philosopher's stone." Traditionally, the philosopher's stone is the magic stone that is supposed to have the power of transmuting base metals to gold or silver. The dwarf turns the philosopher's stone into Zarathustra's own self. Although he tries to throw himself up, the dwarf says, he will fall back on himself like a stone. The attempt to throw up the stone of himself is to make it fly like the eagle and the serpent at the end of Part I. The dwarf is pointing out the futility of Zarathustra's enterprise. The sage was already aware of its futility in "The Wanderer", when he said that the word 'impossibility' was written on his path of ascent. He described his ascent as the adventure of climbing over himself. The dwarf is now taunting him for this futile adventure of self-overcoming by describing it as a foolhardy defiance against the force of gravity.

The dwarf falls silent and his silence exerts an unbearable sense of oppression on Zarathustra. Thus begins a duel between him and the spirit of gravity, and he calls forth his courage for a showdown with the dwarf. After praising courage three times, he asserts his dominance over the dwarf: "It is I or you! But I am the stronger of us two: you do not know my abysmal thought. *That* you could not bear" (Z, 157). Thus he introduces the eternal recurrence as his abysmal thought. When the dwarf jumps off his shoulder and crouches on a stone before him, there appears the gateway scene with two time lines. He explains it to the dwarf as follows. The gate is called the Moment, where two paths meet. One of them stretches eternally to the future and the other eternally to the past. He describes the two time lines in a strange language: "They contradict each other; they strike against each other." Taking this description literally, Heidegger says, "Whoever stands in the Moment is turned in two ways: for him past and future *run up against* one another" (*Nietzsche* 2: 56-57). But it makes no sense to say that past and future run up against one another, because it goes against our normal conception of time as a continuous flow through the present moment. We can make a better sense of the collision of past and future at the Moment by associating the past and the future with the two modes of the will. The future-oriented will and the past-oriented will do collide at the gateway of the Moment. The collision of these two wills was stressed by the end of Part II. Thus the theme of the twofold will is sustained in the vision of eternal recurrence.

Zarathustra then asks the dwarf whether the two time lines would always run in the opposite directions. The dwarf murmurs contemptuously that all that is straight lies, that all truth is crooked, and that time itself is a circle. This is his circular view of time. It is important to note that this view of time is first announced not by Zarathustra, but by the dwarf. Zarathustra rebukes the dwarf for making things too easy for himself. He is clearly annoyed with the dwarf's nonchalance in handling his difficult question. Then he poses a series of questions about the nature of time and the world, which will eventually lead to the endorsement of the dwarf's circular view of time. The first question concerns the relation of possibility to actuality. "Must not whatever *can* happen have happened before?" (Z, 158). This question reflects his presumption that every possibility must already have been actualized. But he does not explain why he subscribes to this presumption. In *WP* 1066, Nietzsche provides the reasoning behind it: "In infinite time, every possible combination would at some time or another be realized." As Bernd Magnus says, he may be assuming that the world is composed of a finite number of atoms (*Nietzsche's Existential Imperative*, 64-65). Assuming that the configuration of these atoms determines the successive states of the world, there will be only a finite number of possible states. But a world of infinite time must have realized an infinite number of states, and any finite number of possible states must be included in the infinite number of these realized states. Relying on the plausibility of this reasoning, Zarathustra asks the dwarf, "Must not this gateway too have been there before?" He then considers the causal connection of all events: "And are not all things knotted together so firmly that this moment draws after it *all* that is to come?" (Z, 158). He ends his talk by asking the dwarf, "Must we not eternally return?"

Zarathustra does not present the doctrine of eternal recurrence as an argument with reasons and proofs. His presentation is made in a series of probing questions. Although I did not restate all those questions in my recount, their number is seven. Those questions probe the plausibility of eternal recurrence. In his preliminary talk to the sailors, he said that they did not like the cowardly method of following a reasoned argument and that they hated to *deduce* where they could *guess*. He is presenting his story of eternal recurrence as a plausible story, which is best suited to his audience's way of thinking. This is an important point to note because some commentators have taken his story as an argumentative proof for the eternal recurrence and pointed out its deductive weakness. For example, Lampert says that the sage gives a deductive argument for the eternal recurrence (*Nietzsche's Teaching*, 165). But David Allison correctly notes that he "does not advance the eternal return as a verifiable truth at all" and that he teaches it only in the conditional and the subjunctive (*Reading the New Nietzsche*, 124 and 169). His questions are meant to be taken as tentative questions for exploring the plausibility of his ideas concerning the eternal recurrence.

By the time Zarathustra says "eternally return," he suddenly becomes afraid of his own thoughts and the thoughts behind his thoughts. This sudden feeling of fear echoes back to the time when he was frightened by his own thought in "On Redemption" of Part II and tried to pierce the thoughts of his disciples and the thoughts behind their thoughts. This was the dreadful thought of determinism that totally paralyzes the autonomous will. The doctrine of eternal recurrence has the same devastating consequence for the autonomous will, which Heidegger describes as follows,

> All being, taken as a whole as a plenitude of details in any of its given sequences, is forged in the iron ring of the eternal recurrence of the identical collective state; whatever enters on the scene now or in the future is but a recurrence, unalterably predetermined and necessary. But then in this ring what are action, planning, resolve—in short, *"freedom"*—supposed to be? In the ring of necessity freedom is as superfluous as it is impossible. (*Nietzsche* 2:132)

This is what I called the most devastating limit of humanity in the last chapter. In "On Redemption", Zarathustra said that the immovable stone of the past crushes the human will and turns it into the spirit of revenge. The stone of the past and its crushing weight are graphically displayed in the vision of eternal recurrence. Prior to this vision, the dwarf presents the philosopher's stone for Zarathustra and generates his spirit of revenge by taunting him. The dwarf is the ultimate source for the spirit of revenge because he is the spirit of gravity. He embodies the crushing weight of the stone that provokes the sense of revenge.

We can say that freedom is equally impossible in the world of determinism with or without the eternal recurrence. This is the abysmal thought that arises from the abyss, the ultimate ground of the physical universe. It is so frightful that Zarathustra cannot bear it, and its frightful character will be demonstrated in the next scene. He hears a dog howl, which takes him back to the howling of a terrified dog in his youth. Now the dwarf is gone, and the gateway and the spider, too. He is totally alone to witness a terrible scene in the bleakest moonlight. While the dog is jumping, bristling, and whining, a young shepherd is writhing and choking and a heavy black snake is hanging out of his mouth. Zarathustra has never seen so much nausea and dread on one face. The snake appears to have crawled into the shepherd's throat and bitten itself fast, while he was asleep. Zarathustra tries to pull out the snake but in vain. So he screams to the shepherd to bite off its head. When the shepherd bites it off and jumps up, he is so transformed that he is no longer shepherd and no longer human. He is radiant and laughing; his laughter is superhuman. Zarathustra says that he is still consumed by his longing for that superhuman laughter.

The shepherd scene and the gateway scene are standardly taken to be the vision of eternal recurrence, the most controversial topic in Nietzsche scholarship, which has produced an endless series of interpretations. Bernd Magnus divides these interpretations into three classes: (1) cosmological, (2) normative, and (3) attitudinal (*Nietzsche's Existential Imperative*, 140-43). In the cosmological version, the doctrine of eternal recurrence is taken to describe the nature of the universe. In the normative version, it is recommended as a mental framework for making normative decisions. In the attitudinal version, it is taken to test the attitude to existence. Let us now consider how the three interpretations fit the gateway and the shepherd scenes. The gateway scene is obviously the cosmological version. But many commentators have resolutely dismissed this ver-

sion as too implausible. Magnus points out that the cosmological version
goes against today's physics (*Nietzsche's Existential Imperative*, 65-66).
That is not a right verdict. The cosmological version is compatible with
the theory of big bangs and big crunches, namely, the oscillation theory
of today's astrophysics. Even in the nineteenth century physics, as Magnus notes, the doctrine of eternal recurrence was regarded as a respectable theory by many scientists, including such thoughtful figures as C. S.
Peirce and Henri Poincare. Zarathustra belongs to this respectable company when he acknowledges the plausibility of eternal recurrence.

Those who cannot accept the cosmological version have advocated
the normative version: one should behave as if the doctrine were true.
But this version has its own problem, as Magnus points out. If you assume its truth, it would have a crippling effect on your behavior. You
have to believe that whatever you do will be another repetition of what
you have done countless times already in the past. You cannot even
properly say that you are making a decision because whatever you may
decide has already been decided in the past. Gilles Deleuze has tried to
eliminate this crippling effect by erasing the past and retaining only the
future in the eternal recurrence. He says that the eternal recurrence pre-
scribes the following practical principle: Whatever you will, you should
will it in such a way that you also will its eternal return (*Nietzsche and
Philosophy*, 68). In employing this practical principle, the agent should
behave as though the entire future were open and never be affected by
the past events in the eternal recurrence. Faced with a totally open future,
the agent functions as a truly creative agent. But such an open future
cannot be permitted in the ring of eternal recurrence.

Dissatisfied with these two interpretations, some commentators have
advocated the attitudinal interpretation of eternal recurrence. Magnus
says that this interpretation has nothing to do with the truth value of the
doctrine, because it is only for testing one's attitude toward existence
(*Nietzsche's Existential Imperative*, 142). One can have either a negative
or an affirmative attitude (or response) toward the thought that everything will be repeated endlessly. If one feels revulsion at this thought,
one is victimized by nihilism. On the other hand, if one rejoices in the

same thought, one has overcome nihilism. Whether affirmative or nega-
tive, one's response to the thought of eternal recurrence reveals one's ex-
istential attitude to the world, that is, whether one is well or ill disposed
toward it. If one has a truly affirmative attitude toward the thought of
eternal recurrence, Magnus says, he has indeed become a superman. The
shepherd writhing with a snake in his mouth may stand for the negative
response to existence, but the same shepherd may stand for the positive
response when he bites off the snake's head and becomes radiant. Hence
the attitudinal interpretation appears to fit the shepherd scene, while the
cosmological interpretation fits the gateway scene. But the normative interpretation cannot be applied to either scene.

There is one important point concerning the relation between the
snake and the dwarf. By the time the gateway scene is replaced by the
shepherd scene, the dwarf disappears. Heidegger says that the dwarf ran
away (*Nietzsche* 2:55). Lampert says that the dwarf is crushed by
Zarathustra's talk (*Nietzsche's Teaching*, 197). But they cite no textual
evidence. Paul S. Loeb points out that Zarathustra never sees the dwarf
killed, but only wonders where the dwarf is gone. When the dwarf disappears, he proposes, it is transformed to the black snake that crawls into
the shepherd's mouth. In support of this hypothesis, he cites a similar
transformation in Richard Wagner's *Rheingold*. When the dwarf Alberich puts on the Tarnhelm, he disappears instantly and then appears as
a monstrous serpent. Loeb notes that Zarathustra's dwarf and the serpent
crawling into the shepherd's mouth are black and heavy like the Wagnerian dwarf and serpent ("The Dwarf, the Dragon, and the Ring of Eternal Recurrence", 101-102). Indeed, Zarathustra describes the serpent in
the shepherd's mouth as "the heaviest and the blackest." This description
may be the author's subtle hint for linking the snake to the spirit of gravity, which is heavier and blacker than anything else in the world. Therefore I am inclined to believe Loeb's thesis that the dwarf has turned into
the snake.

The snake is not simply a time line, but the flow of Life itself. As we
will see in "The Other Dancing Song", Life will be compared to a snake.
In "On the Pale Criminal" of Part I, Zarathustra described a human being

as a ball of snakes, a bundle of desires and passions, which is the breeding ground of all our earthly concerns. The ball of snakes becomes unbearably heavy if our desires and passions are not fulfilled. That is the spirit of gravity. In chapter 1, I quoted Carl Jung's suggestion that the serpent represents the chthonic force. So does the dwarf. Both the snake and the dwarf are heavy because they stand for the chthonic force of Life. The snake is the elusive symbol of Nature in its pristine form. The dwarf is the manifestation of this pristine force in a human form not only in Zarathustra's vision, but also in Wagner's *Ring* cycle. The Wagnerian dwarfs are the denizens of the underworld. Zarathustra's dwarf also arises from the depth of the earth, Mother Nature, as we will see in "The Convalescent". Mother Nature is Life, the cosmic snake that appears as the time line of eternal recurrence. The snake and the dwarf are the interchangeable symbols of Life. In Part II, she taught him by revealing the nature of her will to power. She continues this role by granting him the vision of eternal recurrence through her agents, the dwarf and the snake, because her will to power is embedded in the eternal recurrence.

Zarathustra's relationship with the spirit of gravity is remarkable. He takes the dwarf as his companion for the ascent to his highest peak and forms a partnership with him for the greatest vision in his life. Prior to this astonishing partnership with the dwarf, Zarathustra has never faced or dealt with him as a person. In "On Reading and Writing" of Part I, he mentioned the spirit of gravity as the devil to be killed. In "The Dancing Song" of Part II, he called the devil his most powerful enemy. Why then does he now carry the dwarf, the heaviest burden, on his ascent to the highest peak? But he does not even say where he picked up the dwarf. I propose that he picked up the dwarf from his descent to the abyss, which he began in "On Great Event" and ended in "The Stillest Hour" of Part II. His attempt to climb the highest peak with the dwarf on his shoulder is his attempt to spiritualize the chthonic force, his earthly animal self. In the religious age, the spiritualization of carnal passions was easier because the carnal passions were supposedly uplifted by the celestial force of God. But Zarathustra cannot rely on such celestial support. He has known all along that his soul is his body, an embodiment of the chthonic force or the spirit of gravity. He has to lift the chthonic force by using the chthonic force itself. Hence his ascent of the highest peak is his "impossible" struggle against the spirit of gravity. So he describes it: "Upward—defying the spirit that drew it downward toward the abyss, the spirit of gravity, my devil and archenemy" (Z, 156). He is trying to pull himself up by his own bootstraps. Hence the dwarf has the right to taunt him for the futile attempt.

In the Prologue, Zarathustra launched his ambitious campaign to spiritualize the secular culture. In Part II, as we noted, he realized that the spiritual degradation was his own problem, too. Thus his campaign for others has been transformed to a campaign for himself. This self-directed campaign is his ascent of the highest peak with the dwarf on his shoulder. We also noted that his campaign was transformed from the Faustian to the Spinozan mode, from flaunting the autonomous will to struggling with the heteronomous will. I propose that the dwarf is his physical self, the embodiment of heteronomous will. There is no spiritual self as a separate entity apart from this physical or animal self. Whatever spiritual self he wants to have must be generated from this physical self. Here lies his dire need to rely on his partnership with the dwarf. Since the natural self is his only real self, we should not say that he picked up the dwarf in his descent to the abyss. The dwarf has all along been an essential feature of himself, but this fact was recognized only in his descent to the underworld. He displays this recognition by carrying the dwarf on his own shoulder. His self-understanding depends on his understanding of his relation to the spirit of gravity. When he called the dwarf his archenemy, he took for granted its separateness from himself. But their separateness was an illusion. In Jungian terminology, the dwarf is his shadow, the darkest part of the self that is projected to the external world because the self subconsciously wants to disown it. In Wagner's *Ring* cycle, Robert Donington says, Alberich is the shadow of Wotan and Mime is the shadow of Siegfried (*Wagner's "Ring" and Its Symbols*, 46, 103, 196).

Zarathustra's partnership with the dwarf is far from obvious. Hence it has escaped the attention of most commentators. It becomes most subtle when Zarathustra and the dwarf exchange their views on the eternal recurrence. Many commentators favor Zarathustra's elaborate exposition over the dwarf's terse one.[1] They say that the dwarf's account of the eternal ring is false or too shallow and that it is refuted or amended by Zarathustra's exposition. The volume of a speech is often taken to be the measure of its wisdom. Carl Jung is the only exception to this standard trend. In his view, the dwarf makes the original pronouncement on the eternal recurrence, and Zarathustra only assimilates it in spite of his pretense that the whole doctrine is his own. Regarding the dwarf's pronouncement, Jung says, "This is great language, and Zarathustra assimilates it, but he dilutes it and thinks that they are his own ideas. But the dwarf has brought up these ideas in Zarathustra. These terse pronouncements of monumental short words of wisdom come from the intestines of the world" (*Nietzsche's* Zarathustra, 1272). He says that the words of the dwarf are as terse and as profound as the words of Lao Tzu, Pythagoras, or Heraclitus.

For the substantiation of Jung's unfashionable view, I will assemble some compelling textual evidence. Zarathustra introduces the vision of eternal recurrence as his abysmal thought. When he calls upon his courage to face the eternal recurrence, he makes four references to the abyss or abysses. He is summoning all his courage to face the "dizziness at the edge of abysses." The dizziness comes not only from the abysses, but also from the dwarf and his words that arise from the abysses. The dwarf has the authority to pronounce on the ultimate secret of Mother Nature, Life, because he is her mouthpiece. Zarathustra explicates his terse words exactly the way he explained the secret of Life in "On Redemption" of Part II, where we noted he took on the role of expounding the secret wisdom of Life, namely, the doctrine of the twofold will. On this doctrine, the autonomous will was totally overpowered by the heteronomous will. This was such a terrifying thought that he disowned it when he was commanded to declare it by the voiceless voice in "The Stillest Hour" of Part II. He said, "Alas, is it *my* word? Who am I? I await the worthier

---

1. Stambaugh, *Nietzsche's Thought of Eternal Return*, 38. Strong, *Friedrich Nietzsche and the Politics of Transfiguration,* 264. Lampert, *Nietzsche's Teaching*, 165. Whitlock, *Returning to Sils-Maria*, 198.

one; I am not worthy even of being broken by it" (*Z*, 146). The worthier one has finally appeared in the dwarf and announced the terrifying abysmal thought in his terse words. The fact that the dwarf is the original source for the vision of eternal recurrence can explain why Zarathustra presents his exposition in a series of questions to the dwarf. Alan White says, "Zarathustra clearly anticipates that the dwarf could answer only in the affirmative" (*Within Nietzsche's Labyrinth,* 87). The affirmative answers will confirm that Zarathustra has got it right. He is seeking this confirmation for his exposition from the dwarf, his original authority.

Just before the vision of eternal recurrence appears to Zarathustra, the dwarf jumps off his shoulder and sits on a rock. Roger Hollinrake says that the rock in this scene may allude to Nietzsche's original vision of eternal recurrence near the rock of Surlei in the summer of 1881 (*Nietzsche, Wagner, and the Philosophy of Pessimism,* 81). But he does not connect the dwarf to the vision. I want to make that connection: The vision is coming from the dwarf sitting on the rock. Since the dwarf represents the heavy and hard chthonic elements, he is indistinguishable from the rock. Zarathustra is now reenacting Nietzsche's original vision at Surlei. To say that the vision came to him at the rock does not explain why it happened there, unless the rock was assumed to have some special power of revelation. But Nietzsche attributes no such special power to the rock in recounting his experience of that original vision. The missing explanation is now provided by setting the dwarf on the rock and letting him make the initial pronouncement on the eternal recurrence. Zarathustra only witnesses the vision and elucidates the dwarf's pronouncement. Even more intriguing than this supposition is to assume that the Surlei rock is the dwarf. We already identified the dwarf with the philosopher's stone. As an extension of this identification, we may say that the philosopher's stone is the rock. Therefore the dwarf is the rock. But Zarathustra is not merely reenacting Nietzsche's original vision at the Surlei rock, but articulating it by his probing questions.

In section 345 of *The Gay Science,* Nietzsche calls the eternal recurrence "the heaviest weight." The dwarf, the spirit of gravity, is heavier than anyone else in the whole world. As we noted, the dwarf is interchangeable with the snake, "the blackest and the heaviest." The blackest is the color of the abyss; the heaviest is its weight. The dwarf and the snake have come up from the abyss to elucidate two dimensions of the eternal recurrence. In the gateway scene, the dwarf portrays its cosmological dimension. In the shepherd scene, the dwarf becomes the snake and demonstrates its existential dimension. They are not two versions of the eternal recurrence, but its two dimensions. The existential dimension is subjective; the cosmological dimension is objective. One experiences the devastating impact of eternal recurrence only when one faces it as an existential subject. One does not experience such an impact as long as one considers the eternal recurrence only as an objective fact. These two dimensions of eternal recurrence are given as a vision and riddle to Zarathustra. He is not the author of the vision and the riddle, but only a humble recipient. As far as he is concerned, the eternal recurrence is the most abysmal (blackest and heaviest) thought that strikes him with nothing but horror. For this reason, he had felt that he was not worthy of pronouncing it on his own and had to wait for the worthier one.

The Terror and Mystery of the Abyss (Part III.2-4)

The upshot of the eternal recurrence dramatizes the frightful impact of determinism. In the iron ring of eternal recurrence, everything is predetermined and necessary just as it is in a deterministic world. Whatever happens is only the repetition of what has already happened countless times. The eternal recurrence and the deterministic universe have exactly the same crippling impact on human will and freedom. In the face of eternal recurrence, Zarathustra experiences exactly the same terror he had felt under the weight of the deterministic past in "On Redemption" of Part II. The terror comes from the dwarf because he embodies the chthonic force that determines everything in the physical universe. Now I propose that the dwarf is the visceral part of Zarathustra and that his dialogue with the dwarf is the inner dialogue between his visceral and his cerebral parts. The cerebral part is elucidating and elaborating the intuitive wisdom of the visceral part. In chapter 2, I said that the difference between Life and Wisdom was the difference between the visceral and the cerebral. The dialogue between Zarathustra and the dwarf is the dialogue between Wisdom and Life. Wisdom is his cerebral intelligence that articulates the pronouncement of the visceral intelligence of Life. Without this supposition, Zarathustra's talk with the dwarf would add nothing to the unfolding drama. The dwarf could only play the negative role of saying something false or shallow on the eternal recurrence only to be refuted by Zarathustra. Such a negative dialogue can have no positive significance. To make something out of the refutation, Lampert labels the dwarf as a Socratic rationalist and a Schopenhauerian pessimist (*Nietzsche's Teaching*, 166). To refute such an opponent would be useful. But there is no textual ground for assuming that the poor dwarf is either a rationalist or a pessimist. He never argues like a rationalist, nor laments like a pessimist. He is too visceral to be a rationalist and too stolid to be a pessimist.

We earlier noted Lampert's view that the dwarf is clubbed to death by Zarathustra's lethal thought. But he does not possess the lethal thought, although he calls it his abysmal thought. On the contrary, the dwarf is the lethal thought that terrifies Zarathustra. As we will see, his fear will be fully vindicated when he is mercilessly clobbered by the dwarf in "The Convalescent". The dwarf is the abysmal thought that has come up from the abyss together with the vision of eternal recurrence. That is, the abysmal thought is Zarathustra's knowledge of the dwarf as his darkest and deepest self that rises out of the abyss, the center of the earth. Since the dwarf belongs to the abyss, the center of the earth, he embodies the cosmic force of universal causation that obliterates the autonomous will. This sequence of thoughts terrifies Zarathustra by reviving his terror over the collapse of the autonomous will in the deterministic physical world. So he calls upon courage three times to face the horror of the abyss in bracing himself for his vision of eternal recurrence, because the dwarf has brought up the frightful vision from the abyss. But his vision of eternal recurrence ends with the shepherd's victory over the snake and his superhuman laughter. This sense of victory continues in the next section ("On Involuntary Bliss"), in which he talks to his jubilant conscience, reflecting on his entire teaching mission.

The recollection of his career eventually reaches the abysmal thought, whose burrowing he can still hear with his trembling heart: "My heart pounds to my very throat whenever I hear you burrowing" (Z, 162). He associates his abysmal thought with the call, "It is time!" This was the call for his descent to the abyss in "On Great Events" of Part II. By this association, he indicates that the abysmal thought come up from his descent to the abyss. But his abysmal thought is so terrifying that he cannot face it:

> As yet I have never dared to summon you; it was enough that I carried you with me. As yet I have not been strong enough for the final overbearing, prankish bearing of the lion. Your gravity is always terrible enough for me; but one day I shall yet find the strength and the lion's voice to summon you. (Z, 162)

In this passage, Zarathustra identifies his terrifying abysmal thought with the spirit of gravity. "I carried you with me" refers to his carrying the dwarf on his shoulder for the vision of the eternal recurrence. He is still complaining about the dwarf's gravity. But he seems to have forgotten the advice of the voiceless voice that he must become a child to face the terrible thought. He is still hankering to have the lion's voice and strength to summon the abysmal thought. He looks forward to his victory over the spirit of gravity as the seal of his perfection. His unresolved strife with the spirit of gravity is his most unbearable anxiety. But the burrowing dwarf is still a sleeping worm, which can dampen but not destroy his overwhelming sense of happiness.

Zarathustra's happiness dramatically deepens in the following section ("Before Sunrise"), in which he talks to heaven before sunrise. This is the continuation of his ascent from the abyss. After climbing the highest peak in the previous section, he is now trying to reach heaven. He says, "What I want with all my will is to *fly*, to fly up into you" (Z, 164). His salutation to heaven contains paradoxical statements: "You abyss of light!" and "To throw myself into your height, that is *my* depth." On the

strength of these paradoxes of *coincidentia oppositorium,* Joan Stam-
baugh interprets this section as a record of mystical experience (*The
Other Nietzsche,* 137-39). But there is no mystical communion between
Zarathustra and heaven. There is only one-way talk from him to heaven.
He is using the language of *coincidentia oppositorium* to indicate that the
summit of his ascent is the same as the bottom of his descent. This is the
mystery of the universe that he described in the opening section of Part
III: "It is out of the deepest depth that the highest must come to its
height" (*Z,* 154). In fact, heaven is as dark and as mysterious as the abyss
before sunrise.

His talk to heaven covers the following points. First, he describes
what heaven has done for him before the sunrise. It rose for him silently
over the roaring sea, revealing its love and shyness to his roaring soul. It
came to him, shrouded in its beauty and revealing its wisdom to his loneliest soul. Heaven stands as the god of comfort and wisdom for steadying
his lonely soul. This leads to the next topic, his friendship with heaven.
He says, "We are friends from the beginning: we share grief and ground
and gray dread; we even share the sun" (*Z,* 164). By this reference to
ground and grief, he links heaven to the abyss, which has been the
ground for his grief. Then he says that he hates the drifting clouds and all
that stains heaven, because they prey on what he and heaven have in
common—the unbounded Yes and Amen. His wish is to stand over everything as its own heaven, as its round roof, its azure bell, and eternal
security. Heaven is the azure bell. This image of heaven is transformed
into another image, the well of eternity. The two images have the same
shape: one can be obtained by flipping the other. These are two images
of one universe.

These two images are further elaborations on the image of eternal recurrence presented in "On the Vision and the Riddle". All of them are the
poetic pictures of the universe. Altogether we are given four such pictures. "On the Vision and the Riddle" presents one pair of temporal images, the gateway and the shepherd scenes. "Before Sunrise" presents
one pair of spatial images, the azure bell and the well of eternity. The
former pair represents the temporal perspective on the universe. The lat-

ter pair represents the eternal perspective, which transcends time. The temporal pictures are heavily laden with the spirit of gravity because the temporal perspective is the arena of existential struggle, which can never be freed from the perpetual burden of misery and worry. But the spirit of gravity does not affect the eternal pictures because the eternal perspective transcends the temporal existence. The temporal pictures are experienced in dismal scenes; the eternal pictures are enjoyed in blissful atmospheres. These two pairs of pictures provide two different perspectives on the eternal recurrence. To take the temporal perspective is the human response to the eternal recurrence; to take the eternal perspective is the divine response.

Everything Zarathustra says about the azure bell makes better sense if it is placed in the divine perspective. He says that our purposes and worries are only the drifting clouds in the sky. That is so not from the human perspective, but from the divine perspective. He calls the azure bell "a dance floor for divine accidents" and "a divine table for divine dice and dice players." These descriptions belong to a divine perspective. The paradoxes of *coincidentia oppositorium* also belong to the same divine perspective. I said that the language of *coincidentia oppositorium* indicates that the summit of his ascent is the same as the bottom of his descent. This is a mysterious point that Zarathustra can see because he is taking a divine perspective. He again takes the same divine perspective when he says that the azure bell is the universe of pure chance and that its purity is to be free of all purposes. To be trapped in the chain of purposes is to take the human perspective; to be free of that chain is to take the divine perspective, which can see only cosmic necessity and its innocence in place of human design and intentions. So Zarathustra says, "For all things have been baptized in the well of eternity and are beyond good and evil; and good and evil themselves are but intervening shadows and damp depressions and drifting clouds" (Z, 165-66).

The azure bell is a poetic image of Spinoza's conception of Nature as the infinite substance. Because she is governed by its own eternal necessity, it is beyond good and evil and always affirms itself. Mother Nature is Spinoza's God. The divine perspective belongs to this God of Nature.

By the grace of the azure bell, Zarathustra gratefully acknowledges, he
has gained the power of affirming everything without blaming anyone. In
the world of necessity, it makes no sense to blame anyone. He says that
he has fought for this power of affirmation for a long time. But he does
not exercise his power of affirmation as an act of his will. In his celebration of affirmation, he does not use the word, 'will' or 'willing'. Instead
he says, "I have become one who blesses and says Yes." Since the azure
bell is the heaven of chance, it can have no room for the will. Hence
Zarathustra's affirmation can come as a special gift and blessing from the
azure bell rather than as an outcome of his willing and striving. In that
case, this event echoes back to the prophecy in "The Stillest Hour".
When Zarathustra complained of not having the lion's voice for command, he was advised that he could command only by becoming a child,
who has no will of its own. In the world of pure chance, Zarathustra has
become a happy child of innocence.

Zarathustra's terror in "On the Vision and the Riddle" has been replaced by his sense of bliss under the azure bell. His vision of eternal recurrence terrified him because it demolished his autonomous will. But
the azure bell is a universe of the same chance and necessity that governs
the eternal recurrence. Therefore he should feel the same horror under
the azure bell that he had felt in the vision of eternal recurrence. But he
feels elated instead. This is a stunning change in his view of the eternal
recurrence. In order to appreciate this important change, we should be
clear about the nature of horror he had felt about the eternal recurrence.
He called the idea of eternal recurrence his abysmal thought. In section
55 of *The Will to Power*, Nietzsche states the horror of this abysmal
thought more clearly than anywhere else: "Let us think this thought in its
most terrible form: existence as it is, without meaning or aim, yet recur-
ring inevitably without any finale of nothingness: '*the eternal recurrence*.'" He is now associating the meaning of existence with the aims
and purposes in our life. There can be no aims and purposes in a deterministic world, although we may have the illusion of having them. If
there are no aims and purposes, Nietzsche says, our existence is totally
meaningless. He calls it the most extreme form of nihilism. We may call

it the deterministic nihilism because it arises from determinism, or the nihilism of values because it eliminates all values. Nietzsche attributes it to Spinoza and the European form of Buddhism (*WP* 55).

In "On Redemption" of Part II, Zarathustra talked about determinism without linking it to the eternal recurrence. He was horrified at the idea that everything was determined by the past. He even mentioned the Buddhist way of coping with this existential horror, namely, the view that suffering is the punishment accruing from the inexorable past. This is the Buddhist doctrine of *karma*. With the death of God, Nietzsche says, there is only the European form of Buddhism left, that is, no-doing (*Nein-tun*) after all existence has lost its meaning (*WP* 55). The Buddhist world is very much like the azure bell. There are no aims and purposes in that world because it is completely ruled by the bond of *karma*, the causal chain of pure accidents. If we think that we are operating with our own aims and purposes, we have not awakened yet from our illusion. But when we awaken, we will be free of all our aims and purposes. We will be free from the idea of action. This is the moment of the Buddhist enlightenment and the release from the bondage of *karma*. This is the Buddhist doctrine of no-doing (*Nein-tun*). This is the same teaching as Lao Tzu's doctrine of no action (*wu wei*). In Chinese, *wei* is not only the noun and verb for 'action', but also the preposition for 'for'. Therefore, *wei* means to do something *for* some purpose, and Lao Tzu rejects this notion of action in his teaching of no action (*wu wei*). According to *Tao Te Ching*, Tao flows without purposes or efforts like a river. Lao Tzu says, "Heaven and earth are not humane" (*Tao Te Ching* 5). Just like the azure bell, the Taoist universe stands beyond good and evil. It is totally free of aims and purposes. Hence the very idea of action is pointless. The idea of *wu wei* is to be one with the flow of Tao. This is the way of a Taoist sage.

For Nietzsche, the European form of Buddhism is European nihilism, and he attributes it to determinism and the destruction of the autonomous will. Under the azure bell, however, Zarathustra feels elated instead. Why? His elation is very much like the sense of release from the chain of *karma* that the Buddhists are supposed to experience on their enlightenment. The Taoist sages are also supposed to feel the same sense of elation and release from the crushing weight of worries and anxieties, when they become one with the flow of Tao. They compare their liberation to the release of a bird from a cage. A deterministic world is terrifying only for those who look at it from the perspective of autonomous agents, because it is a perpetual menace to their aims and purposes. As long as you try to fight against this menace, you can only multiply and aggravate your worries and anxieties. But once you recognize the futility of your struggle and accept cosmic necessity, you can strangely gain the sense of relief from the constant pressure of anxieties and worries. Then you are no longer trapped in the human cage of your petty aims and purposes. You have transposed yourself from the individual to the cosmic perspective. So there are two perspectives for approaching the eternal recurrence. In "On the Vision and Riddle", Zarathustra approached it from the individual perspective. He was carrying the dwarf, the worrywart, on his shoulder and was watching a filthy snake crawling into the shepherd's mouth. In "Before Sunrise", he is approaching it from the cosmic perspective of surveying it as an azure bell. The distinction between the individual and the cosmic perspectives corresponds to the distinction I made earlier between the temporal and the eternal perspectives and between the human and the divine perspectives.

Zarathustra's happiness as a child in "Before Sunrise" is the continuation of his happiness, which began in "On Involuntary Bliss". That happiness was called involuntary bliss because it came to him against his will. The notion of an involuntary mood is perfectly in tune with the notion of the universe governed by the Lord Chance. In such a universe, every mood is a matter of accident, whether it reflects a passing cloud or clear sunshine. The will has no control over it. Every mood is involuntary and innocent. Zarathustra experiences the happiness of innocence in the darkness of night. But it cannot last long because the day is coming. The day belongs to the lion, the symbol of an indomitable will, which intensifies the human perspective. He ends "Before Sunrise" by saying, "But the day is coming, so let us part." The reign of day is going to be long for him and the spirit of a lion is going to carry him until it culminates in "On Old and New Tablets". Until then, he will feel that there is nothing impossible under his commanding will. In fact, it will come back roaring in "On Virtue that Makes Small", when he gets off the boat and steps on the firm land.

The Nature of the Will (Part III.5-8)

Instead of going straight back to his mountain cave, Zarathustra wants to find out what has happened to the people during his absence. To his dismay, they have been becoming smaller and smaller. He attributes this deplorable trend to their pursuit of contentment. All this echoes back to the wretched contentment of the last men in the Prologue. What is new is his attempt to restate their situation as the problem of their will. He says, "Some of them will, but most of them are only willed." Even the rulers hypocritically feign the virtue of those who serve and pose themselves as the first servants. He curses all the cowardly devils in a foul language and flaunts his lordly will against their cowardly will:

> I still cook every chance in my pot. And only when it has been cooked through there do I welcome it as my food. And verily, many a chance came to me domineeringly; but my will spoke to it even more domineeringly—and immediately it lay imploringly on its knees. (*Z*, 171)

He offers this imperious posture of his commanding will as a lesson to the small people, who are crawling around like lice. But it is an incredible will. It can cook every chance (or accident) and talk it into submission. This is a drastic reversal of his position in the last section, where repudiated the notion of will as an illusion. As I said in the last chapter, the autonomous will is irrepressible. It keeps coming back even after it was devastated by the vision of eternal recurrence.

The strangeness of his talk is not restricted to his boast of his lordly will; but extends to the way he talks to the people. Angry over the fact that nobody cares about his talk, he says, "But why do I speak where no-

body has *my* ears? And so let me shout it into all the winds: You are becoming smaller and smaller, you small people! You are crumbling, you
comfortable ones" (Z, 171). Evidently, the small people are crumbling
not from their misery, but from their comfort. And yet he warns that they
will perish from their comfort and small happiness. Then he predicts that
their hour will come and his hour, too. When their hour comes, they will
be so small and so weary that they will be fit only for being burned like
dry grass in a prairie fire. When his hour comes, it will be the great noon,
the blessed hour of lightning. This vengeful tone was not in his speech to
the townfolk of The Motley Cow. Nor was the problem of accidents in
that talk. The vengeful tone and the accident go together. Zarathustra
said that the sense of revenge was the wrath against the things beyond
our control and will. The problem of accidents and the sense of revenge
were never discussed in Part I. They became his serious problems in Part
II. Now they are ravaging his heart.

   There is a fairly regular pattern in the waxing and waning of
Zarathustra's will. In the world of night and darkness, all his talks about
the will subside and sometimes completely disappear into silence. But
they come back with a roaring voice as soon as the daylight breaks out.
This is the bipolar rhythm that governs his mood and his will. In addition
to the difference between light and darkness, there is another factor that
seems to influence his mood and will. That is the difference between
land and sky. In "On Involuntary Bliss" and "Before Sunrise", he became keenly aware of the involuntary character of his mood and the indomitable power of accidents. He was then sailing over the sea and talking to the blue sky, where he could vividly feel the immense scope and
depth of the universe, which seemed to overpower his puny will. As soon
as he gets off the boat and lands on the *terra firma* in "On Virtue That
Makes Small", he begins to talk like a lion. On the solid ground, he
seems to regain the sense of his strong will and its mastery over all things.
On the sea, however, he senses not the solid ground (*Grund*), but the
groundless abyss (*Abgrund*). The sky gives the same feeling of the
groundless abyss especially in darkness. The more leonine his will gets,
the more vengeful it becomes, because the sense of revenge is the natural

reaction of the will to its obstacles. Unlike the leonine will bent on control and conquest, the will of a child is free of revenge because it has no interest in control and conquest. This explains why the voiceless voice told Zarathustra to cease to be a lion and become a child.

"Upon the Mount of Olives" reveals another dimension of Zarathustra's will. On the Mount of Olives, Jesus Christ foretells his disciples that they will desert him during the impending critical hour and then prays alone before his arrest (Luke 22:39-46). In "Upon the Mount of Olives", Zarathustra talks about his own loneliness. His only companion is the winter, his wicked guest, and he runs away from this guest to the sunny corner of his mount of olives. But he is not depressed with winter. On the contrary, he plays the game of malice in mocking and teasing it, but the malice is not vengeful but playful. For example, he begins every cold day by taking a cold bath. His game with the winter is a playful battle of will. The long bright silence, which he shares with the bright sky of the cold winter, hides his indomitable sun-will (*Sonnen-Wille*). How does the indomitable sun-will work in coping with accidents? Zarathustra says, "They still have pity on my accidents; but *my* word says, 'Let accidents come to me, they are innocent as little children'" (*Z*, 174). This response is quite different from the one in "On Virtue That Makes Small", where he boasted of cooking every accident. He is now accepting accidents as innocent as little children. To be innocent means to be the products of necessity beyond the control of the will. Even his sun-will has no control over them because it is not a will in the normal sense. Alexander Nehamas says that the sun has no prior intentions and no ulterior purposes ("For Whom the Sun Shines", 166). The sun-will is cosmic necessity.

Zarathustra entertains two radically different conceptions of the will in "Upon the Mount of Olives" and "On Virtue That Makes Small". In the former, he talks about the will that controls and conquers accidents. He assumes that it is a matter of free choice whether one has a strong or a weak will. This is the concept of the autonomous will. He blames the small people for their small virtues because he assumes that they are the agents of free will. In "Upon the Mount of Olives" he is playing a game with the wicked guest of winter as though it had its own will. If it has a will, it is an accident like any other event in the universe of necessity. Such a will may be called the accidental will in distinction from the autonomous will. The accidental will is called the sun-will because it is like the will of the sun. Although the sun rules over the entire world, its will is one with the will of the Lord Chance. It is an innocent accident. The accidental will is the will to power of Life, the cosmic necessity, which rules not only the sun but the whole world. The distinction between the autonomous will and the accidental will is the same as the distinction between the forward-looking Faustian will and the backward-looking Spinozan will. These two labels do not designate two different wills. They are the two ways of looking at one and the same will. One way is to look upon it as an autonomous agent facing an open future. The other is to look upon it as an accident determined by the past. The accidental will is what I called the heteronomous will. In the *Iliad*, Homer calls it the will of fate or the fated will.

Although we must look backward for understanding the nature of the Spinozan heteronomous will, it does not mean that the Spinozan will cannot look forward to make a choice for the future. It can do this as well as the Faustian autonomous will can. But the Spinozan will is aware of its determination by the past even in its decision for the future. On the other hand, the Faustian will does not recognize the power of the past in facing the future. It looks only forward and never backward, whereas the Spinozan will looks backward even when it faces the future. The autonomous will is always future-oriented; the heteronomous will is past-conscious. The Faustian will is conscious of its open future; the Spinozan recognizes no such open future. The former feels free; the latter feels bound. Because of its freedom, the autonomous will feels responsible for its choices and actions and takes credit for its success and blame for its failure. Its freedom is the source of its anxiety. But the heteronomous will feels no responsibility because it has no freedom. It can take neither credit nor blame. It is free of all the anxieties that afflict the free agent. Thus it is truly innocent or beyond good and evil. Under the azure bell, the Spinozan heteronomous will (the sun-will) is the deep reality, while the Faustian autonomous will is the shallow illusion that produces the drifting clouds of good and evil.

In "On Passing By", Zarathustra comes unexpectedly to the gate of a great city and runs into a foaming fool. He is called Zarathustra's ape because he gives scathing sermons just like the master's own. They are a flawless imitation of the master's condemnation of the small people, but he is severely rebuked by the master. So many commentators try to find some difference between the master and his ape. But it is very hard to find any difference. Stanley Rosen says that the fool's speech is a vulgarized version of Zarathustra's (*The Mask of Enlightenment*, 191). But the fool's vulgarity hardly exceeds Zarathustra's. Laurence Lampert says that the ape's speech is different from the master's in being unrelieved by the great longing for something higher (*Nietzsche's Teaching*, 185). But it is hard to see any great longing in Zarathustra's speech in "On Virtue That Makes Small". The great longing usually means the longing for the superman, but there is no such reference in his condemnation of the small people. As a matter of fact, the superman has completely dropped out of his talk since "On Human Prudence" of Part II and is not going to reappear until "On Old and New Tablets". He ends his condemnation of the small people with the phrase, "the great noon." Though the great noon is supposedly the time for the advent of the superman, he associates it not with the superman, but with the prairie fire that will scorch the small people like dry grass. So his promise of the great noon sounds more like the wrath of hellfire than the lofty ideal of the superman.

Zarathustra does not say that the fool says anything wrong. On the contrary, he says, "But your fool's words injure me, even where you are right" (Z, 178). He cannot stand the fool's reviling because he is just pouring out his revenge. He says to the fool, "For all your foaming is revenge, you vain fool; I guessed it well" (Z, 178). Unlike the fool, he claims to speak out of love. This is a dubious claim. As we noted earlier, his condemnation of the small people was revengeful. He is nauseated by the great city under the fool's condemnation. He says to the fool, "Woe unto this great city! And I wish I already saw the pillar of fire in which it will be burned" (Z, 178). The pillar of fire is the same as the prairie fire that he promised would scorch the small people like dry grass at the great noon. This fiery condemnation is dripping with his wrath of hellfire. This time, however, he is not going to pour out his wrath on the people although they are not any different from the small people he just condemned a short while ago. Instead he is going to pass by the great city and advises the fool that "where one can no longer love, there one should *pass by*" (Z, 178). So he saves his own invective against the great city.

This is a surprising development. In "On the Virtue That Makes Small", he had denounced the small people in the same vengeful tone as his ape's. But he did not see the ugliness of his own invective until he was subjected to the invective of the foaming fool. His ape functioned as his mirror image. This is the basic difference between the Zarathustra of Part I and the Zarathustra of Part III. When he denounced the last men in the Prologue, he had no inkling of his own sense of revenge because he had no power of self-reflection. In Part II, however, he completely reoriented his attention to himself by opening his second teaching mission, after he was startled by a distorted image of himself in a mirror. The reflection in a mirror is a metaphor of self-reflection. Since then he came to recognize the sense of revenge deeply simmering in his own heart until it materialized in the shape of the dwarf, the spirit of gravity. The dwarf is the spirit of revenge, the spoil-sport, as Zarathustra said in "The Dancing Song" of Part II. The sense of revenge that comes from the frustration of the earthly concerns makes the dwarf black and heavy. By encountering the dwarf, Zarathustra has placed a human face on his own sense of revenge. Thus his encounter with the dwarf has been the objectification of his own inner self, which has marked notable progress in his self-reflection.

In "On Virtue That Makes Small", Zarathustra was reenacting what he had done to the people of The Motley Cow without realizing that he was exploding with his own sense of revenge. But he comes to see the objectification of his own vengeful behavior in the ugly behavior of his ape. These two episodes are ingeniously separated by "Upon the Mount of Olives", which revives his sense of nobility and the sun-will. Without such a revival, he might very well have welcomed the foaming fool as his companion and joined him by pouring out his own invectives against the great city. But he decides to pass by the city without saying a word against it. About the pillar of fire and the great noon, he says, "But this has its own time and its own destiny" (*Z*, 178). This is the sort of remark that can come only from the owner of a sun-like will, who knows that everything just like the sun is governed not by the puny human will but by the Lord Chance. This is the measure of self-knowledge he has attained since the Prologue.

Zarathustra gives his last talk in the town of The Motley Cow before finally ascending to his mountain cave. This is his talk in "On Apostates". In The Motley Cow, he began to teach his disciples, but most of them have become apostates. Many of them initially responded with courage and enthusiasm. Cheered by the laughter in his wisdom, they lifted their legs like dancers. Then they thought better of it because they became weary and started crawling back to the Cross to become musty mystifiers and hearth-squatters. All of these are cowards. The first wave of his followers were corpses and jesters; the second wave were believers and followers. He says that the latter were not any better than jesters and corpses because they were the fair-weather followers. But his criticism of the apostates is not vengeful. He understands their behavior in terms of their ability: "Were their ability different, their will would be different, too" (*Z*, 179). Their will is determined by their ability. This is their heteronomous will, which is determined by accidents beyond their control. Instead of condemning the apostates, he says, "That leaves wilt—what is there to wail about?" (*Z*, 179). There is no point in blaming the apostates any more than in wailing over the leaves for their wilting. Both events are accidents, the innocent products of natural necessity.

To his surprise, the apostates claim that they have become pious again. What does it mean to become pious again? It means that they can pray again, that is, they have found something mightier than themselves and worthy of their veneration. This echoes back to Zarathustra's own dream of his youth in "The Tomb Song" of Part II: "All beings shall be divine to me." His disciples are also thirsting for something divine, before which they can kneel and pray. This is the religious longing that has afflicted Zarathustra himself. This religious aspiration has made them apostates. He attributes this motivation to the cowardly devil in the apostates rather than to their own autonomous will. Again, he recognizes the operation of their heteronomous will; he would rather blame the devil than the apostates themselves. This is why he is gentle in his rebuke of the apostates. He describes the various attempts the apostates have made for regaining their sense of piety. All of these are the secular surrogates for the traditional religion, as Stanley Rosen says (*The Mask of Enlightenment*, 193). They seek their solace in these surrogates because they cannot go back to the traditional religion.

Some apostates have gone back to the old religion and become its night watchmen. Their job is to blow horns to awaken the old things that have long gone to sleep. Zarathustra overhears a short conversation between two such night watchmen on the role of God as the Father. They agree that he is too old and does not care about his children. But one of them questions whether God has any children and expresses his wish that God would prove it. The other says that God demands faith because proof is difficult for him. Then they toot sadly on their horns. This is the way they sustain the sagging old religion. Their behavior makes Zarathustra almost suffocate with laughter because their hope to awaken the old religion is so pathetic. He then gives his own story of how the old gods came to an end long ago, indeed, a joyful godly end. They did not fade away in twilight, as the lie is told. Instead, they laughed themselves to death. That happened one day when one of the gods made the most ungodly statement: "There is one god! Thou shalt have no other god before me!" An old wrath-beard of a god, a jealous one, thus forgot himself. And then all the gods laughed and rocked in their chairs and cried, "Is it not precisely godliness that there are gods but no God?" The laughter that breaks out of his heart is the continuation of this divine laughter.

For the thematic significance of this laughter, we have to relate it to two other episodes. In "The Soothsayer", Zarathustra was himself a night watchman. To be sure, he was not trying to uphold the old dying religion. But he could not laugh over the death of God because he believed that the whole world had died and become meaningless. When he announced the death of God in the Prologue, he was not in a laughing mood, either. Instead he solemnly offered the superman as the new meaning of the earth. He could not laugh then because he believed that the secularized world was going to the dogs. Now back in The Motley Cow, he does not even mention the superman because to do so may now appear as no more than another laughing stock. He ends his second visit to The Motley Cow with a rocking laughter. That makes a dramatic contrast with his first visit with a solemn message. He can now laugh over the things he used to moan over, which indicates a notable shift in the balance of power between his autonomous and his heteronomous will. As long as he believes in his autonomous will, he will be tense and serious because he feels responsible for all his actions just like the sublime ones in "On Those Who Are Sublime" of Part II. He will be vengeful, too, because he will run into obstacles that will overpower his will. Hence he cannot laugh. On the other hand, when he comes to believe that his will is determined by accidents, he can relax and be spontaneous. Then he can laugh. Laughter cannot come out of a tense and vengeful heart. It can explode spontaneously only from a carefree heart.

The Motley Cow is an important landmark for Zarathustra's career. He has come to love this city since he launched his teaching mission there. He began to recruit and instruct his future disciples in and around this city. He bade his first farewell to the disciples again in this city. Now he has arrived for his final visit to this beloved city, but there is no more teaching on the superman, no more gift-giving virtue, and no more farewell message. He only talks about the disciples who have become apostates. But he does it not in dismay and sorrow, but in humor and laughter. This final visit marks the end of his long teaching career. He is back to Square One and has nothing to show for his teaching mission except for a few apostates. But he has learned much about himself. As we noted in the last chapter, he began as a teacher in Part I and then turned into a learner in Part II. The object of his learning has been chiefly his own self. He came out to teach others, but got to know himself. That is a healthy role reversal for him. So he jubilantly returns to his old cave for the task of completing the perfection of himself in "The Return Home".

Self-Perfection (Part III.9-11)

When Zarathustra finally returns home, he has a long talk with Solitude as though he were talking to his mother. This talk is largely a series of recollections in the same manner as his talk in "On Involuntary Bliss". Whereas the previous talk was a monologue, the present talk is an imaginary dialogue between him and Solitude. Whereas the previous recollections were about his experience of descending to the ultimate depth of reality, the present recollections concern his long career of speaking and preaching. He began this career by storming away from Solitude because he could not stand it any longer only to find that he felt more forsaken among many than in Solitude. He recalls his desperate longing for the joy of receiving ("The Night Song") and the admonition from The Stillest Hour. Then he dwells on the futility of speaking: "Down there, however, all speech is in vain" (Z, 184). So he has learned that the best wisdom is to forget and pass by ("On Passing By"). "But down there everyone talks and no one listens" is repeated five times with some variation. Because these people talk all the time but never listen, he found them unendurable. In order to endure them, he disguised himself and sat among them in "On Human Prudence". But the so-called good people were the most poisonous flies. So he is just happy to leave them in the bog and be back on the mountain free of their evil vapors. Now he has to deal only with himself.

"On The Three Evils" is the story of a morning dream, in which Zarathustra weighs the whole world on a pair of scales. He finds that the world is measurable, weighable, accessible, and divinable. This is the report on the world by his day-wisdom, which mocks all infinite worlds. The same day-wisdom also says, "Wherever there is force, *number* will become mistress: she has more force" (Z, 187). This is another description of the finite world. The infinite world cannot be governed by the day-wisdom. It belongs to the night-wisdom. What can be numbered and measured is finite. He says that his dream offered the finite world to him like a ripe golden apple or a casket to be opened for his delight. It was not so enigmatic as to frighten away human love or not so transparent as to put human wisdom to sleep. The world appeared to be a humanly good thing, though so many evil things were said about it. The upshot of this grandiose talk is the conclusion that the world is good and human contrary to the view that the world is bad and inhuman. The finitude of the world is only a supporting argument for this conclusion. What is infinite defies human will; what is finite is within human control. Because the dream gave him a comforting view of the world, Zarathustra refers to it as a comforter. In an imitation of this comforter, he wants to weigh the three most evil things on his scales: sensuality, the lust to rule, and selfishness. He wants to show that these three are also human and good though they have been widely reviled.

Sensuality is the slow fire for the rabble, but it is the garden of happiness for the free and innocent. Sensuality is a cursed evil to the weak and wilted, but it is a great boon to the lion-willed. The question of whether sensuality is good or evil for you depends on your constitution as a human being. The same is true of the lust to rule. It is the scalding scourge for the hardhearted, the hideous torture for the cruelest, and the malicious gadfly for the vainest. But it breaks all that is rotten and hollow, makes people crawl, teaches the great contempt, and ascends to the self-sufficient height. Zarathustra then blesses selfishness, "the wholesome, healthy selfishness that wells from a powerful soul" (Z, 190). Such a noble soul belongs to a supple, beautiful, triumphant body. It banishes from its presence whatever is cowardly or contemptible, especially those who worry and those who wallow in grief. It holds even in lower esteem the servile and subservient, who cannot resist but only swallow poisonous spittle. But servility and humility have been preached as great virtues for a long time by sham wisdom. The world-weary cowards had good reasons for teaching the virtue of selflessness.

Stanley Rosen says that Zarathustra has nothing radically new to say on these three topics (*The Mask of Enlightenment*, 197). Sensuality was discussed in "On Chastity" of Part I, the lust to rule in "On Self-Overcoming" of Part II, and selfishness in "On the Gift-Giving Virtue" of Part I. But his present discussion introduces one significant rearrangement. In his previous talks, he discussed these three as independent topics. In the present talk, he brings them together as the basic constituents of a healthy and holy ego. That is, a healthy and holy ego should have healthy sensuality, a strong lust to rule, and noble selfishness. Such an ideal of selfhood is the natural topic for Zarathustra's discussion after his return to his cave. After all, he has come home for the task of self-perfection. But why does he talk about the nature of the universe before his discussion on the self? What is the connection between his weighing the world and weighing the three most evils things? This is a really intriguing question because it involves a truly novel feature of the present discussion.

The view that the world is finite and measurable is said to be the gift from Zarathustra's day-wisdom. This view is diametrically opposed to the view from his night-wisdom, which we have encountered more than once. In "The Dancing Song" of Part II, he said that Life was unfathomable. In "The Wanderer" and "Before Sunrise", the ground of reality was called the abyss, the groundless ground. In "Before Sunrise", he called the azure bell the heaven of accidents. All these expressions imply that the world is beyond human control and comprehension. We may use the two labels of "Apollonian" and "Dionysian" to designate these two views of the world. Whereas the Apollonian view stresses measure and number as the essential features of the world, the Dionysian view stresses its immeasurability and its infinity. These two views are closely connected to the twofold will. The autonomous will presupposes a world that can be measured and weighed because what cannot be measured and weighed cannot be controlled. When Zarathustra introduced the commanding will in "Self-Overcoming", he began his talk with the intelligibility of the world: "A will to the thinkability of all things: this I call your will" (Z, 113). But the abyss cannot be an object of our will because it defies our comprehension. Likewise, the Heaven of Accidents transcends our thinkability. Such a world cannot be controlled because our control depends on our knowledge. It overpowers the autonomous will and reduces it to the heteronomous will.

When Zarathustra returned to his cave for self-perfection, he was still struggling with the problem of his twofold will. He was keenly conscious of his heteronomous will while he was on the sea. But he became conscious of his autonomous will as soon as he stepped on the land. Now for his self-perfection, he has to decide which of these two wills is going to be the primary force. In "On The Three Evil Things", he clearly goes for the autonomous will. His talk on the lust to rule is his encomium on the autonomous will. In his praise of healthy sensuality, he treats it as a prerogative of the lion-willed. The healthy and holy ego is said to have the lion-will. In the description of the three evil things, he provides their subtle connection to the autonomous will. Sensuality is now described as forward-looking because it is taken as the sign of higher happiness in marriage. The lust to rule is described as upward-looking because it ascends to the height of self-sufficiency. These two images of upward and forward motions are meant to indicate the active and autonomous will, as we noted in "On Human Prudence" of Part II. Selfishness finally provides the ultimate force for these two movements because it always aspires for the highest and the noblest. All of them are the basic ingredients for the making of the autonomous commanding will.

Lampert correctly notes the similarity of the day-wisdom to the Cartesian aspiration for knowledge and power, which has governed the development of modern science (*Nietzsche's Teaching,* 192). Francis Bacon espoused the same ideal of knowledge and power. For both Bacon and Descartes, the will to science and knowledge was the expression of will to power. But the will to power cannot be restricted to the acquisition of theoretical knowledge, because such knowledge does not deliver power. It has to be converted to the enormous technological power that has devastated the entire natural world. This is the Faustian ethos, the spirit of Doctor Faust, the Renaissance magician, who is determined to conquer and reshape nature, as manifested from Marlowe's *Doctor Faust* to Goethe's *Faust*. The Faustian ethos has inspired the development of modern European culture from science to literature, from music to visual arts, from politics to economics. The scientific spirit of Bacon and Descartes is only the scientific manifestation of the Faustian ethos. Even European expansionism and imperialism have emerged as the global fallout of the same Faustian ethos. Nietzsche usually flaunts the will to power as his proud invention. But he is only expressing the force that has inspired the entire European tradition since the Renaissance.

For the perfection of his healthy selfhood, there is one more chore for Zarathustra. That is to free himself from the spirit of gravity. This is his task in "On the Spirit of Gravity". But what is the spirit of gravity? This has been a controversial topic because Zarathustra never gives a straightforward description in spite of his numerous references to it. Here are some samples in the broad range of opinions on the nature of the spirit of gravity. Werner Dannhauser says that the spirit of gravity is the spirit of objectivity and the spurious universality created by reason (*Nietzsche's View of Socrates*, 267). Bernd Magnus says that the dwarf is the last man, our other self to be uprooted and transfigured (*Nietzsche's Existential Imperative*, 167). Harold Alderman regards the dwarf as the symbol of Zarathustra's own timidity and of his longing for something more immutable and certain (*Nietzsche's Gift*, 96). Greg Whitlock says that the dwarf is the personification of nihilism and despair (*Returning to Sils-Maria*, 197). Robert Gooding-Williams identifies the dwarf as the small man (*Zarthustra's Dionysian Modernism*, 214). Laurence Lampert identifies him with the rational spirit of Socratism and Platonism (*Nietzsche's Teaching*, 162).

Let us now consider Zarathustra's own statements on the spirit of gravity. He opposes his bird's way to the spirit of gravity. He gives the following prescription for becoming like a bird and overcoming the spirit of gravity. The first step is to love oneself with a wholesome and healthy love so that one can bear to be with oneself and need not roam. Such roaming is disguised as love of the neighbor. This recalls the lesson from "On Love of the Neighbor" of Part I. But the art of loving oneself in a healthy way is the subtlest, the most cunning and the most patient of all because whatever is one's own is well concealed from the owner. Of all treasures, it is our own that we dig up last because it is so ordered by the spirit of gravity. How does the spirit of gravity hide and bury our own? We are presented with grave words and values almost from the cradle, and they are called good and evil. From our birth, we are indoctrinated and enchained by the system of values and beliefs of our society. Thus we become a camel, heavily laden with the burden of the past and tradition, which is alien to our true selves.

The alien elements from the outside world are not the only burden on the self. There is the internal burden, which is our own. Zarathustra says that a human being is like an oyster, whose inside is nauseating and slippery and hard to grasp. He does not explain what this metaphor stands for. But its meaning is fairly obvious. It refers to what he described as a ball of snakes in "On the Pale Criminal" of Part I, namely, the tangle of basic drives and passions in the soul. It is the source of all the worldly concerns and anxieties that relentlessly haunt and plague human existence. In short, the spirit of gravity makes life hard and heavy to bear. So there are two elements for the constitution of the spirit of gravity: (1) the value system of the external world and (2) the basic drives of the internal self. But these two elements come from the same ultimate source, Mother Nature, because the values of the herd are created by their basic natural drives. Ultimately, the ball of snakes constitutes the spirit of gravity. Our basic natural drives generate the worries and anxieties that endlessly depress human existence. The spirit of gravity is Dame Care (*Frau Sorge*), a familiar figure in German folklore. In Goethe's *Faust,* this familiar figure appears as an offspring of the Earth Spirit and hounds Faust to the very end of his career. In Richard Wagner's *The Ring of the Nibelung*, Erda is the counterpart of Goethe's Earth Spirit. Wotan calls Erda *Ur-Sorge* (Primal Care) in *Siegfried*, act 3, scene 1. In *Zarathustra*, Life is the counterpart of Goethe's Earth Spirit and Wagner's Erda, and the spirit of gravity is an offspring of Life.

In these three works, the chthonic force of Mother Nature is the ultimate source of earthly concerns and anxieties. The spirit of gravity belongs to the long German tradition of *Frau Sorge*. It is the curse on all human beings as children of Mother Nature. In Christian theology, this sort of curse and evil used to be attributed not to God, but to the devils, the agents of evil. But there are no such agents in Zarathustra's world, which admits no separation between the devils and Life. Natural instincts and passions are called devils when they become ugly, but they are called angels when they become beautiful. Life is Spinoza's Nature, the infinite substance and the only God. She is the all-embracing reality, out-side which nothing can exist. Even the illusion of having an autonomous will comes from this ultimate reality, and the curse of perpetual care is generated by this illusion. We worry ourselves to death because we want to control our existence in accordance with our own will. Hence even the spirit of gravity and his perpetual curse must be attributed to Life. To be free of this curse is Zarathustra's ideal of redemption, which is repre-sented by his metaphor of flying like a bird.

The long German tradition of Care (*Sorge*) lies behind Heidegger's phenomenological analysis of human existence. According to him, Care enslaves individuals to the crowd and their popular culture, which is rep-resented by the market crowd of The Motley Cow in Zarathustra's world. The crushing weight of their secular culture smothers his dream of flying like a bird. This dream is none other than his ambitious campaign for the spiritualization of natural existence, which was represented by the flight of his eagle and serpent in the Prologue. The secular culture displays the most oppressive power of the dwarf, the heaviest and the blackest mon-ster from the abyss, which is the bowel of all desires and passions. Their operation and satisfaction is the essence of secular culture. Hence its val-ues are bound to be cheap and shallow, or inauthentic in Heidegger's word. Moreover, the perpetual strife of our drives and passions strife produces only an endless series of concerns and anxieties, which always renders life hard and heavy to bear. Thus the spirit of gravity enslaves all human beings to the cruel chain of endless worries. This is the worst part of being chained to the ring of eternal recurrence because it is the ring of perpetual care and worries. Zarathustra's campaign of spiritualization is his program to enable human beings to fly above and beyond the cheap secular culture by freeing themselves from the crushing weight of the spirit of gravity. This is what it means to become the superman by tran-scending the limits of humanity. This is why Zarathustra regards the spirit of gravity as his ultimate enemy. Only by defeating this ultimate enemy, he can bring his campaign of spiritualization to the final victory.

In concluding his speech on the spirit of gravity, Zarathustra says that he has reached his truth by trying out many different ways. He has not relied on any one ladder. His preferred method was to try and question every possible way. This is his taste—not good, not bad—just his taste. To anyone who asked about "the way," he said, "This is *my* way; where is yours? For *the* way—that does not exist" (Z, 195). The last statement has provoked the dispute on whether it reflects Zarathustra's relativism. But the claim that everyone should have his or her own way does not automatically lead to relativism because there can be many different ways to the same truth. We should remember that the controversial statement was made in the conclusion of his discourse on authenticity, the uniqueness of every human being. Everyone has to find his or her own way to achieve the uniqueness. To seek a standard way of achieving it will be self-defeating. Zarathustra's disavowal of the way ("For *the* way—that does not exist.") sounds almost the same as the first line of *Tao Te Ching*: "The way that can be named is not the real way." That the way cannot be named (described) means that no one can give a formula for finding it. But *Tao Tae Ching* has never been interpreted as a text for preaching relativism.

The Creative Will (Part III.12)

If Zarathustra has found his own way, he can become his unique self and defeat the spirit of gravity, which enslaves most human beings to the herd. The victory over the spirit of gravity, his archenemy, should be the ultimate end of his self-perfection. With his self thus perfected, what is he going to do? The answer is given in "On Old and New Tablets". In the opening of this section, Zarathustra is engaged in the reminiscence of his entire career. He is surrounded by broken old tablets and new tablets only half written. He is waiting for the sign that the hour has come for him to go down and be with people again. In the meantime he will talk to himself to fill his waiting time. His soliloquy celebrates the victorious career of his autonomous leonine will and totally ignores his heteronomous will until the very end. Let us now go over some salient features of his soliloquy. Subsection 2 of "On Old and New Tablets" is fairly long and covers his entire career from his exposure to the academic chairs of gloomy sages (I.2) to his struggle with the old devil and arch-enemy, the spirit of gravity (III.11). But the central point is his teaching that all values are created by human beings and that he has finally secured his freedom especially from all the constraints imposed by the spirit of gravity. But the spirit of gravity is not totally killed, but only subdued to be the docile floor for his dance. At the beginning of subsection 3, he mentions the superman in an amazingly casual manner, "There it was too that I picked up the word 'superman' off the road (*vom Wege*)."[2] The superman is now reduced from an awesome ideal to a mere word. This makes a dramatic contrast with the solemn announcement in the Prologue, in which he presented the superman as his most important message for the redemption of humankind. Now he talks as though he had picked up the word "superman" somewhere along the road. In fact, as we noted in chapter 1, the superman was already a popular ideal with Herder and Goethe and among the Young Hegelians.

We should note that the superman is appearing for the first time in Part III. The superhuman ideal was the central theme for Part I, which was inseparably connected to the theme of the creative will. In "Upon the Blessed Isles" of Part II, where his talk on creativity reached the highest pitch, he told his disciples that they could well create the superman if they could create a god. Now he mentions none of these things. Instead he recalls his teaching on redemption. In our discussion of this teaching in the last chapter, we identified three different formulae of redemption: (1) the creation formula, (2) the transformation formula, and (3) the acceptance formula. Of these three, he mentions only (1) and (2). These two belong to the Faustian autonomous will, while (3) belongs to the Spinozan heteronomous will. The Faustian will is the creative agent, which is indispensable for the transformation of the past for its redemption or for the creation of a new future. On the other hand, the acceptance formula requires no creative agent because it recommends the acceptance

---

2. Kaufmann translates *vom Wege* as 'by the way', which means 'incidentally' rather than 'off the road'. Hollingdale omits it in his translation for some reason. Thomas Common alone gives a literal translation of it as 'from the path'.

of the past as it was. Zarathustra does not even mention the acceptance formula probably because he is solely concerned with the creative autonomous will.

He makes no attempt to connect redemption to the superman. He mentions them as two independent items. Then he says that he is waiting for his own redemption, but does not say where it is going to come from. Evidently his redemption does not lie within his own power. This is strange and surprising. When he discussed the three formulas of redemption, he surely gave the impression that the first two were under the control of his autonomous will. To be sure, he rejected those two formulas in favor of the third one. But he is now talking about only those two. In speaking of the third and final formula, he indeed confessed that he did not know when and how it could be realized. If redemption can be achieved only by the third formula, then it may indeed lie beyond his power. But he talks as though he had completely forgotten this formula. For these reasons, we have no way of figuring out why he has to wait for his redemption.

In subsection 4, he restates the need to overcome not only oneself as explained in "On Self-Overcoming" of Part I, but also one's neighbor for the sake of the superman as explained in "On Love of the Neighbor" of Part I. In subsection 5, he says that the will of the noble soul desires nothing *gratis* unlike the mob, who want to live *gratis*. In subsection 6, he talks about the importance of self-sacrifice as an essential condition for a strong will. In subsection 7, he says that to be truthful requires a strong will. In subsection 8, he rejects the winter doctrine that everything stands still and frozen and advocates the opposite doctrine that everything is in flux. The winter doctrine provides an inhospitable arena for the operation of a creative will because it can do little in the world where everything is frozen. The world of perpetual flux is the ideal arena for the creative will. But he fails to note that determinism and the eternal recurrence dictate a frozen world of becoming for eternity. In subsection 9, he says that for a long time human beings have lived under illusions whether they believed or repudiated soothsayers and stargazers. It is about time to have knowledge in place of illusions. Knowledge is surely the sound basis for the creative will. Thus the creative will is the central theme for these subsections.

In subsection 10, he repudiates the injunctions against robbery and murder because those injunctions go against the basic instinct of life ("Is there not in all life itself robbing and killing?"). The injury to others is unavoidable in life. In subsection 11, he condemns those who distort the past and reinterpret history as a bridge leading up to their positions. They are despots and the new despot is the rabble. Zarathustra says that a new nobility is needed to fight against the new despot. He talks about this new nobility in subsection 12. This new nobility should look not backward, but forward. Instead of looking back at the father-lands, they should look forward to the land of their children. Their orientation is the same as that of the forward-looking autonomous will. He says, "In your children you shall make up for being the children of your fathers: thus shall you redeem all that is past" (Z, 204). The past should be redeemed not in its own right, but only for the sake of future. This scheme of redemption follows the first formula. He is still banking his hope of redemption on the future and the forward-looking will.

From subsections 11 to 18, he resolutely dismisses the world-weary pessimists. The pessimistic talk ("Why live? All is vanity!") is only an antiquarian babbling, which is no longer relevant for our age of comfort and contentment. Those who renounce the world and those who are weary of all violent desires are suffering from their upset stomachs and can never realize that life is a well of joy. They try to deny their own will: "Nothing is worthwhile! You shall not will!" (Z, 206). This is the ultimate degradation of the creative will. In all these talks about the problem of suffering, he is the Zarathustra of Part I. There is no indication of what he had gone through in Part II. Subsections 19-22 are only a supplement to his talk on the strong creative will. In subsection 23, he talks about the sexual distinction. Man should be fit for war, and the woman for childbirth. In subsection 24, he says that marriage should be not merely for reproduction but for producing something higher, which will eventually lead to the superman. In subsection 25, he says that there will be the new people and their assembly of new experimenters for the for-

mation of a new human society. Thus the creative will is still the center
of his discourse and will remain so until we reach the last subsection.

In the final subsection, his discourse takes a totally different turn. So
far, he has talked to himself and sometimes to "my brothers." Now he
addresses his talk to his own will and the tone of his speech abruptly
changes. To appreciate the full impact of this change, I had better quote
subsection 30 in its entirety:

> Thou my Will! Thou cessation of all my need, thou my
> *own* necessity! Keep me from all small victories! Thou desti-
> nation of my soul, which I call destiny! Thou in-me! Over-me!
> Keep me and save me for a great destiny.
>
> And thy last greatness, my Will, save up for thy last feat
> that thou mayest be inexorable in thy victory. Alas, who was
> not vanquished in his victory? Alas, whose eye would not
> darken in this drunken twilight? Alas, whose foot would not
> reel in victory and forget how to stand?
>
> That I may one day be ready and ripe in the great noon: as
> ready and ripe as glowing bronze, clouds pregnant with light-
> ning, and swelling milk udders—ready for myself and my
> most hidden Will: a bow lusting for its arrow, an arrow lusting
> for its star—a star ready and ripe in its noon, glowing, pierced,
> enraptured by annihilating sun arrows—a sun itself and an in-
> exorable solar Will (*Sonnen-Wille*), ready to annihilate in vic-
> tory!
>
> O Will, cessation of all need, thou my *own* Necessity!
> Spare me for a great victory! (Z, 214f)

I capitalized the first letter of the word "will" to highlight the rhetorical effect of addressing the Will as the second person. Prior to subsection 30, he treated the will as an instrument of creation under his
command. Now he treats it as his master. It is the master of necessity, before whom he feels powerless and helpless. Why has "my Will" become
Necessity? What sort of necessity does it have? It is the necessity of the
azure bell, the whole universe. When he elevates his will to the level of
cosmic necessity, he again calls it the sun-will. So there are two ways of
looking upon his own will: (1) as his instrument and servant for creation

and (2) as an integral element of cosmic necessity and his master. The first is the autonomous Faustian will, which is the creator and liberator for the future. The second is the heteronomous Spinozan will, which is the prisoner of the past. This is the sun-will, the will to power of Life. Since it is coextensive with the whole universe, it is not only in himself ("Thou in-me"), but also over himself ("Over-me"). When he recognizes the inseparability of his will from cosmic necessity, he calls upon his destiny (*Schicksal*). Fate is the simple meaning of the German word, *Schicksal*. Zarathustra mentioned this word for the first time in his entire career at the opening of "On Involuntary Bliss", when he triumphantly stood on his fate. This was shortly after his vision of the eternal recurrence in "On the Vision and the Riddle". Now he sees that his will is none other than his fate as it is determined in and through the eternal recurrence. This is his will of fate, to which he is now presenting his humble supplication.

In "On Old and New Tablets", Zarathustra had gained the right to flaunt his autonomous creative will and its accomplishment because he had presumably conquered his archenemy, the spirit of gravity, in the preceding section. He had also gained the right to ignore the heteronomous will because it is subject to the spirit of gravity. The dwarf is an agent of cosmic necessity. At the end of his long soliloquy, however, he comes back to the mighty sun-will of cosmic necessity. By then he completely drops his posture of mastering the universe and reshaping the entire humanity with his creative will and bows on his knees to present his humble petition to the "inexorable solar will." This abrupt change in his posture has been lurking all along beneath his boastful talk. At the opening of this section, he was waiting for the sign that his hour had come. In subsection 3, he said that he was waiting for his redemption. In "On the Spirit of Gravity", he cursed those who must always wait. Waiting is the sure sign of being dependent on others. So he was all along feeling the power greater than his own autonomous will. Ironically, this greater power turns out to be his own sun-will. If his own sun-will is not an external force, then the spirit of gravity may not be his external enemy either because they are inseparable locked together in his own heart.

CHAPTER FOUR

The Twofold Self

(Part III.13-16)

Let us review Zarathustra's journey in terms of his campaign to spiritual-ize the secular culture. In Part II, as we noted in chapter 2, this campaign was shifted from the Faustian to the Spinozan mode. He moved from the world of light to the world of darkness, where he plumbed the darkness of his soul in "The Night Song", "The Dancing Song", and "The Tomb Song." In "On Redemption", he felt the crushing weight of the past and realized that his will was not autonomous but heteronomous. The shift of his spiritual campaign from the Faustian to the Spinozan mode was dic-tated by the shift from the autonomous to the heteronomous will. In Part III, he made the journey back to his cave and solitude. In the first phase of this journey (III.1-4), he had the vision of the eternal recurrence and then the azure bell, through which he came to understand the Spinozan world and its cosmic necessity, the ground of his heteronomous will. In the second phase (III.5-11), he went back to his old theme of the creative will and consolidated it by his alleged conquest of the spirit of gravity and gave his Faustian speech on the creative will in "On Old and New Tablets." With this speech, his spiritual campaign was reverted to the Faustian mode. But he ended the speech by humbling himself before his own sun-will. The sun used to be the Christian symbol of God; the sun-will is the will of God naturalized. The sun-will belongs to the cosmic self; the autonomous will belongs to the individual self. Thus his spiritual campaign is caught in the tug of two wills, which will turn out to be the battle between his two selves in the remainder of Part III.

The Monster from the Abyss (Part III.13)

One morning, shortly after his return to his cave, Zarathustra jumps up from his bed and screams like a madman. He is screaming to wake up the sleeping abysmal thought. He says, "Zarathustra, the godless, summons you! Zarathustra, the advocate of life, the advocate of suffering, the advocate of the circle; I summon you, you my most abysmal thought! (*Z*, 215)" Zarathustra the advocate of suffering and the circle is different from the Zarathustra, who spoke in "On Old and New Tablets." The latter was the advocate of the creative will and said nothing about suffering and the circle. While he was speaking about the creative will, his most abysmal thought must have gone to sleep in the abyss. That is why he said nothing about it in "On Old and New Tablets." When he jumps up and starts screaming like a madman, he acts as if somebody else were still lying on his resting place and refused to get up. That somebody else is the abysmal thought. Now Zarathustra, the advocate of life, suffering and the circle, is determined to settle his account with it.

For a long time since the terrifying moment in "On Redemption" of Part II, he has thought of calling up the abysmal thought, but he has not been able to muster the courage to do so. In "On Involuntary Bliss" he expressed his fear of the abysmal thought and admitted his lack of courage to face it. He was still waiting for the day when he would be strong enough to have the lion's voice to summon the abysmal thought. Now that he has just roared like a lion "On Old and New Tablets", he has finally earned the right to summon the monster. When the abysmal thought approaches in response to his summons, he says, "Hail to me! You are coming, I hear you. My abyss speaks, I have turned my ultimate depth inside out into the daylight. Hail to me! Come here! Give me your hand!" (*Z*, 216). When the invisible hand seems to touch him, he screams, "Huh! Let go! Huhhuh! Nausea, nausea, nausea—woe unto me!" (*Z*, 216). While speaking these words, he falls down and remains there like a dead person. He behaves as though he had been clobbered by the abysmal thought. This is the devastating outcome of the showdown. When he regains consciousness, he is pale and trembling. He could not eat or drink for seven days, during which he is nursed by his animals.

When Zarathustra finally raises himself, he takes a rose apple into his hands and talks about the difficulty of communication. Every soul has its own world. The unbridgeable chasm between different worlds is covered up by the illusion of speaking. He says, "Speaking is a beautiful folly: with that man dances over all things. (Z, 217)" Indeed, his talk on the difficulty of communication goes over the head of his animals. They only appreciate the word "dance" and tell him that all things in nature are dancing. They look upon the eternal recurrence as a ring of dance, a natural cycle of seasons. The world goes around in an endless dance of renewal. They sing their lyre song on the beauty of nature and its endless return and renewal. In response to their song, Zarathustra talks about the monster that crawled down his throat and the horror of biting off its head. This is his experience of the eternal recurrence, which is the polar opposite to that of his animals. This marks the difference between the natural beings and the human beings. He is quite amused at how lightly his animals are treating his ordeal. He says to them, "But now I lie here, still weary of this biting and spewing, still sick from my own redemption" (Z, 218). It is surprising to note that the terrible ordeal has delivered the redemption he has been seeking so long. But he does not say how he got it. Nor does he say what sort of redemption it is. These are the enigmatic questions that will be considered later.

He begins to describe his ordeal with the abysmal thought by saying: "The great disgust with man—*this* choked me and had crawled into my throat" (Z, 219). This sentence recalls the shepherd scene in "On the Vision and the Riddle", which was a pre-vision of what is taking place now. Enigmatic is the phrase, "the great disgust with man." This may sound like another repetition of his familiar disgust with the rabble and the small men. But it is different. He is now feeling great disgust not with any particular type of human beings, but with all human beings. As far as the smallness of man is concerned, he can see no difference between the small and the great: "Naked had I once seen both, the greatest man and the smallest man: all-too-similar to each other, even the greatest all-too-human. All-too-small, the greatest—that was my disgust with man" (Z, 219). He is using "the small man" as a synonym to "man". Most commentators have missed this semantic link between "man" and "the small man" and assumed that he is talking about the same small man he ridiculed in "On Virtue That Makes Small." Hence they are misled to believe that his disgust is limited to the small men and does not extend to the great ones. In this section, however, every human being is a small man, as Paul S. Loeb points out ("The Dwarf, the Dragon, and the Ring of Eternal Recurrence", 99). Zarathustra's great disgust covers the entire humankind: "And the eternal recurrence even of the smallest—that was my disgust with all existence. Alas! Nausea! Nausea! Nausea!" (Z, 219).

This explosion of "nausea" explains what happened in Zarathustra's encounter with his abysmal thought. When it woke up from sleep and clobbered him, he shrieked the word "nausea" three times. He is now explaining the object of this abominable nausea. It is man as such. Every human being is a disgusting small man. But he never explains why such is the case. As long as 'the small man' is used in contrast to 'the great man', we can understand his outburst against the small man because we have seen it so often. But we have no idea of why he feels horrible disgust with all human beings, including the greatest ones. This is the most baffling feature of his outburst. In order to unravel this mystery, let us take a closer look at the text:

> The great disgust with man—*this* choked me and had crawled
> into my throat; and what the soothsayer said: "All is the same,
> nothing is worth while, knowledge chokes." (Z, 219)

This statement is an adaptation of the Soothsayer's pronouncement in "The Soothsayer" of Part II. But the phrase "knowledge chokes" was not in the Soothsayer's pronouncement: "All is empty, all is the same, all has been" (Z, 133). Why does knowledge choke? The answer may be found in what Zarathustra goes on to say after the quoted passage: "A long twilight limped before me, a sadness, weary to death, drunken with death, speaking with a yawning mouth" (Z, 219). His sadness yawns and says, "Eternally recurs the man of whom you are weary, the small man." Then he says that the human earth (*Menschenerde*) turned into a cave, in which "everything living became human decay (*Menschenmoder*) and bones and decaying (*morsche*) past to me." This statement highlights the sense of decay that pervades the entire earth. The "human earth" has become a cave of "human decay." In this cave of decadence, all human instincts are rotting away. Hence the cave is drunk with death and even his sadness only yawns. The recurrence of the small man is an eternal fixture in this cave of perpetual decadence.

The cave of human decay is different from the dungeon of death Zarathustra saw in his nightmare in "The Soothsayer" of Part II. Whereas he reached the dungeon of death by his descent to the center of the earth, he is exposed to the cave of human decay by the ascent of a monster from the abyss. The descent to the dungeon of death was achieved by scientific reduction, according to which life was supposed to be only an illusion and a surface phenomenon of the earth, because the underlying ultimate reality was believed to be dead matter. But this scientific version of pessimism was blown apart by the exploding laughter, which displayed the irrepressible living force of the physical world. What had initially appeared to be the castle of death was proven to be the castle of living force. But this castle of living force has now become a massive cave of human decay. It is important to understand the difference of Zarathustra's seven-day ordeal from what happened to him in "The Soothsayer." The cave of human decay is real; the dungeon of death was only an illusion. He saw the dungeon of death in the dreamland. But the cave of human decay is situated in broad daylight. The castle of death goes through two transformations. At the end of the nightmare in "The Soothsayer", it was transformed into the castle of inexhaustible life. Then it is again transformed into a cave of pervasive decay filled with countless dwarfs in "The Convalescent." The exhaustible life has become the decaying life, thereby turning the whole earth into a massive dungeon of decay. It is this massive dungeon of decay that provokes Zarathustra's great disgust.

In the dungeon of decay, he now sighs over all human tombs day and night, wailing: "Alas, man recurs eternally! The small man recurs eternally!" (*Z*, 219). In the castle of death, he never encountered any human beings, whether small or great. In fact, he never saw any living things. In the dungeon of decay, the present is smothered under the decaying past ("everything living became . . . decaying (*morshe*) past to me"). This gruesome scene amplifies Zarathustra's pessimism in "On Redemption" of Part II: The present is crushed under the weight of the past. No one can have the creative will under such a crushing weight, but the creative will is the only source of greatness. Thus every human being is a disgusting dwarf. If all human beings are the disgusting dwarfs, there can be no meaningful difference between the smallest and the greatest. Hence all is the same and nothing is worthwhile, as the Soothsayer said. The knowledge of this fact chokes Zarathustra by crawling into his throat ("The great disgust with man—*this* choked me and had crawled into my throat.").

Zarathustra's great disgust came from the monster that crawled into his throat. But who is this monster? We have already associated his ordeal with the shepherd scene in "On the Vision and the Riddle." By virtue of this association, many commentators have assumed that the monster is the snake. But the word "snake" is never used in "The Convalescent." When Zarathustra wakes up the abysmal thought, he first calls it the sleepy worm. That sounds like another name for the snake. But the monster turns out to be quite different from a snake by the time it clobbers him. When the monster approaches him, he says, "Hail! Come here! Give me your hand!" Evidently, the monster has a hand. If so, it cannot be a snake. It must be the dwarf, the spirit of gravity. But the dwarf cannot crawl into Zarathustra's throat. In his report of the seven-day ordeal, both images of the dwarf and the snake are implicated in the description of the monster. We have already noted that the two are the interchangeable symbols of Life. I have accepted Paul S. Loeb's thesis that the dwarf of the gateway scene is transformed to the snake of the shepherd scene in "On the Vision and the Riddle." These two chthonic symbols are not only interchangeable, but also interconnectable. The monster that clobbers Zarathustra is the combination of the snake and the dwarf, which may be called the dwarf-snake monster. This composite monster was hinted by Zarathustra's description of the dwarf as "burrowing" in "Involuntary Bliss", which implies the burrowing worm or snake.

The dwarf and the snake are the agents of Life and her chthonic force. The snake represents not only the time line, but also the instinctual force of life, for example, a ball of snakes as the symbol of desires and passions in "On the Pale Criminal" of Part I. In "The Other Dancing Song" Zarathustra will call Life a snake twice. The dwarf is as repulsive as the black and heavy snake. In "On the Spirit of Gravity" he described the dwarf as something "nauseating and slippery" inside man like the inside of an oyster. You may find it hard to accept the association of Life with these two repulsive creatures. Whereas Life makes her appearance as a majestic woman, the dwarf and the snake cannot be freed from their nauseating appearance. But that is only the appearance. Life is Nature. In "The Dancing Song" of Part II, she told Zarathustra that she is only wild and changeable although men try to impose majestic attributes on her. She can appear in both beautiful and ugly forms. That is the mystery of Life, Mother Nature. The dwarf and the snake are the expressions of Life and her power. Their combination creates the composite monster that is half human and half animal like the satyr. The composite monster is the monstrous agent of Life just as the satyr is a monstrous agent of Dionysus. Life is Mother Nature just like Dionysus. The composite monster is the Dionysian monster.

Roger Hollinrake says that Zarathustra's summons to the abysmal thought is modeled after Wotan's summons to Erda in *Siegfried* (*Nietzsche, Wagner, and the Philosophy of Pessimism*, 84). Erda is the goddess of the earth just like Life. In chapter 2, I said that Life represents Spinoza's conception of Nature, whose divine essence is power. So is Erda. She is the ultimate source of all natural power. Wotan tries to wake her up to benefit from her all-knowing wisdom. Her deep sleep may well stand for the original condition of nature before she is awakened for life. But her sleep is the sleep of wisdom. She says, "My sleep is dreaming; my dreaming, brooding; my brooding, the rule of knowledge" (*Siegfried*, act 3, scene 1). Like Erda, Life has her own wisdom. When Zarathustra was clobbered by the abysmal thought, he said, "Knowledge chokes."

The abysmal thought is the sort of knowledge that belongs to Life. It is the knowledge that the autonomous will is an illusion in the world of Life, because everything is governed by her cosmic necessity. In the Prologue, Zarathustra associated the serpent with knowledge. Now we can see what sort of knowledge the serpent commands and why it chokes him.

Tragic Awakening (Part III.13)

Zarathustra's great disgust with man is his disgust with himself. If all human beings are small men, he should be one, too. He cannot be any different. As the Soothsayer says, "All is the same." This realization is the knockout punch that creates the central crisis of the book. If the small man is someone else, he may have pity or contempt for him as he has done in the past. There is no reason why he should be choked at the eternal recurrence of the small man if he can maintain his separate identity from all the small men. When he turns out to be one of them, however, he can no longer have the distance and height for pity or contempt. He is overwhelmed with the revulsion of his own existence. But he claims to have earned his redemption. How does he get redeemed from this hell of disgust? This is the central question for his redemption. In the last chapter, we called the dwarf his shadow in Jungian language. In reality, the dwarf is more than a shadow. He is the substance. He is Zarathustra's ultimate self as a child of the earth, however disgusting he may be. This shocking self-recognition solves the riddle of his self-identity. By this self-recognition, he accepts the dwarf as his ultimate self and paves the way to his redemption. In "On the Vision and the Riddle" of Part III, the dwarf turned the philosopher's stone into Zarathustra's own self. Now we can see that the dwarf was that stone because he was the abysmal thought, Zarathustra's heaviest thought.

In "The Vision and the Riddle", he presented his vision of the eternal recurrence as a riddle. But he never explained why it was a riddle, or what sort of riddle it was. It now turns out to be the riddle of his own ultimate nature that is embedded in the eternal recurrence. This riddle unravels itself in two stages, first as a general riddle of the universe in "On the Vision and the Riddle" and then as a particular riddle of his own identity in "The Convalescent". These two stages parallel the two stages, in which the Sphinx's riddle of identity unfolded for Oedipus Rex. When Oedipus came to Thebes, he found the city plagued because no one could solve the riddle posed by the Sphinx: "Who goes on four feet in the morning, on two at noon, and on three in the evening?" He vanquished the Sphinx by answering, "Man in the three stages of his life." Although he solved this riddle of general identity for all human beings, he knew nothing about the riddle of his own identity. He knew what man was only in the abstract, but not what sort of man he was in the concrete. Only later when another plague devastated Thebes, he came to see the relevance of the Sphinx's riddle for the mystery of his own identity.

There is a neat parallel between these two stories of riddle. When the riddle of eternal recurrence was given in "On the Vision and the Riddle", the dwarf was crouching on a rock in front of Zarathustra. The dwarf crouching on a rock resembles the Sphinx crouching on a rock and announcing her riddle. We may say that the dwarf is Zarathustra's Sphinx. He is the one who states the riddle of eternal recurrence in terse language in "On the Vision and the Riddle." His statement is terse because it is meant to be a riddle. Zarathustra's elaborate explanation of his terse statement functions as his solution of the riddle. It corresponds to Oedipus's solution of the Sphinx's riddle. The Sphinx is half beast (a lion's body) and half human (a human head). She is a symbol of the chthonic force. We have repeatedly noted that the dwarf is a symbol of the chthonic force. He is also half human and half animal because he is inseparably connected to the snake. Just as the Sphinx's riddle strikes Thebes with a curse, the dwarf's riddle dooms Zarathustra's world. It hangs over his world like a curse, which he sees in his vision of the cave of decay. Like Oedipus, he must save the world from this deadly curse. When another plague descended on Thebes for the unavenged murder of Laius, Oedipus was determined to find and punish the killer to save the city. But he did not know that he was the murderer. When he forces Tiresias to speak against his will, the soothsayer says that he is the murderer he has been seeking. Outraged at this pronouncement, Oedipus reviles the soothsayer, who finally explodes, "Do you even know your parents? You, an oblivious / Enemy to all your kith and kin, both living and dead" (*Oedipus Tyrannus* 415-16). Only later Oedipus recognizes the truth of the soothsayer's pronouncement, when he hears the testimony from the herdsman, who had saved him from abandonment and brought him up as his own child.

Unlike Oedipus, Zarathustra knows the culprit for the plague and curse on his world. He has repeatedly proclaimed that the spirit of gravity is the source of all troubles in this world. But he is like Oedipus in not knowing that he is the dwarf he is determined to hunt down. Again like Oedipus, who does not know his parents, Zarathustra is an enemy oblivious to all his kith and kin. Only when he is crushed to the ground by the abysmal thought, he recognizes his kinship with the dwarf. As the Soothsayer says, "All is the same." He and the dwarf are the same children of Mother Nature. Just as Oedipus identifies himself with the murderer whom he has been seeking as a stranger and an enemy, so does Zarathustra recognize his identity with the dwarf whom he has long loathed as his archenemy. In this critical moment of self-recognition, the heart-rending truth of the Soothsayer's words breaks upon Zarathustra, as it does on Oedipus Rex. Until this critical moment, he had regarded the eternal recurrence only as a general curse on humanity. But he now recognizes this general curse as his own personal fate, just as Oedipus recognized the riddle of the Sphinx as the riddle of his own identity at his tragic moment. Thus the riddle that was initially presented as the riddle of eternal recurrence has become the riddle of Zarathustra's personal identity and condition within the ring of eternal recurrence.

We earlier noted that Zarathustra changed his mission from teaching to learning and that his own self became the object of his learning. The learning mission has climaxed in his recognition of the dwarf as his animal or physical self. His encounter with the monster has been ironically self-reflexive just like Oedipus's search for the murderer of Laius. In his search for the murderer, Oedipus was really looking for himself. Likewise, Zarathustra was summoning himself when he tried to wake up the monster. The highly self-reflexive mode of his self-discovery pervades his talk of the abysmal thought. While he is waking it up, he calls it sleepy worm. But he is the sleepy worm, who is sleepy about his own identity. The sleepy worm is finally woken "out of my depth!" The abysmal thought is not only the knowledge of what the monster stands for, but also the knowledge that he is the monster. This self-reflexive knowledge is his most abysmal thought, which constitutes his existential crisis and his redemption. As long as he looked upon the dwarf as his archenemy, he was alienating himself from his animal self. But he can overcome this self-alienation by recognizing his essential identity with the dwarf and accepting his archenemy as his ultimate self. This is his redemption from the monster that Zarathustra is talking about when he says, "But I now lie here, still weary of this biting and spewing, still sick from my own redemption. (Z, 218)"

What does it mean to bite off the snake's head? Paul S. Loeb gives an excellent account of the standard understanding of this metaphor. To bite off the snake's head has been taken to mean to overcome the nausea that is induced by the eternal recurrence of the small man. Loeb elaborates this standard view by identifying the snake as the eternal recurrence and by dividing the snake into two segments. The head stands for the present moment that is now in the gateway, and the tail for the past that has transpired to the present moment. Loeb holds that to bite off the snake's head means "to end the present existence of the dwarfish humankind" and its future repetition in the eternal recurrence ("The Dwarf, the Dragon, and Ring of Eternal Recurrence", 104-6). This is a highly implausible view. Nobody can bite off the head of the eternal ring and alter its future. The eternal ring is eternally fixed. The more plausible way is to take the snake as one's own life rather than as the eternal recurrence. On this hypothesis, to bite off the snake's head has been taken as the courageous act of accepting life. But to bite off the snake's head means to kill the snake. If the snake stands for one's life, how can you accept it by killing it? Furthermore, to spit out the head after biting it off is clearly an act of rejection rather than of acceptance. For a symbol of acceptance, the act of swallowing the snake would be much more suitable. David Allison says that the shepherd bites off the head of the snake to swallow its truth (*Reading the New Nietzsche*, 163). But the text says nothing about swallowing. After biting off the snake's head, Zarathustra spits it out.

The distinction between the snake's head and body may stand for the distinction between the future and the past, as Loeb says. The head looks forward, while the body trails from behind. The relation of head and body may represent the relation between the forward-looking autonomous will and the backward-looking heteronomous will. Therefore, to bite off the snake's head and to spit it out is to demolish and discard the illusory idea of the autonomous will. This is indeed a devastating blow to human dignity. In our normal understanding, the autonomous will is taken to be our most precious feature. As we noted earlier, the demise of autonomous will forecloses the possibility of creating values. If we cannot create our own values, our existence can have no meaning whatsoever. This nihilism of values is the consequence of realizing that the autonomous will is only an illusion. This realization is so devastating for Zarathustra that he cannot eat or drink for seven days. But he has achieved his redemption, namely, the redemption from the curse of the dwarf. This curse is none other than the paralyzing terror that the autonomous will is overpowered by the dwarf's accidental will.

Zarathustra dissolves the dwarf's curse by two simultaneous strokes. The first stroke is to recognize the illusory character of the autonomous will. If the Faustian idea of autonomous will is illusory, it cannot be a disaster to have this idea quashed. On the contrary, it should be a release from the Faustian yoke of an illusion. The second stroke is Zarathustra's recognition of his identity with the dwarf. This is to accept the heteronomous Spinozan will as his own, thereby identifying himself with the dwarf, the agent of the accidental will. The acceptance of the Spinozan will is equivalent to the third formula of redemption advocated in "On Redemption" of Part II, that is, the act of willing the past as it was. For the Spinozan will is the outcome of past accidents. In short, to reject the autonomous will as an illusory idea is the same as to accept the heteronomous will as the only real will in the world. Zarathustra's recognition of his identity with the dwarf also dissolves the illusion that he is persecuted by the dwarf. This illusion can be sustained only so long as the dwarf is erroneously believed to be his archenemy. By recognizing his identity with the dwarf, he can not only free himself from this illusion of persecution, but also rejoice in the power of his archenemy because it is his own power. This is his redemption.

In "On Those Who Are Sublime" of Part II, he said that the sublime one must redeem his own monsters and solve his own riddles before he can become a superhero. He has indeed solved his own riddles and redeemed his own monsters. In the last chapter, we noted that his remarks on the sublime ones were highly self-reflexive. He is now transforming himself from a stiff monster to a graceful superhero, and this transformation is Spinoza's solution for the problem of determinism and free will. Most of us feel free because we are not critically conscious of the causal conditions of our will. Therefore the uncritical feeling of freedom is an illusion, according to Spinoza. True freedom lies in the acceptance of cosmic necessity; free will is the union of the will and cosmic necessity. Kant's doctrine that human will was free in the noumenal world but determined in the phenomenal world was his way of appropriating Spinoza's doctrine of freedom. But his followers could not accept his demarcation between the two worlds of phenomena and noumena for their theory of freedom. By rejecting this demarcation, they retrieved Spinoza's naturalism and tried to resolve the problem of freedom within the natural world. Fichte took the lead in turning the problem of free will into the primary issue for philosophy and reinstated Spinoza's thesis that freedom lies in the union of the will and cosmic necessity. Fichte's position became the centerpiece of German philosophy and was accepted by all his successors in German Idealism: Hegel, Schelling, and Schopenhauer. In his ordeal with the abysmal thought, Zarathustra is following in the footsteps of these German philosophers and rediscovering Spinoza's teaching on the nature of human will.

On the discovery of his own abysmal self-identity, Zarathustra is not as candid as Oedipus was. At the stunning moment of denouement, Oedipus openly admitted his own crushing identity, "I am exposed— born to forbidden parents, joined / in forbidden marriage, I brought forbidden death. (*Oedipus Tyrannus* 1184-85)." But Zarathustra refuses to make the humiliating declaration that the loathsome dwarf has turned out to be his own self. He wants to keep it as his secret like a sphinx. After all his contempt for humanity and his boast of superhuman aspiration, it should be horrendously difficult for him to divulge this secret. In "On the Way of the Creator" of Part I, he said, "But the worst enemy you can encounter will always be you, yourself; you lie in wait for yourself in caves and woods" (*Z*, 64). Indeed, his worst enemy has turned out to be his own self. But this self-discovery is so devastating that he cannot reveal it even to his animals. His self-revelation cannot keep up with his self-recognition. He is behaving like a sphinx.

This is the most intriguing feature of his tragedy that goes against the standard mode of denouement. Now that he has identified himself as the dwarf, he is indeed a sphinx, partly human and partly animal. But this is not the first time he is playing the sphinx game. He played it in keeping his terrifying thought to himself when he talked of the impossible task of redeeming the past to his disciples in "On Redemption" of Part II. He again refused to express his terrifying thought to the awesome lady of midnight in "The Stillest Hour" of Part II. In chapter 2, we called it the game of masks and concealment. His game of sphinx has evolved out of his game of masks. Although his audience has changed in these games, he has been struggling with the same terrifying thought. But the present round of his sphinx game is not going to be the end of it. He will keep playing the same game to the end of his career and will never openly declare his humiliating identity with the loathsome dwarf. This endless game of secrecy is the main obstacle for recognizing the plotline of his epic journey.

Even if Zarathustra were to declare his crushing thought to his animals, they could not understand it. He is going through a uniquely human agony that can never make any sense to his animals. In his preliminary talk to them, he extensively elaborated on the illusion of communication between two souls, which live in two different worlds. He said that words and sounds are the illusive bridges between things eternally divided and that the smallest cleft is the hardest to bridge. Only now can we see the important function of that strange preliminary talk. His animals could not understand his disgust with his animal self, which is no different from them. This is the chasm that divides the animal and the human world. But the unbridgeable chasm does not lie only between Zarathustra and his animals. It also blocks the communication and understanding between him and his animal self. While his eagle and his serpent were flying high in the Prologue, he called the eagle his pride and the serpent his knowledge. He wished to be as wise as his serpent. Because that was impossible, he said, "so I ask my pride that it always go along with my wisdom. And when my wisdom leaves me one day—alas, it loves to fly away—let my pride then fly with my folly" (Z, 25). In Part I, the pride of Zarathustra's individual self flew without the knowledge of the serpent. But the serpent started crawling back in Part II and almost choked him to death in Part III. But his crushed pride still stands between him and his animals.

The pride of being human and having an autonomous will is the cause of man's cruelty against himself. Just before the outburst of his great disgust with man, Zarathustra says, "For man is the cruelest animal" (Z, 218). With this statement, he opens a long talk on human cruelty. Because human beings are cruel, they greatly enjoy tragedies, bullfights, and crucifixions, and have invented hell as their heaven on earth. But he is not talking about man's cruelty against others. He restates his thesis, "Man is the cruelest animal against himself" (Z, 218). By this enigmatic statement, he is stressing man's cruelty against his animal self. He points out the voluptuous delight in the complaints and accusations of all those who call themselves sinners, cross-bearers, penitents. That is, they are experiencing sadistic pleasure in cruelly treating their own bodies by branding their animal selves as sinners, crucifying them, and chastising them as penitents. They have also invented hell for the chastisement of the body and its devilish passions. In Part I, Zarathustra extensively scrutinized these cruel measures that arise from the hatred of one's own body. Ironically, however, he has used the same measures of cruelty in his relentless war against his own animal self, the spirit of gravity, which he designated as his devil and his archenemy. In "On Reading and Writing" of Part I, he said, "Come, let us kill the spirit of gravity" (*Z*, 41). He even claimed to have conquered the dwarf in "On the Spirit of Gravity." His attempt to fight and conquer the dwarf is his cruelty against his animal self, which is as cruel as the Christian battle against the body. Hence his talk on human cruelty is a self-referential confession. So he says, "And I myself—do I thus want to be man's accuser?" (*Z*, 218). He wants to accuse not man, but himself.

Then he tells his animals, "Alas, my animals, only this have I learned so far, that man needs what is most evil in him for what is best in him— that whatever is most evil is his best power and the hardest stone for the highest creator; and that man must become better and more evil" (*Z*, 218f). What is most evil in man is his body, his animal self, because it has been regarded as the root of all human evils. He now recognizes it as the best in man because it is the ultimate source of all human power as a child of Mother Nature. He calls it the hardest stone. His animal self, the dwarf is the hardest stone of the earth, as we noted in the last chapter. But he could not see this fundamental truth of his own animal self for a long time because his pride stood as the unbridgeable chasm between the humans and the animals. Because of his blindness, he has not only hated the dwarf, but also projected his hatred on all others. When he came down from the mountain cave, he started pouring out his contempt for the various groups of human beings, one after another, for example, the secular crowd in the market place, the preachers of the other world, the despisers of the body, the rabble, the tarantulas, the scholars, and the poets. His hatred of these people culminated in his revenge against time and the past in "On Redemption" of Part II. But his hatred had ironically stemmed from his love of humanity. On his way down to The Motley Cow, he told the hermit that he was taking his gift to humanity because he loved human beings. By asserting his love of humanity, however, he came to hate and despise human beings because they could not measure up to his superhuman ideal. His love of humanity was not love, pure and simple. It was really the assertion of his Faustian will, which bred his great disgust with all humans, because all of them appeared to be pathetic dwarfs when they were measured against his Faustian ideal of the superman.

To be sure, Zarathustra did not share the same reason with the Christians for hating the animal self. He hated it because it had no power to stand against the accidents in the world. He could never have the autonomous will as long as he was saddled with his animal self, because it was only a link in the physical causal chain. He could never be the self he wanted to be, but only the self that was imposed on him by external forces against his will. This harsh enslavement to the physical had made his animal self look like an ugly dwarf. But this ugly animal has now turned out to be his most precious self. He says to his animals, "Alas, my animals, only this have I learned so far, that man needs what is most evil in him for what is best in him." This enigmatic statement is his sphinx way of admitting to his animals that his animal self is his best asset although it looks like the worst. It is important to note that he makes this admission to his animals and that he is talking with his animals for the first time in the book. This rare event indicates that his animals are closely affiliated with his animal self. One of his animals is the serpent, which is interchangeable with the dwarf, his animal self. The conversation between him and his animals can be taken as a symbol of his communion with his animal self. After he was clobbered by the abysmal thought, he was nursed and kept alive by his animals. That may mean that he was sustained by the power of his animal self during the crisis. In that case, it is the testimony in support of his claim that his animal self is his most precious asset. Thus his seven-day ordeal establishes the critical position of his animals and his animal self in his epic journey.

Mother Nature and her Poetic Images (Part III.2, 4, 13)

After Zarathustra's explosion of his great disgust with man, his animals ask him to stop speaking and go out to the world that awaits him like a garden. They recommend singing for his convalescence and then sing a long song to cheer him up. Suspecting that he wants to die, they try to fathom his fear of death, that is, he may fear that he will become nothing when he dies because the soul is as mortal as the body. They try to dissolve this presumed fear by saying that he will come back again and again because he is entangled in the causal chain of eternal recurrence. That is, his immortality is secured in the eternal recurrence. Bernd Magnus says that the doctrine of eternal recurrence may express *kronophobia*, the fear that time will destroy everything (*Nietzsche's Existential Imperative,* 190-95). This fear may be attributed to Zarathustra's animals, but not to him. Hence their attempt to console him backfires. Their talk of eternal recurrence and its immutable causal chain only aggravates Zarathustra's revulsion, because it reminds him of the inevitable recurrence of the disgusting small man. But the animals have no understanding of his disgust because of the unbridgeable chasm between the humans and the animals.

The animals conclude their final song by predicting that Zarathustra will return again and again to teach the eternal recurrence of all things and to proclaim the superman. Then they add an intriguing sentence: "I spoke my word, I break to pieces (*zerbreche*) at my word: thus my eternal lot wants it; as a proclaimer I perish." This sentence, which is supposed to represent Zarathustra's thought, echoes back to the stern command from the voiceless voice in "The Stillest Hour" of Part II: "Speak thy word and break (*zerbrich*) to pieces." What is the word to be spoken? It is the unspeakable 'it'. It is the collision of two wills, which are now stated in terms of Zarathustra's two missions mentioned by the animals: to teach the eternal recurrence and to proclaim the superman. In proclaiming the superman, he placed all his hope on the autonomous creative will, but its possibility has been shattered by the heteronomous will embedded in the iron ring of eternal recurrence.

If Zarathustra had spoken "it" out loud, he would have broken to pieces long ago. So he refused to say it to the hunchback and to his disciples in "On Redemption" of Part II. For this refusal, the awesome lady in "The Stillest Hour" of Part II became angry and told him: "Speak thy word and break (*zerbrich*) to pieces." He was then resisting her command for him to go through the metamorphosis from a lion to a child. He has now finally spoken "it" and is indeed broken to pieces. In "On Self-Overcoming" of Part II, he said, "But a more violent force and a new overcoming grow out of your values and break egg and eggshell" (*Z*, 116). His leonine self is an old egg, whose shell has to be broken for the birth of his new self as a child of innocence. His breaking to pieces is his going under. So the animals conclude their final song: "The hour has now come when he who goes under should bless himself. Thus *ends* Zarathustra's going under" (*Z*, 221). His going under was prefigured by the tightrope walker's death in the Prologue. Just before this accident, Zarathustra warned against the grave hazard of crossing over the abyss. This warning has come true. He has been shattered by the monster from the abyss, who has played the jester for tripping the tightrope-walker.

The conclusion of the animal's last song states the mystery of Zarathustra's redemption: He is redeemed by being broken to pieces and by going under. This is the Dionysian form of redemption: Dionysus is dismembered for his rebirth. By being broken as a lion of the autonomous will, he takes the decisive step for becoming a child of the heteronomous will. This has been accomplished by the shattering recognition that the autonomous will is an illusion. This simple idea does not really come from the eternal recurrence. It is dictated by determinism. A glimmer of this thought terrified him well before his vision of the eternal recurrence in "On the Vision and the Riddle." He was so scared of it that he had to stop his discourse in "On Redemption" and it became the unspeakable "it" in his dialogue with the voiceless voice in "The Stillest Hour" of Part II. These two events take place prior to the official announcement of eternal recurrence in "On the Vision and the Riddle." There is no need to deploy the intricate notion of eternal recurrence. In "Before Sunrise" the same simple idea of determinism is restated as the cosmic necessity that governs the azure bell without any reference to the eternal recurrence, even though this doctrine has already been announced by then. The doctrine of eternal recurrence is not required to generate the abysmal thought. It is the thought from the abyss concerning the deterministic universe and its consequent nihilism. Nietzsche attributes the horror of European nihilism to the determinism of the Buddha and

Spinoza and points out that the eternal recurrence only depicts this horror of deterministic nihilism in its most terrible form (*WP* 55).

So there are two ways of representing the abysmal thought and its nihilism. One is to understand it as the crushing weight of determinism, and the other as the stifling prison of eternal recurrence. The former is situated in a linear world, and the latter in a circular world. The linear picture is largely Zarathustra's own; he presented it in "On Redemption." The circular picture is closely associated with the dwarf and his animals. In "On the Vision and the Riddle" he appeared to expound the doctrine of eternal recurrence as his own. But we noted that his talk was only an elaboration on the dwarf's bald statement that the time line was a circle. This bald statement is restated by his animals when they take the eternal recurrence as a natural cycle of seasons that goes around in an endless dance of renewal and return. This highly natural view of eternal recurrence need not entail the recurrence of every particular individual and events. Zarathustra himself seldom dwells on such recurrence. His statement "The small man recurs eternally!" may sound like it. But he never talks about the return of any particular individual in "The Convalescent" because he uses "the small man" as a generic term. Even a linear deterministic world can guarantee the return of the small man forever, because it eternally creates the puppets of cosmic necessity.

The story of eternal recurrence may be no more than a poetic parable for describing a deterministic universe. Roger Hollinrake says that the dread of determinism is conveyed by Zarathustra's disgust with the eternal recurrence of the smallest man in "The Convalescent" (*Nietzsche, Wagner, and the Philosophy of Pessimism,* 9). In the last chapter, we noted that Zarathustra's discussion with the dwarf on the eternal recurrence was a reenactment of Nietzsche's vision of 1881 at the rock of Surlei. That must have been only a poetic or metaphoric vision. In addition to determinism, the metaphor of eternal recurrence signifies the eternity of the world. Whereas the Christian world has a beginning and an end, the world of eternal recurrence has no beginning and no end. The conception of the world as an eternal existence had ruled antiquity before it was replaced by Christian creationism. This point is well documented by

Bernd Magnus in his brief genealogy of eternal recurrence (*Nietzsche's Existential Imperative*, 47-68). The eternity of the world was usually conceived as an endless repetition of the cosmic cycle. In *Ecce Homo* (*The Birth of Tragedy* 3), Nietzsche notes that the doctrine of eternal recurrence could have been taught by Heraclitus and that its traces can be found in the Stoic writings. He indeed advocated a cyclic cosmology: The universe is made of fire and oscillates between chaos and order. Magnus cites a Stoic exposition of this view by Zeno of Citium: "Next, the whole cosmos at certain fated periods is dissolved by fire, and then again formed into a world" (*Nietzsche's Existential Imperative*, 52).

In the ancient world, the cyclic cosmology was not a Stoic monopoly. The Pythagoreans had developed their own version, which is much closer to Nietzsche's than the Stoic-Heraclitean version, although he may not have been aware of it. These two versions differ on two points. According to the Stoic-Heraclitean version, every cosmic cycle begins and ends with a cataclysmic conflagration, but no cycle is the exact repetition of a previous cycle. These two features were not retained in the Pythagorean version: There are no catastrophes to mark the beginning and the end of a cycle, and every cycle is the same as every other cycle (*Nietzsche's Existential Imperative*, 60). Although the doctrine of eternal recurrence sounds strange to our ears, it was a prevalent view of the world in the pagan antiquity. It was so prevalent in the ancient world that Augustine felt the need to explain the motivation for this cosmic view. Because the pagans had assumed the eternity of the world, they could not accept the linear view of time and history that had a definite point of beginning. Hence they were compelled to accept the cyclical view that had neither the beginning nor the end (*The City of God*, bk. 12, ch. 13).

The cyclic cosmology was also dominant in ancient India, where the universe was understood to be the endless cycles of creation and destruction. In Hinduism, those endless cycles were pictured as the cosmic dance of Shiva. Although such cyclic views lasted a long time in India and many other parts of the world, they faded away in Europe with the ascendancy of Christian cosmology. The Christians rejected the eternal existence of the world because it was incompatible with their dogma of divine creation. But the eternity of the world came back with the recovery of classical learning in modern Europe. Their advocates such as Giordano Bruno had to brave the brutal persecution by the Christian Church. Even in the seventeenth century, Baruch Spinoza was not safe. By the nineteenth century, European scientists could accept the eternity of the world without the fear of persecution. Some of them even revived the cyclic cosmology (Magnus, *Nietzsche's Existential Imperative*, 64-65; Paul Davies, *The Fifth Miracle,* 248). This revival provides the background for Nietzsche's and Zarathustra's vision of eternal recurrence. In this vision, they are trying to restore three features of the universe, its eternity, necessity, and independence, which had been suppressed and forgotten in the long reign of Christianity. The natural world is eternal because there is no god to create or destroy it. The eternal world is also the necessary world. The Christian world is not necessary but contingent, that is, it may or may not exist, depending on God's will. The necessary world does not depend on such contingencies. It exists necessarily. Necessity also governs its operation. It acts out of its own necessity. Hence it is free of teleology unlike the Christian world. This is Spinoza's conception of Nature as the infinite substance or the eternal all-embracing reality. Because Nature is the cause of its own being, *causa sui,* it does not serve any external function.

Spinoza's repudiation of teleology can easily lead to a gross misunderstanding of his conception of Nature. His assertion that the physical world is free of teleology and governed by its own necessity may give the impression that he is advocating a mechanistic universe, that is, Nature is made of dead matter. But nothing could be further from his view of Nature. On the mechanistic view, matter has no power of motion. It can move only by being pushed by external forces. Neither can it have any purpose of its own unless it is given by an external agent. That is the Christian conception of the world. It can move only when God gives it the power to move. Its history can have a purpose only because God gives it. This is the picture of the world that is portrayed by Saint Augustine in *The City of God.* Spinoza is repudiating this Christian picture of the world by rejecting teleology. On Christian theology, God is *causa sui* and the world is an effect of this ultimate cause. In Spinoza's philosophy, on the other hand, Nature is not an effect but *causa sui*. She is God. She does not need any external force for motion because her essence is power. She cannot derive any power from anything outside her because there is nothing outside her. For the same reason, she can gain no purpose from outside for her motion. She moves by the necessity of her own nature. Her actions only express her nature. That may be regarded as her purpose or teleology. Let us call it internal or immanent teleology in distinction from the Christian external or transcendent teleology. Thus understood, Spinoza's teleology is the same as Hegel's. In fact, Hegel's teleology is an adaptation of Spinoza's. The teleology that Spinoza rejects may well be Aristotle's teleology. The latter may appear to be internal teleology because the final cause is built into the essence of each species. But the final causes are derived from the Prime Mover, which stands above and beyond all species. Hence Aristotelian teleology is external and transcendent rather than internal and immanent because it is under the control of an external and transcendent power.

Nietzsche's conception of Nature is equally open for serious misunderstanding. Like Spinoza, he repudiates teleology and all its paraphernalia (aims and wishes, intentions and purposes). Again like Spinoza, he also emphatically rejects mechanistic reduction. On these two issues, Zarathustra faithfully follows Nietzsche. We have seen that he rejects the mechanistic view of Nature in "The Soothsayer" of Part II, where he affirms the inexhaustible power of life as the essence of the physical world. This is his doctrine of will to power. We have noted that the will to power is Life, Mother Nature. In that case, he cannot easily repudiate teleology because it is indispensable to the will to power. But we have seen that he repudiates all aims and purposes in "Before Sunrise" of Part III. This goes against his own preaching. When he announces the superman in the Prologue, we noted, he appeals to the cosmic principle of creative evolution. We also noted that his theory of evolution is not the Darwinian principle of chance mutation, which is totally devoid of teleology. Zarathustra presents his theory of evolution as a matter of the will rather than chance. This obvious discrepancy between his preaching of the superman and his repudiation of teleology can be dissolved by adopting the distinction between the internal and the external teleology. If the superhuman ideal is imposed on humanity externally, it will be an external teleology like the Christian ideal of obeying God. On the other hand, if the same ideal arises out of human nature by necessity, it will be an internal teleology. The Faustian superman acts as an agent of external teleology by hoisting his ideal as his own creation and tries to dictate it to all human beings. On the other hand, the Spinozan superman acts as an agent of internal teleology by recognizing his ideal as a necessary expression of Mother Nature. Whereas the Faustian superman claims his creativity as the expression of his autonomous will, the Spinozan superman recognizes it as his fatality or the necessity of his nature.

Nietzsche explains the teleology of inner necessity by his notion of *how one becomes what one is* (*EH* II.9). At the outset of his career, he did not have the remotest idea of what he was. He describes how his task of *a revaluation of values* has worked itself out subconsciously:

> In the meantime, the organizing 'idea' destined to rule grows and grows in the depths—it begins to command, it slowly leads *back* from sidepaths and wrong turnings, it prepares individual qualities and abilities which will one day prove themselves indispensable as means to achieving the whole. (*EH*, II.9)

This subconscious process had nothing to do with his desires or goals. He explains,

> To 'want' something, to 'strive' after something, to have a 'goal', a 'wish' in view—I know none of this from experience. Even at this moment, I look out upon my future—a *distant* future!—as upon a smooth sea: it is ruffled by no desire. I do not want in the slightest that anything should become other than it is; I do not want myself to become other than I am. (*EH*, II.9)

By his disavowal of desires and goals, he appears to repudiate teleology altogether from his life. But there is a mightier teleology at work than that of desires and goals. This is the teleological movement of the "organizing idea", which is hardly distinguishable from Hegelian teleology. Such an epochal event as Nietzsche's revaluation of values may not be only an individual affair any more than such historical events as the decline of master morality and the emergence of slave morality. All of them are cultural or spiritual developments. Spiritual health and sickness do not fall upon natural animals because they arise from human culture rather than directly from human nature. Hence decadence may be not an individual problem but a cultural one, as Daniel Conway has astutely argued in *Nietzsche's Dangerous Game*. The distinction between healthy and decadent cultures is primary; the distinction between healthy and decadent individuals is derivative. Nietzsche indeed takes such a cultural approach to the problem of masters and slaves. Although slave morality has developed a terrible spiritual sickness, he says, "something so new, so deep, so unprecedented, so enigmatic *and pregnant with the future* came into existence that the earth's aspect was essentially altered" (*GM* II.16). The earth's aspect cannot be affected by individual events. He goes on to say that it took divine spectators to appreciate fully this drama. He is talking about a cultural and historical drama. Then he identifies someone pregnant with the future as Zarathustra the godless (*GM* II.25). That is, he looks upon the advent of the superman as the final outcome of this historical and cultural drama.

John Richardson says that there is a dialectical development in the transformation of healthy and decadent cultures (*Nietzsche's System*, 68). Master morality produces slave morality, which in turn prepares a fertile ground for the genesis of the superman. Richardson regards the superman as the synthesis of master and slave. The masters had never developed the spiritual dimension of human existence; the slaves developed it through their suffering. The superman combines the spiritual dimension of slaves with the lordly dimension of masters. If this is the correct account of the nature of superman, it follows the Hegelian schema of cultural dialectic, that is, the development of conflicting cultural ideals. Hence Nietzsche's philosophy of culture is as teleological as Hegel's. But we will later see that the schema of Nietzschean existential dialectic clearly diverges from the Hegelian schema. Nevertheless, both of them are the dialectical schemata of inner necessity. They have been devised as two different developmental frameworks for Spinoza's philosophy.

Let us get back to Christian theology and teleology. The three attributes—eternity, necessity, and sovereignty—were assigned to God. The Christians had transferred these attributes from Nature to their God. In ancient Greece, Nature alone was the only eternal and necessary being, while their gods and goddesses were her contingent products. Spinoza restored these three attributes to Nature and then endowed her with one attribute, which was never associated with Nature in ancient Greece. This is the attribute of thought or mind, which had been assumed to be the special attribute of the gods and the living beings. With the addition of this attribute, Spinoza's Nature has gained all the attributes that had been assigned to the Christian God. Therefore, he has the right to say that Nature is God. This is his naturalization of God, and Zarathustra is revising it in his doctrine of eternal recurrence. He replaces the attribute of thought with the attribute of life. This refinement of Spinoza's doctrine has been made by Goethe, who regarded life as more basic than thought.

In chapter 2, we compared Zarathustra's descent to the abyss to Faust's descent to the underworld of the Eternal Mothers, which Mephistopheles describes as the everlasting void containing only Nothing (*Faust* 6246-56). When Faust descends there, he finds it totally devoid of life. Although nothing lives there, the moving forms of life swarm around in the eternal mode (*Faust* 6429-32). The eternal void full of the moving forms of life becomes Zarathustra's dungeon of death that explodes with force of life in "The Soothsayer" of Part II. This explosion blows apart his misconception that the world is made of dead matter and revives his faith in Life's teaching that she is the eternal fountain of universal living force. She is Mother Nature, Nietzsche's counterpart to Goethe's Eternal Mothers. As we will see later, the ring of eternal recurrence is the eternal dance of Mother Nature, Spinoza's God. The existence of living beings is not a fluke that may or may not happen in the course of Nature's history. As one of the essential features of Nature, Life is as eternal and as necessary as the ring of eternal recurrence. Life is coextensive with the eternal ring. Zarathustra's cosmology is very much like Fred Hoyle's theory of steady-state universe, in which eternal life produces an infinite number of biosystems on an infinite number of planets (*The Intelligent Universe*). The inexhaustibility of life force is expressed in the endless cycles of biosystems. Likewise, the eternal recurrence expresses the inexhaustible power of Life. This is Zarathustra's contribution to Spinoza's project of naturalizing the Christian God. The eternal recurrence is being used as a poetic device in this contribution. This is my reason for treating it as a poetic parable.

We should remember that Zarathustra gained the vision of eternal recurrence after his descent to deep reality as a penitent poet. To take the eternal recurrence as a poetic image has theoretical and practical advantages. Many commentators have pointed out the implausibility of eternal recurrence for two reasons. First, it violates Leibniz's principle of identity. If the repetition of an object or event is truly identical with its previous incarnation, it cannot be a repetition because the two cannot be distinguished from each other. Second, it is scientifically groundless. Hence Babette Babich regards the eternal recurrence as the stumbling block for the interpreters of Nietzsche's thought (*Nietzsche's Philosophy of Science*, 262-63). Regarding the enormous difficulty of accepting the eternal recurrence as a cosmological theory, she says, "How incredulous would we need be! Better to ask, how naïve *should* we get!" (*Nietzsche's Philosophy of Science,* 285). The cosmological version is to take the eternal recurrence in its literal sense. Surely, it would take the extremely naïve and gullible ones like Zarathustra's animals to accept the eternal recurrence in its literal sense. Those brutes are the only ones who take it literally in Zarathustra's world. This point has not escaped Maudemarie Clark's attention. After noting Zarathustra's own ambiguous attitude to the truth of eternal recurrence, she says, "Only the animals express belief in recurrence." She hastens to add that Zarathustra responds to their version of eternal recurrence by calling them buffoons and barrel organs (*Nietzsche on Truth and Philosophy,* 256). If it is naïve and ludicrous to take it literally, the only sensible alternative is to take it metaphorically. That is the only way to avoid behaving like Zarathustra's naïve animals.

In addition to this theoretical advantage, it can provide the practical advantage in portraying the rigor of cosmic necessity. Determinism is not limited to Western scientific materialism. The Christian doctrine of pre-destination was a form of determinism. So was the Buddhist doctrine of *karma*. Determinism is one of the most ancient doctrines that know no cultural and historical boundaries. But it has always provoked the temp-tation to soften its rigor for the practical purpose of coping with human existence by finding some escape hatches from the wheel of cosmic ne-cessity. Some Buddhists have maintained that one can change one's fate by one's effort, although it is subject to the chain of *karma*. Many Chris-tian theologians have proposed similar revisions and taught that human beings can participate in the fulfillment of their predestination by the ex-ercise of free will. These are the typical attempts to dilute the rigor of de-terminism. But the poetic picture of eternal recurrence leaves no room for such attempts of dilution. There is no way to tinker with the present and the future that are destined to be the exact repetitions of the past.

To be sure, the abysmal thought of determinism could have been stated without the poetic imagery of eternal recurrence. But such a sim-ple straightforward exposition would never have generated the sort of poetic mystification that has grown around this imagery. As Zarathustra says in "On Poets" of Part II, the poets love to mystify their audience. He also said that a poet's trick and trade is to make up parables. As a poet, he is entitled to a few tricks of poetic mystification. In addition to the po-etic metaphor of eternal recurrence, he employs another one, the monster from the abyss who clobbers and leaves him almost dead for seven days. It is far more difficult to take this story in its literal sense than the eternal recurrence. But the monster unloads the full force of the devastating doc-trine contained in the metaphor of eternal recurrence. If the monster is taken as a metaphor, the eternal recurrence should also be so taken be-cause these two metaphors go together hand in hand. It offends our po-etic sensitivity to take one of them literally and the other allegorically. The same problem arises with the azure bell. In the last chapter, we noted that the azure bell is a cosmic metaphor equivalent to the ring of eternal recurrence. The latter is a two-dimensional image; the former is a three-dimensional image. In spite of this difference, both of them poetically express Spinoza's conception of Mother Nature as the infinite substance, the all-embracing eternal reality. There can be nothing outside (spatially and temporally) the azure bell or the eternal ring. The equivalence of these two metaphors becomes obvious when the eternal ring is described as the well of eternity, which is three-dimensional like the azure bell. The poetic image of the eternal ring is given in a long series of metaphors, which may be called the imagery of eternal recurrence. By understanding the flow of this imagery, we should be able to see through the poetic tricks of mystification instead of turning them into our stumbling blocks.

The imagery of eternal recurrence has been progressively ramified and elaborated in response to Zarathustra's expanding knowledge of the universe. The expanding imagery finally explodes in "The Convalescent", when he is clobbered by the composite monster of the dwarf and the snake. This is his existential encounter with the eternal recurrence. He now realizes that he is only one of the countless helpless dwarfs forever chained to the iron ring of eternal recurrence. This is the eternal curse from the abyss. He secures his redemption from this curse by identifying himself with the dwarf and by denying the autonomous will and accepting the heteronomous will as the only real will. This is his simple solution for the problem of suffering in the ring of eternal recurrence.

The Hero and the Superhero (Part III.13)

This simple solution is Spinoza's teaching. It only requires the wisdom and courage to accept the fact that the very idea of the autonomous will is only an illusion. We have to give up the idea that our aims and goals are the products of our own will. On the contrary, they are the manifestations of cosmic necessity, the sun-will. This is again Spinoza's teaching, which is cited by Nietzsche:

> Can we remove the idea of a goal from the process and then affirm the process in spite of this?—This would be the case if something were attained at every moment within this pro-

cess—and always the same. Spinoza reached such an affirmative position in so far as every moment has a logical necessity,
and with his basic instinct, which was logical, he felt a sense
of triumph that the world should be constituted that way. (*WP
55*)

In Spinoza's philosophy, there is no teleology: no external goals or ideals
can ever be imposed on the world. This is not to say that we can have no
desires or make no choices. Whatever desires we may have or whatever
choices we may make, they all belong to the cosmic process of working
out the necessary essence of the infinite substance. Whether our desires
and choices are fulfilled or frustrated, every moment of our existence is
governed by the same cosmic necessity. By understanding such a comprehensive necessity of the universe, Nietzsche notes, Spinoza felt "a
sense of triumph." This sense of triumph is reflected in the superhuman
laughter of the shepherd in "On the Vision and the Riddle" of Part III.

Spinoza's simple solution, however, is not easy to embrace, especially for those who cherish their creative will and try to seek their meaning of life in their project of self-creation. That is why Zarathustra has to
go through a complicated maneuver of evasion and detour in his ordeal
of nausea and disgust. It is emotionally devastating to concede that the
autonomous will is only an illusion. But to recognize this illusion is the
prerequisite for accepting cosmic necessity as one's real will. The transition from the autonomous Faustian will to the heteronomous Spinozan
will is the transformation of a lion into a child in the scheme of three
metamorphoses. The difference between a lion and a child can be restated as the difference between the hero and the superhero, which
Zarathustra talked of in "On Those Who Are Sublime" of Part II. The
hero is like the lion, who asserts its strong will to conquer and control the
world. He is a battle-scarred warrior. But the superhero is like the child,
who "stands with relaxed muscles and unharnessed will." His unharnessed will is the will of a child. The child is relaxed and beautiful; the
scarred warrior is stiff and ugly. In "The Stillest Hour", Zarathustra was
ordered to become a child. In "The Convalescence" the animals conclude
their final song with a reference to this order.

The hero is the Faustian superman; the superhero is the Spinozan superman. The former has the audacity to assert his power against the whole world; the latter has the wisdom to see the whole world as the matrix of his power. These two correspond to the two worldviews we discussed earlier: the Apollonian view given by Zarathustra's day-wisdom and the Dionysian view given by his night-wisdom. On the Apollonian view, the world is measurable and controllable; on the Dionysian view, the world is immeasurable and uncontrollable. The Faustian hero stands on the Apollonian worldview in asserting his autonomous will; the Spinozan superhero thrives under the Dionysian worldview in accepting his heteronomous will. Zarathustra feels inordinate pride in his image of himself as the Faustian superman. When that self-image is shattered, however, his pride turns into unbearable despair. Spinoza says that the greatest pride and the greatest despair arise from the ignorance of oneself (*Ethics,* pt. 4, prop. 56). Zarathustra's pride and despair have been generated by his illusion about his own self, which he can overcome only by recognizing the dwarf as his ultimate self. By this move of self-understanding, the force of nature and its cosmic necessity cease to be alien and hostile to his own self because they are embodied in the dwarf, his ultimate self. Thus he dies as the Faustian superman, but emerges as the Spinozan superman. This is what Richard Schacht calls the transformation of Zarathustra from an Apollonian to a Dionysian figure ("Zarathustra/*Zarathustra*", 232). This important event is his destiny or fate (*Schicksal*). The word 'destiny' is seldom used lightly in *Thus Spoke Zarathustra*. It is used never in the Faustian phase of Zarathustra's career, but only in its Spinozan phase. It is used for the first time "On Involuntary Bliss", shortly after the vision of eternal recurrence. Zarathustra uses it twice when he kneels before his sun-will in "On Old and New Tablets". In "The Convalescent", his animals mention it four times in urging him to bear his great destiny as the teacher of eternal recurrence. This shows not only that his destiny is determined by the eternal recurrence, but also that his animals know it because they are the agents of destiny.

The difference between the two types of superman can be restated as the difference between the epic and the tragic hero, as it was understood in ancient Greece. The epic hero has the power to conquer his world and control his destiny, but the tragic hero is not blessed with that sort of power. On the contrary, he is overpowered by fate, over which he has no control. Zarathustra's career as an epic hero begins in the Prologue and culminates in "On Old and New Tablets", but this section already contains the seed of tragic reversal. It opens with Zarathustra in the humble position of waiting for the signs that his hour has come and ends with his earnest entreaty to his sun-will. The sun-will begins to emerge in this section and crushes the autonomous will in "The Convalescent". Zarathustra as the Faustian hero breaks to pieces, but he emerges as a new subdued superhero of the Spinozan superhero.

Let us now review the difference between the Faustian and the Spinozan supermen in reference to Zarathustra's speeches in Parts I and II. The Faustian superman is striving for absolute individual sovereignty. Such an individual cannot even depend on friends and neighbors and must flee from the rabble and the state. We noted that Max Stirner advocated such unlimited individual independence as his ideal of self-possession. But his ideal is so unreal that it can be realized only in the Christian God, who depends on no one but himself. Stirner usually takes the Christian God as the model for his ideal of self-possession or self-ownership. We can now see that the Faustian superman is the humanization of the Christian ideal of God. The Faustian superman understands himself as a highly spiritual agent, as spiritual as the Christian God. But the Spinozan superman understands himself as a physical agent, that is, as physical as Spinoza's conception of nature.

In chapter 1, we noted that the Faustian superhuman ideal was the secular version of Lutheran individualism, which had developed from Martin Luther's revolt against the oppressive framework of the Roman Catholic Church for the sake of religious conscience. By the eighteenth and the nineteenth century, however, radical individualism had the danger of trapping the individuals in their narrow self-interests. To counter this dangerous tendency, many social critics advocated ideal communities for the realization of individual freedom. At the end of his long career, for example, Goethe's Faust tries to build an ideal community on a vast track of reclaimed land. Hegel exalts the state as the arena for the fullest realization of humanity, and his follower Bruno Bauer faithfully upholds this ideal as we saw in chapter 1. Ludwig Feuerbach advocates the more ambitious ideal of building a universal community of all human beings, and this universal ideal is further developed in Karl Marx's ideal of the communist utopia. Like these Hegelians, Zarathustra is also trying to work himself out of his radical individualism. But he does not accept collectivism as an adequate solution because it can also suffocate the individuals. His solution is to recognize his animal self and its connection to the entire physical world. This is his cosmic self, which is much broader than his individual self. This is the Dionysian self that stands against the Apollonian self of every individual. The Dionysian self is represented by the dwarf, the ultimate basis of Nietzschean selfhood.

Many Nietzsche scholars have said that Nietzsche has taught the virtue of egoism and the vice of altruism. But that is not the really important issue for Zarathustra because everybody is selfish by nature. What is overlooked in this debate is the scope of the self. Its scope can be narrow or broad. The ancient Chinese made the distinction between a small person (*xao ren*) and a big person (*dai ren*). A small person has a self, whose heart is too narrow to include any other interests than the paltry individual interests. On the other hand, a big person has a self, whose heart is broad enough to include the interests of many other people. Only such a person was regarded to be fit to govern the state. The Mahayana Buddhist idea of Boddhisattva is even more magnificent than the Chinese concept of a big person. The Boddhisattva identifies himself with all the living beings in the world. That is his cosmic identity of feeling and compassion. Likewise, Zarathustra identifies himself with the whole physical world when he recognizes his cosmic self. He can do this only by realizing that the idea of individual self stands on the illusory demarcation between the mental and the physical. One is usually aware of oneself in terms of one's consciousness, which appears to be independent of the physical world. But self-awareness belongs to the body, especially the brain and sense organs. Here the boundary between mind and body is an illusion. The recognition of this illusion is the essential step for recognition of the cosmic self and for the liberation from the suffocating yoke of radical individualism.

Zarathustra's conception of self is even broader and deeper than that of the Hegelians. Because of their idealistic bent, they have never fully appreciated the physical dimension of human existence as he does in his great moment of awakening and redemption. In his words, the Hegelians have never recognized themselves as the dwarfs of the earth. They have always conceived themselves as spirits. Even Marx is no exception to this Hegelian trend in spite of his trenchant critique of Hegel. The material conditions he stresses for social evolution are not really physical conditions, but social forces such as the class structure and the mode of production that are shaped by human spirits. The dialectic of these social forces is the driving force of history. In his discussion of material conditions, he rarely includes such purely physical events as our bodies and their physiology. In chapter 1, we noted the close affinity of Zarathustra's superhuman ideal with the aspiration of the Young Hegelians. But the Spinozan superman rejects this idealistic heritage and seeks its roots in the physical world. But the ultimate source for these two superhuman ideals is the concept of the almighty God that was created by the Feuerbachian projection of human ideals. These alienated ideals are reappropriated in two stages. First, the concept of God is humanized in the Faustian superman. Then, the concept of God is not only humanized but also naturalized in the Spinozan superman. The latter will appear in the cosmic self in the next section.

The Cosmic Self (Part III.14)

In "On the Great Longing", Zarathustra has a strange talk with his soul, which goes through three stages. On the first stage, he recounts everything he has done to make his soul perfect. On the second stage, he laments over the fact that his soul is still suffering from melancholy. On the third stage, he foretells his soul about her future redeemer. He has done many things to make her free, pure, and complete. The most important of all these things is to teach his soul to be one with the eternal ring. He says, "I taught you to say 'today' and 'one day' and 'formerly' and to dance away over all Here and There and Yonder" (*Z*, 221). This passage is restating what his animals said about the dance of the eternal ring: "In every Now, being begins; round every Here rolls the sphere There" (*Z*, 217-18). Since the soul has become one with the eternal ring, he asks his soul, "Where would future and past dwell closer together than in you?" (*Z*, 223). In "On the Vision and the Riddle", the Moment was described as the gateway where past and future collide with each other. In the eternal ring, however, they do not collide, but dwell close together. Thus he has given his soul the eternal perspective of eternal recurrence. Having brought his soul into this state of super-perfection, he has given her new names, 'the destiny', 'the circumference of circumferences', 'the umbilical cord of time', and 'the azure bell'. These names are different labels for the eternal ring or the universe. His soul has become coextensive with the entire universe.

There are two strange points about Zarathustra's talk with his soul. First, why does he assign a series of cosmic epithets to his soul? Second, why does he talk to his soul as though he were talking to another person? Never before has he done this. The cosmic epithets cannot apply to his soul if she is an individual entity. Robert Gooding-Williams says that his soul is envisioned as "an omnipresent, pantheistic deity" (*Zarathustra's Dionysian Modernism,* 295). In fact, Zarathustra's description of his soul in terms of cosmic attributes comes right out of Spinoza's pantheism. In his theology, the mind of God is not separate from the individual minds. The thought of God is realized in the ideas of countless individual minds. The totality of these ideas constitutes a system of ideas, the infinite idea of God, whose scope is coextensive with the world. The human mind can be viewed from two perspectives. It is seen as an individual mind from the individual perspective. But it is only a mode of the divine attribute of thought from the cosmic perspective. Insofar as an individual mind approaches the infinite divine idea, it becomes coextensive with God. The human mind can gain such a cosmic status by intellectual intuition. Then, it becomes like a pantheistic deity. In Spinoza's philosophy, the relation of human mind to divine mind mirrors the relation of human body to divine body. He says, "The order and the connection of ideas is the same as the order and connection of things [bodies]" (*Ethics,* pt. 2, prop. 7). Our bodies are individual objects only from the individual perspective, but they are parts of the divine body from the cosmic perspective. This is also true of Zarathustra's animal self, the dwarf, and his soul.

In Spinoza's philosophy, there is only one substance, which is infinite and eternal. This substance is God or Nature. The so-called individuals are the modifications of one of the infinite divine attributes. The cosmic connection of individuals to the infinite substance can be made in terms of both mind and body, because they are two of the infinite divine attributes. In Zarathustra's philosophy, the cosmic connection is chiefly made in terms of body. In "On the Despisers of the Body" of Part I, he had advocated the identity of soul and body. His soul is coextensive with the world because his body is integrally connected to it. Thus the identity of the soul and the body leads to the recognition of the soul as a cosmic entity. Hence Zarathustra talks to his soul as though it were a pantheistic deity. His soul is his cosmic self. In the last section, he took a decisive step for becoming a child by breaking his leonine self to pieces. The lion is an individual self that asserts itself against the world. To break the leonine self to pieces is to dissolve the illusory boundary between the individual and the world and to reveal the integral connection between them. Thus emerges the cosmic self, which knows, like a child, no separation from the world. Zarathustra's cosmic self and his soul is none other than the dwarf he accepted as his bodily self. The dwarf has revealed himself as his ultimate self by shattering his leonine individual self. Zarathustra ended the last section by talking with his soul and the present section is the continuation of that talk.

Because of its integral connection to the world, his soul deserves the cosmic epithets of the destiny, the circumference of circumferences, the umbilical cord of time, and the azure bell. These cosmic labels are equally applicable to the dwarf. But Zarathustra failed to recognize its cosmic attributes in "The Convalescent". Consequently, his animal self appeared to be an ugly dwarf, whereas it is now revealed as a cosmic giant. But the animal self is only a brute that has no power to recognize its own cosmic attributes. The recognition has been made by Zarathustra's individual self. That is why he claims to have given his soul its super-perfection, namely, its perfection on the cosmic level. Thus he has realized the cosmic conception of his own self that he announced at the beginning of Part III. This is the positive outcome of his seven-day ordeal in "The Convalescent". In the next section, he will encounter Life as the principle of life for his cosmic self. Zarathustra became conscious of his soul for the first time when he was overwhelmed by the immense domain of night in "The Night Song" of Part II. The cosmic self belongs to night; the individual self belongs to day. The day-world is the world of individuation; the night-world is the world of cosmic union. In the last chapter, we distinguished between the cerebral and the visceral self. The individual self rides on the cerebral (day) consciousness; the visceral feelings arise from the subconscious (night) cosmic self.

In "The Night Song", Zarathustra said, "Night has come; now all the fountains speak more loudly. And my soul too is a fountain" (Z, 107). He knew then that his soul was one of the fountains flowing out of the abyss of night. This is a poetic description of his soul from the cosmic perspective. Just as the fountain flows out of the abyss, so does the dwarf, his animal self. When you understand your self as an animal, you can readily see its connection to the entire physical world because every physical object is causally connected to every other physical object. This is the consciousness of your cosmic self. On the other hand, when you think of your self as an autonomous agent acting on the world, you instinctively feel your individual independence. This is the consciousness of your individual self facing the whole world. But the individual self and the cosmic self are not two separate entities. One and the same self can be understood from the individual and the cosmic perspectives. The consciousness of your cosmic self is not anything mysterious. Let us consider the relation of your self to your body. You regard yourself as the owner of *your* arms and *your* legs. They belong to *you* as their master and controller. So does your whole body; you call it *your* body. This is the consciousness of your individual self, which is demarcated from your body. But such demarcation is dissolved in the theory of identity between the body and the soul. On this theory, you are identical with your body. Therefore, you can neither possess, nor control your body because possession and control make sense only on the presumed demarcation between you and your body. When you completely identify your self with your body, you are your animal self, which is defined as its body ("I am my body."). But your body is physically linked to the whole world.

Consider your self-consciousness. It is causally determined by your brain state, which is in turn determined by the condition of your body, which is in turn determined by the state of the solar system, which is in turn determined by the state of the cosmos. Such a cosmically determined self cannot set its desires and feelings against the world. Even its will should be understood as an extension of cosmic necessity. You understand your cosmic self by combining two items: (1) the identity of your self with your body and (2) the physical link of your body to the world. This is not the normal conception of the self. Our normal conception naïvely presupposes the independence of the self from the world. This naïve feeling of an individual subject is abrogated by the cosmic perspective. Therefore, the consciousness of a cosmic self is much more sophisticated than the consciousness of an individual self.

The two different perspectives are important for understanding the role of the dwarf. When he is perceived as an individual, he looks like a helpless dwarf chained to the iron ring of eternal recurrence. His connection to the iron ring appears to be an accidental misfortune. This perception stands on the assumption that there is a clear boundary between the dwarf as an individual and the eternal ring. But that boundary is illusory from the cosmic perspective. The dwarf is one with the eternal ring. His inseparable connection to the ring is not accidental but essential to his nature. When this essential connection is understood, we can recognize the dwarf as a cosmic giant. He is not a puppet of the iron ring, but the master of its revolution. That is why Zarathustra called the spirit of gravity "master of the world" in "The Dancing Song" of Part II. There is only one spirit of gravity reigning over the eternal ring, but there are a countless number of dwarfs chained to that ring. But each of those numerous dwarfs is really a cosmic giant, who function as an agent of the cosmic will. When Zarathustra takes an individual perspective by asserting his individual will, all those dwarfs appear to be his enemies, who are buffeting him, individually or collectively. But when he looks upon them from the cosmic perspective, they are the essential features of his cosmic self.

Just like the dwarf, the snake can manifest itself as an individual or a cosmic entity because they are the two interchangeable symbols of Life. The cosmic snake is Life. The individual snakes make up the ball of snakes in every human soul. Because the snake can be either a cosmic or an individual entity, to bite off its head can also be taken in two ways. As we noted earlier, Paul S. Loeb takes it as the cosmic act of biting off the ring of eternal recurrence. But I have proposed to take it as the individual act of repudiating the autonomous will. The dual perspective also obtains for the will to power, which belongs to the snake. From the cosmic perspective, there is only one will to power, which belongs to Life. However, there are many individual wills to power from the individual perspective. Each individual is a dwarf, who asserts his will to power and strives to realize his project. In this existential mode, every individual becomes subject to worries and anxieties over their purposes and projects, because they can be crushed under the cosmic will to power. Thus the spirit of gravity arises from the joint operation of the individual and the cosmic will to power. In "Before Sunrise", Zarathustra said that purposes and worries are only drifting clouds in the azure bell. He called it the heaven of accident and innocence. Situated in such a heaven, one can free oneself from the spirit of gravity only by taking the cosmic perspective and completely disregarding all purposes and worries. This is to transcend the individual self and identify with the cosmic self.

The individual self is the Faustian self; the cosmic self is the Spinozan self. The latter is not an individual; it transcends the illusory idea of individuation. The distinction of these two selves concerns the important dispute on Nietzsche's conception of the self. There are two contending views on this dispute: self-creationism and fatalism. Alexander Nehamas is the leading advocate of self-creationism. According to Nietzsche, he says, human beings are totally free agents who give themselves laws and create themselves (*Nietzsche,* 174). In support of this view, some commentators have attributed the doctrine of free will and indeterminism to Nietzsche. Richard Rorty says that he recognizes no predestined place for any human being because everyone creates his or her own future. It is his understanding of Nietzsche's teaching that one does "not simply take one's place within a predetermined scheme, but change the scheme." In that regard, Nietzsche is the forerunner of existentialists like Heidegger and Sartre (*Contingency, Irony, and Solidarity,* 99, 108).

Though this is a highly popular view in Nietzsche scholarship, it can be maintained only by closing our eyes to Nietzsche's well-known determinism, which Charles Hartshorne attributes to modern scientific culture. Before the emergence of statistical mechanics and quantum mechanics, which have introduced indeterminism into scientific inquiry, he says, most European philosophers were determinists because they were trapped in the Laplacean determinism of classical mechanics. Nietzsche was no exception. Hartshorne says, "Nietzsche is a remarkable example of the grip of determinism upon the modern mind." He concedes that Nietzsche talks a lot about creativity. But for Nietzsche, he points out, "Creativity is only the unwinding of an eternal pattern" (*Insight and Oversights of Great Thinkers,* 235, 238). Peter Berkowitz also complains that Zarathustra's ideal of creativity is abrogated by his doctrine of eternal recurrence (*Nietzsche,* 199-201). Lately, Brian Leiter has given a rigorous critique of the popular Nietzschean self-creationism. He holds that all the passages cited in its support are compatible with Nietzsche's determinism. In fact, they are meant to be understood within the framework of Nietzschean fatalism ("The Paradox of Fatalism and Self-Creation in Nietzsche"). These two views, fatalism and self-creationism, are indeed in strife in *Thus Spoke Zarathustra.* Self-creationism belongs to the Faustian individual self, and fatalism to the Spinozan cosmic self. But these two are not equal. The Faustian self is Zarathustra's initial ideal for the superman, but it is vanquished by the recognition of the Spinozan self. This is the outcome of the battle between the two selves in Nietzsche's epic of the soul.

Zarathustra recognizes his soul as his cosmic self for the first time in "On the Great Longing". Although I identified his soul with the dwarf, the recognition of the dwarf as his animal self in "The Convalescent" was not yet the recognition of his cosmic self. As we noted earlier, the recognition of a cosmic self requires two components: (1) the identification of the self with the body and (2) the physical connection of the body to the world. He accomplishes only (1) in "The Convalescent" and then (2) in "On the Great Longing". The recognition of his cosmic self is the final outcome of the self-perfection he has undertaken under the command of the awesome mistress in "The Stillest Hour" of Part II. This is on his mind when he says that he has done everything to make his soul perfect and super-perfect. The task of self-perfection involves both the individual and the cosmic self. He talked chiefly on the perfection of the individual self in sections 5 through 12 of Part III. But he began to shift his attention to the cosmic self in section 13 ("The Convalescent"). In "On Involuntary Bliss" he prophesied that his self-perfection would be sealed by his victory over the borrowing abysmal thought. But this prophecy was turned upside down. Instead of a glorious victory, he suffered a humiliating defeat. Through this humiliation, however, he recognized his identity with the Dionysian monster and accepted it as his cosmic self. Thus he was transformed from a Faustian hero to a Spinozan superhero. This was his transformation from a lion to a child. Throughout his talk with his soul, in fact, he treats it like an infant with tender love and care.

In his talk with his soul, Zarathustra is reordering his relation to his cosmic self. He has changed from a warrior to a lover. He talked about this transformation in "On Those Who Are Sublime" of Part II. He said that the combative warriors were ugly and nervous and that they ought to become graceful and beautiful. If they do, he assured them, their souls will shudder with godlike desires. He gave this advice as a big secret for dealing with one's soul. This secret is now fulfilled for his own soul. For a long time, it has been the object of conquest by a combative hero. But it is now being courted by a graceful superhero for the first time. The difference between hero and superhero is the difference between war and love, which in turn reflects the difference between the self and the other. The self is the proper object of love and the other is the proper object of war. Zarathustra had to wage war against the dwarf because he regarded the dwarf as the other. But he can now love the same dwarf because he recognizes the dwarf as his own soul. The Faustian self is always combative because it has to assert its will against others. But the Spinozan self is like a child because it has no will of its own or rather its will is nothing other than cosmic necessity. In this regard, the Spinozan self is like a Taoist sage. Lao Tzu says that the contentious will can only bring war and death because it goes against Tao (*Tao Te Ching* 29-31). To be one with Tao is to become like an infant. Because the infant has no will of its own, Lao Tzu says, it overflows with the power of Tao and never contends against the world (*Tao Te Ching* 55). This is the Taoist ideal of cosmic union with Tao, the force that governs the natural world. The same cosmic ideal is guiding Zarathustra in his struggle to bring his individual self in harmony with his cosmic self.

Even in his fight against the Dionysian monster in "On the Spirit of Gravity", he stressed the importance of loving oneself and the difficulty of recognizing one's hidden self. He noted that the art of loving oneself in a healthy way is the subtlest, the most cunning and the most patient of all because whatever is one's own is well concealed from the owner. Of all treasures, he preached, it is our own that we dig up last because it is so ordered by the spirit of gravity. He now realizes that the spirit of gravity is his ultimate self that has been dug up last from the abyss because it has been so well concealed from himself by his own illusory view of himself. Now that this hitherto concealed physical self is revealed as his cosmic self, it can be as magnificent as the entire universe. With this recognition, his hatred of the dwarf is being transformed into his love of his ultimate self. In "On the Way of the Creator" of Part I, Zarathustra said that your devilish self is your worst enemy as long as you hate and despise it and that you can love your devilish self only by turning it into your best friend. He called it the process of self-creation. He is now performing this process and transforming his self-hatred into self-love. But this process is impossible without the recognition and acceptance of the dwarf as one's own ultimate self. Self-love and self-hatred are deeply rooted in self-knowledge, and the conversion of self-hatred to self-love marks the ultimate outcome of Zarathustra's self-perfection.

The perfection of Zarathustra's soul, however, has led to her strange happiness, which makes her suffer from melancholy. This is another subtle connection that links his soul to the dwarf. The spirit of gravity is the spirit of melancholy (*Schwermut*). We will see this point more clearly in "The Song of Melancholy" of Part IV. The German word *Schwermut* literally means the heavy mood, and the spirit of gravity is the spirit of heaviness because gravity is the source of heaviness. The Dionysian monster is not only the source of melancholy but also its perpetual victim. In her sorrow and melancholy, Zarathustra's soul is looking out over roaring seas, searching, and waiting for the redeemer. Her waiting is so painful, he says, that it will dissolve even the angels to tears. But he can do nothing to help her. He asks her to pour out her longing by singing until the golden bark comes over the sea. The master of the golden bark will be the vintager, her great redeemer. He is Dionysus, the god of intoxication. Because his soul is the Dionysian monster, she can be redeemed only by Dionysus. The redemption by his hand will not be merely redemption from suffering, but intoxication in the bliss of love. The absence of love must have been the real cause of melancholy for Zarathustra's soul. In speaking of her perfection, he says that there was not a single soul more loving than his soul. But she is still waiting for the appearance of someone to love.

Cosmic Dance with Life (Part III.15)

In "The Night Song" of Part II, Zarathustra said, "And my soul too is the song of a lover" (Z, 107), and then proceeded to sing it in "The Dancing Song." But he will be much more ambitious this time. Instead of merely singing of his love, he will try to dance to it in "The Other Dancing Song", in which the great redeemer finally arrives in the golden boat. This section opens by repeating the first line of "The Dancing Song":

"Into your eyes I looked recently, O Life." In the earlier song, this line was followed by the story of how Life saved him from drowning with her golden fishing rod. Now the opening line is followed by: "I saw gold blinking in your night-eye; my heart stopped in delight: a golden boat I saw blinking on nocturnal waters, a golden rocking boat, sinking, drinking, and winking again" (Z, 224). This is the golden bark of the vintager, whose coming was promised in the previous section. But the vintager turns out to be a flirtatious woman, who entices Zarathustra to a dance by casting her melting glance and by waving her clapper. In his previous encounter, he could not dance with her because he was still fighting against the spirit of gravity and sinking to the bottom of the ocean under its weight. Now that he has appropriated the dwarf as his own ultimate self, he feels fully prepared for a dance. When he leaps forward in response to her enticement, however, she flees away from his leap. Her fleeing motion is described in the imagery of a leaping and darting snake: "and the tongue of your fleeing, flying hair darted toward me. Away from you did I spring and from your snake."

Life is the serpent, the principle of cosmic life. The dance turns out to be a game of catching the snake. Zarathustra cannot keep up with Life. He suffers and hates her. It is a game of love and hate. That has not changed from the previous encounter, where he said, "Deeply I love only Life—verily, most of all when I hate Life." Now he says, "I fear you near, I love you far; your flight lures me, your seeking cures me: I suffer, but what would I not gladly suffer for you?" (Z, 225). But he cannot get hold of her because she is wild and fleeting like a snake. In the chase, he gets lost in the caves and thickets, in which owls and bats are whirling around. She fools him by barking and howling like a dog. He calls her an untamable prankster and a guileless temptress. He tries to be the hunter. But he leaps and falls when he tries to run down the swift and malicious leaping belle. While still lying on the ground, he asks her whether she has become exhausted from running around. But he suddenly finds that she is no longer in sight. She can never be caught or tired. So he curses her, "Oh, this damned nimble, supple snake and slippery witch! Where are you?" (Z, 226). In his curse, Life is again identified as the snake. The ring of eternal recurrence is the snake biting its own tail, and the dance of the eternal ring is the cosmic dance of the snake. But Zarathustra cannot get into this cosmic dance because he cannot get a grip on the slippery and slithering Life.

I have identified Life as Dionysus. This may sound strange because Dionysus is not a woman. In fact, my identification goes against the prevailing practice of identifying Zarathustra with Dionysus. Lampert points out that Nietzsche originally titled "On the Great Longing" as "Ariadne". On this basis, he says that Zarathustra's soul waiting for her redeemer can be compared to Ariadne's relation to Dionysius and that the union of this fundamental pair and their love are celebrated in the last two sections of Part III. In "The Other Dancing Song", he says, "Ariadne or Dionysos's quarry appears as Life, while Dionysos or Life's hunter appears as Zarathustra" (*Nietzsche's Teaching*, 234). This point is further elaborated by Robert Gooding-Williams in his identification of Zarathustra as Dionysus-Zagreus, who is also called as Zarathustra-Zagreus (*Zarathustra's Dionysian Modernism*, 261-64). Indeed, Zarathustra poses himself as a hunter in chase of Life, but he turns out to be a clumsy hunter. The relationship between a hunter and his quarry does not really fit the relationship between Zarathustra and Life, because he is far from enjoying the commanding position associated with the hunter. On the contrary, it is Life who takes the commanding position over him.

Lampert has one more reason for his identification of Zarathustra with Dionysus: In *Ecce Homo,* Nietzsche says that Zarathustra is Dionysian (*Nietzsche's Teaching,* 233). But this piece of textual evidence is not strong enough. Nietzsche regards him as Dionysian because he has the Dionysian power of binding all opposites in a new unity. But to have a Dionysian attribute is not the same as being Dionysus. One does not have to be Dionysus to be Dionysian any more than one has to be Christ to be Christian. The biggest obstacle to identifying Zarathustra as Dionysus is his description of Life's arrival: "a golden boat I saw blinking on nocturnal waters, a golden rocking boat, sinking, drinking, and winking again." As we noted earlier, the golden boat in this passage clearly refers to the vintager's golden bark: "the bark floats, the golden wonder around

whose gold all good, bad, wondrous things leap." Life arrives as the redeemer in a golden boat. If Zarathustra is identified as Dionysus, he
should play the role of a redeemer for Life. But Life needs no redeemer
and Zarathustra has no power of redemption. On the contrary, he or his
soul is the one waiting for the great redeemer.

The only obstacle for the identification of Life with Dionysus is their
gender difference. To be sure, the gender problem does not arise in
Lampert's identification of Dionysus with Zarathustra. But the gender of
Dionysus is notoriously ambiguous because he is the god of fertility. In
the history of religion, Thorkild Jacobson says, the goddesses of fertility
constitute the first wave of divine beings, which is followed by the second wave, the gods of warfare (*The Treasures of Darkenss*). The goddesses of fertility reigned over ancient human societies, whose economy
was largely agricultural and whose social structure was usually matriar-
chal. The highest of those goddesses was identified with Mother Earth,
as in the case of Demeter of ancient Greece and Isis of Egypt. The Israeli
version of these deities was Asherah. The Goddess of Amaterasu is still
the highest reigning deity of Japanese Shintoism. The most popular deities of ancient China were the Spirit of Earth and the Spirit of Grains,
both of which were later downgraded by the elevation of *Ti* (The Lord on
High) and then *Tien* (Heaven) to the highest position. The chief concern
of these ancient societies was the fertility of the earth, but it was replaced
by the problem of warfare with the development of metallurgy and other
technology, which led to the emergence of warriors. The warrior culture
became patriarchal and produced the warrior gods such as Zeus, Apollo,
and Aries. The emergence of warrior gods demoted the goddesses of fertility to the lowest positions and sometimes to their extinction, as in the
case of the mother-goddess Asherah's disappearance after the elevation
of Yahweh as the god of warfare. The two sexes of divinity shared the
same fate with the two sexes of humanity.

The Greek belief that Dionysus stood for a flood of passion, which
could be ordered only by Apollo, was an imposition by male chauvinism,
the same chauvinism that demoted the goddesses of fertility to the lowest
stations. In the heyday of fertility cult, the female deities were believed

to be wise and sober, while the male deities were believed to be slaves of the irrational impulses. In Japanese Shintoism, Amaterasu is the queen of peace and order, while her brother-husband Susa-no-o is a uncontrollable villain of violence and wild temper. She is the Sun Goddess, the ultimate source of light and wisdom. Likewise in the Egyptian myth, Isis is the queen of order and peace, while her brothers are prone to commit the crimes of malice and violence. In the age of fertility cult, the feminine is the principle of not only fertility but also immortality because it is the source of life, while the masculine is the principle of violence and mortality. Isis is the goddess of eternal life; her brother-husband Osiris is the god of the dead.

When Mount Olympus became the Greek pantheon of warrior gods, Demeter could not find a place there. But Dionysus was a rare exception in this pantheon. Although he was male, he was a god not of warfare, but of fertility. Perhaps for this reason, he was believed to be male and female, human and animal, at the same time. This ambiguous gender of Dionysus is matched by the equally ambiguous gender of Life. In "The Dancing Song" of Part II, Life is given the feminine gender, but it changes to the neuter gender in "On Self-Overcoming" of Part II. But the gender ambiguity of Life is not primarily to mimic that of Dionysus. Its main function is to indicate the important transformation of Dionysus from *The Birth of Tragedy* to *Thus Spoke Zarathustra*. The Dionysus of *The Birth of Tragedy* is still hampered by the Olympian male chauvinism. He is the antithesis of Apollo; his relation to Apollo is the relation of night to day. Dionysus is the god of orgy and frenzy; Apollo is the god of reason and order. Walter Kaufmann says that the Dionysus that appears in Nietzsche's later writings is no longer opposed to Apollo, because he is the synthesis of himself and Apollo (*Nietzsche*, 282). He locates the union of Apollo and Dionysus in *Twilight of the Idols*. But their union takes place much earlier in Nietzsche's career. In *Zarathustra*, Life stands not merely as the union of two gods, but the fusion of Dionysus with the whole natural world. This point is rarely noticed largely because the name of Dionysus is not even mentioned from the beginning to the end of *Thus Spoke Zarathustra*.

Kaufmann says, "The will to power is the heir of Dionysus and Apollo" (*Nietzsche,* 238). We should remember that the will to power is introduced for the first time in *Zarathustra* and that Life is the will to power. But Kaufmann can recognize neither the will to power nor Life as the new appearance of Dionysus. Therefore, he can see only "the heir of Dionysus and Apollo." Bruce Detwiler offers the following incisive description of the difference between the old and the new Dionysus in Nietzsche's writings. In *The Birth of Tragedy*, the Dionysian genius is praised as the force of art. In his later writings, however, the fine arts lose their privileged status and the artists are reviled for their superficiality and mendacity. Nietzsche now associates Dionysus with the eternal recurrence and the will to power. This is the true Dionysian genius that is "clearly the new philosopher" (*Nietzsche and the Politics of Aristocratic Radicalism,* 145). But Detwiler fails to see that the eternal recurrence and the will to power are none other than Life. As the god of tragedy, Dionysus constitutes one of the two principles of art along with Apollo. In *The Birth of Tragedy*, these two are the highest principles because "only as an *aesthetic phenomenon* is existence and the world eternally *justified.*" But the poets are indeed chastised for their superficiality and mendacity in "On Poets" of Part II. Even at its best, art can be no more than a cheap substitute for the real and a clever mechanism for escape and delusion. In his later writings, therefore, Nietzsche assigns a higher principle to Dionysus than that of art. This is the principle of reality, the ultimate principle of philosophy. Thus his notion of Dionysus has evolved from an artistic to a philosophical conception. Nietzsche owes this evolution largely to Spinoza, who has admitted no other philosophical principle than that of reality (the infinite substance). The Life-Dionysus is the ultimate ground of all reality. She is the original source even for the gold of the sun, the symbol of Apollo. In "The Other Dancing Song", gold is blinking in her eye and she comes in a golden boat. She is Spinoza's ultimate philosophical principle, that is, Mother Nature, the all-embracing reality.

In classical mythology, Dionysus was believed to be too elusive to be hunted down. This point is demonstrated by Zarathustra's difficulty of chasing and catching Life. She is hard to catch because she can appear and disappear in so many different forms. For Zarathustra, Life has appeared in many forms: the snake, the dwarf, the azure bell, the well of eternity, the eternal ring, and night and darkness. All these forms are the different expressions of her will to power that produces every event and every object in the vast natural world. Hence she can assume all the shapes of Nature. She is as elusive as Dionysus. She told Zarathustra that she is changeable and untamable in "The Dancing Song" of Part II. We may give her the hyphenated name of 'Life-Dionysus' because she has come as the vintager and redeemer for Zarathustra. Whatever name we may give her, we should understand that she is Nietzsche's counterpart to Richard Wagner's Erda in *The Ring of Nibelung* and Goethe's *Erdgeist* (the Earth Spirit) in *Faust*. These three goddesses are the poetic renditions of Spinoza's God, that is, Mother Nature as the all-embracing reality or the infinite substance.

The Game of Love (Part III.15)

Let us get back to the game of love between Zarathustra and Life. Since the game of chasing Life leads nowhere, he decides to change his game plan and tame Life with a whip. But she admonishes him not to crack the whip so frightfully because that may kill the tender thoughts that are just coming to her. Then she shares the tender thoughts with him as follows. Both of them are good-for-nothings and evil-for-nothings, but they alone have found their island and green meadow beyond good and evil. The green meadow beyond good and evil is the natural world. Since they share this green meadow, she says, they should be friendly with each other. Even if they do not love each other from the heart, they should not bear a grudge against each other. Then, she softly tells him that he is not faithful enough to her and does not love her as much as he says. For this reason, he is thinking of leaving her soon. She even designates the exact hour when he wants to leave her, that is, the hour of midnight when the old bell strikes between one and twelve. Hesitantly affirming what she has said, he whispers something into her ear, which takes her by surprise.

She replies, "You *know* that, O Zarathustra? Nobody knows that" (Z, 227). Then they look at each other and weep together and he feels that Life is dearer to him than all his Wisdom has ever been.

This dialogue is the story of power and love. Zarathustra confronts Life with power, first as a hunter and then with a whip. But he gets nowhere. He wants to control and dominate her. This is incredible in view of the fact that she had clearly established herself as his commander by fishing him out of deep waters in "The Dancing Song" of Part II. It appears that he has completely forgotten that humiliating episode. He may have forgotten it because he has been perfecting his leonine will by smashing the old tablets and inscribing the new ones in "On Old and New Tablets". He must have also forgotten that his leonine will was clobbered by the monster from the abyss. He came on to Life like a lion. Henry Staten says that this scene "clearly undercuts the blustering ideology of masculine dominance that the whip symbolizes" (*Nietzsche's Voice*, 172). Alexander Nehamas says, "As long as Zarathustra wields the whip in an effort to master and subdue life, he is incapable of coming to terms with her" ("For Whom the Sun Shines", 177). Nevertheless, Life responds with soft words and tender thoughts to his power play, and he hesitantly replies, "Yes, but you also know. . ." The secret whisper is indicated by the blank sign. What is represented by this blank sign? This question is as enigmatic as the riddle we encountered in "The Stillest Hour" of Part II: What is the unspeakable "it"?

Just like this enigma, the question of the secret whisper can be resolved only contextually because the blank sign carries no textual meaning. Let us now consider a few proposals for the solution. Laurence Lampert proposes the following solution,

> His answer to her final words—"You want to leave me soon!"—affirms his mortality: "yes," he will leave her soon. However, this necessity is not a refutation of life, for his "yes" is followed by a "but"—"but you also know . . . ," and this "yes . . . but" suggests that the whispered words are some variant or other of the expected phrase, "I will return eternally." (*Nietzsche's Teaching*, 238)

According to this construction, Zarathustra's inevitable mortality is the central concern in the secret exchange between him and Life. Lampert believes that the secret whisper affirms life against the necessity of mortality by the power of eternal recurrence. He calls the secret whisper a "holy open secret" because the eternal recurrence has already been made public. It is so open that there is no need to speak it aloud. In this contextual construction, Lampert assumes that "You want to leave me soon!" refers to Zarathustra's inevitable natural death. But that is unlikely. The quoted sentence refers to his desire to die, not to his inevitable mortality. The word "want" has no place in talking about the latter.

I have already pointed out that we can read the blank sign only contextually. Let us go over the conversational context for the blank sign. It can be divided into two phases: what Life and Zarathustra say to each other before the secret whisper and what they say thereafter it. Just before the whisper, Life complains that he does not love her enough. At the outset, she says, "O Zarathustra, you are not faithful enough to me. You do not love me nearly as much as you say; I know you are thinking of leaving me soon." Then she specifies the time for his planned departure: He wants to leave her soon when he hears the midnight bell. In response to this complaint, he whispers something into Life's ear. Hence his secret whisper cannot be contextually linked to his inevitable mortality because it is never mentioned either by him or by her. Let us now consider what happens after the secret whisper. It takes Life by surprise. She says, "You *know* that, O Zarathustra? Nobody knows that." If the secret whisper were a "holy open secret" of overcoming mortality by the eternal recurrence as Lampert says, she would not say, "Nobody knows that." Instead, she would say, "Everybody knows that." How can Lampert account for Life's surprise at the secret whisper? He may be trying to answer this question when he says, "Zarathustra, the teacher of eternal recurrence, teaches even Life eternal return" (*Nietzsche's Teaching*, 238). If the eternal recurrence is known to nobody, not even to Life, Zarathustra has the right to teach it to her and his teaching can take her by surprise. But this goes against Lampert's earlier view that the eternal recurrence is the "holy open secret."

In the guessing game of the secret whisper, Michael Platt entertains three hypotheses: (1) You [Life] are barren, therefore I [Zarathustra] want to leave you soon, (2) You are leaving me, therefore I want to leave you, and (3) I shall return, although I want to leave you soon ("What Does Zarathustra Whisper in Life's Ear?"). He regards (1) and (2) as implausible. These two hypotheses cannot be linked to Zarathustra's dialogue with Life because they never talk about Life's barrenness or her plan to leave him. By ruling out the first two hypotheses, Platt regards (3) as the only plausible answer. But this answer cannot be contextually justified because it relies on the doctrine of eternal recurrence like Lampert's interpretation. Alan White also believes that the answer lies in the eternal recurrence. He says that there is an obvious answer to the question: "I'll leave you soon, but I'll be back!" (*Within Nietzsche's Labyrinth*, 97). But he raises a number of questions against this presumably obvious answer. First, how does Zarathustra know that? This question is evidently in response to Life's assertion: "No one knows that." If nobody knows it, it is surely a mystery that he knows it. This leads to White's second question. Even if he knows it, why should he be the only one to know it? As White points out, the eternal recurrence is known even to his animals and the dwarf. If his "obvious answer" is correct, Life should say, "Everybody knows that", as I said earlier.

Although these two questions cast serious doubt on his own construction of the secret whisper, White does not attend to them. Instead, he raises the third question: What does it mean for Zarathustra to leave or forsake life? He says that death is the obvious answer. This leads to his final question: Why should he want to die, even if he knows that he will return? This cannot be explained if "death" is taken in the normal sense. So White proposes an unusual notion of death, that is, it should be understood in terms of eternity. The secret whisper is followed by Zarathustra's roundelay, which constitutes the third subsection of "The Other Dancing Song". Because the roundelay ends with a triumphant affirmation of deep eternity, White says, Zarathustra's death should be understood as an event taking place in eternity. But what is eternity? White says that this question is answered, if at all, in the final section of Part III, in which Zarathustra expresses his passionate love of eternity. So White tries to find the meaning of eternity in "The Seven Seals". The following is his interpretation of what is meant by "eternity" (*Within Nietzsche's Labyrinth,* 100-104). Eternity is neither Christian-moral eternity, nor the infinite repetition of earthly life, that is, the eternity of dwarfs and buffoons. It should be understood as the ubiquity of the moment within earthly life. White is injecting the notion of eternity into the domain of temporality. This may be the only way to save eternity in the world of Zarathustra, who has repudiated the traditional notion of eternity together with God and the other world.

According to White, every moment of time is the intersection of two time lines, the past and the future. The past is closed; the future is open. Situated in this ubiquitous moment, one can perpetually create a new self. This perpetual process of self-creation is a constant resurrection: The old self constantly dies to be reborn as a new self. To accept this self-creative death is to will the eternal recurrence. But this perpetual process is a new form of eternity because it is taking place in the eternal Now. Zarathustra is longing for this form of eternity, when he expresses his passionate love of eternity in "The Seven Seals". He is dying every moment to be reborn in the next moment. White says that Life is referring to this perpetual process of dying, when she says that Zarathustra is thinking of leaving her soon. But he replies in his whisper that his death will prepare for the birth of his new self. The two lovers are exchanging their secret understanding of this mystery of the eternal Now. So White uses the eternal recurrence in a completely different sense from its official doctrine. In "The Seven Seals", he holds, the ring of eternal recurrence is not a ring of repetition, but a ring of unification and reconciliation. What recurs is only the perpetual process of death and resurrection, and this endless process is the meaning of eternity in "The Seven Seals". The perpetual creative process is eternally present everywhere. That is, eternity is none other than the ubiquity of the eternal Now.

Let us see how this view of eternity can illuminate his construction of the secret whisper: "I'll leave you soon, but I'll be back!" Let us restate White's thesis that "to leave Life" should be taken not as the natural death, but as the perpetual process of self-creation. Hence "I'll leave you soon, but I'll be back!" means "I will be dying every moment only to be reborn." As White says, this statement involves the eternal mystery of life. It is so mysterious that Life can say, "You *know* that, O Zarathustra? Nobody knows that." Thus it can explain Life's surprise at the secret whisper. But it does not fit what Life says before the secret whisper. When Life talks of Zarathustra's desire to die, according to White, she must be referring to the perpetual process of death and resurrection. But such a process is not even intimated in her talk. She only says, "I know you are thinking of leaving me soon." What is going to happen "soon" cannot be the same as what is happening at every moment or the eternal Now. The "soon" indicates a moment in the future, but the eternal Now is the present moment. She even specifies the time of his departure as soon after the midnight bell. But the eternal Now cannot be pinned down on any particular future moment. She depicts Zarathustra's impending departure as one-shot deal, whereas White turns it into a perpetually re-peatable process. This is the contextual obstacle to his proposed con-struction.

Robert Gooding-Williams takes Zarathustra's projected death as a one-shot deal. When Life says to him that he is thinking of abandoning her, Gooding-Williams claims, she is recalling his pronouncement made in III.12.3: "For I want to go to men once more; under their eyes I want to go-under; dying I want to give them my richest gift" (*Zarathustra's Dionysian Modernism*, 265). This is his death wish, which Gooding-Williams calls his soul's secret. In his secret whisper, he affirms this se-cret to Life by saying "yes" and then explains his motive behind it by saying "but. . ." By his death, Zarathustra can reclaim his ability to go-under. After this secret exchange, Gooding-Williams says, Life is aston-ished to discover that she shares this secret with him. So she says, "You *know* that, O Zarathustra? Nobody knows that" (*Zarathustra's Dionysian Modernism*, 267). But "You know that. . ." seems to indicate her surprise of finding out not that they share a secret, but that he knows something he is not supposed to know. That "something" cannot be his own secret wish because he must know it even if nobody else does. Life does not stop with "You know that. . ." Instead she says "Nobody knows that." This statement makes no sense as a response to Zarathustra's presumed confession. Instead of this statement, Life should say, "Nobody else knows that."

These remarks concern what happens after the secret whisper. Let us now relate Gooding-Williams' construction to what happens before the secret whisper, namely, Life's complaint about the quality of his love and fidelity. His gift of death may well be the last and the richest gift to the people as Gooding-Williams says, but it may have nothing to do with the quality of his love and fidelity to Life. So we had better find a way to connect his death wish to his love of Life. But this may be an impossible task because death wish and love of life go against each other. Perhaps we can do it by linking them to eternity, as Alan White has tried. We should note two important textual details. First, Eternity is introduced as the object of joy in the roundelay for the first time in the book. Second, the same Eternity becomes the object of passionate love in "The Seven Seals". But what does Eternity have to do with the love between Zarathustra and Life? If we can answer this question, we may be able to figure out the content of the secret whisper. To this end, let us reconsider Zarathustra's game of love with Life.

Their game of love is the game of power between Zarathustra's Faustian individual self and his Spinozan cosmic self. The cosmic self has appeared in two different forms. First, it appeared as the dwarf in "On the Vision and the Riddle" and "The Convalescent". Second, it appeared as Zarathustra's newborn soul in "On the Great Longing". In both cases, we encountered only his potential cosmic self, which had yet to be actualized. The dwarf was still only an animal that could become his cosmic self only when Zarathustra accepted it as his own and recognized its cosmic dimension. His soul was again a potential cosmic self in another sense. She was not yet activated. She showed no sign of power and action. That is why she needed the redeemer, who could provide the power for her activation. Life is the cosmic force for activation because she is the principle of cosmic life. This cosmic principle is Dionysus, Mother Nature. Hence Life comes as the redeemer for Zarathustra's soul.

With the infusion of cosmic force, his soul can become one with Life. Hence the ultimate form of his cosmic self is Life, the ring of eternal recurrence. Although Zarathustra's animal self and soul are his potential cosmic self, they will appear to be more or less as individual entities until their complete union with Life, because they cannot become fully cosmic without her. Thus there are many stages for the elevation of the individual self to the cosmic level.

The three forms of the cosmic self mark the different stages of Zarathustra's redemption. The first stage is his recognition of the dwarf as his animal self. Although he is crushed by his animal self, he claims to have achieved redemption because he overcomes his alienation from his animal self by accepting him as his own self. But his animal self is not yet fully redeemed. The ugly dwarf still appears to be an individual animal because its cosmic dimension is still unknown. When its cosmic dimension is recognized, his animal self is revealed as his soul with all her cosmic attributes of perfection. This is the second stage of his redemption. For all its cosmic attributes, his soul still suffers like an individual self because it is yet to be activated. Its activation is the third stage of his redemption, which takes place with the advent of Life. The fully activated cosmic self would be one with Life. She is the ultimate cosmic self. But she is too wild and too nimble for Zarathustra. He cannot join the dance of his cosmic self. The fourth and final stage of redemption will be their joyful union in the cosmic dance. These four stages constitute Zarathustra's Ladder of Redemption. They are distributed to the last four sections of Part III. The first stage takes place in "The Convalescent", the second stage in "On the Great Longing", and the third stage in "The Other Dancing Song". The fourth stage does not take place by the end of Part III. It is projected as Zarathustra's ultimate longing in "The Seven Seals". Eternity is the object of this ultimate longing.

In "The Other Dancing Song", Zarathustra is still struggling in the third stage of redemption. When his soul is activated, he tries to impose his individual will on Life. By this Faustian move, his soul is reverting from the cosmic to the individual mode. The distinction between the individual and the cosmic self is functional. The same dwarfish monster can appear as the individual soul or as the cosmic agent of Life, depending on its function. I said earlier that the distinction of the individual from the cosmic self is perspectival. But the perspectival distinction coincides with the functional distinction because functions and perspectives define each other. Those distinctions are as fluid and as slippery as those functions. Just as the shattering of the Faustian self led to the emergence of the cosmic self, so the assertion of the individual will transposes Zarathustra's soul from the cosmic to the individual mode. By this transposition, it loses the innocence that it had gained by its metamorphosis from a lion to a child. No metamorphosis can ever become really real as long as the Faustian will is not completely extinguished. But it can never be extinguished in the temporal world. Hence the final metamorphosis can be fully realized only in the eternal ring toward the end of Part IV.

In chapter 2, I talked of how hard it is to discard the autonomous will. Even if you believe that your will is already determined by the past, you must still make your decisions by exercising your will. There is no way to avoid the assertion of your individual will in the temporal world. The autonomous will may be an illusion, but this illusion is the practical necessity for every action. In every phase of temporal existence, the individual will is irrepressible and ineliminable. This relentless spirit is exemplified by Goethe's Faust and his forever striving will. In the Faustian manner, Zarathustra tries to impose his will on Life. But that is not the way of dance and love. It takes two to tango, that is, the fusion of two partners into one seamless team. But he cannot free himself from his Faustian will. What is the moral of his game of love? It demonstrates the insurmountable difficulty in loving the cosmic self because it is inextricably interwoven with the whole world. But the world is full of accidents that go against the individual will. This is the ground for the endless collision of the individual self with the cosmic self.

There is no way to resolve the conflict of the individual self with the cosmic self. This is the heart of Nietzschean existential dialectic. It cannot be resolved by a Hegelian synthesis because there is no third term for the mediation of the two protagonists. Nor can this existential dialectic be resolved by the Kierkegaardian decision of Either/Or, because neither of the protagonists can be eliminated by such a decision. Therefore, their irreconcilable tension generates an interminable dialectic. But there is one sure way to terminate this conflict. It is to terminate life itself, which is the source of this conflict. For this reason, many believed in the nineteenth century that love could be fulfilled only in death. The intimate connection of love and death was most hauntingly dramatized in Richard Wagner's *Tristan and Isolde*. Incidentally, this was Nietzsche's favorite opera. He exults over its hero's yearning for love and death (*The Birth of Tragedy* 21). Tristan and Isolde yearn for their ecstatic union in death because such a union of two lovers is impossible in life. Their love is perpetually frustrated in this world, just like Zarathustra's love of Life. The game of love involves not only the loving relation between two individuals, but also their hazardous relation with the cosmic self, a massive tangle of frightful accidents. Such is also the love between Brynhilde and Siegfried. But she also tries to fulfill their love in death, which obliterates the separation of individuals from Mother Nature. Hence it is plausible to attribute a death wish to Zarathustra, as Robert Gooding-Williams suggests. Surely, death is a way to Eternity. This morbid thought may lie behind Zarathutra's death wish.

A Rendezvous with Eternity (Part III.15)

What sort of death is Zarathustra contemplating when he whispers his secret wish to Life? As a preliminary to answering this question, let us note that Zarathustra's love of his cosmic self is what Nietzsche calls *amor fati* (love of fate) because his cosmic self determines his fate. Nietzsche's *amor fati* is equivalent to Spinoza's *amor dei* (the love of God), which is the love of the entire natural world. But Yirmiyahu Yovel points out the difference between the two: "Spinoza's *amor dei* expresses a harmonious agreement with the universe, whereas *amor fati* involves an inner rupture and distance, bridged by an act of defying affirmation" ("Nietzsche and Spinoza", 200). Because *amor fati* requires the defiant affirmation of the self against the world, he says, it precludes the possibility of mystical union between the self and the world, the salient feature of *amor dei*. The inner rupture and distance that Yovel speaks of are reflected in the interminable tension and strife in Zarathustra's love of his cosmic self. But *amor dei* is supposedly free of such tension and strife because it takes place in the highest level of knowledge that can intuitively understand the whole world from the eternal perspective. Spinoza's Nature can be viewed from two perspectives, temporal and eternal. The mystery of a*mor dei* is attainable in the eternal perspective, but not in the temporal perspective because it is full of conflict (*Ethics,* pt. 5, prop. 33). 'Love' is an ambiguous word. It can mean two different states: (1) love fully realized and (2) love still striving. Yovel is speaking of *amor dei* realized in the eternal perspective. But there is *amor dei* unrealized in the temporal perspective. This is Spinoza's doctrine of *conatus* and its perpetual striving in the temporal world. In that case, *amor fati* can also be understood on two levels. In the temporal domain, it may be perpetually frustrated. Zarathustra may have come to feel that it can be realized only in the eternal domain.

Just like Spinoza's Nature and God, Life can also be viewed from two perspectives, temporal and eternal. In the eternal mode of her existence, she is the eternal ring. Although Zarathustra has talked about the eternal ring or the well of eternity, he has never lived in it. All his life, he has struggled with Life in her temporal mode only to be teased and frustrated by her perpetually changing character. Since all his frustrations have arisen from the temporal dimension of Life, he may have hit upon the idea of leaving her in the temporal mode and trying his luck in the eternal mode. On this basis, I propose that he whispers this new plan to Life. In response to her statement that he wants leave her soon, he says, "Yes, but you also know . . ." This short statement may be read as the contraction of: "*Yes,* you are right about my wish to leave you soon, but *you also know* that I can rejoin you in the eternal mode." In response to this stunning idea, Life says, "Nobody knows that." Surely, nobody knows this sort of thing. This brilliant plan is far better than the yearning of Tristan and Isolde for their ecstatic union in death and Brynhilde's scheme of self-immolation for her eternal union with Siegfried. His plan can be accomplished in life rather than in death. In Spinoza's and Zarathustra's world, one does not have to die physically in the temporal world to reach the eternal world. One only has to ascend from the temporal to the eternal mode within the same natural world. In his secret whisper, Zarathustra is announcing the reorientation of his love for Life from the temporal to the eternal mode.

We have noted the contextual similarity between the unspeakable 'it' and the secret whisper. Their similarity does not end there. They are functionally similar, too. Just as the thematic development of Part II is crystallized in the unspeakable 'it', so does the thematic development of Part III culminates in the secret whisper. One is an unspeakable secret; the other is an unhearable (to others) secret. The unspeakable 'it' leads to Life's command to Zarathustra to become like a child, which is fulfilled in the birth of his soul as a child in "The Great Longing". The secret whisper leads to his passionate longing for Life in "The Seven Seals", which will be fulfilled in Part IV. The two secret events constitute two momentous turning points in Zarathustra's epic journey. With the unspeakable 'it', Life issued her order for him to change the mode of his epic struggle from a lion to a child. In the secret whisper, he takes the initiative for changing the mode of his love from temporal to eternal. This is his ingenious contrapuntal move to Life's earlier stern command.

Zarathustra's ascent to the eternal domain, however, is different from Spinoza's. The latter is purely intellectual; the former is existential. Unlike the intellectual ascent, the existential ascent cannot be achieved by the exercise of the individual will, because such an exercise is a defiant act of the individual agency that belongs to the temporal perspective. One can assert one's will and perform an action only in the temporal perspective. But assertion of the individual will always traps the self firmly in the temporal world. This is the existential paradox of the will. This paradox appears in the Stoic ideal of *apatheia*, that is, the ideal of freeing the soul from all passions. Anyone who tries to fulfill this ideal will still be trapped in one passion, namely, the passion to be free of all passions. Hence the Stoic ideal is self-defeating if it is pursued consciously. The same problem arises in the Buddhist ideal of being free from all desires and attaining *nirvana*. If you try to fulfill this ideal, you will find your-self still trapped in one desire, namely, the desire to be rid of all desires and attain *nirvana*. Therefore, the Buddhists never try to achieve enlight-enment by their will and self-imposed discipline. Instead, they patiently wait for the mysterious coming of enlightenment in the meditative state of total inaction. It can come upon them only by some mysterious power beyond their control and discipline. If they have any will, theirs is the will of a child. This is the symbolic meaning of a child in the allegory of three metamorphoses, and this was the meaning of the instruction by the voiceless voice when Zarathustra was told to drop his leonine posture and become like a child in "The Stillest Hour" of Part II.

Like the Buddhists, Zarathustra realizes that his transcendence from the temporal to the eternal perspective does not lie within his individual power. In that regard, he is different from Spinoza. The latter's *amor dei* is supposed to be achieved by his act of intellectual intuition. But the sage Zarathustra has come to realize through his long frustrating experi-ence that his *amor fati* can never be fulfilled by his own effort. We have noted Yovel's assertion that *amor fati* precludes the possibility of mysti-cal union between the self and the world. Zarathustra now realizes that the preclusion has been dictated by his defiant individual will. Instead of willing, therefore, he can only wish for the fulfillment of his *amor fati* by the mysterious power that lies beyond his individual will. His notion of transcendence is as mysterious as the Buddhist's notion. It can be ful-filled only by a stroke of fate. The Buddha has no will of his own. He be-comes one with the whole world by accepting his *karmic* bond. Hence he may look like a child. Likewise, as we noted earlier, the Taoist sage claims to take no action (*wu wei*) because to act is to assert one's will. The sage is supposed to move with the flow of Tao. This is to become like an infant or water. There is no way to describe the flow of Tao, Lao Tzu says. As soon as it is described, it becomes an object of the will. The only way to become one with Tao is to be without the will, but freedom from the will can never be achieved by the willful action. It can be given only by the mysterious flow of Tao. Hence Tao is called the gateway to all mystery in the first chapter of *Tao Te Ching*.

By reorienting his love from the temporal to the eternal mode, Zarathustra wants to abandon the world of action and ascend to the world of
mystery. This idea is not totally new to him. In "On Involuntary Bliss",
he felt a mysterious sense of happiness against his will. In "Before Sunrise", he again felt a mysterious mood of elation under the azure bell.
Both of these mysterious experiences came to him in the world of darkness and inaction. The temporal world is the theater of individual wills; it
is the domain of decision and action. The world of darkness is a symbolic
token of the eternal world. No one can act in the eternal world because it
transcends time, the basic condition for all actions. For the fulfillment of
his love, Zarathustra now wishes to transcend from the domain of action
to the domain of mystery that can never be controlled by the individual
will. This notion of transcendence was already reflected in his attitude of
supplication, which he showed by patiently waiting for "the sign" in the
opening scene of "On Old and New Tablets" and by humbly praying for
the fulfillment of his destiny at the end of the same section. He assumes
the same humble position by the time he sits down (no action) with Life
before their separation in "The Other Dancing Song". He says, "But then
life was dearer to me than all my wisdom ever was" (Z, 227). His wisdom is the day-wisdom, the instrument of his Faustian self. He now recognizes the greater power of his Spinozan self.

His game of love was his Faustian struggle to control his Spinozan
self. We can further explore the nature of this game by comparing it with
the cosmic dance of Shiva. Life is equivalent to Shiva because she is
Dionysus, the god of perpetual creation and destruction. Hence her dance
has the same significance as Shiva's. The allegorical meaning of Shiva's
dance is portrayed in the bronze statutes of Nataraja (The King of
Dance). The King is dancing within a ring of fire, which stands for the
world of *samsara*. He stands on his right foot supported by a crouching
dwarf, while his left foot is in motion. He has four arms. He holds a drum
in one of his right hands and a flame in one of his left hands. At every
moment, the dance of Shiva continually destroys old things and produces
new things. The drum sets forth the rhythm of his perpetual creation,
while the flame signals his perpetual destruction. A cobra, which is

coiled around his waist or one of his arms, is also dancing with him. The Dance of Shiva symbolizes not only the cosmic cycles of creation and destruction, but also the daily rhythm of life and death.

Let us now try to see the dance of Shiva as the interaction between the individual and the cosmic self. The crouching dwarf, on whom Shiva stands in his dance, is the individual self. Shiva is the cosmic self. The dwarf is crushed under Shiva's dance. This is the way Zarathustra is treated in his dance with Life, his cosmic self. His individual self can never get into the flow of Life's dance as long as he tries to impose his Faustian will on her. The dwarf under Shiva's foot is sometimes taken as the symbol of ignorance. The notion of an individual self is based on ignorance, that is, the ignorance of one's inseparable connection with the cosmic self. This ignorance is *maya*, the illusion that obstructs the union of the individual with the cosmic self. Shiva's dwarf serves the same function as Zarathustra's dwarf, the small man victimized by his own illusion of autonomous will. While Shiva's dwarf is crushed, his cobra fully displays its power. This snake is Kundalini, which is supposed to lie at the base of everybody's spine. But its cosmic energy cannot be tapped without becoming one with the cosmic self. In Zarathustra's dance, Life is the cosmic snake, whose energy is inaccessible to his Faustian self. Thus the dwarf and the snake play similar roles in the two stories.

Why does Shiva dance? Before the dance, Shiva is totally absorbed in meditation and feels neither pleasure nor pain. He is totally free of motion and feeling. But his dance is called the dance of bliss (David Smith, *The Dance of Siva,* 1). This is the reason for his dance. When he moves out of his meditation into his dance, he experiences the bliss of activity. This transition is similar to the transformation of Zarathustra's soul. In "On the Great Longing", his soul was totally inactive for all her cosmic attributes. That was his cosmic self in stasis. It can become the active cosmic self only by joining the dance of Life. She holds the clapper in her hands just as Shiva holds the drum in his. Again like Shiva, she runs all over the world in her dance. She is so wild and so fast that Zarathustra cannot keep up with her. He feels just like the crouching dwarf crushed under Shiva's dancing foot. If he still tries to love his cosmic self even in this humiliating position, his love will indeed be a matter of defiance as Yovel says. But Zarathustra has now learned that such defiance can only lead to a perpetual quarrel with Life.

This lovers' quarrel is similar to the one between Shiva and his consort Parvati. When they play the game of dice, they always wind up in an acrimonious dispute, accusing each other of cheating and many other unfair tricks. Shiva's game of dice is another mythological account of how the world runs, although it is not so well known as the myth of his cosmic dance (Don Handelman and David Shulman, *God Inside Out*). The game illustrates the conflict between the individual and the cosmic self. The game of dice is also Zarathustra's favorite metaphor along with the metaphor of dance. In "Before Sunrise", he compares the world to a game of dice by calling the azure bell "a divine table for divine dice and dice players." In fact, he equates the cosmic game of dice with the cosmic dance of the world. He says to the azure bell, "You are to me a dance floor for divine accidents (Z, 166). The dance of Life is the cosmic dance of the azure bell. Just like Shiva's dance, the cosmic dance of Life is a game of dice. That explains why Zarathustra cannot control it. By its nature, the game of dice is beyond control. Parvati gets into vicious arguments with Shiva because she is trying to control what is beyond control. For the same reason, Zarathustra cannot avoid fighting with Life. He cannot resist the temptation to control her.

Prior to the game of dice, according to the Hindu myth, Shiva and Parvati are one in their eternal peace and harmony. But they get separated from each other for the sake of their game because there is no way to play a game without the competing parties. Their separation is dictated by the necessity of their game. But the game takes place in the turbulent temporal world because every move in the game takes time. Thus, the eternal world is the domain of unity and harmony; the temporal world is the domain of separation and conflict. This may be true of Zarathustra's universe. In that case, he has every reason for wishing to transcend this world of conflict for the world of harmony. This dear wish may well be his secret whisper to Life. Their secret exchange is followed by the metrical composition that is known as Zarathustra's roundelay.

Zarathustra's Roundelay

One!	O man, take care!
Two!	What does the deep midnight declare?
Three!	"I was asleep—
Four!	"From a deep dream I woke and swear:
Five!	"The world is deep,
Six!	"Deeper than day had been aware,
Seven!	"Deep is its woe;
Eight!	"Joy—deeper yet than agony:
Nine!	"Woe implores: Go!
Ten!	"But all joy wants eternity—
Eleven!	"Wants deep, wants deep eternity."
Twelve!	(Silence)

(Z, 227-28)

Who is the author of this song? There is no textual indication. I propose Life as its author. I take the song as her response to Zarathustra's secret wish to see her in the eternal mode. But she does not make this response while she is sitting with him in the temporal world. After exchanging her tender thoughts with him at the end of subsection 2 of "The Other Dancing Song", she vanishes altogether never to be seen again in the temporal world. She is sending this song from the eternal domain. That explains why the roundelay is not physically associated with her presence. Its eleven lines are distributed to the twelve sounds of the midnight bell. That is the exact time when Life predicted that Zarathustra wanted to leave her. The deep midnight speaks in the roundelay. Midnight belongs to the cosmic self. She is none other than Life. She says that she was asleep and woke from a deep dream. Her speech ends with the affirmation of the desire for deep eternity. This is her emphatic endorsement of Zarathustra's secret wish to see her the eternal mode. With this endorsement, he can expect that she will grant his wish and that his frustrated love will be fulfilled in the eternal domain. But the fulfillment will not come until the midnight bell rings again in "The Drunken Song" of Part IV. The roundelay is the prophecy for this fulfillment. Until then, he can only express his passionate longing for Life in her eternal mode. This passionate longing is already expressed by the last line of the roundelay: "Wants deep, wants deep Eternity." Life in her eternal mode is Eternity and his longing for Eternity will be fully elaborated in the next section ("The Seven Seals"). Stanley Rosen says, "The section does not require detailed analysis; it is a song of self-explanation and resumes the main themes of the work to this point" (*The Mask of Enlightenment*, 205). Unfortunately, this is one of the most difficult sections in the entire book.

Longing for Eternity (Part III.16)

"The Seven Seals" presents many difficult problems for interpretation, but those problems are rarely recognized. This section is a song of seven stanzas, but the title does not directly show what function the song serves. This is the first problem of interpretation. Laurence Lampert says that it is the marriage song between Zarathustra and the ring of eternity. In proposing this view, he chiefly relies on the biblical symbolism of the seven seals: "The eschatological symbolism of the Bible is also reflected in the marriage that ends *Zarathustra*, for the final event in the book of *Revelation* is the marriage of the victorious, imperial Christ to the purified Church, the New Jerusalem" (*Nietzsche's Teaching*, 241). If we are faithful to the symbolism of seven seals in Revelation, it is hard to take "The Seven Seals" as the song celebrating the marriage of Zarathustra to Eternity. The biblical seven seals announce the prophecy of Christ's marriage to the purified Church in his second coming. In that case, "The Seven Seals" should be read as the prophecy of Zarathustra's marriage rather than as its celebration. As a matter of fact, every stanza of "The Seven Seals" repeats one line: "Oh, how should I not lust after eternity and after the nuptial ring of rings, the ring of recurrence?" "To lust after" means to have a passionate longing. Therefore, we should say that "The Seven Seals" expresses Zarathustra's passionate longing for his marriage with Eternity rather than describes its celebration.

The second problem of interpretation is the identity of the lady called Eternity. There are two theories. One of them identifies Eternity as Life; the other distinguishes the two. David Krell says that Zarathustra appears to spurn Life and become ardent for Eternity (*Postponements*, 56). Gary Shapiro recognizes three women of Zarathustra as Wisdom, Life, and Eternity (*Nietzschean Narratives*, 95). Stanley Rosen elaborates and expands this view. Because a genuine love of Life is impossible, Zarathustra turns to Eternity, who is neither Life nor Wisdom. He understands Eternity as "the great womb of chaos, the confluence of creation and destruction. It is no life but the mother of life, and hence too of death" (*The Mask of Enlightenment*, 206). This view may be supported by the fact that Life never appears again after "The Other Dancing Song". Before her disappearance, she said that Zarathustra was not faithful enough to her and wanted to leave her soon. Although nothing was said about where he wanted to go after leaving Life, it is possible to assume that he was planning to leave Life to find another woman. He has now found that woman in Eternity. Just as he discarded Wisdom after finding Life in Part II, he has now found Eternity after deserting Life. That should make him an adventurous opportunist, hopping from one woman to another in response to his ever changing desires and situations. This may be the reason behind Life's complaint about his fidelity. But this view clashes with his last statement in "The Other Dancing Song" that Life was dearer to him than ever before.

If Eternity were indeed different from Life and Wisdom, there should be some indication that Zarathustra has met her somewhere before expressing his ardent wish to be married to her. But there is no such indication. It is inconceivable for him to express his passionate longing for a marriage to a total stranger. In "The Seven Seals", he talks to her like an old friend. If so, Eternity must be either Life or Wisdom. Of these two, Life is far more likely to be the object of his lust because he has never shown any erotic impulse for Wisdom. Finally, if Eternity is different from Life, Eternity must be the mother of Life as Rosen says. But there is no textual ground to assume that there is any higher power than Life in the Zarathustrian world, or that there can be a mother to Life. For all we know from the text, Life is the ultimate force and the mother of all. She is Mother Nature. For these reasons, we had better identify Eternity with Life. But what is the ground for this identification?

This is not an easy question because Life is never identified as Eternity in any part of *Thus Spoke Zarathustra*. But Laurence Lampert offers an elaborate theory for the identification of Life with Eternity. He reads "The Seven Seals" as a continuation of "The Other Dancing Song" without a break. He takes the roundelay as the song of the midnight bell, which the two lovers hear together. The roundelay is the expression of his deepest thought for her (*Nietzsche's Teaching*, 239). His deepest thought awakens in midnight and issues two conflicting commands. Its woe commands Life to depart, but its joy commands her to eternally return. Lampert says, "The commanding voice of joy sings the marriage song after the twelfth toll" (*Nietzsche's Teaching*, 240). This nuptial song is "The Seven Seals". In this song, Lampert says, Zarathustra commands Life to become Eternity and names her as "Eternity":

> "Eternity" is the name Zarathustra wills Life to take. As is appropriate for a bride, Life receives a new name from her husband. Just as Dionysos, in marrying mortal Ariadne, raised her to the heavens and placed her immortal among the stars as Corona Borealis, Life is valorized "Eternity" by Zarathustra's love. (*Nietzsche's Teaching*, 240)

In this account, Lampert assumes that there is no break of any kind between the last two sections of Part III. The identity of Life with Eternity is established by Zarathustra's command to Life to become Eternity and his bestowal of the name "Eternity" on her in the wedding ceremony.

None of these claims can be supported by textual evidence. The alleged wedding never takes place. Hence there can be no celebration of the wedding. Lampert assumes that Zarathustra and Life are still together for their wedding in "The Seven Seals" as they were in "The Other Dancing Song". But there is no textual evidence for this assumption, either. If Life were still there with him for the wedding, she would say something in the course of the alleged ceremony. But he is the only speaker in "The Seven Seals". It would be surely strange if he were to conduct and celebrate the wedding all by himself. In "The Seven Seals", he is expressing his passionate love for someone far away, who is called Eternity. She is not even there to respond to his passionate longing. The tone of his speech accentuates the absence of his beloved rather than her presence. Her absence is also the objection to Alan White's thesis that Eternity should be understood as the present Now, which we considered earlier. White may say that the present Now is equivalent to Life. Although Eternity may be far away, the present Now is perpetually present. It makes little sense to wish to be wed to Eternity if she is the eternal Now, because everyone is already wed to it.

By bestowing the name of "Eternity" on Life, Lampert further claims, Zarathustra immortalizes Life as the god of Dionysus elevated the mortal woman Ariadne to the immortal level. Throughout his account, Lampert assumes that Zarathustra holds a commanding position over Life. But this is to misunderstand their relation. As we noted earlier, it is Life who takes the commanding position over him. She firmly established this position by saving him from drowning with her fishing rod in "The Dancing Song" and maintains it by teasing and taunting him throughout "The Other Dancing Song". He is in no position to change her name or give her a new name. Even if he had the power to rename Life, why does he choose the name of Eternity for her? This point is not explained by Lampert. He may say that the name of Eternity is used to immortalize Life. This may sound like an obvious answer, but it is really a senseless one. All the Olympians are immortal, but none of them is called Eternity. None of their names carry the sense of eternity. Any name can be used for immortalization, even the name of Dawn or West Wind. If so, why is the name of Eternity used for the immortalization of Life? All these questions stand on the premise that Life is in need of immortalization. But she needs no immortalization because she is the only immortal in Zarathustra's world if there is any. Nor does she need renaming to be called Eternity. She is Eternity because she is the ring of eternal recurrence. As we have noted in a number of occasions, Life is the ring of eternal recurrence because she is Mother Nature. Eternity is the ring of recurrence in its eternal mode. Hence Eternity is Life in her eternal mode.

Let us next consider the third problem of interpretation for "The Seven Seals". Each stanza is composed of two parts: the main text and the refrain. There is nothing problematic about the refrain. It simply expresses Zarathustra's love of Eternity: "Never yet have I found the woman from whom I wanted children, unless it be this woman whom I love: for I love you, O eternity! *For I love you, O eternity!*" But the structure of the main text is highly peculiar. It consists of two segments: (1) the if-segment and (2) the question-segment. In all seven stanzas, the question-segment repeats the same question: "Oh, how should I not lust after eternity and after the nuptial ring of rings, the ring of recurrence?" But the if-segments of the seven stanzas are all different; they recount Zarathustra's career in seven different roles: (1) a prophet, (2) a destroyer of the old gods and their churches, (3) a breather of creative spirit, (4) a universal mixer and reconciler, (5) a boundless seafarer, (6) a dancer of happiness, and (7) a flier of bird-wisdom. Each of these roles is narrated in a strange description, which begins with the word 'if'. It is not a straightforward description such as, "I am a soothsayer. . ." but a conditional one such as, "If I am a soothsayer. . ." Each of these conditional descriptions is followed by the same rhetorical question: "Oh, how should I not lust after eternity and after the nuptial ring of rings, the ring of recurrence?"

Why is an if-clause used to describe Zarathustra's achievements? There is nothing iffy about his achievements. They are well-known facts. What is the point of using the conditional form for describing those well-known facts? This is the first question about the structure of each stanza. The next structural question concerns the connection of the if-segment to the question-segment. How does the if-statement lead up to the question-segment? It is hard to see the connection between the two. Let us now consider the question-segment. It contains an emphatic ("Oh") rhetorical question ("how should I not lust after Eternity?"), which amounts to saying, "I have every reason to lust after Eternity." Let us again assume that to lust after Eternity is to lust after Life in her eternal mode. "How should I not lust after Eternity?" should be read as "How should I not lust

Life in the eternal mode?" Thus the rhetorical question expresses his desperate need for the reorientation of his love of Life from the temporal to the eternal mode. Its meaning can become even clearer if it is expanded to read: "Oh, how should I not lust after Eternity, given the condition of my love of Life in her temporal mode?" What is the condition of his love in temporal mode? It is implied by the if-segment, the conditional description of his heroic achievement. Thus, the conditional statement leads to the rhetorical question.

The heroic achievements recounted in the seven if-segments have taken place prior to the last four sections of Part III. All of them belong to Zarathustra's attempt to advocate the creative will as the new way of life in the godless world, that is, the ideal of instituting the supreme sovereignty of human will to supplant the traditional divine sovereignty in the universe. In pursuit of this epochal ideal, however, he has run into the insurmountable problems of redeeming the past, releasing the creative will from the burden of the past, and getting crushed under the abysmal thought only to realize that the very idea of the creative will is an illusion. His creative will culminated in the leonine pronouncements in "On Old and New Tablets", but that momentary triumph was shattered by a series of tragic reversals in the next three sections. In desperation, he had to tell Life his secret wish to leave her in the temporal mode and approach her in the eternal mode. The if-segments give the reasons for this secret wish for reorienting his love from the temporal to the eternal mode.

Zarathustra's epic deeds recounted in the seven stanzas are of the highest heroism, and yet it does not deliver the ultimate bliss. *If* he cannot experience the ultimate satisfaction even after reaching the summit of human achievements in the temporal world, *then* why should he not feel the lust for the eternal world as his last resort? The conditional description of his heroic achievement implicitly contains the poignant sense of his frustration in the temporal world, as described in the three sections preceding "The Seven Seals". The if-segment of each stanza consists of two elements: (1) the description of a heroic achievement and (2) the unmentioned frustration as its consequence. The second one is left unmentioned because it was the central point of exposition in the preceding three sections. To mention it again would be too repetitious and cumbersome. The first and the second jointly lay the ground for posing the rhetorical question for the reorientation of his love. The force of the if-segment can be given a more forceful expression by translating the German word *wenn* not simply into 'if' as usually done, but into 'even if' or even better into 'even when'. Instead of deflating his heroic achievements, let us take them at face value as most commentators do. Then Zarathustra would come out as a pompous braggart. The poignant lament over his perpetual frustration would sound like a blatant boast over his countless heroic achievements, by which he tries to present himself as a warrior worthy of the love of Eternity, presumably a lady even more exalted than Life as Stanley Rosen understands the two ladies. It is hard to accede to this disgraceful picture of our epic hero. This is my main objection to the standard reading of "The Seven Seals". I will now try to justify my reading by going over each stanza of "The Seven Seals".

The first stanza of "The Seven Seals" describes Zarathustra's audacious activities as a soothsayer. In his prophetic spirit, he wanders on a high ridge between two seas like a heavy cloud between past and future. Textually this passage alludes to "The Wanderer" of Part III, where he appears as a wanderer and a mountain climber about to ascend his ultimate peak, and to "On Redemption" of Part II, where he struggles with the clash of two wills spanning over past and future. In "The Wanderer" he ended his talk, laughing at himself in melancholy and bitterness. In "On Redemption" he became terrified by his own talk and thought. Now he describes himself as pregnant and compares himself to a heavy cloud loaded with lightning bolts, which are waiting to explode someday. But this waiting game is neither easy nor glorious for him because it is the pathetic game of those who cannot command their destiny. In "On the Spirit of Gravity" of Part III, he said, "Cursed I call those too who must always *wait;* they offend my taste" (Z, 195). He proudly said that he waited only for himself. But his pregnant self is not waiting for himself.

His boasting game of not waiting did not last long. He opened the next section by sitting and waiting in the middle of old and new tablets, and ended it by becoming a humble suppliant to his own sun-will. He could no longer command his own will. On the contrary, he had to wait for it to unfold as his fate. This was the final recognition he achieved as a soothsayer. By the nature of their profession, the soothsayers cannot dictate their will on the fortunes they foretell. Instead they must wait on the accidental will of those fortunes, their cosmic necessity. One can free oneself from the ubiquitous accidental will only moving from the temporal to the eternal world. The causal necessity obtains only in the temporal world because causation is a temporal relation. In the eternal world, there is no need to wait. Tired of the waiting game, Zarathustra has every reason to reorient his love of Life from the temporal to the eternal mode. So he says, "Oh, how should I not lust after Eternity and after the nuptial ring of rings, the ring of recurrence?" Then he expresses his ultimate hope: "Never yet have I found the woman from whom I wanted children, unless it be this woman whom I love: for I love you, O eternity! *For I love you, O Eternity!*" He hopes that the children he will get from Life in the eternal mode will be much more fortunate than the ones he has gained from her in the temporal mode. By "children" he may mean not necessarily the carnal offspring, but the fruition of his love in all forms.

The second stanza describes Zarathustra's activities of breaking tombs, shattering old law-tables, and rejoicing over the death of gods, but ends by leaving him to sit, like grass and poppies, on broken churches. This scene may appear triumphant and exhilarating. But it is a scene of defeat. Disgusted with the cheap secular culture of The Motley Cow, he launched his campaign to spiritualize godless humanism in the Prologue. Then in "The Tomb Song" of Part II, he realized that his own sense of sanctity had dissolved with the death of God. But he expressed his dear wish to redeem his old dream of divinity ("All beings shall be divine to me") and sanctity ("All days shall be holy to me"). In the next section, he reaffirmed his longing for divinity and sanctity: "You still want to create the world before which you can kneel: that is your ultimate hope and intoxication" (Z, 113). But his ambitious campaign to spiritualize secular culture has only shattered churches and shrines, the traditional fortress for the sense of divinity and sanctity, and his "ultimate hope and intoxication" has been buried under their ruins. Mired in the profanity of the temporal world, he cannot avoid feeling the passionate longing for the sanctity of the eternal world. This longing justifies the reorientation of his love from the temporal to the eternal mode because the temporal world has turned out be irredeemably profane.

The third stanza praises his creative spirit. But he has faced the stark truth that the creative spirit is not under the command of his autonomous will. The creative spirit came to him as a breath of heavenly necessity that compels even accidents to dance star-dances. In short, it came to him as a gift of cosmic necessity. Even his laughter of creative lightning was also the same kind of "accidental" gift. To live with these gifts of cosmic necessity is to play the game of dice with the gods and use the earth as the table for this game, as he recognized it in "Before Sunrise". That may look like an exciting scene, but it is described as a game of horror, which goes on until the earth quakes, bursts, and snorts up floods of fire. The earthquakes and the floods of fire indeed belong to a game of horror. The dice game is a game of horror because it is governed by the Lord Chance. There is no guarantee that the Lord Chance will send only the gifts of blessing. The earthquakes and any other natural disasters are equally his gifts. There is no way to avoid the sense of horror in the temporal world, where everything is a matter of chance. But you can avoid it in the eternal world because it is free of accidents.

The fourth stanza describes Zarathustra's power of blending all things, the farthest and the nearest, pain and joy, good and evil. These have been traditionally kept apart from each other as the incompatible opposites, but he is the redeeming salt that can blend them all together. When he was about to climb the highest peak, he said, "Peak and abyss—they are now joined together" (Z, 152). This is the synthesis of the highest and the lowest. In *Ecce Homo* (*Zarathustra* 6), Nietzsche singles out the awesome power of universal synthesis as the salient feature of Zarathustra ("all opposites are in him bound together into a new unity"). In support of this claim, he then gives an exegesis of Zarathustra's description of the most comprehensive soul in subsection 19 of "On Old and New Tablets". In his encounter with the twofold will in "On Redemption" of Part II, however, Zarathustra found out that the universal synthesis was an impossible task. There was no way to reconcile the autonomous and the heteronomous will. In "On Human Prudence" of Part II, he experienced the same difficulty in coping with his twofold will that was pulling him in the opposite directions. The upward will was his longing for the superman; the downward will was his attachment to the vain herd, the good and the just. It was extremely tortuous and dangerous to hold on to both. Every synthesis of opposing forces appears to generate a painful conflict in the Zarathustrian world. Especially his mixing of love and hatred in his game of love with Life has yielded only frustration and disappointment. Thus he has severely suffered in the conflict of opposites. Sadly, their conflict is inevitable and interminable in the temporal world. Hence it is quite natural for him to turn to the eternal world.

The fifth stanza sings Zarathustra's love of sea and his courage for exploring the boundless space in search of new shorelines. But the endless seafaring guarantees nothing beyond the raging sea and the great seasickness, as he said in subsection 28 of "On Old and New Tablets". The purpose of seafaring was to find the country of man and man's future, but the voyage itself produced nothing but the great sickness and the great nausea. He recalls a moment of jubilation when he said, "The coast has vanished, now the last chain has fallen from me; the boundless roars around me, far out glisten space and time; be of good cheer, old heart!" (Z, 230). This word of good cheer is ironic. More than once we noted that his leonine will waxes and roars on the land, but wanes and whines when it goes on the sea and encounters the boundless space and time. The open sea promises the open future and freedom ("the last chain has fallen from me"), but the open future and freedom have turned out to be an illusion because the temporal world is governed by the necessity of Lord Chance. One can be released from the illusion of freedom and open future in the eternal world, which admits no distinction between past and future. That surely gives a strong incentive to reorient one's love from the temporal to the eternal world.

The sixth stanza recapitulates Zarathustra's recurrent themes of dance and laughter, his two favorite devices for overcoming the spirit of gravity. But he has never succeeded in getting rid of the dwarf. The

dance requires a dancing floor. In subsection 2 of "On Old and New Tablets", he proudly said that moles and heavy dwarfs constitute the floor for
his dance. If his dance depends on the floor of moles and dwarfs, there is
no way to free his dance from the spirit of gravity. In "On the Vision and
the Riddle", the dwarf talked of Zarathustra's inevitable subjection to the
spirit of gravity in his parable of the philosopher's stone. In "On the
Spirit of Gravity", he pitched his final battle against the dwarf, but all in
vain. In "The Convalescent", he was crushed by the monster. Even when
he accepted dwarf as his ultimate self, he could not fully solve his problem. His newborn soul was still suffering from melancholy. In "The
Other Dancing Song", he tried to fulfill his dream of dancing with Life.
But his attempted dance turned out to be a perpetual process of humiliation and frustration. He now says, "If my sarcasm is a laughing sarcasm . . ." Whether laughing or crying, he has every reason to be sarcas-
tic about his vaunted ambition of dancing because it has crumbled. There
appears to be no way to be free from the oppression of the spirit of gravity because he is indeed master of the temporal world. The only way to
be freed from its oppression may be to fly up to the eternal world.

   If you cannot fly up to the eternal world, you can try the next best.
This is the attempt to flee from the dwarf by flying up to the sky like a
bird in the temporal world. Zarathustra's attempt to do so is the theme of
the final stanza. This bird-like flight gave him his bird-wisdom, which
told him two things. First, it said, "Behold, there is no above, no below!
Throw yourself around, out, back, you who are light" (Z, 231). There is
no more distinction between high and low, noble and ignoble, good and
bad. It makes no difference which way one flies. The flight becomes
pointless. The freedom of this flight is the freedom of indifference, that is,
the freedom that makes no difference. Zarathustra always wanted to fly,
but fly upward. Levitation is wonderful only when it is counterbalanced
by gravity. Without gravity, levitation becomes a pointless game because
there can be no distinction between high and low. Second, the bird-
wisdom said, "Sing! Speak no more! Are not all words made for grave
and heavy? Are not all words lies to those who are light? Sing! Speak no
more!" (Z, 231). The elimination of the distinction between high and low,

noble and ignoble, good and bad, also eliminates the semantic distinctions, without which there can be no words. The semantic distinctions also depend on the spirit of gravity. The words may lie, but to live without words is much more difficult to live with them. To sing through life may be wonderful, but singing without words may be pointless. Just imagine what Zarathustra's career would have been like if he had to sing without words. In the end, the bird-wisdom is not any weightier than the birdbrain. Since the flight into the sky can get you nowhere, it is high time to try the flight to the eternal world.

Each of the seven stanzas begins with the description of Zarathustra's heroic deeds. But those deeds belong, one and all, to his Faustian self, which has given him nothing but endless frustrations in the temporal world. In that regard, he is truly Faustian. Throughout his life of perpetual striving, Goethe's Faust gains nothing but an endless series of dissatisfactions and frustrations. Zarathustra was so frustrated with his Faustian self that he finally decided to give it up altogether. So he whispered to Life his secret wish to reorient his love from the temporal to the eternal mode. The Faustian self belongs to the temporal world because it is the theater of action. Hence to give up the temporal world for the sake of the eternal world is to sacrifice the Faustian self. Let us now consider how this sacrifice is related to the biblical symbolism in "The Seven Seals". As we noted earlier, Lampert locates the eschatological significance of Revelation in the marriage of Christ to the New Jerusalem. But this is an unbalanced reading of Revelation, in which the Apostle John sees the sealed scroll in the right hand of God. When the Lamb of God opens it by breaking the seven seals, it reveals the endless series of disasters in the war between God and Satan. The seventh seal presents seven angels, who blow seven trumpets, each of which announces its own frightening events of the war. After the seven trumpets, the seven angels pour out seven bowls of horror, each of which displays its own phase of the holy war. Then, one of the angels announces the destruction of Babylon and the wedding of the Lamb to the New Jerusalem. But this prophecy is only the coda of Revelation, not its body that reveals the continuous horrors of the protracted war between God and Satan. This protracted war corresponds to the war between Zarathustra's individual self against his cosmic self. Satan's war against God is the defiant assertion of his individual will against the Creator. The same principle governs Zarathustra's war: it is the defiance of the individual self against the cosmic self.

In "The Seven Seals", Zarathustra recites only his supposedly victorious feats and never mentions his humiliating defeat. But we know that he was clobbered by the monster from the abyss. The biblical seven seals have its own monster in Satan. This devil is the beast that comes up from the abyss to make war and defeat all (Rev. 11:7). This monster is also the serpent of the primal age (Rev. 12:9). As we noted earlier, Zarathustra's monster from the abyss combines the dwarf and the serpent, the two interchangeable agents of Life, Mother Nature. The two monsters are further connected by the number seven. Zarathustra's monster from the abyss gives him his seven-day ordeal; the biblical monster generates all the horrors revealed by the seven seals, the seven trumpets, and the seven bowls. In the Bible, the number seven connotes a countless number. In response to Peter's question on the old rule of forgiving a brother seven times for his sin, Jesus tells him to forgive him not seven times, but seventy times seven (Matt. 18:21-22). By this expression he means countless times. Zarathustra's seven-day ordeal implies that his ordeal has been as endless as the protracted war portrayed by the seven seals, the seven trumpets, and the seven bowls. That makes three times seven. His ordeal is not limited to his showdown with the monster from the abyss in "The Convalescent". It has been going on all his life. His showdown with the monster from the abyss was only the Armageddon of his endless war. The seven-day ordeal of his great disgust is now transformed into the seven stanzas of his love song.

The biblical seven seals conceal the divine secret that can be broken open only by the Lamb of God. Zarathustra's secret whisper corresponds to this sealed divine secret. Only the Lamb of God is worthy to open the sealed document in God's right hand. Jesus Christ is the Lamb of God, who gives up his own will and takes on the cross for the will of his Father (Matt. 26:39-45). Likewise, only Zarathustra is worthy to reveal the secret of his whisper to Life because he has become the Lamb of Life by sacrificing his individual self for the love of his cosmic self. Each of the seven stanzas of "The Seven Seals" corresponds to the breaking of one of the seven seals by the Lamb of God in Revelation. Each stanza describes Zarathustra's Faustian feat in his war against Life, just as the breaking of each seal reveals Satan's prodigious battle against God. The Faustian self plays the role of Satan in the war between the individual and the cosmic selves. But the Faustian feat is perpetually self-defeating like Satan's defiance against its Creator because it is the defiance against the ultimate source of its own power. So Zarathustra concludes every stanza by declaring his love of Eternity. This declaration is the reorientation of his love of Life from the temporal to the eternal mode. As I said before, this is to sacrifice his Faustian self, that is, its crucifixion, which will lead to its reconciliation with the cosmic self. This corresponds to the future wedding of the Lamb to the New Jerusalem. Thus the allegorical parallel between the book of Revelation and "The Seven Seals" lies in the opening of sealed secrets. This parallel is not limited to the prophecies of Christ's marriage to the New Jerusalem and Zarathustra's marriage to Eternity. Most important of all, the prophecy of a wedding should not be mistaken for its celebration.

On this last point, I am going against the standard view that the ending of Part III is the real coda of the entire poem and that Part IV is an embarrassing addition. R. J. Hollingdale says that the glowing conclusion of Part III is the book's true climax (*Nietzsche*, 190). Tyler Roberts believes that "The Seven Seals" expresses Zarathustra's ecstasy and love of Eternity ("Ecstatic Philosophy", 204). Lampert says that Zarathustra concludes his marriage with Eternity and achieves happiness in "The Seven Seals" (*Nietzsche's Teaching*, 241, 287-88). These commentators believe that Zarathustra's love is finally fulfilled in his marriage to Life in "The Seven Seals." But his love is far from fulfilled by the end of Part III. "The Seven Seals" only expresses the passionate longing that erupted in "On the Great Longing". Hence Heidegger locates the climax of the entire book and its divine suffering in this section rather than in the last section of Part III ("Who Is Nietzsche's Zarathustra?", 68). In my view, the last three sections of Part III present a series of passionate lamentations on this divine suffering and they culminate in Zarathustra's passionate longing for Eternity in "The Seven Seals". This painful longing stands like an open wound. Such an open wound cannot be the conclusion of Nietzsche's poetic work. There is no way to bind this open wound and stop its bleeding except by writing Part IV.

In his letter of February 12, 1885 to Carl von Gersdorff, Nietzsche refers to Part IV as "a sort of sublime finale." In this finale, we will see, Zarathustra will be given the mysterious power to ascend from the temporal to the eternal domain and fulfill his frustrated love. This sublime ending will be the fulfillment of what was prefigured in the flight of the eagle and the serpent at the end of the Prologue, which we took as the symbol of his spiritual campaign. The serpent was coiled around the eagle's neck. This is an extraordinary scene. The eagle and the serpent are naturally hostile to each other; the serpent usually chokes and kills the eagle by coiling itself around the eagle's neck. But this hostile act is now converted to an act of erotic embrace. Now we can recognize the eagle as the symbol of the individual self and the serpent as the symbol of the cosmic self. Their circular flight is the symbol of their spiritual dance, the ultimate end of the spiritual campaign that Zarathustra launched at the end of the Prologue. When his spiritual campaign was shifted from the Faustian to the Spinozan mode in Part II, Wisdom was replaced by Life. Now the Spinozan campaign is transformed from the temporal to the eternal mode, and this transformation is marked by the replacement of Life by Eternity. Life vanishes altogether after "The Other Dancing Song" never to be seen again, just as Wisdom vanished in Part II. Zarathustra's epic journey is guided by three ladies, Wisdom, Life, and Eternity, who correspond in their roles roughly to Dante's three guides for his epic journey, Virgil, Beatrice, and St. Bernard of Clairveaux. Just as St. Bernard guides Dante to his beatific vision in the Empyrean, so Eternity will give Zarathustra his mystical vision.

CHAPTER FIVE

The Higher Men

(Part IV.1-16)

By the opening of Part IV, Zarathustra is back in his cave. He is still waiting for the sign that his time has come, sitting on a stone and looking out on the sea over winding abysses. Those abysses are always ominous because they are the ground of nausea and despair. So his animals have every reason to be concerned with his happiness. They ask him whether he is looking out for his happiness, and he replies that happiness does not matter to him because he is concerned with his work. But his animals refuse to drop the question of happiness and ask him, "Do you not lie in a sky-blue lake of happiness?" (*Z*, 237). Changing their metaphor for his happiness, he says, "But you also know that my happiness is heavy and not like a flowing wave of water: it oppresses me and will not leave me, and acts like molten pitch." Responding to this new metaphor of molten pitch, the animals ask him, "Is *that* why you are growing ever yellower and darker, although your hair looks white and flaxen? Look, you are sitting in your pitch!" He replies that he was verbally abusive in using the word 'pitch'. What is happening to him is what happens to every fruit when it ripens. It is the honey in his veins that makes his blood thicker and his soul calmer.

The change of his metaphor from "pitch" to "honey" cannot change the stickiness and heaviness of his happiness. When he compares his happiness to the ripeness of fruit, he seems to refer to the perfection of his soul attained in "On the Great Longing" of Part III. Even then his soul still suffered from melancholy. Her condition was like that of the virtuous pagans in the Limbo of Dante's Hell. Although they are free of sin, they cannot enjoy the heavenly bliss because their existence is devoid of divine love. The Limbo is filled with the sighs of sadness without torment (*Inferno* 4.25-28). Zarathustra's happiness is like the natural happiness of his animals. Such natural happiness is sticky and heavy because it does not provide an outlet for the overflowing love of his soul, as we noted in "On the Great Longing" of Part III.

Laurence Lampert says that Zarathustra has achieved happiness but conceals it from his animals (*Nietzsche's Teaching,* 292). But he cites no textual evidence for this hidden happiness. Nor does he explain the motive for this alleged concealment. He only claims that Zarathustra achieved happiness in his marriage to Eternity in "The Seven Seals". It is surely strange that he celebrated his marriage all alone. It is equally strange that his spouse is not here with him now. Why is he now living not with her but with his animals? This mystery question cannot arise if "The Seven Seals" is taken not as the celebration of his marriage with Eternity, but as his passionate longing for it. In Part IV, he is still waiting for its fulfillment. His unfulfilled love heavily shrouds his natural happiness with the sense of melancholy. So he compares his happiness to the stickiness and heaviness of sweet honey. In the Prologue, Zarathustra also used the metaphor of honey. He came down from the mountain to dispense his wisdom that had accumulated like honey. When he greeted the sun at the outset of his descent, he looked upon it as the symbol of his radiant wisdom. But he said to the sun, "You great star, what would your happiness be had you not those for whom you shine?" (Z, 9). The great star is the star of happiness. The problem of happiness has all along been on his mind throughout his epic journey. It has now become the primary concern for his animals and will relentless haunt him and his guests, the higher men, throughout Part IV.

In order to lighten his mood, the animals encourage him to climb the mountain for better scenery. Taking up this advice, he proposes to offer a honey sacrifice on the mountain. When they reach the mountaintop, however, he sends back the animals and announces his stratagem. He has used the honey sacrifice as a trick to fool his animals. His real intent is to use the honey as bait for fishing human beings in the abysmal sea. He says that the most colorful abysmal groundlings will come up to him in response to his honey bate. His use of honey for baiting fish is quite different from its use for sacrificial offering. The honey sacrifice is an offering that a humble suppliant makes to a mighty god. Roger Hollinrake says that the honey sacrifice was made in the cave of Trophonius to pacify the serpents (*Nietzsche, Wagner and the Philosophy of Pessimism*, 274). For Zarathustra, the serpents represent Life and the cosmic self. On the other hand, the honey bait is an instrument for controlling the lowly creatures. These two represent two diametrically opposed positions Zarathustra takes toward the world. With the honey bait in his hand, he asserts his individual self and his Faustian will. He is arrogantly determined to rule over the sea of abysses. With the honey offering, he is reverently bowing before his cosmic self. The sea of abysses provides the fishing ground for his Faustian self, but it also shrouds the cosmic self that can clobber him. The difference between the two selves is the difference between reverence and arrogance.

He shows his reverent attitude to his animals by proposing the honey sacrifice. His animals are closely affiliated with his cosmic self because the cosmic self is an animal self. He talked with his animals for the first time in his life in "The Convalescent" of Part III, when he recognized his own animal self. His talk with the animals was the sign of his communion with his animal self. As soon as the animals leave him at the mountaintop, however, his Faustian arrogance comes right back. There is a perpetual struggle between these two attitudes because he cannot sever his link to either the individual or the cosmic self. The same tension had generated all his horrendous problems in the last four sections of Part III. This tension will again be the central problem until its resolution in the loving union of his individual self with his cosmic self in the last two sections of Part IV. The appearance of his animals and their speech in the opening scene of Part IV portends that his cosmic self will exert its enormous power in Part IV. They will stay in his cave to the end of Part IV and their presence will be magnified by the arrival of countless birds and a laughing lion in "The Sign". This dramatic event will mark the blissful union of his individual self with his cosmic self.

For the moment, let us note the same tension in his soliloquy on the mountaintop, which is given after the departure of his animals. He flaunts his Faustian self when he shouts to the sea of abysses: "Open up and cast up to me your fish and glittering crabs! (*Z*, 239)" But he immediately identifies himself as the one who counseled himself: "Become who you are!" (*Z*, 239). Although many things have been written about this enigmatic motto, it may be the simple advice to accept the cosmic self. The individual self cannot become what it already is. It becomes what it is by changing its old self and creating a new one. This is the mode of self-creation that Zarathustra taught in the Prologue and "The Way of the Creator" of Part I, where he said, "And your way leads past yourself and your seven devils" (*Z*, 64). Because the Faustian self must perpetually surpass itself, it can never become who it already is. On the other hand, if the individual self is determined by the fate of the cosmic self, it can become only what it already is. The Spinozan self can do nothing other than becoming what it already is. To become what you are is to follow your destiny or fate that is embedded in your cosmic self. "Destiny" was the first of the four cosmic attributes Zarathustra gave his soul as his cosmic self in "On the Great Longing" in Part III. He extols the magic of relying on his destiny and links it to eternity ("my eternal destiny"), probably because it is inscribed in the eternal ring of recurrence. With this sense of eternal destiny, the great *Hazar*, his kingdom of a thousand years. He is now sitting on the highest peak that will be the center of this kingdom, which will be set up for the redemption of those foundering in the sea of abysses all over the world.

The announcement of Zarathustra's kingdom comes as a big surprise. Nothing in the first three Parts of the whole book has given any indication for the establishment of such a kingdom. He had never talked of himself as the founding father of a new kingdom. But we may be able to make some sense of this surprising announcement by connecting it to "The Seven Seals". The seven seals in the Book of Revelation is the prophecy of the kingdom that will be established by Christ on his second coming. Just as Christ's marriage with the New Jerusalem will establish his universal kingdom, so Zarathustra's marriage with Eternity will lead to his universal kingdom. The great *Hazar* may be the final form that his cosmic self will take, just as the New Jerusalem was the final form for the realization of Christ's cosmic self, the mystical body of Christ. He is following Jesus Christ in laying the foundation of his future kingdom by becoming a fisher of human beings. He is now casting out his fishing line from the center of his future kingdom to all the seas, telling his fishing rod to bite into the belly of all black affliction. The black affliction is the nausea that has afflicted his own heart for a long time. He wants to call up all those who have been struggling with the same affliction. They are the higher men who will be coming up from the abysses and become the foundation of his great *Hazar*. But their arrival is announced with the cry of distress. Thus the problem of misery and happiness is reaffirmed as the central theme of Part IV.

The Rising Tide of Despair (Part IV.2-6)

The Soothsayer is the first of the higher men to show up at Zarathustra's cave the next day. While the hermit of the cave is tracing his shadow on the ground, he is startled by another shadow, which turns out to the Soothsayer, the proclaimer of the great weariness. The Soothsayer is inseparably connected to Zarathustra and his abysmal thought. In "The Convalescent" of Part III, he used the Soothsayer's words in describing his encounter with the abysmal thought. The Soothsayer has come to announce the ascent of the higher men from the abyss to Zarathustra's mountain cave. As soon as Zarathustra recognizes the Soothsayer, there begins a subtle duel between the two old men. When Zarathustra looks into the eyes of the Soothsayer, he is frightened to see many evil prophecies pass over the face of the Soothsayer. Noticing what is going on in Zarathustra's mind, the Soothsayer wipes off his face with his hand. When both of them compose themselves, they shake hands as a sign that they want to recognize each other. And then they try to size up each other. Thus begins a struggle of mutual recognition between the two, as Robert Gooding-Williams points out (*Zarathustra's Dionysian Modernism*, 278).

In this struggle of mutual recognition, Zarathustra presents himself as a cheerful old man to the Soothsayer, inviting him to eat and drink with him again. This invitation should be the reminder to the Soothsayer that Zarathustra had overcome his terrible last encounter with the Soothsayer by inviting him to a hearty meal in "The Soothsayer" of Part II. This is his first punch against the Soothsayer. But he scoffs at Zarathustra for his pretense to be a cheerful old man and delivers his counterpunch by predicting the disaster that will soon overwhelm him. The following is the gist of his prophecy on the impending disaster. Zarathustra's bark is now resting on dry, but it will be swept away by the waves of great distress and melancholy that are now climbing and rising to the mountaintop. This prophecy takes Zarathustra by surprise, and the cry of distress indeed rises up from the abysses and the black sea. It unsettles him because it appeals to his sense of pity, which he calls his last sin. Fully aware of this weakness, the Soothsayer says that he has come to seduce Zarathustra to his final sin. The Soothsayer tells him, "The cry is for you." He hesitantly asks the Soothsayer who is calling him. The Soothsayer rebukes him for pretending not to know it. He says, "Why do you conceal yourself? It is the *higher man* that cries for you" (Z, 242). The mention of "higher man" terrifies Zarathustra and this is the Soothsayer's second punch against him.

Zarathustra has become giddy with fear and trembling, and the Soothsayer ridicules him by saying that his giddiness does not seem to come from happiness. The question of happiness is again the center of their discussion. The Soothsayer says that anybody coming to this height for Zarathustra would find many caves for hiding, but no mines of happiness. This is his third punch. Zarathustra counters it by calling him the sighing bag of sadness and the rain cloud of melancholy. He wants to go away and look for the higher man in the woods, from which the cry of distress came. He says that the higher man shall not come to grief in his domain. This is his counter-punch. He is asserting his authority over his domain. The Soothsayer counters this move by calling him a rogue, who makes up a clever excuse to run away from him. But this roguery will never work, he says confidently. In the evening Zarathustra will come back and find him waiting like a heavy log in his cave. This is the final challenge in his showdown with Zarathustra, who accepts it confidently by saying, "So be it!" When they get together again in the evening, he predicts, both of them shall be cheerful and the Soothsayer shall dance to his songs like a dancing bear. He is now telling the Soothsayer that he will win the showdown when the evening comes. But the Soothsayer only shakes his head. His chief contention is that Zarathustra's happiness is only a mask. The Soothsayer is set upon exposing the game of masks that Zarathustra has been playing for a long time. Their struggle of mutual recognition, which Robert Gooding-Williams talks about, is the struggle to pierce the masks of concealment and dissemblance. Even before the Soothsayer's appearance, Zarathustra had already resumed the game of masks in his talk with his animals. And this game will be more and more complicated with the thematic development of Part IV.

In "Conversation with the Kings", two more higher men appear in Zarathustra's domain. Dressed in colorful regalia, the two kings are driving a laden ass. One of the two kings is talkative and the other is reticent. When Zarathustra sights the kings, the talkative king is lamenting over the degeneration of social order. It is ruled by the gilded, false, painted mob. The mob is a hodgepodge, although some of them dare call themselves nobility. The only healthy people left are the peasants; they are the noblest species today. This degenerate social condition gives only nausea. He is equally critical of the kings for failing to play their role. Still dressed in their garb of ancient pomp, they have become only showpieces of the real power. They only pretend to be masters and their self-deception also gives only nausea. The two kings are trying to get away from the rabble because they cannot stand their foul breath and noise. They are now wallowing not only in nausea but also in self-pity ("What do we kings matter now?"). The two kings are restating what Zarathustra has preached many times over. At this point, he comes out of his hiding and greets the two kings. He says to them, "Here, however, is my kingdom and my dominion: what might you be seeking in my kingdom?" (Z, 246). He is behaving like a king who has his own kingdom. He talks as though his great *Hazar* were already established.

Taken by surprise, the kings tell him that they are looking for the higher man, higher than even kings, and that they are bringing the ass as their tribute to the highest man on earth, who should be the highest lord on earth. This episode alludes to the Magi's travel with their gifts for the baby Jesus, the future king of the world. This allusion is in line with Zarathustra's announcement of his future Empire, the great *Hazar*. When the talkative king condemns the social degeneration of the day, Zarathustra composes and recites a rhyme, placing its beginning at the birth of Christ. This rhyme clarifies the parallel between the two kings and the Magi. Just as the Magi paid their tribute to Jesus Christ as the future king of decadence, so the two kings are now paying their tribute to Zarathustra as the future king of the great Hazar, the new kingdom destined to replace the old kingdom of decadence. The talkative king explains how they have decided to seek out Zarathustra. They were especially enthralled by his teaching on war and bravery, which made them feel the blood of their fathers stirring in their bodies. They are still proud of their ferocious fathers. The talkative king concludes his talk with a bloodthirsty line: "For a sword wants to drink blood and glistens with desire" (Z, 247). When Zarathustra sees these old timid kings waxing in their nostalgia of their fathers' bravery, he feels the temptation to mock their eagerness. But he restrains his temptation and cordially invites them to go to his cave and wait for his return. Although it may be discourteous to ask the kings to wait, he candidly adds, the ability to wait is all the virtue left to today's kings.

After parting from the kings, Zarathustra walks deeper and farther into the woods and steps on a man, who is lying on the ground and sticking his bare arm into a swamp to study leeches ("The Leech"). He is a natural scientist specializing in the study of leeches. In anger for being stepped on, he tells Zarathustra that this is his home and his kingdom. He is a different kind of king from the two kings Zarathustra just sent to his cave. He turns out to be the king over the leech's brain. Zarathustra says to him, "This is not your kingdom but mine, and here nobody shall come to grief" (Z, 249). Here again he asserts his royal authority. In fact, everyone seems to be conscious of his own kingdom. When Zarathustra declares his identity, the Scientist tells him that Zarathustra and the leech are the only two important things for him. He links these two by calling Zarathustra the great leech of conscience and then he establishes his identity with Zarathustra by calling himself "the conscientious in spirit". The leech-like conscience shapes this man's scientific spirit. He is so strict and so narrow as a scientist that he does not presume to study the whole leech. He specializes on the leech's brain; he is a peerless master and expert on that narrow topic. For the pursuit of this one small truth, he has sacrificed everything in his life and become an intellectual ascetic. Zarathustra sends him to his cave with his compassion for his suffering.

In "The Magician", Zarathustra runs into a trembling old man, who is throwing around his limbs like a maniac and then falls down to the ground with vacant eyes. This is the Magician or the Poet. The man appears to be in such a pitiful condition that Zarathustra takes him to be the higher man, from whom the terrible cry of distress must have come. After many convulsions and contortions, the pitiful old man recites a long poem with all the air of poetic possession. With this playacting, he is trying to trick Zarathustra. But the old sage sees through him and starts beating him until he stops his game. The Magician confesses that he was playing a game of his trade and that Zarathustra's stick was hard enough to force the truth out of him. Adamantly refusing to be flattered, Zarathustra tells the Magician that he has no right to talk of truth because he is "the peacock of peacocks." This is the expression Zarathustra used in "On Poets" of Part II in accusing the poets of lying too much and of being victimized by their own vanity. In his defense, the Magician says that he was playing "the penitent of the spirit", the poet who repents their sin of vanity and untruth. In "On Poets", Zarathustra indeed talked about the penitent poets who became weary of the dubious profession and decided to devote their work to the search of truth.

Zarathustra attributes the Magician's penitence to his own despair. He says to the Magician, "I solve your riddle: your magic has enchanted everybody, but no lie or cunning is left to you to use against yourself: you are disenchanted for yourself. You have harvested nausea as your one truth" (Z, 256). This is the cruel verdict on the Magician. He may be able to deceive and enchant others, but he is condemned to his own dis-enchantment. This is his nausea. At this remark, the Magician becomes defiant and rebukes Zarathustra for talking so insolently to the greatest man alive today. But immediately he changes the tone of his voice and terminates his game of dissemblance for greatness. He says, "O Zarathustra, I am weary of it; my art nauseates me; I am not *great*—why do I dissemble?" (Z, 257). He goes on to say that he indeed sought great-ness. He wanted to appear as a great man and persuaded many. But this lie has gone beyond his power and it is now breaking him. Thus the Ma-gician ends his performance by confessing that he has been broken by his own game of dissemblance for greatness.

Zarathustra honors the Magician's confession. He tells the Magician that it is to his credit that he sought greatness. The Magician says that he was seeking a man of all honesty, a vessel of wisdom, a saint of knowl-edge, a great man, whom he identifies as Zarathustra. But he repudiates the Magician's designation of himself as a great man by declaring that he has never seen one in his entire life. He has seen many who have inflated themselves and who are called the great by the mob. What it means to be great and how one can seek greatness constitute the central topic of dis-cussion between Zarathustra and the Magician. What is the Magician's special connection to greatness? He should have something to do with greatness because he sought it more than anything else. Although that is an obvious point, I propose, the discussion of greatness should be seen in a broader context that goes well beyond the Magician's personal pursuit. To pursue greatness only to be defeated by nausea at the small man is the central theme of this discussion. This was also the central theme of "The Convalescent" in Part III, where Zarathustra suffered from his disgust with the small man. As we noted there, the small man does not mean any particular group of human beings. For Zarathustra, every human being is a small man because no one has the creative will, the essence of great-ness. When he tells the Magician that he has never seen a great man, he is just repeating what he said in "The Convalescent". The poet has played an important role in Zarathustra's conception of greatness, be-cause he creates the great ideals of gods and heroes and the superman.

But he has come to see that all those creations are cheap poetic fabrications, which make up the game of dissemblance. Now this point is finally conceded by the poet himself.

The burning desire to achieve greatness is the common bond that ties Zarathustra to all the higher men. That is why every one of the higher men behaves like a king. Zarathustra's kingdom turns out to be a domain of these would-be sovereigns. In chapter 1, we noted, the superman is an absolute sovereign, whose will is subject to no one else. Every one of the higher men has tried to be such a sovereign in pursuit of greatness. But none of them has attained it. The Soothsayer cannot even think of attaining greatness because of his pessimism. The two kings cannot attain it because they are too weak to exercise their royal authority. The Scientist cannot attain it because he has sacrificed everything to become the master of a tiny subject. All of them have turned out to be the small men that nauseated Zarathustra in "The Convalescent". Thus, the despair over the impossibility of achieving greatness is the most dismal feature of his abysmal thought. This is the ultimate source of pessimism and nausea that is shared by all the higher men who have come up from the human abysses. Before parting from the Magician, Zarathustra advises him to seek advice from his animals. As natural beings, they are free of the spiritual sickness of the higher men. Their uniquely human sickness is deeply rooted in their pretension for greatness, which is exemplified by the Magician's game of dissemblance. After sending him to his animals for counsel, Zarathustra feels that his heart is comforted probably because he himself feels relieved from the game of dissemblance. This is the first time he feels some comfort in his encounter with the higher men.

In "Retired", Zarathustra runs into a tall man deeply muffled under melancholy. He turns out to be the last Pope, who served his old God until his last hour and retired after his death. But he has neither recovered from his bereavement, nor become free of his old master. He is still haunted by the sense of piety. He longs to see a festival of pious memories and divine services. He looked for the last pious man, the hermit, only to find that he had expired. So he had to seek Zarathustra, the most pious atheist. Zarathustra wants to hear from the former Pope how his

God died. He wants to know whether it is true that God was strangled by his pity for human beings. But the former Pope declines to answer this question. Zarathustra then counsels him to forget his dead God and be free of him. In response, the former Pope describes the secret character of his old God he spied on as his servant. The old God was addicted to secrecy and even got a son in a sneaky way of adultery. He was young when he came out of the orient and he was harsh and vindictive, too. As he grew older, he became old and soft and behaved more like a grandfather or grandmother than a father. He became weary and wilted. One day he choked to death on his great pity. This is a funny but witty summary of how Yahweh has changed from the God of terror in the Old Testament to the God of mercy in the New Testament, and the ending of this summary confirms the rumor Zarathustra has heard about the cause of the old God's death.

It is now Zarathustra's turn to give his view of the situation. Because the old God was equivocal and indistinct, he had a great deal of difficulty in communicating with his people. He got angry with his people because they understood him badly. Zarathustra asks, "But why did he not speak more cleanly?" (Z, 262). This point concerns the problem of theodicy. Many theologians have tried to argue that the world is governed by God's providence in spite of all the evils and sufferings. But they have found it impossible to make even a plausible case for their view. So they have had to resort to the idea that God does not reveal himself manifestly in the world. This is known as the mystery of the hidden God. Zarathustra, who is not tricked by this theological ploy, would rather see the Christian God as a bungler, who has never finished his apprenticeship. He not only bungles his work out of clumsiness, but becomes angry over his own frustration. This is the best way to account for all the disasters and sufferings God has produced in this world. Since this is a far more charitable way of looking at God's governance of the world than the traditional theodicy, the former Pope compliments him for his piety. He says that Zarathustra has been converted to atheism by his sense of piety.

In talking about the death of God, remarkably, both the former Pope and Zarathustra fully appreciate the deep-seated sense of piety in each other. A while ago, we noted that the pursuit of greatness is the common bond between Zarathustra and his higher men. There can be no greatness without the sense of piety. "Piety" should be understood as the sense of reverence. In "On Self-Overcoming" of Part II, Zarathustra said, "You still want to create the world before which you can kneel." You can kneel only before something truly sacred, and piety is the sense of reverence for the sacred. Although both Zarathustra and the former Pope are deeply reverent, they cannot find proper objects for their reverence. This is the source of their melancholy. When Zarathustra sends the Pope to his cave, he repeats his motto that no one shall come to grief in his kingdom. But he confesses that he is too weak to lift the dark blanket of melancholy off the former Pope's heart. The blanket of melancholy can be lifted only by restoring the sense of sanctity, which lies beyond his power. For that, he says, someone has to awaken the old god again. This is a shocking statement from the man, who has been celebrating the death of God. But the revival of a dead god may take place when he returns to his cave for the evening and the higher men perform their own religious ceremony.

Alter Egos and Shadows (Part IV.7)

In "The Ugliest Man", Zarathustra runs into a truly miserable creature. Just before this dreadful encounter, he feels elated over the people he had met on this day. But the scenery abruptly changes and he enters a kingdom of death, which bristles with black and red cliffs. There is no grass, no tree, and no bird's voice. It is a valley avoided by all animals, even the beasts of prey. Only a species of ugly fat green snakes come there to die when they grow old. Therefore the shepherds call this dead land the valley of serpent-death. Zarathustra sinks into a black reminiscence because he feels as though he had stood in this valley once before. With what scenery is he associating the valley of serpent-death in his black reminiscence? This valley may revive his memory of the steep mountain path devoid of all vegetation, where he had the vision of eternal recurrence in "On the Vision and the Riddle" of Part III. But the two landscapes are quite different. One is a steep mountain; the other is a valley. Moreover, there were no old ugly snakes dying on the mountain path. The valley of serpent-death may resemble the lonely mountain castle of death that Zarathustra saw as a guardian of tombs in his dream in "The Soothsayer" of Part II. As we noted before, however, the castle of death was a totally dead world. It contained no living creatures, not even the dying old snakes. The place that really looks like the valley of serpent-death is the cave of human decay where Zarathustra felt the great disgust with man in "The Convalescent" of Part III. He is about to relive his greatest disgust with man.

When Zarathustra opens his eyes after his black reminiscence, he notices something that looks like a human being. But it is exceedingly horrible. This is the Ugliest Man. We have noted that the dwarf and the serpent are the interchangeable symbols of Life. The Ugliest Man is one of the dwarfs and snakes that are dying in the valley of serpent's death. The sight of this disgraceful being overtakes Zarathustra with shame. When he starts walking away from it, the wasteland gets filled with a noise, which sounds like the gurgling and rattling of clogged pipes. This strange noise turns out to be the voice of the Ugliest Man. He challenges Zarathustra to solve the riddle: What is the revenge against the witness? Then he says that this riddle concerns his own identity ("who am I?"). He is reenacting the riddle of self-identity Zarathustra encountered for his own identity in "The Convalescent". We noted that he solved it by recognizing the dwarf as his ultimate self. But the question of self-identity appears to revive his frightful sense of identity with the ugly dwarf and provoke his empathy with the Ugliest Man. He is seized by empathy and sinks down on the ground, but immediately arises and solves the riddle by recognizing the Ugliest Man as the one who murdered God in his revenge for seeing him through for all his ugliness. He can solve the riddle because he has gone through the same ordeal as the Ugliest Man has.

Zarathustra again tries to leave him, but the ugliest one detains him by holding on to his garment and says something intriguing, "Stay! Do not pass by! I have guessed what ax struck you to the ground: hail to you, O Zarathustra, that you stand again!" (Z, 264). He claims to know what has struck down Zarathustra. He knows it because he was felled by the same ax. When Zarathustra was clobbered by the abysmal thought, he found himself in the cave of human decay, which looked like the valley of serpent-death. The great disgust he felt then was exactly the same disgust he is now feeling with the Ugliest Man. But he is now being admired by the Ugliest Man ("hail to you") for having stood up again. Evidently, the Ugliest Man could not. This is the common bond and the difference between the two. The image of Zarathustra standing up again after being felled by an ax recalls the image of the shepherd who rises up triumphantly after biting off the snake's head. But the Ugliest Man could not bite it off. Consequently, he is still choking and decaying in the valley of serpent-death. His choking is indicated by his voice, which sounds like the gurgling and rattling of clogged pipes. The connection of this valley to the shepherd scene of eternal recurrence is further suggested by the earlier remark that the shepherds called it the valley of serpent-death. What does it mean to say that the Ugliest Man dies a lingering death like old snakes, whereas Zarathustra can stand up? In chapter 4, we noted that to bite off the snake's head and spit it out means to recognize the autonomous will as an illusory idea and to accept cosmic necessity as the only real will. This courageous act is to smash the illusory sense of a bloated ego, which is based on the illusory idea of autonomous will. But the Ugliest Man cannot do it. But the assertion of the autonomous will severs the individual's lifeline from the whole world. Such an isolated individual is bound to decay and die a slow death. On the other hand, to accept cosmic necessity is to affirm one's integral connection with the world, the matrix of all life. Zarathustra has secured this lifeline by sacrificing his bloated ego. That is why he can stand up again.

The Ugliest Man went through the same trial and test as Zarathustra's seven-day ordeal with the abysmal thought. But they have come out with different results. Because of this common background, Zarathustra feels greater empathy with the Ugliest Man than with any other higher men. The Ugliest Man is his alter ego or his counter ego. The other higher men are various versions of this alter ego, insofar as they resemble the Ugliest Man. They represent the various features of Zarathustra's repulsive earthly animal self. Hence all of them are his alter egos with the exception of the two kings, which will be explained later. It may be more accurate to say that the Ugliest Man is his primary alter ego. As we will soon see, the Ugliest Man will be singled out from all the higher men to be crowned for the evening festival. He is now grateful to Zarathustra for not pitying him as everyone else does. He still has a sense of greatness in spite of his ugliness. Bemoaning the virtue of the small people, he says, "They have no respect for great misfortune, for great ugliness, for great failure" (Z, 265). His failure may be ugly, but it is a great failure. He disdains the success and happiness of the small people. His contemptuous attitude toward the small people is the same as Zarathustra's former attitude. He has never outgrown it.

In "Retired", Zarathustra told the former Pope the story that pity strangled God. This story is amplified by the Ugliest Man. Here again he functions as a replica of Zarathustra. Though pity eventually led to the death of God, he says, it was not the immediate cause. God saw everything about human beings, all their ugliness and paltriness, and his pity for them knew no shame and no bound. This is an allusion to the Christian view of humanity as ugly and paltry in contrast with the power and glory of the almighty God, as perhaps most vividly depicted by Pope Innocent III in his *On the Misery of Human Condition*. The Ugliest Man could no longer stand God because He was the witness to his own ugliness and paltriness. So he had to kill God. It was his revenge against God for his most intrusive surveillance and excessive pity. After parting from the Ugliest Man, he muses over the ugliness of human beings. But he recognizes that this ugly creature has the secret virtue of self-love. For all his ugliness, man still loves himself. This self-love is amazing because it involves great self-contempt. About the Ugliest Man, he says, "This fellow too loved himself, even as he despised himself: a great lover he seems to me, and a great despiser. None have I found yet who despised himself more deeply: that too is a kind of height" (Z, 267). The height of self-contempt is the only reliable mark of greatness available to humans.

The Ugliest Man's story of why he had to kill God is taken as a fable of self-love and self-contempt by Zarathustra. This fable should be understood in reference to Feuerbach's theory of God. According to him, God was created by the projection of human ideals, that is, He was the idealization of what human beings wished to be. The more beautiful projections were made, the more ugly creatures the human beings became because they were measured against the projected ideals. This was the feeling of shame the Ugliest Man felt against God's witness of his own ugliness. To kill God is to disown the ideal created by the projection of human ideals. God can be killed because He exists only as an ideal. By killing God, ironically, the Ugliest Man was exercising his Faustian will, the hallmark of greatness. Because of his Faustian will, he could not accept his Spinozan self, the only way to achieve greatness. Alienated and isolated from the cosmic self, he is destined to shrivel to an ugly dwarf because the cosmic self is the ultimate fountain of all power. This is the paradox of the Faustian struggle to achieve greatness.

The Cure for Nausea (Part IV.8)

In "The Voluntary Beggar", Zarathustra leaves the cold oppressive atmosphere in which he encountered the Ugliest Man and walks into a warm and cheerful scenery. He soon finds a bunch of cows surrounding a preacher talking to them. This is the Voluntary Beggar. He is trying to find out the secret of happiness from the cows. He identifies the secret as the art of chewing the cud or rumination. In the domain of nausea, he can see no distinction between the rich and the poor. He has known both. He had given away great wealth, become a beggar, and gone to the poor. But the poor were as nauseating a mob as the rich. They are all suffering from nausea. The only cure for this universal affliction is the art of rumination. He claims to have learned this from the cows. Laurence Lampert identifies the Beggar as Jesus Christ because he speaks in a parody of Christ's sermon on the mountain (*Nietzsche's Teaching*, 297-98). Peter Berkowitz endorses this identification by calling the Beggar a thinly veiled Jesus (*Nietzsche*, 219). But this identification does not fit the text well because Jesus neither had any great wealth to give away, nor advo-

cated the art of rumination. Greg Whitlock says that the Voluntary Beggar's personal history reflects that of Gautama Buddha (*Returning to
Sils-Maria*, 256). This suggestive idea is in need of substantiation.
Whitlock does not explain how the Beggar's personal history reflects that
of the Buddha. Gautama Buddha gave up great wealth and much more,
but did not give them away. But he was a mendicant. That appears to be
the only point of resemblance between the Buddha and the Beggar. Instead of an outright identification of the Beggar as a Buddha-figure, I
would rather take him as a naturalized figure of Gautama Buddha because his existence is totally contained in the natural world of cows. In
support of this view, let us consider what Nietzsche says about Buddhism
in his other writings.

In *The Will to Power* 342, Nietzsche says that the Buddhist is the
perfect cow. His scattered remarks on the bovine existence of Buddhists
generally fall into two groups. Some of these remarks imply that the bovine existence is the predisposition for becoming a Buddhist. For example, the world-weary souls get attracted to the peaceful Buddhist life.
Robert Morrison protests against this view on the ground that it misrep-
resents the character of the Buddha and his followers. He says that Gautama Buddha and his followers were renowned for their vitality and that
the Buddha was often compared to a bull bursting free of his bonds or an
elephant tearing down creepers (*Nietzsche and Buddhism*, 36). But
Nietzsche's other remarks on the Buddhists imply that their bovine existence is the consequence of their religious training. In *The Will to Power*
342, he calls it their achievement. In *Anti-Christ* 20, he explains how the
Buddhists achieve their bovine existence. Though Christianity and Buddhism are two great nihilistic religions, he says, Buddhism is a hundred
times more realistic in coping with human existence than Christianity.
Whereas Christianity is obsessed with sin, Buddhism struggles against
suffering. The Buddhists have gone beyond good and evil by dispensing
with the moral concepts that lie behind the concept of sin. They treat suffering, especially depression, as a physiological problem. As a remedy
for this problem, the Buddha devised hygienic measures such as the open
air, the wandering life, the moderation with food, the avoidance of emo-

tions that heat the blood, and no anxiety for oneself or others (*A* 20). These hygienic measures appear to be exemplified by the Voluntary Beggar and his cows ruminating in the fresh open meadow.

What is meant by the art of rumination? This is a baffling metaphor, for whose understanding the text provides little clue. So again we had better seek some extra-textual assistance. In the Preface to *On the Genealogy of Morals*, Nietzsche uses "rumination" as a synonym for interpretive meditation. By chewing the cud, the Beggar says, the cows refrain from all heavy thoughts that inflate the heart. Rumination appears to serve the same function as the Buddhist meditation, probably the most important of all the hygienic measures devised by the Buddha. Buddhism is the religion of meditation. When the young Gautama began his religious life, he spent the first six years with the ascetic yogis only to realize the futility of their discipline. By their grueling exertions, he has only ruined his health without going a single step beyond the common human condition in the domain of knowledge. After he abandons the ascetic discipline, he recalls the meditation he had under a rose-apple tree sometime before entering the religious life. But he realizes that he cannot carry out meditations because he has been physically exhausted by his ascetic life. After refreshing his body with proper nourishment, he meditates and achieves enlightenment. While he was practicing the yogic discipline with the ascetics, he had believed that the exhaustion of the body was essential for the purification of the eternal self, *atman*. He now realizes the error of this doctrine. He will eventually reject the doctrine of *atman* and advocate the doctrine of *anatma*, thereby admitting the identity of the self with the body. As Freny Mistry notes, his position is equivalent to Zarathustra's teaching in "On the Despisers of the Body" of Part I (*Nietzsche and Buddhism*, 58).

The doctrine of *anatma* drastically changes the direction of meditation for Gautama Buddha. In the old yogic practice, the aim of meditation was to transcend the world of phenomena to achieve a union with *atman*, the eternal and immutable self, which is one with Brahman, the undifferentiated ground of the universe. For the transcendent union with *atman*, the yogin is supposed to shut out all awareness of this world from his mind. Let us call it the *atman*-meditation because it is based on the doctrine of *atman*. Gautama Buddha cannot follow this old tradition because he denies the existence of *atman*. He says that he can never find the eternal enduring self. He distrusts all metaphysical entities that transcend human sensibility. After repudiating the invisible transcendent self, he focuses his attention solely on the phenomenal world. As Nietzsche notes, he practices a strict phenomenalism (*A* 20). *Nirvana* is sometimes known as a metaphysical entity and some Buddhists look upon it as the other world. Although this is a popular belief in the vulgar version of Buddhism, *nirvana* is supposed to be an object of insight meditation for the sophisticated Buddhists. Since Gautama Buddha can find only the evanescent phenomenal self, he makes it the object of his meditation. Thus he has developed a new method of meditation for meticulously observing and analyzing the minute details in the perpetually changing human existence (Michael Carrithers, *The Buddha*, 46). This new form of meditation is called the *vipassana* meditation, which Michael Carrithers translates as insight meditation (*The Buddha*, 52). We may call it the *anatma*-meditation because it is based on the doctrine of *anatma*. Whatever this new method of meditation may be called, it is the method of ruminating on the phenomenal self in minute details the way the cows chew the cud. Carrithers says that Gautama Buddha gave his followers this new method of meditation as a spiritual discipline and encouraged them to develop the ability to witness with full lucidity their inner and outer states in dispassionate and clear perceptions (*The Buddha*, 50).

The Buddha's insight meditation eventually led to his understanding of the Four Noble Truths, all of which are given as hygienic measures in Nietszchean sense. Michael Carrithers says, "These [the Four Noble Truths] are phrased after the pattern of a medical diagnosis: this is the disease, these are the causes of the disease, this is the judgment of whether it is curable, this is the method of treatment" (*The Buddha*, 54). He explains how each of the Four Noble Truths is based on the Buddha's insight meditation. For example, the first Noble Truth concerns the existence of suffering as a universal phenomenon: "Birth is suffering, ageing is suffering, sorrow and lamentation, pain, grief, and despair are suffering" (*The Buddha*, 55). It is phenomenologically shown that suffering is the ubiquitous concomitant of human life as a whole from birth to death. This large scale overview of suffering is further reinforced by the small intimate view of suffering ranging from petty irritations and frustrations to the catastrophic failures and misfortunes. All our sufferings ultimately stem from the impersonal flow of our lives, over which we have no control and which never deliver durable satisfactions. The uncontrollable flow of human existence is further analyzed to five aggregates: materiality, feeling, perceptions, impulses, and consciousness. The second Noble Truth concerns the cause of suffering. It is craving that drives ceaseless human activity and produces the endless stream of suffering. This is the impersonal active principle behind suffering (*karma*). From this follows the treatment for suffering: the extinction of craving in the third Noble Truth. This in turn leads to the cessation of suffering: the attainment of *nirvana* in the fourth Noble Truth.

The Buddha's insight meditation does not merely describe the surface phenomena of human life. It explores and exposes its deeply hidden features such as the ubiquity of suffering and craving as the cause of suffering. The thesis that everything in human life is suffering clearly goes against our surface understanding of life. It is our commonsense belief that human life contains not only suffering but also happiness. It also goes against our commonsense understanding to note that not a single moment of our life can escape the causal determination. The thesis that craving is the cause of suffering also goes against our superficial understanding. Most of us would locate the cause of suffering in our failures and misfortunes rather than in our cravings and desires. The Buddha's insight meditation reveals the deeply hidden dismal layers of human existence by the interpretation of everyday phenomena. In this regard, it is again like the art of rumination. When the cows chew the cud, they bring it up from their stomachs. Likewise, before we can mull over our deeply buried thoughts, we have to bring them up from their storage place. They are deeply buried there largely because they are unpleasant to face. Hence rumination is an ingenious metaphor for the art of reaching the deepest layer of mind, the abyss in Zarathustra's favorite expression, and taming the abysmal thought by meditation. So I am taking rumination as a metaphor for the art of meditation.

The art of meditation is practiced not only by the Beggar, but also by Zarathustra. At the end of "The Convalescent" of Part III, Zarathustra goes into meditation: "Rather he [Zarathustra] lay still eyes closed, like one sleeping, although he was not asleep; for he was conversing with his soul" (Z, 221). To converse with one's soul in silence is to meditate in the Buddhist mode. He has been practicing it for a long time. His long soliloquies in "The Night Song" and "The Tomb Song" of Part II are the vocalized self-reflections. If they were made silent, they would be hardly distinguishable from the self-reflective observations made by the Buddhist insight meditation. They are proto-meditations or vocalized meditations. His discourse on the nature of time and causation in "On Redemption" of Part II is as meditative and as phenomenological as the Buddha's discourse on the nature of suffering and *karma*. His discourse on the eternal recurrence in "On the Vision and the Riddle" is also given in the same meditative mode. Although this discourse is conducted as a dialogue between Zarathustra and the dwarf, we noted in chapter 3, it is really a soliloquy because the dwarf is his earthly animal self. We have also noted that this discourse is delivered in a series of questions. These questions reflect Zarathustra's meditative approach for exploring the world of phenomena. For these reasons, we can say that Zarathustra has been practicing the Buddhist form of meditation for a long time.

The Voluntary Beggar says that the art of rumination is the cure for nausea. Let us consider the Buddhist meditation as a remedy for the same illness. This illness comes from Zarathustra's abysmal thought. In chapter 4, we noted that the abysmal thought stems from determinism, the common ground for both the eternal recurrence and Buddhist *karma*. To be sure, as Freny Mistry points out, there is a conspicuous difference between the Zarathustrian doctrine of eternal recurrence and the Buddhist doctrine of reincarnation, although they resemble each other (*Nietzsche and Buddhism*, 141). The Buddhist reincarnation does not exactly repeat the previous life. But this point does not matter for the abysmal thought. What matters is the Buddhist notion of universal causal determination, which is duly noted and stressed by Nietzsche (*WP* 55). The Buddhists believe that the universal causal determination makes all human beings mere puppets (*Samyukta Nikaya* I: 133-35). Of these puppets, the Buddha says that "as the aggregates arise, decay, and die, O monk, from moment to moment you are born, decay, and die" (*Paramatthajotika* I: 78, translated by Michael Carrithers in *The Buddha,* 59-60). This sounds like Zarathustra's description of the earth as the cave of human decay in "The Convalescent" of Part III, when he was clobbered by the abysmal thought. The decaying puppet is what Zarathustra called the disgusting small man. He is disgusting because he has no autonomous will whatsoever for creating values. The monster from the abyss is his animal self that has no autonomous will. As a puppet in a deterministic world, the ugly dwarf embodies the inevitability of suffering and the nullity of all values. This is the universal fate of all human beings, and Zarathustra's recognition of this universal fate corresponds to the Buddha's enlightenment on the bondage of *karma.* Zarathustra's seven-day ordeal with his abysmal thought corresponds to the Buddha's seven-day struggle.

Following his enlightenment, the Buddha continued to sit at the root of the Bodhi Tree for seven days in order to cope with the terrifying truth he has discovered about human existence. This was his struggle with the abysmal thought, which became the basis for his teaching on suffering and redemption. For seven days, the Buddha tackled the problem of nihilism and despair with meditation. The Buddhist sect that has taken meditation as the central remedy for suffering has been known as Zen Buddhism in the West. The Japanese word *zen* is the phonetic transcription of the Chinese character *chan*, which means meditation. In the Far East, the Zen meditation has been popularized by the allegory of oxherding in a series of annotated paintings.[1] These paintings tell the following story. The ox-herd has lost his ox and feels hopeless. He searches and finds the ox's footprints in the forest and by the stream. By following those footprints, he finds the ox. But he has enormous trouble in controlling the ox because it is wild and unruly. He works hard to tame it until

---

1. There are several versions. Some of them can be found in Fletcher and Scott, *Way of Zen,* 88-103, and Kapleau, *The Three Pillars of Zen,* 301-13.

he can ride on its back. He can even play the flute, while riding on its back. When he rides the ox home, lo and behold, the beast disappears. Then the ox-herd also disappears, leaving only one blank circle on the canvas in the series of annotated paintings. All illusions are dissolved; even the idea of holiness vanishes. When the ox-herd returns to town, he is indistinguishable from all other folk. Oneness and twoness have been transcended, and *samsara* has been revealed as *nirvana*. The ox-herd has finally realized his Buddha Mind or his True Nature. He has achieved his enlightenment and become a Buddha.

The ox stands for the Buddha Mind. As we noted earlier, the Buddha was often compared to a bull. By the time this metaphor was transported to China, the metaphor of a bull was translated into the Chinese character *nieu*, which can mean a bull, an ox, or a cow. The Chinese character *nieu* is gender-neutral. The Chinese have no gendered bovine terms. The Chinese story of *nieu*-herding should have been translated as "bull-herding" rather than as "ox-herding" for two reasons. First, there are not many oxen in the Far East, where the bulls are seldom neutered. Second, the annotated pictures feature a wild bull, which stands for the unruly character of the Buddha Mind. But "ox-herding" has become the standard translation because "ox" is closer to the gender-neutral term *nieu* than "bull" or "cow". In the story of ox-herding, the animal changes from a wild beast to a gentle one. In another version of paintings, it changes from a black beast to a white one. The important point of this story is that the word *nieu* designates a wild animal that has to be found and tamed. Since the wild animal is the Buddha Mind that lies hidden in each individual, it is comically absurd for the herdsman to lose it and make a big search to find it. Only after taming the wild beast, the herdsman realizes that it is none other than his own self. Hence the animal vanishes and so does the herdsman. Their external relation turns out to be internal. The herdsman struggles against the wild beast only so long as he mistakes it for an alien force, just as Zarathustra fights against the dwarf, the spirit of gravity, only so long as he mistakes the dwarf for his archenemy.

The ox is the herdsman's animal self; the dwarf is Zarathustra's animal self. The herdsman's recognition of his identity with the wild beast corresponds to Zarathustra's recognition of his identity with the dwarf. The herdsman recognizes the Buddha Mind as his cosmic self, just as Zarathustra recognizes the dwarf as his cosmic self. When Zarathustra recognizes his identity with the cosmic self, he becomes the superhero. When the herdsman realizes his Buddha Mind, he becomes a Buddha. Any human being who can become a Buddha is a superman. The Sanskrit word, which is usually translated as "superman", is *Maha-purusa*. This word literally means a great person and does not have the Zarathustrian technical sense we have given "superman" in chapter 1, namely, someone who transcends the limits of humanity. It only means an extraordinary human being who can become either a great king in the secular world or an arahant, a Buddha Supreme, by leading a religious life (*Digha Nikaya* III, 1:142). When he becomes a Buddha Supreme, however, he is a superman in the Zarathustrian sense. He transcends the limits of humanity and stands even higher than the gods. The Buddha is finally released from the chain of *karma*, whereas the gods are still subject to it. When Gautama Buddha attained perfect knowledge, the gods worshiped him with exultation.

By highlighting the parallel between the two stories, I do not mean to indicate any historical influence of Buddhism on Nietzsche's Zarathustra. The parallel obtains neither by any historical influence, nor by a fortuitous coincidence. It arises from the fact that the Buddha and Zarathustra are engaged in solving the same problem of nihilism and despair in a deterministic world. The similarity of their problems is fully recognized by Nietzsche as we noted earlier. Because their problems are similar, their solutions are likely to be similar, too. How then does Buddhism resolve the problem of nihilism and despair? When the demarcation between the ox and the herdsman vanishes, all psychological disturbances vanish, too. That is freedom from the spirit of gravity in Zarathustra's language. Such peaceful condition can be found in the Buddha's description of his monks: They "do not repent the past nor brood over the future. They live in the present. Hence they are radiant" (*Samyutta Nikaya* I: 5, translated by Michael Carrithers in *The Buddha*, 75). The radiant monks remind us of the shepherd, who becomes radiant after biting off the snake's head stuck in his throat in "On the Vision and the Riddle". In the last chapter, we noted that to bite off the snake's head and to spit it out is to reject the illusory idea of autonomous will and to accept the cosmic sun-will as the only real will. By the same method, the Buddha's monks free themselves from the emotional strains over the past and the future. This is the secret of their radiance and peace.

Nietzsche fully understands the radiance and peace that the Buddhists achieve by their religious discipline:

> The Buddhist religion is the expression of a fine evening, a perfect sweetness and mildness—it is gratitude toward all that lies behind, and also for what is lacking: bitterness, disillusionment, rancor; finally a lofty spiritual love; the subtleties of philosophical contradictions are behind it, even from these it is resting: but from these it still derives its spiritual glory and sunset glow. (*WP* 154)

These lovely features are fully exemplified by the Voluntary Beggar and his cows chewing the cud and lying in the sun. He must have achieved them by the art of rumination, the Buddhist meditation. He has overcome the greatest affliction of nausea. That is a clear victory over the abysmal thought. The Beggar is also like the Buddha in being a peaceful vegetarian, who avoids the joys of the flesh. Like the young Beggar, Gautama Buddha began his mendicant life as a relatively young man. But Beggar says nothing about *nirvana*; he knows nothing beyond the natural world of cows. He has obliterated the demarcation between *samsara* and *nirvana* just as the distinction between the ox and the ox-herd has vanished for the Zen master. So I am inclined to take the Beggar as a Buddha-figure naturalized.

The Beggar is the first one to claim that he has found the cure for the great affliction of nausea. Hence his pronouncement marks a huge milestone in Zarathustra's search for redemption, because nausea is the greatest affliction in his world. This milestone is the counterpoint to the discovery of the Ugliest Man, who has been crushed by the same great affliction. When the Beggar recognizes Zarathustra, the former calls the latter the man without nausea, the man who has overcome the great nausea. This is an extraordinary pronouncement. In his long struggle against nausea, Zarathustra has never shown any sign of having conquered it. To be sure, when he descended from his mountain cave for the first time, he had the appearance of having conquered it. The hermit said that his mouth hid no nausea (Prologue 2). But this perception was proven wrong in Parts II and III. He may have conquered it in "The Convalescent". That may be what the Ugliest Man meant by saying that Zarathustra stood up again after the ax-blow. The talk over nausea establishes an immediate rapport between Zarathustra and the Beggar. One of them has found the remedy for nausea; the other has overcome it. This common ground sets them apart from the other higher men, who are still suffering from nausea. There can be no clearer sign of becoming a superman than the conquest of nausea. This sign was established by the shepherd when he bit off the nauseating snake's head and jumped up with a superhuman laughter in "On the Vision and the Riddle". The Beggar is a shepherd, who has achieved his superhuman victory by learning the secret of cows. He may also be a Western version of the ox-herd in the Zen fable.

Two Models of the Superman (Part IV.9)

Shortly after sending the Beggar to his cave, Zarathustra runs into the last higher man in "The Shadow". Although he turns out to be his own shadow, Zarathustra has trouble in recognizing him because he looks like a ghost. The Shadow has spent all his life in wandering and following Zarathustra from one remotest corner of the world to another and in pursuing the most dangerous wishes. The Shadow eventually discarded all values and tried to live by the nihilistic motto, "Nothing is true, all is permitted." The father of this motto is Max Stirner. As long as you believe in the truth, he says, the truth is the master and you are the servant. You should assert your mastery over the truth by making it your servant and creature (*The Ego and Its Own,* 311-14). But this willful posture had its own hell, the Shadow admits. By his willful game with truth, he has been reduced to a shadowy ghost. In "On Self-Overcoming" of Part II,

Zarathustra said that the will to truth was only a shadow of the will to power. If there is no truth, every assertion must be only a show of power.

After all these tribulations on truth and falsity, the Shadow adopted a new motto: "To live as it pleases me, or not to live at all" (Z, 274). Unfortunately, he found it impossible to live up to this new motto. He could not tell which way of living was pleasing to him, because there was no goal for his sailing. So he is now left only with a weary heart, a restless will, fluttering wings, and a broken backbone, and he is desperately trying to find his home. He has searched for his home everywhere, but he has found it nowhere. This is about the most pathetic moment in the entire Part IV, and it is the ultimate outcome of perpetual wandering, which is another expression for perpetual self-overcoming. But the Shadow expresses his despair of homelessness in the language of eternity: "O eternal everywhere, O eternal nowhere, O eternal—in vain" (Z, 274). Why does the Shadow use the language of eternity? Perhaps he may be betraying his secret wish to find his home in the eternal world, because he cannot find it in the temporal world. That is what Zarathustra did in "The Seven Seals" of Part III. In fact, the Shadow's desperation restates and amplifies Zarathustra's, which was described in the last stanza of "The Seven Seals". Perhaps for this reason, he is indeed deeply moved by the Shadow's lament. But he warns against the temptation for the restless to seek security even in prison. He wishes the Shadow will find a home and rest in his cave at least for the evening.

The Shadow is not only the last but also the first higher man to appear on Zarathustra's domain. Just before the appearance of the Soothsayer, he was tracing his shadow on the ground. Thus his shadow marks the beginning and the end for the presentation of all the higher men. This shows that all the higher men are his shadows. But what is a shadow? As Zarathustra says, his shadow follows him from behind. Although many theories have been proposed on the nature of the higher men, none is better than the simple view that they are his shadows from his past.[2] Those

---

2. Kathleen Higgins says that the higher men function as mouthpieces "for mental attitudes that bear some distorted relationship to those Zarathustra has promoted" (*Nietzsche's* Zarathustra, 209). Bernard Magnus, Stanley Stewart,

shadows still haunt him mercilessly. The cry of distress was their collective cry. That is why he was terrified, when the Soothsayer told him that the cry came from the higher man. Because the higher men are his shadows, I called them his alter egos. His relation to his shadows takes on different grades of self-identification. The first sign of self-identification is given by the Ugliest Man in his riddle of self-identity. Zarathustra's identity with the Beggar is also established by a disguised riddle. When he identifies the Beggar as a vegetarian, who dislikes meat and loves honey, the latter says, "You unriddled me well." By this remark, he recognizes that Zarathustra solved the riddle of his identity. By solving this riddle, Zarathustra is establishing his own identity with the Beggar just as he did with the Ugliest Man. His identification with the Shadow is most obvious, though he has some trouble in the recognition of his own Shadow. By identifying himself with these three figures, he is reenacting the ordeal of solving the riddle of his own self-identity in "The Convalescent" of Part III. The Ugliest Man and the Shadow represent his condition before his identification with the dwarf, while the Beggar stands for his own self after his acceptance of the animal self. Just as Zarathustra talked with his animals after this event, so the Beggar talks with the cows. Their talk stands for the communion with their animal self. These three are the closest shadows of Zarathustra's own self.

Let us compare these three. The Beggar is the polar opposite to the Ugliest Man. The latter is victimized by nausea; the former has found the remedy for this affliction. The Beggar is the loveliest of all the higher men; the Ugliest Man is the ugliest of them all. One is found in the cold valley of serpent-death, and the other in a sunny beautiful meadow. As we noted, these two scenes are the variations of the same pastoral scene. The Shadow is also the polar opposite to the Voluntary Beggar. The latter is a peaceful man, but the former is a daredevil. The Shadow is the Faustian self. By arrogantly flaunting the autonomous will, the Shadow

---

and Jean-Piere Mileur say that each of the higher men reflects Zarathustra back at himself (*Nietzsche's Case*, 163). Alexander Nehemas says that the high men are laughable characters because they have wrong understandings of Zarathustra's "message" ("For Whom the Sun Shines", 184).

has overthrown all boundary stones and manipulated the truth at will. But this willful posture has brought him the disastrous consequence of being reduced to his shadowy existence. His condition is the same as that of the Ugliest Man shriveling and decaying in the valley of serpent-death. The Shadow and the Ugliest Man are two shadows of Zarathustra's same past. Whereas both of them are the Faustian figures, the Voluntary Beggar is a Spinozan figure. He has learned the bovine art of rumination for living with his animal self in peace and harmony. He is the Buddha-figure, who embraces the karmic bond. At the beginning of "The Shadow", the Beggar starts running away and Zarathustra runs after him. Then the Shadow appears and starts running after him. So there are three runners. The Beggar is ahead of Zarathustra and the Shadow is behind him. This scene of three runners portrays their relationship. The Shadow is Zarathustra's past self and the Beggar is his future self. The former is the reminder of his past suffering; the latter is the promise of his future happiness.

The other higher men are not so closely related with Zarathustra's identity as the Ugliest Man, the Shadow, and the Beggar are. There are nine higher men altogether, but only seven of them function as his shadows or alter egos. The two kings are the exceptions to this stage function. In terms of their personality, they do not at all reflect Zarathustra's character or his past, as the other higher men do. The presentation of the two kings takes a notably different form from that of the other higher men. Whereas the latter appear singly on Zarathustra's domain one after another, the former present themselves jointly in a parade and bring an ass as a tribute to the future king of the great *Hazar*. One usually pays a tribute to someone other than oneself. As the tribute-bearers, the two kings set themselves apart from Zarathustra's own self. Beside the two kings, the Ugliest Man, the Shadow, and the Beggar, there are four more higher men. They are the Soothsayer, the Scientist, the Magician, and the Retired Pope. They represent Zarathustra's social functions. He played the role of a soothsayer in "The Soothsayer" of Part II and called himself a soothsayer in "The Seven Seals" of Part III. In "On Poets" of Part II, he included himself in his scathing critique of poets and became a penitent poet. In "On Great Events" and "The Soothsayer" of Part II, he acted as a scientist in undertaking the descent to the abyss, which I interpreted as the operation of scientific reduction. In "On Priests" of Part II, he said that his blood is related to the blood of priests. The Pope is one of those priests. Thus these four shadows represent Zarathustra's outer (or social) self, while the other three represent his inner (or existential) self.

With the Voluntary Beggar, we had better broaden our notion of Zarathustra's shadows. They are not restricted to his past. One of them is running ahead of him. The Beggar represents not only Zarathustra's past, but also his present and future. He is the only past Zarathustra that is still alive in the present Zarathustra. In that regard, the Beggar stands out in the company of the higher men. As we already noted, he is the only lovely higher man. He is also the only healthy one. Zarathustra shows extraordinary respect and fondness for him, whereas he does not hide his distaste and contempt of the other higher men. Since we have identified the Beggars as a Buddha-figure, we should say that he represents the Buddhist dimension of Zarathustra. Freny Mistry says that the name of Zarathustra's favorite town "The Motley Cow" is a literal translation of the name of the town Kalmasadalmya visited by the Buddha on his wanderings (*Nietzsche and Buddhism,* 17). There are a couple of other links that can also connect Zarathustra to the Buddha. When Zarathustra meets a hermit on his descent from the mountain cave, the hermit calls him an enlightened one. Gautama was called the Buddha, which meant the Enlightened One. When a mendicant met the Buddha on his wandering shortly after his enlightenment, he said, "Your form shines like the moon in the night-sky, and you appear to be refreshed by the sweet savor of a wisdom newly tasted. Your features shine with intellectual power, you have become master over your senses, and you have the eyes of a mighty bull" (Edward Conze, *Buddhist Scriptures,* 53). This sounds like the hermit's description of Zarathustra: "His eyes are pure, and around his mouth there hides no disgust. Does he not walk like a dancer?" (Z, 11). Zarathustra also resembles the Buddha in his mode of existence, that is, his wandering, his preaching, and his solitary seclusion.[3] It is impossible

---

3. Graham Parkes closely examines the resemblance of Zarathustra's mission to that of the Buddha ("Nature and the Human 'Redivinized'").

to designate any other historical figure, whose modality of existence comes so close to Zarathustra's.

Even more important than these formal features of resemblance is the substantive affinity between Zarathustra and Gautama Buddha in their approaches to the problem of nihilism. The Buddhist superman serves exactly the same function that is served by the Zarathustrian superman. Both of them are meant to perform the epochal mission of providing new meaning to the world by creating new values after the death of gods. The world has been rendered meaningless not only by the death of gods, but also by the collapse of morality under the crushing weight of determinism. Atheism and amoralism constitute the common ground that defines the nihilism of values in the two worlds of Zarathustra and the Buddha. To attribute atheism to the Buddha may sound like a gross misrepresentation of his teaching because he talks about the gods. But his gods are derivative entities, who cannot perform the awesome function of creating the world. They are harmless residuals of the old theism in his de facto atheism. Along with atman, Buddha denies Brahman, the ultimate source of all phenomena in the Hindu tradition. The cycle of reincarnation is claimed to take place in such an atheistic deterministic world. It is beyond the control of the gods and demons because they are also subject to the chain of *karma*. *On the Genealogy of Morals* III.27, Nietzsche says that the Buddha popularized and made into a religion the absolute and honest atheism developed in the Sankya philosophy. In his view, the evolution of atheism from theism and its consequent nihilism that is taking place now in modern Europe had run its course five centuries before Christ in India. This point has been substantiated by Robert Morrison (*Nietzsche and Buddhism,* 7-29).

As a chain of cosmic necessity, the cycle of reincarnation is like the eternal recurrence. But the latter has one advantage over the former. Some Buddhists have tried to soften the chain of *karma* by moral exhortations. They have taught that the future reincarnations can be affected by moral and immoral behaviors in the present life. This looks like an escape hatch from the iron chain of karmic bondage. But this escape hatch is an illusion because our moral and immoral behaviors are also determined by prior causes such as our inherited dispositions, education, and environment. Nietzsche says that both Buddhism and the eternal recurrence allow no possibility of aims and goals if they are taken the objects of autonomous choice (*WP* 55). Therefore, human existence is meaningless, that is, if it is assumed to be the arena of an autonomous individual who is in control of his life. Our aims and goals should be understood as the manifestations of cosmic necessity. In Buddhism, he says, the moral precepts such as benevolence are accepted not for their own sake, but only as hygienic means for promoting health, repose, and cheerfulness (*A* 20). The links between means and ends in human actions are as firmly embedded in the chain of *karma* as the links between desires and actions. In the Buddhist world, where the relation of means and ends, desires and actions, is understood in the context of universal causation, Nietzsche says, there is no categorical imperative (*A* 20). Kant's categorical imperative requires free will that is alleged to break the causal chain. The Buddhist denial of the categorical imperative is entailed by *pratitya-samutpada*, which is generally translated as the doctrine of interdependent origination (or causation): Everything is causally determined and nothing can be an original or uncaused cause. The cycle of reincarnation is as deterministic as the eternal recurrence, when all the escape hatches are closed for the integrity of the karmic chain. These two are in turn as nihilistic as Spinoza's deterministic universe. Hence Nietzsche treats these three universes as one set of three equivalent matrices for generating the most extreme form of nihilism (*WP* 55).

Zarathustra, Spinoza, and the Buddha share the common ground of accepting determinism and going beyond good and evil. All three of them are seeking one thing: the redemption of human beings trapped in a deterministic universe. Consequently, Zarathustra's remedy for nihilism turns out to be equivalent to the Buddha's and Spinoza's. His remedy is Spinoza's naturalism and Buddhism naturalized. But the Zarathustrian superman is not always similar to the Buddhist superman because he advocates two models of the superman. One of them is the superman of autonomous will; the other is the superman of heteronomous will. The former is the Faustian superman; the latter is the Spinozan superman.

The Faustian superman is crushed by the eternal recurrence. But his death leads to the birth of the Spinozan superman, who can rejoice in the eternal recurrence. The Spinozan superman follows Spinoza's ideal of loving cosmic necessity as one's own will. He is hardly distinguishable from the Buddhist superman. The birth of the Buddhist-Spinozan superman takes place in "The Convalescent" of Part III, where Zarathustra's meditation is transformed from the proto-Buddhist mode to the fully Buddhist mode. The Shadow is the crushed Faustian superman; the Voluntary Beggar is the newly emergent Buddhist-Spinozan superman.

The appearance of the Voluntary Beggar in Part IV is the scenic station to mark the complete transformation of Zarathustra from a Faustian hero to a Spinozan superhero. The scene of the Beggar's preaching to a bunch of cows echoes back to the first scene of Zarathustra's preaching in the market place in the Prologue. The market place was located in the town called The Motley Cow. He castigated the market crowd for their bovine existence and their wretched contentment. That was the old Faustian Zarathustra, but the situation is now reversed with the new Spinozan Zarathustra, the Voluntary Beggar. Instead of denouncing the wretched contentment of cows, he is trying to learn the secret of their happiness. The real problem with The Motley Cow was not their bovine existence, but its contamination. David Allison says that a motley cow is a variegated cow with splotches of two colors, usually black and white (*Reading the New Nietzsches,* 129). Like a spotted sheep, such a cow is not a pure breed. The people of The Motley Cow are already spiritually contaminated by the Faustian ethos. Its market crowd are eager to have the last man and his invention of happiness by science and technology, a salient legacy of Faustian culture. True bovine existence is beyond their reach and comprehension. They have no idea of what it is like to be a cow and have its peace and happiness. The Voluntary Beggar could not find the secret of happiness in any group of human beings, whether they were rich or poor. He has finally found it among the cows. But the peace and harmony of cows can never come naturally to the culturally diseased human beings. They can be achieved only by a highly sophisticated meditative self-understanding. This is the Buddha's teaching.

As we have repeatedly noted, Zarathustra's mission has changed from teaching to learning. His preaching to the market crowd in The Motley Cow was the opening salvo of his teaching mission. The end point of his learning mission is marked by his alter ego, the Voluntary Beggar, who learns the secret of rumination from the cows. The lesson from the cows is the continuation of the lesson that Zarathustra received from his animals in "The Convalescent" of Part III, where he perceived the illusory character of his autonomous will and recognized the heteronomous will as the common bond of all living beings. This was his valuable lesson from his animals. It was the illusory idea of the autonomous will that had alienated human beings from natural existence and generated their resentment against Mother Nature. But his animals were spared of this spiritual ailment because they were free of the illusion of freedom. Hence they could take the eternal recurrence as the ring of dance and joy. Although he recovered his natural health with the help of his animals, he never solved the problem of his happiness to the end of Part III. Hence his animals opened Part IV by questioning the quality of his happiness, and their questioning was further intensified by the Soothsayer and by the gathering of the higher men, all of whom were suffering from nausea and despair. As they arrived for his help, he sent all of them to his cave and asked them to consult his animals on the secret of happiness because he did not have it. But he finally runs into the Voluntary Beggar, who has learned it from the cows. But his meditative peace is not the ultimate end for the Buddhists. It is only their hygienic means to cope with the turbulent world of *samsara*. Their ultimate end is the bliss of *nirvana*. Likewise, the peace and harmony of bovine existence cannot be the ultimate end for Zarathustra, whose heart has been pulsating with the great longing for Eternity ("The Seven Seals").

A Mystical Respite (Part IV.10)

"At Noon" gives a foretaste of Zarathustra's future bliss in the eternal ring. He lies down under a tree and enjoys a few moments of solitude af-

ter rounding up the company of higher men. The old tree is covered by a
lot of yellow grapes. He falls into a strange sleep and starts talking to his
heart. It is a strange talk, which begins as follows,

> Still! Still! Did not the world become perfect just now? What
> is happening to me? As a delicate wind dances unseen on an
> inlaid sea, light, feather-light, thus sleep dances on me. My
> eyes he does not close, my soul he leaves awake. . . . He
> touches me inwardly with caressing hands, he conquers me. (Z,
> 276)

Joan Stambaugh takes this unusual sleep as a mystical event, in which
Zarathustra experiences the sense being out of time or being in eternity
(*The Other Nietzsche*, 141-46). In this strange blissful state, he says to
his soul, "O happiness! O happiness! Would you sing, O my soul?" He is
talking to his soul just as he did in "On the Great Longing" of Part III,
where he asked his soul to sing a roaring song to express its melancholy
and promised his soul the coming of the vintager, its great deliverer. The
happiness he is now experiencing may be coming from that vintager. It is
taking place under a grove of grapevine, which is associated with Dionysus, the vintager. But he immediately changes his mind and tells his soul
not to sing and not even whisper, because he notices something far
greater than his soul, namely, a god.

This god is Pan, who is supposed to sleep at noon. In Greek mythology, there was a close affinity between Pan and Dionysus. Both of them
are the gods of fertility. Pan combines the human and animal attributes;
he has the goat's head, hoofs and tail. Because he is half human and half
animal, he is very much like satyrs and sileni, the companions of Dionysus. He even joins in Bacchic revels. For these reasons, Pan and Dionysus were linked by the vase painters of the fifth and fourth centuries BCE
(Philippe Borgeaud, *The Cult of Pan in Ancient Greece*, 178). They were
so closely associated that their distinction sometimes became hard to
maintain. This appears to be the case with Nietzsche in *The Birth of
Tragedy* 11, in which he links the death of tragedy with the devastating
announcement that the Greek sailors heard at the time of Tiberius: "The

great god Pan is dead." For Nietzsche, Dionysus is the god of tragedy; he takes the death of Pan for the death of Dionysus. For these reasons, the sleeping Pan can be taken as the sleeping Dionysus. In "The Dancing Song" of Part II, Zarathustra mentioned a sleeping god along with the spirit of gravity to a group of dancing girls before recounting his encounter with Life. He said that the god had fallen asleep in bright daylight beside the well probably because he had been tired after chasing butterflies. This sleeping god, who was then identified as the spirit of gravity and Life, now turns out to be Pan (or Dionysus). Thus Zarathustra's brief mysterious sleep under the grapevine is a Dionysian intoxication that reveals the identity of Dionysus, the spirit of gravity, and Life, all of whom were introduced in "The Dancing Song".

When Zarathustra wakes up from his strange sleep, sunlight falls on him and he feels as though he had slept half an eternity. But no time really passed at all. He finds the sun still straight above his head, that is, exactly the same spot it occupied when he fell asleep. Bewildered over this strange happening, Zarathustra asks himself, "What happened to me?" Time seems to have flown away and he feels as though he had fallen into the well of eternity. Mystical experience is supposed to take place in the eternal world, which lies beyond the passage of time. The Dionysian intoxication transports Zarathustra from the temporal to the eternal realm. At the onset of his mysterious sleep, he compares his soul to a ship that has sailed into its stillest cove and leans against the earth, weary of long voyages and uncertain seas. This poignantly echoes back to his Shadow's lamentation on his perpetual wandering and his endless search for home. The sense of perpetual wandering and homelessness is the inevitable stress of temporal existence, because time never remains the same. The stress of temporal existence can be relieved only in the eternal realm. But Zarathustra's soul has not yet fully entered the eternal realm. She has just sailed into a cove and is leaning against the land.

Because Pan is the god of shepherds and nymphs, Greg Whitlock says, Zarathustra's bright happiness at noon provides a counter-image to the dark misery of the shepherd, who is suffocated by a snake biting into his throat in a dreary evening landscape in "On the Vision and the Rid-

dle" of Part III (*Returning to Sils-Maria,* 258). There is another scene of
suffering associated with the shepherds: the desolate place, where the
ugly fat green snakes came to die and where Zarathustra found the Ugliest Man. That place was called the valley of serpent-death by the shepherds. In a dramatic contrast to these two gruesome scenes of pastoral
suffering, Zarathustra under the grapevine has become a shepherd enjoying a moment of pastoral happiness in the company of Pan. In this happy
moment, the whole world becomes perfect. This blissful scene is indeed
a counter-image to the gruesome pastoral scenes. These two types of pastoral experience are two ways of experiencing the same ring of eternal
recurrence, Mother Nature. Perhaps to indicate this point, the world that
has become perfect in Zarathustra's mysterious sleep is described as "the
golden round ring". The ring of eternal recurrence can be golden and
beautiful when it is seen from the eternal perspective, though it may look
ugly and gruesome if it has to be endured in the temporal perspective.

At the beginning of Part IV, Zarathustra showed his new sense of
eternity. In his mysterious sleep, this new sense of eternity to initiates
him into Eternity, for which he expressed his passionate longing in "The
Seven Seals". In the last chapter, we stressed that the transcendence to
the eternal could not be achieved by conscious effort because it lies beyond our control. This point is proven by the mysterious sleep, in which
his individual self relinquishes its control. When he wakes up from this
mysterious sleep, he suddenly asks his soul, "Who are you? O my soul!"
Now he begins to suspect that his soul must be in communion with mysterious reality. So he asks heaven above him, "When will you drink this
strange soul?" (*Z*, 278). Heaven is the azure bell. He then puts the same
question to the well of eternity and the dreadful abyss of noon. These two
are the same mystical sphere as the azure bell. He is longing for the ab-
sorption of his soul into the mystical sphere. This mystical union will
take place later in Part IV. He is now experiencing a foretaste of what
will come later. He is given not a full vision, but only a fleeting vision of
the golden ring: "Oh, the golden round ring—where may it fly? Shall I
run after it?" (*Z*, 277). Instead of running after it, he must meet with the
higher men who have been sent to his cave.

Convocation of the Higher Men (Part IV.11-13)

In "The Welcome", Zarathustra returns to his cave and faces the higher men to realize that the cry of distress was their collective voice. In welcoming the higher men, he uses the word "despair" six times and calls them the men of despair. But he wishes they will find rest and strength in the security of his kingdom. On behalf of the higher men, the talkative king delivers a speech of homage to Zarathustra. After praising his strong and lofty will as the earth's most beautiful plant, the king identifies the higher men as the men of great longing, of great nausea, and of great disgust. By these three epithets, the higher men become indistinguishable from the Zarathustra of "The Convalescent" of Part III. They are indeed his shadows, a collective representation of his despairing self. The king says that the higher men have come up with the waves of despair. This was the Soothsayer's prediction. Zarathustra's response to the king's speech is blunt and brutal. He says that the higher men are not strong enough to be his warriors. They are no more than bridges to better and stronger human beings because they are still suffering from great longing, nausea, and disgust. He is waiting for those who are stronger, more cheerful, and more triumphant. He calls them the "laughing lions." These new people will be his children.

At the end of this speech, the higher men are treated to a banquet ("The Last Supper"), during which he gives a long speech on the higher men ("On the Higher Men"). In its format, this speech resembles his earlier speech in "On Old and New Tablets" of Part III. He begins both speeches by recollecting the spiritual campaign he launched against the mob and their secular culture in the Prologue. In the earlier speech, he stressed his mission of destroying old values and creating new ones. In the present speech, he stresses the superiority of the higher men against the mob's egalitarianism. He stresses the danger of facing the abyss (subsection 2). The abyss was not even mentioned in "On Old and New Tablets". To overcome the fear of the abyss is to overcome man; this is what it means to be the superman (subsection 3). He expresses his nausea of the small man three times as he did in "The Convalescent" of Part III and calls the small man the superman's greatest danger. He urges the higher men to overcome the small man, his small virtues and his ant-like riffraff. He treats overcoming man as equivalent to overcoming the small man and looks upon the higher men as clearly superior to the small men. Evidently, they have earned this respect for having strived for greatness although they have failed, whereas the small men find their wretched happiness in their paltry existence and knows nothing about greatness.

In subsection 4, he comes back to the danger of the abyss and asks the higher men whether they have the courage to face it. Thus the abyss and its danger is the keynote for his present speech. In subsection 5, he says that the greatest evil is necessary for the superman's best. This is the repetition of what he said about the danger of facing the abyss in "The Convalescent". He has not come to take care of the higher men's small miseries (subsection 6). He says that his suffering is different from that of the higher men. He explains, "For you suffer from yourselves, you have not yet suffered *from man*" (Z, 289). Indeed, he has suffered *from man*, namely, "the great disgust with man" in "The Convalescent". Thus his seven-day ordeal with the monster from the abyss is the basic framework for his entire speech. He advises the higher men against willing great things beyond their capacity (subsections 8 and 13). In subsections 11 and 12, he calls on them as the creators. But he describes their role not as destroying old values and creating new ones as he did "On Old and New Tablets", but as giving birth to one's own child. This is again what he did in giving birth to his new soul by accepting the dwarf as his ultimate self in "The Convalescent".

In subsection 14, he says that life is a big jesting-and-gambling table. He introduced this idea in "Before Sunrise" of Part III, but it was never mentioned "On Old and New Tablets". He advises the higher men never to take their failures seriously because they are determined by the dice game. For the same reason, they should not take themselves seriously, either. Instead they should laugh over themselves. He urges them to learn the art of laughing over themselves and dancing over themselves. The remaining six subsections (15-20) are devoted to the art of laughing and dancing, the essential requirement for the spirit of all free spirits. The target of this free spirit is the spirit of melancholy (subsection 19). It is the crushing weight that the monster from the abyss inflicts on human existence. He concludes his speech by throwing the crown of roses to the higher men and pronouncing laughter holy. Thus the central theme for his speech is how to cope with the danger arising from the abyss and the spirit of gravity. This is markedly different from the central theme of creating values in "On Old and New Tablets". The earlier speech was Faustian; the present speech is Spinozan. The earlier speech laid out the agenda for his spiritual campaign in the Faustian mode; the present speech does the same for his spiritual campaign in the Spinozan mode. The earlier agenda is revamped by the later agenda.

The Last Skirmish with the Spirit of Gravity (Part IV.14-16)

After this long speech, Zarathustra withdraws with his animals from the higher men and walks out of his cave for fresh air. He wants to get away from their bad smell. On his departure, the Magician holds the court in "The Song of Melancholy". He wants to counter Zarathustra's cheerful spirit of laughing and dancing with his heavy spirit of dark melancholy. This is the spirit of gravity, but its name is never mentioned. The Magician refers to it as his melancholy devil and an adversary of Zarathustra. The spirit of gravity is the father of melancholy (*Schwermut*), the heavy and black feeling of depression. He has been Zarathustra's devil and his archenemy for all his life. This devil is fond of all those suffering from the great nausea, Zarathustra's favorite sickness. Though he wears the beautiful mask of a saint, the Magician says, his evil spirit of melancholy takes pleasure in this masquerade. If Zarathustra's cheerful demeanor is only a mask, he has not really defeated the spirit of gravity. The Magician is restating the Soothsayer's earlier suspicion that Zarathustra's happiness was only a pretense. The Magician now wants to summon his devil to expose Zarathustra's deep-seated hidden melancholy. To this end, he reaches out for his harp and recites the song dictated by his spirit of melancholy.

The first stanza of the song sets the melancholy tone by recalling the old heavenly tears and dripping dew. In the next stanza, the spirit of melancholy presents itself as a poet, who was mocked as "the suitor of truth". The mocking critique is none other than Zarathustra's attack on the poet for making up too many lies in "On Poets" of Part II. In the third stanza, the poet becomes vengeful because his work is exposed as lies. Instead of becoming a pillar of God and building statues before temples as he used to do, he now wants to knock them down. He behaves like a beast of prey, laughing and tearing to pieces the god in man no less than the sheep in man. In this iconoclastic mood, the spirit of melancholy becomes a free spirit like Zarathustra's Shadow, who has no faith in any truth and suffers from skepticism. In the last stanza, the spirit of melancholy goes crazy over the question of truth and sinks downwards into shadows. This is the pathetic condition of Zarathustra's Shadow. At this point, all the higher men are engulfed by the sense of melancholy. In "On Science", the Scientist comes up to battle the spirit of melancholy. He takes the harp away from the Magician and warns him to be careful in fussing about truth. This outburst does not affect the old Magician at all. He enjoys his magic spell over the higher men and blames the Scientist for lacking the poetic sensitivity to appreciate his song.

The Scientist now tells the other higher men that they are not really free souls because they do not have the freedom not to be bewitched by the Magician's cheap trick of deception. He is seeking security in this day of insecurity when everything is tottering and all the earth is quaking, and that is why he came to Zarathustra because he is the firmest tower and will today. But the other higher men are seeking insecurity in cheap thrills and excitement, and that is why they are mesmerized by the Magician's song. To seek thrill and danger is the life of wild animals, the Scientist says. But the original human instinct is to overcome the fear of danger. He says that even science has grown out of this basic instinct. It is the spiritualization of the fear of wild animals and the inner beast. His picture of human existence is not any brighter than the Magician's, although he is presenting a scientific account of human existence. His duel with the Magician is the battle between science and poetry. But his sense of fear and insecurity indicates that he is oppressed by the spirit of gravity no less than the Magician is. Hence his attack on the Magician can do nothing to dissolve the air of melancholy. At this point, Zarathustra comes back into the cave and tries to brighten the atmosphere by throwing a handful of roses at the Scientist and laughing at his "truths". He contends that it is not fear but courage that has governed human history. At his invocation of courage, the higher men cheer up and the Magician concedes his defeat. He says that the evil spirit of melancholy has departed. But the Shadow wants to offer his own entertainment lest the higher men may be seized by another assault of melancholy after their dinner. He wants to sing an old after-dinner song he once composed ("Among Daughters of Wilderness").

This song describes a European who wants to assert his moral authority while enjoying the sensuous beauty of two houris in an African oasis. It is known as one of the most difficult pieces for interpretation in Nietzsche's corpus because it lays out a series of images, without clearly revealing their thematic framework. C. A. Miller says that it is arguably the most bizarre and perhaps the most obscure of Nietzsche's poems ("Nietzsche's 'Daughters of the Desert'", 160). Though there have been many interpretations of this song, none of them can explain its thematic fit to the unfolding of Part IV. I will propose the following thematic role for the song. The Magician and the Scientist have handled the problem of melancholy as a matter of truth and knowledge, but that is too intellectual an approach to the problem. They have said nothing about sensuality, which has a much more direct connection to melancholy than the intellectual problem of truth and knowledge. Therefore, the Shadow addresses his song to the problem of sensuality in a mocking tone, thereby making fun not only of the withered European sensuality, but also of the Magician and the Scientist's response to the problem of melancholy.

According to Nietzsche's sister, "Among the Daughters of the Wilderness" was a parody of Ferdinand Freiligrath's "desert poetry". The poetic imagery of the former is largely derived from that of the latter: the roaring lion, palm trees, oases, houris, and deserts (Miller, "Nietzsche's 'Daughters of the Desert'", 166). Gary Shapiro makes a similar observation. He says that the Shadow's song is a parody on the exotic and romantic poetry of the Orient written by Europeans in the late nineteenth century. This genre tended to celebrate the passion and mystery of the East in contrast to the boredom and exhaustion of the West (*Nietzschean Narratives,* 116). The Shadow's song is a parody, which ridicules the withered passion of Europe in contrast to the primitive vitality of Africa. In the nineteenth century, many Europeans were fascinated by the primitive vitality of Africa. Suffering from their own exhausted culture and longing to return to the primitive nature, they took Africa as their model of pristine natural existence. This trend of African primitivism became fashionable in music and painting. For the same reason, Nietzsche stressed the need of overcoming the European alienation from *homo natura* and took special interest in African naturality and vitality portrayed in Bizet's *Carmen* as a mark of healthy sensuality over against the European wilted sensuality represented by Richard Wagner's *Parsifal* (Miller, "Nietzsche's 'Daughters of the Desert'", 188-92).

"Wilderness grows: woe unto him that harbors wilderness!" This sentence opens and closes the Shadow's song. "Wilderness" stands for the untamed primitive sensuality, which is a frightful woe to the Europeans, because they are too wilted to cope with it. In "On the Three Evils", Zarathustra said that sensuality was a sweet poison for the wilted, but the great invigoration of the heart for the lion-willed. The content of the song is given as a narration by a European of his experience in an African oasis. In the first stanza, the European poses himself as a lion of solemnity. But he is not a sensual but a moral lion. The notion of a moral lion is a big joke in the land of Zarathustra, who presented the lion as the slayer of the dragon, "thou shalt" of morality. Hence the image of a moral lion is immediately changed to "a moral howling monkey." A monkey loves to imitate. A howling monkey is imitating a roaring lion. The European solemnity is presumably the moral superiority over the Africans. But the European says to his two sensuous friends that his moral solemnity is nothing to them. He knows that he is only a howling monkey to them. So he places himself in a humble position before the two African girls: he is allowed to sit at their feet under the palm trees.

He is sitting near the wilderness, but safely far away from it. He is afraid of the wilderness of sensuality. But he falls into the well of a small oasis and compares it to a mouth. By extending this metaphor, he then compares his fate to that of Jonah, who was swallowed by a whale. Like Jonah, he has become an object of appetite for someone else mightier than himself. He wonders whether the whale's belly was as lovely as his oasis. He cannot be certain because he is racked by European skepticism. He is expressing his uncertainty and discomfort in being a captive slave for someone else's sensuality. The European moral lion is not invading and ruling over the oasis of sensuality. On the contrary, he is a helpless captive for the two houris, who want to play with him for their own pleasure. In the third stanza, he views himself as the object of African sensual appetite. He is sitting in the small oasis like a sweet date for the round mouth of a girl, especially for her cutting incisors. Now the metaphor of mouth reveals the frightful image of its cutting incisors. In the fourth stanza, he is sniffed at and played about by little winged bugs, the two girl-cats, Dudu and Suleika. Although they provoke his sensuous wishes and fancies, he has no sexual vitality to respond to them. So he becomes skeptical of his virility and prays to God for its revitalization.

In the fifth stanza, since he cannot do anything with the two houris, he shifts attention to a palm tree, which sways like a dancer. Noting with alarm that the dancer is standing only on one leg, he looks for the other leg under the dancer's most delicate skirt but in vain. Wondering about the missing leg, he imagines that it was perhaps gnawed and nibbled away by a lion monster. He cannot enjoy even the dance of a palm tree because he instinctively associates it with a woman's sensuous body and its voracious appetite that may devour him. His morality alienates him from the world of nature; his sensuality suffers and withers from this alienation. In the final stanza, he calls upon European dignity and virtue to roar like a moral lion before the daughters of the wilderness. Presumably, the moral roar should scare away those African maidens. He tells those girls that his virtuous howling is more than anything else European fervor and European ravenous hunger. Then he concludes his soliloquy by reciting Martin Luther's words of defiance against the Church: "And I stand even now / As a European; / I cannot do else; God help me" (*Z*, 309). He cannot do anything else with the sensuous African girls because his sensuality is totally withered.

C. A. Miller says that the narrator is a moral ascetic and that his impotence is the effect of Christian moral asceticism ("Nietsche's 'Daughters of the Desert'", 187). But there is no textual support for this view. The song says nothing about moral asceticism or Christian morality. The European's sexual impotence is presented as an independent fact. His posture as a moral lion does not represent his morality or moral asceticism. It is his desperate ploy to ward off the sexual advances of the African maidens. It is like the devious erotic ploy that an old husband uses against his young wife in the tenth story of the second day in Boccaccio's *Decameron*. A wealthy judge of Pisa obtains a young beautiful woman for his wife, but he is too withered to satisfy her vibrant sexual need. So he devises many excuses to exempt himself from carnal relation with her as much as possible. He shows her the religious calendar, which records all religious holidays and all feast days of saints. He tells his wife that they should never have sex on any of those holidays and feast days in order to maintain their proper reverence for God and the saints. His posture of religious reverence is serving the same function as the European's posture of morals and virtues does. The African oasis presents the erotic resources and opportunities that would invigorate a sensual lion, but the withered European is deeply embarrassed over his impotence and tries to cover it up by posing himself as a moral lion. This comical posture provokes the laughter of the higher men. Thus the Shadow succeeds in sweeping away the sense of melancholy that has been cast over the higher men by the Magician's magic spell.

What is the moral of the Shadow's song? It locates the ground of melancholy in shriveled sensuality. The Shadow's song is highly self-reflective. It portrays his own shriveled sensuality and his own shattered will before anyone else's. We noted earlier that the Shadow is Zarathustra's Faustian self, who has been shattered and reduced to a mere shadow of his previous existence. His Faustian self screamed for the superman and the creative will, and this was his howling as a moral lion. Like the pathetic European, he was howling to hide his exhausted sensuality. All the higher men are like the Shadow. The Magician's song satirized their pathetic condition as the intellectual victims of skepticism. But the Shadow has now described them as the instinctual victims of withered sensuality. His description is a deeper and truer revelation of the spirit of melancholy that is plaguing the higher men. They are trapped in the noose of their own shriveled sensuality in the mountain cave, just as the European is in the African oasis. That makes the mountain cave just like the cave of human decay that gave Zarathustra the horrible nausea in "The Convalescent". No wonder, he cannot stand them. He has to get away from them frequently for fresh outside air. Their withered sensuality makes them more disgusting than anything else. Thus the abysmal thought and the nausea with shriveled humanity continue to be the central theme for the three sections following "On the Higher Men".

The relation of these three sections to Zarathustra's speech on the higher men is functionally similar to the relation of "The convalescent" to his earlier speech on the creation of values in "On Old and New Tablets". After his earlier Faustian speech, he was clobbered by the spirit of gravity in "The Convalescent". After his Spinozan speech in "On the Higher Men", his cave is assaulted by the spirit of melancholy, which we identified as the spirit of gravity. But this second assault is only poetic, whereas the first assault was real. The former is a dramatic reenactment of the latter, as we will discuss it in the next chapter. The reenactment goes through three phases. First, the Magician treats the spirit of melancholy as an external force. Second, the Scientist tries to counter this poetic creation by his scientific truth. Third, the Shadow exposes the shallowness of both the Magician and the Scientist by showing that the spirit of melancholy is not an external force, but the internal condition of shriveled sensuality. This pathetic condition is exemplified by the small man that provoked the outburst of Zarathustra's disgust with all humanity in "The Convalescent". This internal diagnosis of dwarfism is deeper than the external diagnosis given in "The Convalescent", where the smallness of all humans was attributed to their being crushed under the weight of eternal recurrence. Thus the reenactment provides a deeper understanding of Zarathustra's disgust with man and the nature of dwarfism, which we called the curse of the dwarf on humanity in the last chapter.

The external diagnosis is only one half of the story. To be sure, everyone is enchained to the eternal ring. But there are two ways of being in the eternal recurrence, the Faustian and the Spinozan ways. The Faustian way leads to dwarfism. The Faustian self becomes small and its sensuality shrivels because it defiantly asserts its individual will and severs its lifeline to the cosmic self, the ultimate source of its power, as demonstrated by the Ugliest Man and the Shadow. On the other hand, the Spinozan way produces a cosmic giant, who can draw the Dionysian vitality from the ring of eternal recurrence, as Zarathustra and the Voluntary Beggar have done. In the next chapter, we will see some Dionysian heroes such as Napoleon Bonaparte and Cesare Borgia, who become great by drawing their exuberant power from Mother Nature. Arc these Dionysian figures then the exceptions to Zarathustra's great disgust with all humanity? No, they are not. They are no longer human but superhuman. Unfortunately, the higher men are still in Zarathustra's cave of human decay. But this cave will become the cave of revival in the Ass Festival. As a symbol of inexhaustible sensuality, the ass stands for Dionysus and his dynamism. The worship of the Ass-God will lead to the birth of Dionysian faith for the completion of Zarathustra's spiritual campaign.

CHAPTER SIX

The Dionysian Mystery

(Part IV.17-20)

In the "The Awakening", the higher men become merry after warding off the spirit of melancholy. Zarathustra claims it as his triumph over the spirit of gravity. He is announcing his victory for the first time in his long battle against his archenemy. He boastfully says that his bait is working. But the bait of his honey could not have done it. His honey was sticking like molten pitch. In his cave, nothing turns out exactly the way he has planned, and yet everything turns out better than he has expected. These reversals demonstrate the working of not his individual will, but the cosmic will of the universe. But he wants to take all the credit for the dramatic change in the mood of the higher men. He claims to have fed them the warrior's nourishment and their hearts are stretching out. He feels his own happiness. Here is another reversal of roles. He was going to make them happy, but they are now making him happy. Just then he is startled to note that the cave has suddenly become quiet. Here is another unexpected accident. He goes to the cave only to find out that the higher men are worshiping an ass as their god, and the Ugliest Man begins to recites a strange litany for the adoration of the Ass-God.

The Ass Festival (Part IV.17-18)

The worship of an ass is a sheer absurdity, if it is taken literally. To avoid such an absurdity, many commentators have tried to take the ass allegorically. For example, Laurence Lampert takes the ass as the mob (*Niertzsche's Teaching*, 308), and Stanley Rosen takes it as the spirit of the mob and modern progress (*The Mask of Enlightenment,* 241). In order to determine the validity of these claims, let us consider the history of the ass. The two kings brought this animal loaded with wine as a gift to Zarathustra. On this occasion, Lampert says, the ass stands as a symbol of the mob (*Nietzsche's Teaching*, 293). Expanding this symbolic function, Stanley Rosen says that the two kings wish to transfer their burden, the mob, to Zarathustra when they present the ass as a gift to him (*The Mask of Enlightenment*, 214). If this is what the kings are doing to their host, they must be grossly discourteous. They have the nerve to present as a gift what is really a disgusting burden to them. They repeatedly tell him that they are disgusted with the mob and the rabble. Even If the ass represents the mob, the kings do not have the power to hand over the beast as a gift to anyone because they are only an appendage to the mob rule. Nor do they have any reason to worship the ass because they repeatedly express their contempt of the mob and the rabble. When Zarathustra takes the king's lament on the mob rule as his theme and composes a rhyme, the ass resoundingly endorses it by saying "Yea-Yuh". If the ass were to stand for the mob, it would be denouncing its own rule. Greg Whitlock takes the ass as a symbol of the state (*Returning to Sils-Maria*, 273). This thesis runs into the same objection as the thesis that it represents the mob, because the state is a mob rule.

These three views are the recent variants of Gustav Naumann's century old thesis that the ass is the symbol of democracy, a joint product of the mob and the state (*Zarathustra-Commentar* 4:172-78). In "On the New Idol" of Part I, Zarathustra talks about the state as a new idol. Although this new idol is indeed an object of worship for the mob, the higher men have no reason to participate in this worship. All of them share Zarathustra's nausea at the rabble and the state, the mob rule. Hence it is absurd to assume that they have come all the way to his cave to enact the mob cult of the state worship. When the ass is presented to Zarathustra, it carries a load of wine, which has been closely associated with Dionysus. So I propose to take it as a symbol of Dionysus. In the ancient Greek medallions, Dionysus is often pictured as riding on an ass (Caroline Houser, *Dionysos and His Circle*, 50). His coming was envisaged by Zarathustra right after his announcement of the triumph over the spirit of gravity in "The Awakening": "Even now evening is approaching: he is riding over the sea, this good rider. How the blessed one, returning home, sways in his crimson saddle!" (*Z*, 310). It is Dionysus who sways in his crimson saddle. He is the vintager whose coming was prophesied in "On the Great Longing" of Part III. If the ass stands for Dionysus, the god of fertility, the worship of the Ass-God is the worship of Mother Nature as God. Dionysus is not a supernatural deity created and placed above heaven by some poets, but a natural deity of the earth. Instead of taking Mother Nature as God's creation, the higher men are worshiping her as the only and ultimate God, who creates all things.

The identification of the ass as the symbol of Dionysus can explain a few important textual details. There is a notable fanfare to mark the advent of the ass. When Zarathustra sights the ass with the two kings, he says, "Strange! Strange! How does this fit together? Two kings I see—and only one ass!" (*Z*, 244). There are three exclamation marks in this short statement. The repetition of the word "strange" is indeed strange. What then is truly so strange? There are two kings but only one ass. The ass is more precious than the kings. It is their mission to escort this precious gift to the highest man on earth. Let us now connect the ass to the rhyme Zarathustra composes to mark the conclusion of his talk with the kings. This rhyme describes the emergence of Christianity and the rampant decadence of Rome, the two historical phenomena that reflected the expulsion of Dionysus from Western culture. Now coming back in the form of an ass, Dionysus resoundingly endorses the rhyme by saying "Yea-Yuh". The Ass Festival is a Dionysian festival that marks the return of nature-religion, that is, the worship of Nature as God. The Ass Festival is naturalizing God in the spirit of Spinoza's naturalism.

The notion of Nature as God comes from Spinoza's pantheism, which became influential in Europe of the late eighteenth and the nineteenth centuries. With the emergence of scientific naturalism, it became exceedingly difficult to hold on to the traditional theism, which postulates God as totally transcending the natural world. Kant was the last great German philosopher to hold on to the theistic conception of God. But most post-Kantians such as Fichte, Schelling, Hegel, and Schopenhauer took it almost as their mission to convert Kant's theism to pantheism and found their inspiration in Spinoza's naturalism. In Fichte'e philosophy, God is identified with the universe: the latter is nothing but the material for the realization of the former. In Schelling's philosophy, all distinctions disappear in the ultimate Nature, the mother of all things, even the distinction between God and the world. In Hegel's view, this is too crude a way to grasp the ultimate reality ("All cows are black at night"). His philosophy of the Absolute Spirit is a Neoplatonic version of pantheism, which purports to display the logical emanation of all distinctions from the ultimate reality. Although the Absolute Spirit is spiritual rather than material, it is not a transcendent deity. Schopenhauer's philosophy of the world as the cosmic will is his Hindu version of pantheism. Zarathustra's higher men are now treading this long trail of pantheistic naturalism to institute their religion of Dionysian pantheism.[1]

In the late eighteenth and the nineteenth centuries, Spinoza's pantheism became a ground swell not only for philosophy but also for literature. The Romantic poetry of this period revolted against the separation of God from Nature. The German leader of this Romantic revolt was Friedrich von Schlegel, who found his inspiration in Spinoza's identification of Nature with God. He countered the prevalent charge of atheism against Spinoza by praising the sage as "the God-intoxicated philosopher." Goethe also enthusiastically accepted Spinoza's concept of Nature as the infinite divine substance and praised the infinite creativity of Nature. Hölderlin believed in the oneness of God and Nature. Novalis's pantheism led to his poetry of mysticism. In England, Coleridge became a keen student of German pantheism and mysticism. Tennyson's conception of a Great Soul is pantheistic; it fuses God and Nature into One. Wordsworth's conception of God and Nature is no different. The spirit of

---

1. Keiji Nishitani says that Nietzsche advocates a new religion of Dionysian pantheism in *The Will to Power* (*The Self-Overcoming of Nihilism*, 48, 65). This point is discussed by Graham Parkes ("Nature and the Human 'Redivinized'").

Romantic pantheism is well expressed by the title of a nineteenth century book: *Nature and the Supernatural, as together Constituting the One System of God*. The author was Horace Bushnell and the book was published in 1860. A little more than a century later (1973), the same pantheistic Romantic ethos was portrayed by M. H. Abrams in his *Natural Supernaturalism: Tradition and Revolution in Romantic Literature*. Pantheism is the transformation of naturalism into a mystical form. In accepting the natural world as the only ultimate reality, the Romantics could not take it merely as a world of dumb and dead matter. They wanted to believe that some spiritual principle gives the material world its vitality and creativity. Their natural supernaturalism was Spinoza's pantheistic naturalism; their Romanticism was Spinozism popularized. Whereas Spinoza had conceived knowledge and intellect as the highest attribute of Mother Nature, the Romantics exalted her creative vitality as her highest power. The same Romantic conception of Nature is reflected in the higher men's worship of the ass, as we will see in the Ugliest Man's litany.

The litany states the theology of Dionysian pantheism. No doubt, it is a parody of the Christian adoration of Jesus Christ as the God Incarnate. It opens with the familiar expression of "praise and honor and wisdom and thanks and strength" to God. The second stanza praises his role as a humble servant: "He carries our burden, he took upon himself the form of a servant" (Z, 312). Just like Jesus Christ, the Ass-God carries our burden, taking upon himself the form of a servant. Nature is the God that carries the burden of sustaining all life. The third stanza talks about his speaking ability: "He does not speak, except he always says Yea to the world he created: thus he praises his world" (Z, 312). This passage is an allusion to the identification of Christ as the Word in the opening sentence of the Gospel according to John. The Greek word for the Word is *logos*, which means "speech" and it is associated with wisdom. Unlike the supernatural God, the Ass-God does not speak. Although he does not speak, he is not dumb. His is the hidden wisdom of Nature, the wisdom beyond words. The fourth stanza praises the plain-looking appearance of the donkey. Unlike the supernatural deities, Nature is plain looking, but produces all the natural wonders.

The fifth stanza praises his wisdom of creation: "What hidden wisdom it is that he has long ears and only says Yea and never No! Has he not created the world in his own image, namely, as stupid as possible?" (Z, 313). This line alludes to the Christian dogma that God created the world in his own image. If the world is created in the image of the omnipotent and omniscient God, it should be the most perfect world as Leibniz claims. But it is far from perfect. It is riddled with so many defects and disasters that some theologians have regarded it as a work of a bungling deity. In his talk with the last Pope on theodicy in "Retired", Zarathustra said that the Christian God was only an apprentice who bungled too much. But all those defects can be excused and explained if the creator is understood to be the Nature-God, who employs natural selection as the method of creation. Since natural selection is not guided by any design or foresight, it appears to be stupid if it is mistaken as the work of an intelligent agent. But this seemingly stupid method hides its own wisdom, that is, the inventive genius of creating the wonders of life ranging from the single cells to the complex organs of sensation and reproduction. Some biologists are so impressed with these wonders of life that they regard the entire biosphere as a huge inventive brain. The Ass-God has long ears. His virtue lies not in speaking but in listening. Nature listens to everything that takes place in her dominion; it has a wonderful feedback mechanism for natural selection.

Especially impressed with Nature's way of creation, the Scientist says, "God is supposed to be eternal, according to the witness of the most pious: whoever has that much time, takes his time. As slowly and as stupidly as possible: in *this* way, one like that can still get very far" (Z, 315). The Nature-God takes billions of years for creation, whereas the Christian God takes only six days. This long stretch of time belongs to the eternity of Mother Nature. Such a long period is required for the creation of Nature-God because its method of creation is natural selection, the blind process of fortuitous happenings. Hence the Ass-God can be said to take both straight and crooked paths (the sixth stanza). These are the same crooked paths that Life claimed for self-overcoming in "On Self-Overcoming" of Part II. Life is Mother Nature, the Ass-God, and Life's self-overcoming is Nature's self-creation. But the distinction between straight and crooked paths is not the consequence of design and intent, but the outcome of accidents in the domain of cosmic necessity. The God of Nature is the god of innocence, whose kingdom lies beyond good and evil and knows no distinction between straight and crooked. Hence it refuses to recognize all human distinctions, even the distinction between the beggars and the kings (the seventh stanza). That is exactly the way Jesus Christ treated all human beings. Like Christ again, the Nature-God loves children and embraces sinners.

Finally, the last stanza praises the sensuality of the Ass-God: "You love she-asses and fresh figs; you do not despise food. A thistle tickles your heart if you happen to be hungry. In this lies the wisdom of a god" (Z, 313). Whereas the previous stanzas play on the subtle mixture of resemblance and difference between the Ass-God and the Christian God, this stanza starkly points out their unbridgeable difference. The Christian God-man led the life of chastity and celibacy, thereby disowning his reproductive instinct. His sensuality must have shriveled like that of the European in the Shadow's song. But the Ass-God loves sex and food. This shows its exuberant sensuality, which is natural for the Nature-God because its method of creation is reproduction. Traditionally, the ass has been known as a notorious beast of inexhaustible sexual energy. No wonder, the worship of the Ass-God takes place after the Shadow's song revived the higher men's shriveled sensuality. Their asinine festival can be taken as the celebration of their resurgent sensuality.

At the end of every stanza, the ass heartily brays Yea-Yuh. Without having any chance to appreciate the theological significance of the litany, Zarathustra storms into the cave and scolds the higher men. He calls upon them, one by one, and orders them to account for their childish and stupid behavior. But their responses are thoughtful and startling. The last Pope appeals to his motto: "Better to adore God in this form than in no form at all!" (Z, 314). Now that he has found something on earth to adore, he says, his old pious heart leaps and jumps. When Zarathustra asks his Shadow how a free spirit can do this sort of silly thing, the Shadow says that the fault lies with the Ugliest Man, who has awakened God again.

The Magician candidly admits his own stupidity in worshiping the ass. But the Scientist takes a strong stand. He says that there is something in this spectacle that even pleases his conscience. Even if he may be an atheist, God in this form is most credible to him. When Zarathustra finally turns to the Ugliest Man, he notices something unusual. The Ugliest Man has awakened not only God, but himself. This is an important point. The Ass Festival has awakened not only God, but also the spirit of the higher men. The religious revival is not merely the revival of religious practices, but the spiritual revival of human beings. Amazed at this development, Zarathustra congratulates the higher men for having become truly joyful again. This is clearly their triumph over the spirit of melancholy. He says that the higher men have blossomed by the magic power of the festival. They were like withered plants when they came to the cave. They are now experiencing a new sense of vitality and elation.

This stunning outcome of worshiping the Ass-God immediately changes Zarathustra's heart. He exhorts the higher men not to forget this night and proceeds to consecrate the Ass Festival: "And when you celebrate it again, this ass festival, do it for your own sake, and also do it for my sake. And in remembrance of *me*" (Z, 317). This is a parody of the words that Christ used in consecrating the Last Supper. By using these words, he is instituting a religion of Nature-God. This is the new religion of Dionysian pantheism. The function of this new religion is to revitalize human beings by the renewal of their connection to Mother Nature, as manifested in the Ass-Festival. In this new religion, Zarathustra finally fulfills his lifelong dream of regaining the sense of divinity and sanctity that he once had in his youth. He can also bring to fruition the ambitious campaign that he launched for the spiritualization of secular culture in the Prologue. He has found a new God to sanctify our natural existence. If Mother Nature is holy and sacred, all her creation must equally be holy and sacred. Nikolai Berdyaev calls this spiritual move the religious renaissance that moves humanity out of godless humanism to divine humanism (*The Meaning of the Creative Act*, 82).

Because the Ugliest Man's litany and Zarathustra's words of consecration are parodies, the Ass Festival is usually assumed to be a ritual of satire and derision. But this is a mistake due to our misconception of parody. Nowadays, the word 'parody' indeed carries the overtone of satire and derision. But the model of parody for the Ass Festival is the parody mass of the Renaissance, a popular genre of musical compositions written by Mouton, Pontio, Cerone, Palestrina, and many other musicians. Because the parody mass imitated, in its form and content, the Roman Catholic Mass, it was also called the imitation mass. Unfortunately, even 'imitation' has become a derogatory word for us. In the Christian tradition, however, 'imitation' was a word of veneration as it was shown in "the imitation of Christ," which meant reverent emulation. The word 'parody' in "the parody mass" simply means imitation and emulation. There is no sense of satire or derision in the parody mass. On the contrary, it is solemn and reverent. Likewise, though the Ass Festival is a parody, it is equally solemn and reverent. Textually, it is impossible to detect any sense of satire or derision in the whole affair. It can be imputed to the text only by the reader's ignorance and prejudice.

The Ass Festival and Nature-Religion (Part IV.17-18)

The Ass Festival of Part IV is usually taken as Nietzsche's poetic invention. Gustav Naumann is one of the rare exceptions. He talks about the Christian Ass Festival and its influence on the Ass Festival of *Zarathustra* (*Zarathustra-Commentar* 4:172-90). But this valuable historical observation has been ignored by most of the later commentators, who have uncritically adopted his groundless identification of the ass as the symbol of democracy, a joint product of the mob and the state. The ass festival of Part IV is a parody of the medieval Christian Festival, which was popular especially in France from the eleventh to the sixteenth century.[2] It was an annual feast celebrated on the day of Circumcision, Epiphany, or the

---

2. My account is largely drawn from Ingvild Gilhus, "Carnival in Religion: The Feast of Fools in France," *Numen* 37 (1990): 24-52. Other accounts can be found in Carl Jung, "On the Psychology of the Trickster Figure" and Joseph Campbell, *The Masks of God: Primitive Mythology*, 274.

octave of the Epiphany. The original name for the Ass Festival is *asi-naria festa*, which is sometimes translated as "the Feast of Asses". It is a special version of the Feast of Fools, in which the ass takes the center stage. The Feast of Fools, never an officially approved festival, was often condemned for its vulgarity by the Church authorities. The feast was led by the lowest members of the clergy, especially the subdeacons, who played the role of bishops and clowns at the same time. It began as a service in a church and ended as a procession to the outside. The entire event was built around the ass. For the service, an ass was sometimes brought into the church, and a litany of praise was sung to the braying of the ass. Whether the ass was led into the church or left standing outside, the celebrant and the congregation heartily brayed like ass, repeatedly saying "Amen".

How did the ass come into the Feast of Fools? The historians have located the probable sources in both the pagan and the Judeo-Christian traditions. According to Ingvild Gilhus, the ass is likely the transmutation of a little deer or hind in the pagan festival games called Cervulus or Cervula. Gustav Naumann says that many features of the Christian Ass Festival have been directly taken from the ancient Dionysian mystery cult (*Zarathustra-Commentar* 4:190). But the ass was also connected to the biblical tradition. In the Bible, the ass was perhaps the most important work beast for carrying heavy loads. This point is noted in the Ugliest Man's litany for the ass. The ass also served as a palfrey for patriarchs, prophets, and even kings. Abraham rides a donkey on his way to sacrifice Isaac to God (Gen. 22:3), and the Mesopotamian diviner Balaam travels on a donkey, which has the miraculous power of seeing an angel, who is invisible to human eyes (Num. 22:23). Jesus rides a donkey in his triumphant entry into Jerusalem on Palm Sunday (Matt. 21:1-9). He not only ends his divine mission on a donkey, but also begins it in the stable of a donkey. The baby Jesus was born in a manger evidently located in the stable of a donkey. Hence the Nativity was closely associated with the ass. In the medieval Christian iconography, the ass is represented at the crib of the baby Jesus and used as a palfrey for him and his mother in their Flight to Egypt. In the procession of the Ass Festival, a real ass was used to enact Balaam's ass and the Flight to Egypt. Because of the intimate connection between Jesus and the ass, Ingvild Gilhus says, the Christians are reported to "have worshiped the Ass, the head of an Ass, or a man with the head of an Ass as their God" ("Carnival in Religion," 38-39). This report was so strange and so widespread that Tertullian took it seriously and tried to explain it away (P. G. Walsh, *Apuleius: The Golden Ass*, xxxviii).

This is the story of how the ass came to play the central role in the Ass Festival. The ruling idea of this festival was the reversal of roles and the inversion of statuses. The lower clergy played the role of the higher clergy; human beings played the role of animals by wearing animal masks. Men dressed themselves in the feminine garb to pose as women. This reversal of roles indicates the transformation of a higher into a lower nature in opposition to the Christian teaching for the transformation of a lower into a higher nature. It was the reversal of the doctrine of transubstantiation. Instead of striving for the transformation of human beings from their natural state into the promised supernatural state, the Christian Ass Festival was designed to celebrate the transformation of human beings to beasts. Just as God has become human, a human being should become a beast, or God who has become human should finally become a beast. To facilitate the entrance into the kingdom of beasts, the Ass Festival was meant to open up the human body to the sensory world in opposition to the Christian teaching that the bodily senses should be closed to open up the spiritual senses for the supernatural world. This Christian teaching was based on the ascetic premise that the spiritual senses can be cultivated only by suppressing the carnal senses, which are assumed to be basically evil. The Ass Festival stood this ascetic doctrine on its head by vouching for the goodness of carnal senses and celebrating the physical dimension of human existence. It used blood pudding and sausage for the Eucharist. Consequently, the feast was denounced as a detestable mockery of the sacrament by the Church authorities.

The spirit of the Ass Festival is to invert the Christian teaching: instead of trying to become like God, we should all rejoice in becoming healthy animals. Moreover, this inverted message was taken to be the message of redemption delivered by Jesus Christ himself, whose life was closely associated with the ass. In this inversion of the Christian dogma, God takes on the humble form of a donkey when he comes down from the supernatural to the natural world. The same spirit of inversion is taking place in the Ass Festival of the higher men. Their Ass-God is the God who has come down from the supernatural to the natural world, that is, their god is being naturalized. The Ugliest Man, who has killed God as the supernatural being, is now sanctifying Nature as God. By worshipping this new God, the higher men are rejoicing over their status as healthy beasts just as the Christians did in the medieval festival. The Ass Festival also restores their sense of reverence. The higher men have become pious again by finding something before which they can kneel. Prior to this event, they were all seeking the sense of reverence because its loss was the chief cause for their despair in the Godless world. This point was well articulated by the Retired Pope in his conversation with Zarathustra. The sense of reverence has also haunted Zarathustra throughout his career. If Nature is recognized as the creator of all things, its awesome power is overwhelming and worthy of reverence. To worship Nature as God is to institute a Nature-religion, and the higher men are instituting one by reviving and parodying the medieval festival.

Some people have the wrong impression that Nietzsche is opposed to all religions. On the contrary, he stresses the importance of religion for all social strata (*BGE* 61). He is against only the otherworldly religions because they alienate human beings from the natural world. The function of a Nature-religion is to reinforce the human connection to Mother Nature. He seems to think that the teaching of Christ was originally for natural religion, but it was perverted to an anti-natural religion by his followers. If so, the inversion of Christianity can not only institute a Nature-religion but also restore Christianity to its original spirit. Although I have no strong textual evidence in support of this view, I will cite the following for your consideration. In "On Old and New Tablets" of Part III, Christ is depicted as the creator, who breaks the tablet of old values and institutes the tablet of new values. The tablet of old values was the rigid, petrified value scheme of the Pharisees. Zarathustra says, "O my brothers, one man once saw into the hearts of the good and the just and said, 'They are the pharisees.'" Then he adds, "The good *must* crucify him who invents his own virtue. That is the truth" (*Z*, 212).

What new values was Jesus creating against the old values of the Pharisees? In Nietzsche's account (*A* 25), the old Judaism originally thrived as a natural religion. Yahweh was the god of nature, to whom the old Jews were grateful for their livestock and husbandry. But they lost faith in their God after the Assyrian invasion. They thought that the old God could no longer do for them what he formerly had done. So they had to alter their conception of God: He was changed from the God of nature to the God of morality. Whereas the old God operated with natural causality, the new God operated with moral reward and punishment, the anti-natural causality. This was the denaturalization of Yahweh that was engineered by the priestly class. By this transformation of their God, the priests also desecrated nature (*A* 26). As long as Yahweh was believed to be the God of nature, nature was regarded as sacred. But nature was degraded as soon as their God became anti-natural. Together with nature, all natural instincts and values became also degraded and desecrated.

The Pharisees were heirs to this systematic degradation of nature, which was achieved by the exaltation of God above nature. According to Nietzsche, Christ rejects this Pharisaic dogma of anti-naturalism and the separation of nature from God. Jesus had no reason to deny the natural world because he never accepted the ecclesiastical concept 'world' (*A* 32). Because he rejects the separation of the world from God, he seeks eternal life here and how (*A* 29). Finally, Christ completely transcends the Pharisaic notion of guilt and punishment:

> In the entire psychology of the 'Gospel' the concept guilt and punishment is lacking; likewise the concept reward. 'Sin', every kind of distancing relationship between God and man is abolished—*precisely this is the 'glad tidings'*. (*A* 33)

Nietzsche believes that Christ's mission to restore the unity of God and man was aborted by the trickery of Paul, a faithful product of the rabbinical tradition (*A* 41-44).

For a dramatic contrast to Paul's sickly and decadent instinct, Nietzsche cites the healthy and cheerful instinct of Cesare Borgia, a pre-eminent specimen of the Renaissance (*A* 46). In his view, the Renaissance has been "the only great war" for the revaluation of Christian values, namely, for restoring the sanctity of nature. In this war, the Papacy was the target of Cesare Borgia's most fundamental attack:

> Neither has there been a form of *attack* more fundamental, more direct, and more strenuously delivered on the entire front and at the enemy's center! To attack at the decisive point, in the very seat of Christianity, to set the *noble* values on the throne, which is to say to set them *into* the instincts, the deepest needs and desires of him who sits thereon. . . . I see in my mind's eye a *possibility* of a quite unearthly fascination and splendour—it seems to glitter with a trembling of every refinement of beauty, there seems to be at work in it an art so divine, so diabolically divine, that one might scour the millennia in vain for a second such possibility; I behold a spectacle at once so meaningful and so strangely paradoxical it would have given all the gods of Olympus an opportunity for an immortal roar of laughter—*Cesare Borgia as Pope.* (*A* 61)

This long passage portrays Nietzsche's fantasy for the successful outcome of Cesare Borgia's attempt to become the Pope. With his success, he could have placed "the *noble* values on the throne," thereby fully realizing the Renaissance ethos of natural values. This fantasy is not too unrealistic. Under the powerful impact of the Renaissance, the Vatican was fast becoming a secular state and its sacraments were being used as theocratic devices for controlling political power. This was the corruption of the Church that was later to provoke Martin Luther's passion for the Reformation. But the corruption of the Church was her regeneration in Nietzsche's view. He says, "What Luther saw was the *corruption* of the Papacy, while precisely the opposite was palpably obvious: the old corruption, the *peccatum originale,* Christianity *no* longer sat on the Papal throne! Life sat there instead! The triumph of life!" (*A* 61). Cesare Borgia as the Pope could have completed the regeneration of Christianity, which had embodied the priestly degeneration of a nature-religion. He was the Renaissance prince, who served as the model for Machiavelli's secular manual for power politics, *The Prince*. The cultural conflict between the Renaissance and the Reformation was the war between the princes of natural values and the priests of anti-natural values.

Daniel Conway says that Nietzsche was intrigued with Borgia's ambition to occupy the Petrine throne (*Nietzsche's Dangerous Game*, 204-5). In Peter Berkowitz's view, the image of Cesare Borgia as Pope is Nietzsche's fantasy over the lost chance to abolish Christianity (*Nietzsche*, 122). With Borgia on the papal throne, Nietzsche indeed adds, Christianity would have been abrogated or abolished. But the Popes do not have the power to abolish Christianity any more than American Presidents have the power to dissolve the Union. But the Popes can subvert or abrogate Christianity by transforming its anti-natural values into natural ones. Nietzsche is imagining Cesare Borgia's bold venture on the Petrine throne for the transformation of Christianity to a completely natural religion. Such audacious move is made in the Ass Festival of Part IV, when the former Pope gives his pious defense of the nature-religion: "My old heart leaps and jumps that there is still something on earth to adore" (Z, 314).

In the ancient world of primitive religions, the earth was universally assumed to be the only thing to adore. As we noted in chapter 4, the goddesses of earth and fertility were the highest deities before the emergence of the gods of warfare and heaven. Nothing could be more sacred than Mother Nature because she was believed to be the eternal source of all life. Her sanctity was the focus of all primitive religions. Their rituals and festivals celebrated her sacred power and blessings. But Mother Nature was desecrated and degraded by the Pharisees when they denaturalized Yahweh, according to Nietzsche. This decadent Pharisaic tradition was passed on to Christianity, which reduced naturality to profanity and equated supernaturality with sanctity. Even the death of God has not restored the sanctity of Nature. On the contrary, Mother Nature is humiliated even more severely by the secular humanists and scientists because they view the earth as nothing more than a massive cluster of inert material objects. Such a degrading view of Nature was the basis for the cheap secular culture that Zarathustra despised and reviled in The Motley Cow. Spinoza tried to restore the sanctity and divinity of Nature by transferring all divine attributes from the Christian God to her and exalting her as the only Divinity. Zarathustra and the higher men are performing the same restoration project in their worship of the ass. The donkey is a plain animal. It is too plain to be taken as the symbol of a god. So is Mother Nature. But that is the misleading appearance that hides her divinity and sanctity from the uninitiated. Only the initiates can appreciate her divinity and sanctity that are praised by the Ugliest Man in his litany.

In Spinoza's scheme of restoration, the Christian God is replaced by Mother Nature and the sanctity of the former is transferred to the latter. But Spinoza does not advocate religious rituals for the adoration of Mother Nature. This is the vital element missing from his scheme of restoration. Zarathustra secures this vital element by instituting a religious worship of Nature. If Mother Nature is really divine, we should express our reverence to her through rituals and display our sense of gratitude in festivals. To have such rituals and festivals for Mother Nature is to have a nature-religion. Such a natural religion is instituted by Zarathustra's consecration of the Ass Festival as a permanent ritual. By the power of natural devotion, he can redeem the lost dream of his youth: "All beings shall be divine to me" and "All days shall be holy to me." If Mother Nature is holy and divine, all things from her must also be holy and divine. Such a positive development can be secured not by abolishing Christianity, but by converting it from an anti-natural religion to a natural one. Merely abolishing Christianity can only lead to the cheap secular culture of the market place.

The Religion of Nature and the Cult of Isis (Part IV.17-18)

Let us now consider the connection of the Ass Festival of Part IV to the pagan tradition. Our best guide is Kathleen Higgins, who traces the ass of Zarathustra's festival back to *The Golden Ass* by Apuleius (*Nietzsche's*

Zarathustra, 211-19). It is the story of one Lucius, who is transformed into an ass by a mistake in magic and goes through a series of horrible treatments at the hands of his successive owners until he regains his human form with the grace of Isis. *The Golden Ass* has also been known as "(Eleven Books of) Metamorphoses", because it chronicles the transformation of Lucius from one animal shape into another. In the first ten books, it presents a series of entertaining events Lucius witnesses as a suffering ass over a long period of time. But its tone abruptly changes and becomes pious and solemn in the last book. Still trapped in the body of an ass, Lucius is awakened by the brilliant light of a full moon and prays to Isis, the queen of heaven, for his salvation, that is, his release from the beastly form. When he falls to sleep, Isis miraculously appears to him and announces herself as the mother of nature, first-born in this realm of time, the loftiest of all deities, and the ruler of the whole world (bk. 11.5). For his salvation, she gives him the following instruction. There will be a procession in the religious observance of her the next day and a priest will be carrying a wreath of roses. If Lucius eats some of those roses, he will regain the human form. The following day, this miraculous transformation takes place: his body is changed from an ass to a human form.

The procession takes place in a carnival atmosphere. A she-bear is dressed up as a matron and carried in a chair, a monkey in a woven cap and saffron garment is holding a golden cup like the shepherd-boy Ganymede, and an ass with wings stuck to its shoulders is walking along beside an old man (bk. 11.8). In the middle of this funny fanfare, where animals are impersonating human beings, Lucius eats the wreath of roses and feels his asinine body changing into a human body. To the spectators, this metamorphosis must have looked like the climax of the carnival. He now finds himself totally naked and tries to hide his privities, thereby presenting another comic scene. Thus his metamorphosis is a comic spectacle within a huge comic event. For Lucius, the wreath of roses serves as a sacramental meal for his transfiguration in the same manner as the sacrament of the Eucharist is supposed to work. The roses play the same sacramental function for Zarathustra and his higher men; they are supposed to transform the life of suffering and depression into the life of laughter and elation. As Higgins points out, Zarathustra may be alluding to Lucius's eating of roses when he crowns himself with a wreath of roses and calls it the crown of laughter during his speech to the higher men (*Nietzsche's* Zarathustra, 214-15).

On Lucius's liberation from the asinine imprisonment, the priest says that he has finally reached the harbor of peace and the altar of mercy after the heavy storms of Fortune. For he has been delivered from the slavery to blind Fortune (*Fortuna caeca*) into the care and protection of open-eyed Fortune (*Fortuna videns*). Shortly after his liberation, Lucius is initiated into the mystery cult of Isis in a special ceremony and dedicates his life to the service of the Goddess by becoming her devotee. He rejoices in his life as a pastophor of Isis. Finally, he is initiated into the mysteries of Osiris, the brother and husband of Isis and becomes a devotee of this god as well. With this ceremony, the story of *The Golden Ass* comes to an end. The last book of *The Golden Ass* celebrates the mystery cult of Isis. She has saved Lucius from his enslavement in the same manner that she had revived her husband Osiris, who had been killed by his jealous brother Seth and whose body had been trapped in a pillar. She is the Mother of all Men. The adaptation of her cult in the medieval Christian Church became the cult of the Virgin Mary, the Queen of Heaven and the Mother of all Men.

What significance can we draw from this story for our understanding of Zarathustra's Ass Festival? We can take it as a story of redemption. In the first ten books, Lucius goes through an endless series of torments and disasters; in the final book, he gains salvation and bliss. These two series of his life belong to two Fortunes. He suffers as a child of blind Fortune (*Fortuna caeca*), but he rejoices as a child of open-eyed Fortune (*Fortuna videns*). But these two Fortunes are one and the same Goddess, Isis, viewed from two different perspectives, temporal and eternal. But who is Isis? She is Mother Nature. While imprisoned in the form of an ass, Lucius can see only *Fortuna caeca*. In his mystical vision, however, he can see *Fortuna videns*. *The Golden Ass* was a religious testimony for the mystical journey from the realm of *Fortuna caeca* to that of *Fortuna videns.* The religion of Isis was an old fertility cult, a nature-religion, whose influence was being eroded by the rise of Christianity in the days of Apuleius. P. G. Walsh has long maintained that book 11 of *The Golden Ass* was meant to be Apuleius's fervent recommendation of the religion of Isis as a counterblast to the meteoric spread of Christianity in Africa in the later second century (Apuleius, *The Golden Ass*, xxxvii).

By stressing Isis's *numen unicum multiformi specie*, Walsh holds, Apuleius was trying to counter the Christian jibes about the pagan polytheism. The cult of Isis was not a vulgar natural religion. Imbued with a profound sense of sanctity, it led its votaries into mysteries and services of devotion. Like the Christian God, the Isis of book 11 not only has the power of salvation, but also demands of her followers the consecration of their entire lives (P. G. Walsh, *The Roman Novel*, 188). In Walsh's view, this demand for consecration, which was practically unknown among the ancients, makes sense if it is taken as Apuleius's way of building up the cult of Isis to fight against the new cult of Christianity, which was making a magical appeal to many by its message of purity and sanctity. The cult of Isis was an attempt to save the sanctity of Nature from the profanity of secular culture.

In its spirit, the cult of Isis is very much like Zarathustra's nature-religion. In both cases, Nature is the ultimate source of both suffering and redemption. Lucius was transformed into an ass because he tried to control Nature with magic, just as Zarathustra reduced himself to an ugly dwarf by his Faustian will to control his fate. We should remember that Faust was a magician. Lucius and Zarathustra produced their own tragedies by their arrogant and defiant approach to Mother Nature. But they can be redeemed only by the power of Mother Nature because she is the absolute sovereign of the whole world. Just as Lucius was delivered from his slavery to blind Fortune (*Fortuna caeca*) into the care of open-eyed Fortune (*Fortuna videns*), so Zarathustra can be redeemed from his slavery to Life in the temporal mode to the bliss with Life in the eternal mode. The cult of Isis was advocated as the natural religion to replace the supernatural religion of Christianity in its original ascendancy. Zarathustra's Ass Festival is designed as his natural religion to replace Christianity in its final decline. The medieval Christian Ass Festival served as the spiritual link between the cult of Isis and Zarathustra's nature-religion.

The distinction between natural and anti-religion is crucial for understanding Part IV. In Nietzsche's view, ancient or primitive religions emerged as the institutions for communion with Mother Nature. Their gods and goddesses represent natural powers and values, and the rites of their worship express the gratitude for the bounty of their gifts. These natural religions are the cults of fertility that I discussed in chapter 4. Their festivals celebrate the seasons and cycles of Mother Nature. Even the ancient Judaism began as such a natural cult. Passover was originally a festival celebrating the planting of spring wheat crop, and Pentecost was a festival celebrating the harvest of wheat fifty days after planting (Al Martinich's lecture notes). But this natural religion was denaturalized by the priests after the Babylonian captivity (*A* 25). When the Israelites were routed by hostile forces, their priests had two choices. They could abandon their God by recognizing that he no longer had the natural power to sustain and protect them, or maintain their allegiance to him by transforming him from a nature-god to a moral judge. The priests took the latter alternative and interpreted the conquest of Israelites not as the defeat of their god by the god of their enemies, but as the moral punishment by their own god on his own people. Thus Judaism was transmogrified from a natural to an anti-natural religion, which denies natural values. Accordingly, Passover was reinterpreted as a commemoration of a historical event. Likewise, the pagan festival for the winter solstice was transformed to Christmas, the feast day commemorating the birth of Christ. Pentecost was also transformed to the feast day commemorating the descent of the Holy Spirit for the founding the Christian Church. With natural religions, Time is cyclical and seasonal, just the way Zarathustra's animals praise the ring of recurrence in "The Convalescent" of Part III. With anti-natural religions, Time is linear and historical as it is portrayed in Christianity.

Whereas a natural religion is the expression of gratitude to Mother Nature, Nietzsche believes, an anti-natural religion is the expression of resentment to her. The latter alienates humans from Mother Nature; the former nurtures their union with her. Hence he regards a nature-religion as an essential institution for maintaining the natural integrity of human psyche. One of the critical functions of Part IV is to restore the anti-natural religions to natural ones. The Voluntary Beggar is a Buddha-figure trying to naturalize Buddhism by his communion with the cows. The Ass Festival is the attempt to naturalize Christianity by reviving the spirit of the medieval Ass Festival. By the naturalized Buddhism, the Beggar claims to have found the cure for nausea. If so, this is a clear sign that he has regained his spiritual union with Mother Nature. Let us now consider what impact the Ass Festival of Part IV has on the psychological condition of the higher men. During the festival, they all behave like a bunch of donkeys, as Higgins says (*Nietzsche's* Zarathustra, 226-27). By "an ass", she means a fool and a buffoon. She says that Zarathustra makes himself into a big ass in being trapped by the higher man's cry of distress, while vainly talking about catching some great human fish. The ass is repeatedly identified with Zarathustra and his higher men. Their asinine behavior has been a troublesome puzzle for many commentators. Why does Nietzsche turn his hero Zarathustra and his company of higher men into a bunch of donkeys? Does he really want to end his entire book in an embarrassing asinine farce? Is he closing his book "by ridiculing its hitherto serious protagonist out of existence?" (*Nietzsche's* Zarathustra, 227). Higgins asks these sensitive questions. If such a paltry ending is the ultimate outcome of the Ass Festival, Part IV should turn out to be a mockery of the whole book instead of being its sublime finale as intended by the author. This is the main reason why most Nietzsche scholars want to take Part III rather than IV as the real ending of the book. They would rather dismiss Part IV than witness the whole book fizzle out in a buffoonery. This may be the most sensible way to dissolve the impending gloom of the Ass Festival.

I want to propose a better way of coping with this asinine problem. The ass may have a place in Zarathustra's story of metamorphoses, as it has in *Eleven Books of Metamorphoses*. The spirit of humankind is supposed to undergo three metamorphoses: it first becomes a camel, then a lion, and finally a child. In their worship of the Ass-God, the higher men are kneeling like children. In this foolish behavior, they are also likened to the ass. By this casual reference, the ass is identified with a child. In the litany that follows, the Ugliest Man says to the ass, "Beyond good and evil is your kingdom. It is your innocence not to know what innocence is." In response, the ass brays, "Yea-Yuh." Innocence is a common attribute of the child and the ass. We have already identified the ass as the symbol of Dionysus, Mother Nature. She is as innocent as a child. The higher men have become like children by emulating the innocence of Mother Nature. This is the secret for the final metamorphosis. Everybody seems to know what it means to be obedient like a camel or to be fierce like a lion. But nobody seems to know what it means to become a child. Hence the final metamorphosis has baffled many commentators, as we noted in chapter 1. Although Zarathustra was given the stern command to become like a child by the voiceless voice in "The Stillest Hour" of Part II, he has not been able to execute this command because he has never discovered the secret of becoming a child. But the higher men have just shown the secret.

What appears to be their asinine buffoonery reveals their transformation into innocent children. Innocence is the ground for their roguish and prankish behavior. They are behaving like Life, the personification of Mother Nature, whom Zarathustra called a prankster for teasing him with her roguish tricks in "The Other Dancing Song" of Part III. With the final metamorphosis, we noted in chapter 4, the individual self is supposed to be in a complete union with the cosmic self. The higher men are now taking the first step for this union in the Ass Festival. Their worship of the Ass-God is the subjection of their individual selves to their cosmic self, Mother Nature, which transforms them into children. To be a child is to have no individual self to assert. On the other hand, to be a camel or a lion presupposes the separation of the individual self from the cosmic self. But their separation should be preceded by a childlike state. Therefore, the state of innocence should obtain before the spiritual development as well as at its end. The first one is to be a child literally and physically, but the second one is to be a child only metaphorically and spiritually. The first one is the first or original innocence; the second one is a second or consequent innocence.

In chapter 4, we noted that the conflict between the individual and the cosmic self can never be resolved by any human effort because such an effort is always a self-defeating defiance against the cosmic self. We further noted that their true harmony can be realized only by some mysterious power beyond human control. But such power cannot come into play until and unless the higher men relinquish their individual wills and become like children. This point is demonstrated by the Ass Festival and its strange happening. It was never planned by anyone. It took place spontaneously. It came upon the higher men like "a roaring that blows your souls bright" as Zarathustra says. They had become receptive for the flow of mysterious force through their innocence. Even Zarathustra becomes like an innocent child and gracefully embraces the childlike behavior of the higher men. Surrendering his stubborn will to oppose their worship of the ass, he happily blesses their foolish ritual. In their childlike mood, he and his higher men have just seen the God of Nature in the tangible form of an ass. That was to see the Nature-God in the temporal mode. He is now about to encounter it in its eternal mode and finally fulfill his passionate longing for Eternity expressed in "The Seven Seals" of Part III. To see the Nature-God in a tangible form is the mythical approach, which was taken in the Ass Festival. A ritual or a festival is an enactment of a myth. To see the Nature-God in the eternal mode is a mystical experience, the climatic event in a mystery cult. The celebration of the Ass Festival prepares the spiritual mood for the mystical communion with the Ass-God in "The Drunken Song".

The Midnight Bell (Part IV.19.1-3)

After the Ass Festival, the higher men feel elated and step out into the open air of the cool night. Zarathustra leads the Ugliest Man by the hand to show him the beauty of his night-world and the big round moon. As we noted earlier, there is a special bond between the two. The higher men stand together there in silence, secretly amazed at feeling so well on this earth. But the secrecy of the night comes closer and closer to their hearts, that is, they feel closer and closer to the mystery of the Nature-God. Zarathustra again thinks, "How well I like them now, these higher men" (Z, 317). Just at that moment, the most amazing thing of this amazing day happens. The Ugliest Man, again gurgling and snorting, says that he is for the first time satisfied for having lived his whole life on earth. Now he wants to say to death, "Was *that* life? Well then! Once more!" (Z, 318). Then he asks the higher men whether they want to say the same thing to death. "Was *that* life? Well then! Once more!" is the statement introduced by Zarathustra as an expression of courage to face the eternal recurrence in "On the Vision and the Riddle" of Part III. The Ugliest Man has modified it to make his personal declaration to death. In the valley of serpent-death, he wanted to die rather than to live his miserable life of failure. To die in the valley of serpent-death is to choose death over life; the old serpents come there to die when they get weary of life. The Ugliest Man is now saying that he would rather live than die, even if he has to repeat the same miserable life of failure.

The Ugliest Man's declaration of "Once more!" announces his new love of life over death. This is his resurrection. The valley of serpent-death looked very much like the valley of dry bones, in which Ezekiel had received God's assurance that He would bring those dead bones back to life (Ezek. 37:1-6). The Ugliest Man's sense of resurrection is contagious. When the other higher men hear his jubilant announcement, they all become conscious of their own transformation and offer thanks and reverence to Zarathustra. Even the old Soothsayer is dancing with joy, thereby signaling Zarathustra's victory in the contest between the two of them for the evening. The Ugliest Man's love of life has now spread to all the other higher men. What is the cause of this transformation? The Ugliest Man attributes it to the Ass Festival. He says, "Living on earth is worthwhile: one day, one festival with Zarathustra, taught me to love the earth." His love of life is restored by the overflowing sensuality of the Ass-God. This sudden overflow of erotic impulse even overtakes Zarathustra. He stands like a drunkard: his eyes grow dim, his tongue fails, and his feet stumble. And his spirit flees and flies to remote places, wandering like a heavy cloud between past and future. These are the typical symptoms of a mystical flight of the soul from the temporal to the eternal world. They signal the onset of Zarathustra's mystical experience.

Let us note one important point about this onset. When the Ugliest Man announces the eternal recurrence, he is moved by his love of life. This joyful behavior makes a dramatic contrast with the terrifying act of courage that is supposed to be required for accepting the eternal recurrence. In "On the Vision and Riddle" of Part III, Zarathustra called upon "courage" for three times before facing the vision of eternal recurrence. The act of courage to accept the eternal recurrence is like the shepherd's attempt to bite off the snake's head in his mouth. It is gruesome and defiant. But we noted in chapter 4 that such a defiant approach is self-defeating for the harmonious acceptance of the eternal recurrence. The defiant approach is not the Ugliest Man's response. He responds with an overflowing joy and love of life. It has come to him mysteriously because he has surrendered his will and become like a child through Dionysian intoxication during the Ass Festival. The ass had arrived with a load of wine. The same intoxication has prepared for Zarathustra's mystical union Life. In chapter 4, I suggested that the roundelay contains Life's prophecy of his future encounter with her at the sounding of a midnight bell in the eternal domain. He will now use it as a framework for describing his mystical union with her as Eternity.

Most commentators have taken "The Drunken Song" as an interpretation of the roundelay. Walter Kaufmann says that the roundelay is interpreted in "The Drunken Song" (Z, 151). Laurence Lampert takes "The Drunken Song" as a commentary on the roundelay (*Nietzsche's Teaching*, 310). Greg Whitlock says that "The Drunken Song" is "a type of mini-commentary" on the roundelay (*Returning to Sils-Maria*, 277). It is hard to make a plausible case for this standard view because there is too long a gap between the text and the alleged commentary or interpretation. Why does Zarathustra have to wait so long before presenting his commentary? Why does he choose this occasion to do it? Strangely, nobody has ever raised these questions against the prevalent view. In addition to these troublesome questions, Lampert's account generates one more problem. He says that the last silent line of the roundelay in "The Other Dancing Song" is filled out by the marriage song of "The Seven Seals" (*Nietzsche's Teaching*, 239). But we noted in chapter 4 that "The Seven Seals" is not a marriage song because the alleged marriage never takes place there. There is no way to take "The Seven Seals" as the filler of the last blank line of the roundelay. If you compare the text of the roundelay with that of "The Drunken Song", you can clearly see that the last blank line of the roundelay is filled out in "The Drunken Song". This is meant to indicate that the prophecy contained in the roundelay is finally fulfilled. So the relation of the roundelay to "The Drunken Song" is not that of a text to a commentary, but that of a prophecy and its fulfillment.

What sort of song is "The Drunken Song"? The title appears to record the song of a drunkard, that is, the drunken Zarathustra. But he is not said to be drunk or even have taken any wine, as Stanley Rosen correctly notes (*The Mask of Enlightenment*, 242). However, he may be under Dionysian intoxication since he has just participated in the Dionysian feast of the Ass Festival. In that case, "The Drunken Song" is the song of a Dionysian mystic. To the best of my knowledge, Joan Stambaugh is the only one who has attempted a mystical reading of this song (*The Other Nietzsche*, 146-51).[3] She first points out that Zarathustra's mystical experience does not conform to the traditional pattern of mystical vision. In her view, this is what makes it hard to recognize the mystical dimension of "The Drunken Song". Whereas the sense of vision is the traditional mode of mystical experience, she says, Zarathustra's mystical experience is associated not with the sense of vision, but with the sense of hearing. His mystical experience begins with the sound of a bell at midnight, when nothing can be seen. It employs not only the sense of hearing but also the sense of smell. Whereas the sense of vision demarcates subject from object, she says, the senses of hearing and smell fuse subject and

---

3. Regarding Stambaugh's mystical reading, Tyler Roberts says that "The Drunken Song" reprises the mystical ecstasy at the end of Part III ("Ecstatic Philosophy", 204). That appears to be his way of saying that "The Drunken Song" is a commentary on the mystical event that took place in "The Seven Seals".

object into one. She believes that the unity of subject and object is high-lighted by detaching Zarathustra's mystical experience from the sense of vision and by shrouding it in the senses of smell and hearing.

What is truly strange about Zarathustra's mystical experience is the full use of natural senses, whether they be the sense of smell, hearing, or vision. As his mystical experience deepens, his natural senses become keener and keener. In this regard, his experience also diverges from the traditional mold of mystical experience. Traditional mysticism is theistic. It presupposes the separation between the eternal and the temporal, God and the world, and the mystical vision is the flight from one to the other. But this cannot happen in Zarathustra's world because it is Spinoza's Nature. But Mother Nature can be approached from two different perspectives. When it is approached from the eternal perspective, it is called God or the eternal reality. When it is approached from the temporal perspective, it is called the temporal world or Nature. Therefore, when one takes the eternal perspective, one experiences the same natural world instead of abandoning it for another reality. Spinoza's scheme of two perspectives for one reality is also operating in Zarathustra's mystical experience. It is not a flight from the natural to the supernatural world. It takes place in the midst of nature, where the moon shines and the bell tolls. But the same natural world can be approached from the temporal or the eternal perspective, and the temporal perspective is indicated by day and the eternal perspective by night. The day-world is governed by the sun, whose movement in the sky is the most prominent sign of temporal succession. On the other hand, the night-world is indicative of the eternal reality, the natural world viewed from its eternal perspective, because its darkness renders invisible the motion of physical objects. Zarathustra's mystical experience takes place in midnight where all motions are covered in darkness.

When Zarathustra regains his senses, he seems to hear something mysterious, which turns out to be the voice of midnight. Just before the arrival of midnight, he puts one finger on his mouth and says, "*Come!*" Just then the sound of a bell slowly comes up from the depth of midnight, just as Life prophesied in "The Other Dancing Song" of Part III. He puts one finger on his mouth for the second time and says, "*Come! Come! Midnight approaches*" (Z, 319). As it grows even more quiet and mysterious, he says, "*Come! Come! Come! Let us wander now! The hour has come: let us wander into the night.*" Then he wants to whisper to the higher men what is whispered by the old bell. This metaphor of whisper echoes back to his whispered secret into Life's ear in "The Other Dancing Song". He whispered this secret to her when they were exchanging tender thoughts. The whisper of the midnight bell will complete their tender exchange. The midnight bell is the voice of Life. He tells the higher men that midnight has something to say in this still hour that can never be heard in the clamor of the day. His mystical experience is going to take the form of midnight's secret speech to him, and he will convey this secret message to the higher men. This is the format for the composition of "The Drunken Song". Zarathustra says thrice "Come!" in inviting the higher men to the mystical vision. The same word of invitation is spoken in Revelation, when the Lamb of God opens the scroll by breaking each of the first four seals. Zarathustra is going to reveal the hidden mystery of Eternity just as the Lamb breaks open the sealed scroll in God's hand.

Mystical Flight (Part IV.19.4-9)

In subsection 4, Zarathustra loses his sense of time ("Where is time gone?") and feels as though he had fallen into deep wells. There is no time in the deep well of eternity. The well of eternity does not flow because it transcends time. On the other hand, the temporal world is like a flowing river. When he falls into the well of eternity, he says, "Now I have died." If life is taken as a temporal phenomenon, it should cease in the eternal world. He is dying away from the temporal world to be born into the eternal one. This is the death that Life had in mind when she mentioned his plan to leave her at the stroke of the midnight bell in "The Other Dancing Song" of Part III. It is happening now. As Paul S. Loeb points out, his death has been an intriguing mystery for those who want to see him as a martyr. For the parallel between his career and that of Jesus, F. A. Lea says, he must suffer martyrdom. But Nietzsche cannot accept such a tragic ending (*The Tragic Philosopher,* 226). Daniel Conway compares Zarathustra's career with that of Socrates. Whereas Socrates has to die in the *Phaedo,* Zarathustra is granted a stay of execution so that he can impart Nietzsche's teaching ("A Moral Ideal for Everyone and No One", 23). David Krell says that Zarathustra cannot fulfill his tragic destiny because of his persistent refusal to die (*Postponements,* 53-69). Against all these commentators, Loeb makes the shocking claim that Zarathustra really dies at the end of Part III and fulfills his tragic destiny ("The Conclusion of Nietzsche's *Zarathustra*", 145f and n. 32).

There is something truly strange about this whole debate. None of the participants even mentions the only passage in which Zarathustra says, "Now I have died." Why do they have to compare his career with that of Jesus or Socrates rather than with that of the Buddha, as Graham Parkes does? They expect a martyr's death for Zarathustra for two reasons. His story is called a tragedy in *GS* 342 and he announces his going-under at the outset of his career. Then, this prophetic announcement is allegorically illustrated by the tragic death of the tightrope walker in the Prologue. But his going-under has taken place in "The Convalescent", as witnessed and announced by his animals. His story is called a tragedy for the same reason that Goethe's *Faust* is called a tragedy. That is, it is dealing with a serious theme rather than a light-hearted one.

While Zarathustra is going through his mystical death, he shivers and freezes. He still asks the important question, "Who shall be the lord of the earth?" He once proposed the superman as the lord of the earth in place of God. He opens subsection 5 by stating his question once more, "I am carried away, my soul dances. Day's work! Day's work! Who shall be the lord of the earth?" (*Z,* 320). He associates the lord of the earth with day's work, but says nothing about it because it is now midnight. Instead he begins to talk about dancing and flying. He asks the higher men, "Have you flown high enough yet? You have danced: but a leg is no wing" (*Z,* 320). They may be good dancers on the earth, but they cannot fly high to the eternal world. They can only vicariously participate in his experience of flying up to Eternity. In comparison with the flight to

Eternity, however, all the temporal existence is drudgery. So he says, "You good dancers, now all pleasure is gone: wine has become dregs, every cup has become brittle, the tombs stammer" (*Z*, 320). The temporal existence is no more than stammering tombs. He exhorts the higher men to redeem the tombs and awaken the corpses, that is, the corpses like the Ugliest Man dying in the valley of serpent-death. Like the Ugliest Man, all the higher men are no more than stammering tombs. Zarathustra sighed over these human tombs day and night in the massive cave of human decay and slow death in "The Convalescent" of Part III. We have already noted the sense of resurrection that the higher men experienced when the Ugliest Man announced his love of life over death. Zarathustra is now issuing his call for the resurrection of all human beings from their living tombs. He now connects those tombs to the burrowing heartworm, the dwarf-snake that is decaying and dying in every human heart. This heartworm will keep burrowing and pounding as long as time keeps running and will turn every human being into a living tomb. But there is no one else in the whole world beside this worm, the dwarf, who can be the lord of the earth. In "The Dancing Song" of Part II, Zarathustra called him the master of the world. He was then the master of grief. But he is now becoming the master of joy because he will be redeemed from his living tomb. Even at the end of subsection 5, Zarathustra is still concerned with the fate of the dwarf in the temporal world. He is still going through the preliminary pain of leaving the temporal world for Eternity.

In subsection 6, Zarathustra's mood changes abruptly. The humming bell becomes a sweet lyre, whose intoxicated sound delights him. Its sound comes from all ages and all places. The sweet lyre is the music of midnight, Life, who has experienced all the joys and woes of the earth. The smell of Eternity is secretly welling up. It is the fragrance of roseate bliss and ancient happiness, the drunken happiness of dying at midnight. The drunken happiness sings: "the world is deep, *deeper than day had been aware*" (*Z*, 321). In subsection 7, Zarathustra becomes pure. He says, "Leave me! Leave me! I am too pure for you. Do not touch me! Did not my world become perfect just now?" (*Z*, 321). The world is becoming perfect, too. By becoming pure, he will be fit to be the lord of the earth. He says, "The purest shall be the lords of the earth—the most un-known, the strongest, the midnight souls who are brighter and deeper than any day" (*Z*, 321). The midnight soul is the most unknown because it is the dwarf from the abyss, the deepest and darkest depth of the whole world. The dwarf is also the strongest, who clobbered Zarathustra in "The Convalescent" of Part III. But this monster has become the purest in the eternal ring. The ugly dwarf is now being transformed into a heav-enly being, as Zarathustra said in "On Those Who Are Sublime" of Part II. But he says, "but I am yet no god, no god's hell: *deep its woe*" (*Z*, 321). He has not yet become a god yet because god's hell has not be-come his own.

In subsection 8, Zarathustra finally plunges into divine woe. He says, "God's woe is deeper, you strange world!" (*Z*, 322). In the theistic tradi-tion, the eternal world of God and angels is supposed to be free of the woe and suffering that afflict the temporal world. But this cannot be true of Zarathustra's world, whose eternal dimension is inseparable from its temporal dimension. Therefore the gods have their own woes, which are even deeper than ours, because they are greater. The woe of suffering is inevitable in both the temporal and the eternal world. The flight to Eter-nity is not a flight from the world of woe. On the contrary, the woe of Eternity is even deeper and greater than the woe of temporal existence because Eternity is deeper than the temporal world. This is the essential distinction between Zarathustra's nature-mysticism and traditional mys-ticism. The latter is a flight from the world of suffering to the world of bliss. But the former is a joyful plunge into the world of suffering.

Zarathustra tells the higher men to reach for God's woe, not for him, because he is only a drunken sweet lyre and an ominous bell-frog. At this dramatic moment, he hears the dog howl and the wind whine. This re-calls the shepherd scene of "On the Vision and the Riddle" of Part III. In that scene, Zarathustra heard the howling dog and the whining wind only as natural phenomena. But he now experiences them as the cries of di-vine suffering. They come from the midnight, who sighs and laughs, rat-tles and wheezes, reflecting all the joys and sorrows of the world. He says, "How she speaks soberly now, this drunken poetess!" (*Z*, 322). She is drunken with the Dionysian intoxication. Even then she speaks soberly when it comes to suffering. Zarathustra says, "She became overwake? She ruminates?" (Z, 322). Because the problem of suffering is so difficult to cope with, he seems to think, even the drunken poetess perhaps becomes wakeful and ruminate. This observation echoes back to the Voluntary Beggar, who learned from the cows that rumination was the secret art for coping with the unruly animal self. After all, all sufferings belong to the animal self. But the midnight's rumination includes not only her woe, but also her deeper joy: "For joy, even if woe is deep, *joy is deeper yet than agony*" (Z, 322).

In subsection 9, the midnight lyre talks as the vintager, who cruelly cuts the vine. But blessed be his knife that cuts the vine. When the vine is cut, the grape is made into wine. This is the symbol of transforming humanity to divinity. This is the same symbol as the transubstantiation, in which wine is transformed to the blood of Christ. In subsection 7, he said that he had not yet become a god because he had not made god's hell his own. In subsection 8, he took on divine suffering as his own, thereby becoming ripe for the vintager's knife. The coming of this vintager has been predicted many times since "On the Great Longing" of Part III. He came in "The Other Dancing Song", but Zarathustra was not ripe yet for the harvest. Now he has come again and says that what has become perfect and ripe wants to die. But this is the bliss of dying as a temporal being and becoming a god in the eternal world. Therefore blessedness belongs to death. On the other hand, all that is unripe wants to live and woe belongs to this desire to live. All that suffers wants to live so that it may become ripe and joyous. It is lured by the longing for what is farther, higher, and brighter. This is the perpetual drive for self-overcoming, which generates all the sufferings. Even the desire to have children is the extension of this drive for self-overcoming: "thus speaks all that suffers; 'I want children, I do not want *myself*'" (Z, 322). On the other hand, joy does not want to have any children because it is already in the perfect world: "joy wants itself, wants eternity, wants recurrence, wants everything eternally the same" (Z, 322).

There are two important items in subsection 9: (1) the eternal recurrence and (2) the heirs. The howling dog in the preceding section recalled the shepherd's gruesome act of biting off the snake's head in "On the Vision and the Riddle" of Part III. That was an act of courage, which is different from an act of joy that wants eternity and recurrence. This is the response to the eternal recurrence from the eternal perspective, while the shepherd's courageous act was the response from the temporal perspective. The eternal recurrence combines two notions. The 'eternal' is linked to eternity, and the 'recurrence' to temporality. The concept of recurrence or even occurrence presupposes the temporal world. But nothing can occur or recur in the eternal world because it is timeless. Because the eternal recurrence combines the attributes of both eternity and temporality, it can be viewed from both perspectives. When it is viewed from the temporal perspective, it is an object of woe, that is, the abysmal thought, which provokes disgust with the whole world. But when it is viewed from the eternal perspective, it is an object of joy, which can be gladly accepted without any struggle. In such a blissful state, there is nothing to overcome. Joy simply wants itself and its eternity.

In the temporal world of woe and suffering, it makes no sense to wish for the repetition of one's life without variation, if there is a chance for changing it for better. Just imagine that you spent ten years in a concentration camp and that you are now given the option of having your life repeated with or without variation. You would be crazy to take the option of having your life repeated without any variation. In the temporal world of suffering, we are bound to look for a better future. If we cannot hope any better future for us, we would at least want a better future for our children. Our hope for our children is an extension of our hope for ourselves. This point is addressed in subsection 9: "But all that suffers wants to live, that it may become ripe and joyous and longing—longing for what is farther, higher, brighter" (Z, 322). Those who suffer now place their hope in their children and say, "I want heirs" or "I want children. I do not want *myself*" (Z, 322).

Zarathustra has repeatedly talked about the children of the future, and the superman is the most eminent specimen of the future children.

His longing for the superman is the expression of his discontent with the present. In "The Seven Seals" of Part III, he concluded every stanza by expressing his desire to have children: "Never yet have I found the woman from whom I wanted children, unless it be this woman whom I love: for I love you, O Eternity." He can now say that he was burning with that desire because he was still suffering in the temporal world. But he no longer wants any children or any heirs because he is now in the eternal world of joy. The need and desire for heirs arise from the unfulfilled love, but there is no unfulfilled love in eternity. So the woe of the temporal world says, "Break, bleed, heart! Wander, leg! Wing, fly! Get on! Up! Pain!" (*Z*, 322f). The heart breaks and bleeds in the temporal world. So it wanders on its legs, but it cannot get away from woe. The only way to get away from woe is to fly up to Eternity. So Zarathustra says to the old heart, "*Woe implores, 'Go!'*"

Mystical Union (Part IV.19.10-12)

In subsection 10, Zarathustra asks the higher men about his identity, that is, who they think he is, whether he is soothsayer, a dreamer, a drunkard, an interpreter of dreams, etc. Why does he raise this question of his own self-identity at this point? This is because his identity was changed in the last subsection. When he had a foretaste of mystical experience in "At Noon", he questioned the identity of his soul and said, "Still stretching, yawning, sighing, falling into deep wells? Who are you? O my soul?" (*Z*, 278). In the eternal well, he has been cut by the vintager's knife and made into wine, the symbol of divinity. He has gained a new identity that is unknown to the higher men. As he has become a god, so his world has become perfect. He says, "Just now my world became perfect" (*Z*, 323). In Spinoza's philosophy, reality and perfection are the same (*Ethics*, pt. 2, def. 6). Reality may appear to be imperfect only because we try to impose our own ideals on it. We can see the perfection of reality only when we can comprehend it in its essential nature. In this regard, Nietzsche says, the eternal recurrence is no different from Spinoza's pantheism:

"So one understands that an antithesis to pantheism is attempted here: for 'everything perfect, divine, eternal' also compels a faith in the 'eternal recurrence'" (*WP* 55). But the perfection of reality can be seen only in perfect understanding.

In Spinoza's philosophy, perfect understanding is the intellectual intuition that sees the totality of Nature in its eternal mode (*Ethics,* pt. 5, prop. 30). Zarathustra has now achieved his perfect understanding in his mystical vision of the eternal ring. He describes this mystical moment in a string of paradoxes: "midnight too is noon; pain too is a joy; curses too are a blessing; night too is a sun—go away or you will learn: a sage too is a fool" (Z, 323). In this mystery of Eternity, he says, "Have you ever said Yes to a single joy? O my friends, then you said Yes to *all* woe." Why should you say "Yes" to all woe because of a single joy? The following is his answer,

> All things are entangled, ensnared, enamored; if ever you wanted one thing twice, if ever you said, "You please me, happiness! Abide, moment!" then you wanted *all* back. All anew, all eternally, all entangled, ensnared, enamored—oh, then you loved the world. Eternal ones, love it eternally and evermore; to woe too, you say: go, but return! *For all joy wants—eternity.* (Z, 323)

"All things are entangled, ensnared, enamored" describes the same mystery of Eternity that was described by the string of paradoxes. The ring of eternal recurrence is the ring of love that binds together all things, for example, pain and joy, midnight and noon. To become a god in the eternal world is to be entangled, ensnared, and enamored in this cosmic bond of love. This cosmic bond establishes his new identity.

The cosmic bond is the union of the individual self with the cosmic self, because the eternal ring is the cosmic self in its eternal mode. The Zarathustra who has become perfect is his individual self; the world that has become perfect is his cosmic self. The union of these two is their ultimate perfection. In chapter 4, we noted the difficulty of resolving the conflict of the individual self with the cosmic self in the temporal world because the temporal world is the world of individuals and their conflict. Perpetually frustrated in the temporal world, Zarathustra longed for the eternal world for the fulfillment of his love with Life. In the eternal ring, he has finally achieved a mystical union with her. In this mystical union, even the heart of the burrowing worm that breaks and bleeds in the temporal world, becomes a fountain of joy. Thus his love of the ugly dwarf as his ultimate self becomes complete and absolute in the eternal ring of love. But there is no need for him to say it because his love of the whole world is obviously his love of his cosmic self in the eternal domain. In the early phase of his career, he expressed his hatred of himself as his hatred of others. Only later in his career, he came to realize that his hatred of others only reflected his hatred of his own being. Just as his hatred of himself involved all others in the world, so his love of himself now encompasses the whole world. He comes to love his own being by falling in love with the whole world. This is the secret of self-love.

This expansive notion of love is elaborated in the opening of subsection 11: "All joy wants the eternity of all things, wants honey, wants dregs, wants drunken midnight, wants tombs, wants tomb-tears' comfort, wants gilded evening glow" (Z, 323). This passage indicates another important difference of Zarathustra's mysticism from the traditional one. According to the latter, all our desires are extinguished in the joy of the eternal world. In the eternal ring, on the contrary, all desires become more active and vibrant than ever. Joy is thirstier and hungrier than all woe. Joy is so rich that "it thirsts for woe, for hell, for hatred, for disgrace, for the cripple". It even longs for the failure and agony of the higher men. Everything becomes an object of joy in the eternal ring, because all things are connected in the chain of eternal love. Zarathustra says, "Joy wants the eternity of *all* things, *wants deep, wants deep eternity*" (Z, 324). The ring of eternal recurrence is the ring of intense desire and joy. Even the ugly dwarf and the gruesome shepherd scene become the objects of joy. Zarathustra never calls upon his courage to face the eternal ring. There is no need for it because he is overflowing with love and joy. His passionate longing and love for Life, which was expressed in "The Seven Seals" of Part III, is now fully realized. In the final subsection, he invites the higher men to sing his roundelay with him. Thus he fills out the twelfth and last line of the roundelay, which was left blank at the end of "The Other Dancing Song" of Part III. This indicates that the prophecy of Life in "The Other Dancing Song" is now finally fulfilled at the twelfth stroke of midnight in "The Drunken Song".

Zarathustra's love fulfilled is his love of the eternal ring. It is his *amor fati* (love of fate), his love of the cosmic self. The eternal ring is the ring of fate that governs his life. But his *amor fati* in the eternal ring is different from his *amor fati* in its temporal mode. As we noted in chapter 4, the latter is his love of Life in the defiant mode as demonstrated by Zarathustra's power play in his game of love in "The Other Dancing Song" of Part III. By its nature, love can never be truly fulfilled in its defiant mode. But there can be no defiance in his *amor fati* in its eternal mode because there is no conflict in his mystical union with the eternal ring. The eternal recurrence in "The Drunken Song" is notably different from its original version of "On the Vision and the Riddle" of Part III. The latter stressed the notion of recurrence and repetition, that is, everything, big and small, will be eternally repeated without any variation. In "The Drunken Song," however, the word "recurrence" appears only once: Joy "wants recurrence" (subsection 9). In this case, Zarathustra is still talking about joy in the temporal domain. The word "recurrence" does not appear at all in the description of eternal recurrence from the fully eternal perspective, which is given in subsection 10: "All anew, all eternally, all entangled, ensnared, enamored." This line consists of three phrases, each of which begins with "all", because the eternal ring includes all things. The first phrase ("all anew") indicates anything but repetition; what is repeated cannot be new. Strictly speaking, nothing can be new or old in the eternal domain because it is timeless. To say that everything is new in the eternal domain is just a rhetorical device for saying that nothing is old there.

The timeless character of the eternal ring is expressed by the second phrase ("all eternally"). Because all things are eternally present in the eternal ring, there can be no repetition. The notion of repetition makes sense only in the temporal world, where one thing happens after another.

Nothing happens or becomes in eternity. To indicate the timeless modality of eternal existence, Zarathustra uses the word "ring" in subsection 11. So there are two metaphors for describing the ultimate reality: the eternal recurrence and the eternal ring. These two metaphors correspond to the two modes of reality, temporal and eternal. The third phrase ("all entangled, ensnared, enamored") describes another feature of eternal reality: all of its elements are tightly entwined with one another in the cosmic chain of love. This notion of cosmic interconnection can also be found in the original description of eternal recurrence in "On the Vision and the Riddle": "And are not all things knotted together so firmly that this moment draws after it *all* that is to come?" (Z, 158). But the two descriptions of the universal connection are different. One is described as the temporal connection of succession and repetition, and the other as the timeless connection of eternal presence. The temporal connection provokes disgust and nausea because its causal power crushes the autonomous will. The eternal connection generates love and joy because it assures the harmonious union of the individual with the cosmic self. In the temporal world, it takes courage and defiance to love one's fate. But there is no need either for courage or defiance in the eternal world because it is the world of eternal joy.

The nature of the will changes when it moves from the temporal to the eternal world. The joy of eternal love belongs to the will of the eternal ring: "it [joy] wants itself, it bites into itself, the will of the ring strives in it" (subsection 11). In this mystical mode, the will of Zarathustra becomes one with the will of the eternal ring. The fusion of his will with the eternal ring resolves the problem of redemption propounded in "On Redemption" of Part II, where Zarathustra says that the spirit of revenge arises from the fact that the will has no control over the past. The will is supposed to be the liberator and bringer of joy for the future, but unfortunately it is also a prisoner of the past. Everything in our life is determined by the causal chain from the past, and every life is a series of *sufferings* in its technical sense, that is, a series of accidents beyond one's control. Since nothing is of our own making and everything is an accident, our lives are shattered fragments. The redemption from this world of shattered lives can be achieved only by the will that can over-come the causal chain from the past. The liberation from the causal chain is fully realized in the world of eternity. There is no causal chain in the realm of eternity because it admits neither the past nor the future, but only the eternal presence. Hence the revenge against the past is dissolved in the eternal world. In the eternal realm, Zarathustra wills not any single item, but the whole world in its entirety, "the eternity of all things." By this universal willing, he can bring the shattered human experiences into a unified whole. In *Ecce Homo* (*Zarathustra* 6), Nietzsche says that Zarathustra binds together in a new unity all opposites from the highest to the lowest forces of human nature. By this universal synthesis, Nietzsche claims, the concept of superman reaches the greatest reality.

Zarathustra has gone through many levels of the superhuman ideal. He started out with the Faustian ideal of superman and changed it over to the Spinozan ideal. In the fourth stanza of "The Seven Seals", we noted in chapter 4, he boasted his enormous power of synthesis, but could not achieve the union of his individual self with his cosmic self. He has secured their union in his mystical union with the eternal ring, and his ideal of superman has indeed reached "its greatest reality". This outcome may clarify the enigmatic remark at the end of "On the Thousand and One Goals" of Part I: "Only the yoke for the thousand necks is still lacking: the one goal is lacking. Humanity still has no goal" (*Z*, 60). The final yoke that was still missing is the yoke of eternal recurrence. He has secured it in love and joy. Heidegger stresses the connection between the superman and the eternal recurrence:

> Zarathustra is *not* a teacher of two things. Zarathustra teaches the Superman *because* he is the teacher of the Eternal Recurrence. But conversely, Zarathustra teaches the Eternal Recurrence because he is the teacher of the Superman. Both doctrines belong together in a circle. By its circling, the doctrine accords with what is, with the circle that constitutes the Being of things—that is, the permanent within Becoming. ("Who Is Nietzsche's Zarathustra?", 75)

In support of this view, Heidegger quotes from Nietzsche's own note #617: "To *impress* the character of Being upon Becoming—that is *the highest will to power*." The distinction between Being and Becoming is supposed to correspond to the distinction between the eternal and the temporal modes of reality. Being is the eternal mode: it simply is. Becoming is the temporal mode: it perpetually becomes. To impress the character of Being upon Becoming would indeed require the highest will to power. In his mystical experience, however, there is no need for Zarathustra to impress the eternal mode of reality on its temporal mode because the eternal and the temporal modes belong to the same reality. Being is Becoming. Heidegger's metaphysics is too old-fashioned for understanding Zarathustra's world. But he rightly stresses the inseparable connection between the superman and the eternal recurrence. In chapter 2, we noted that the stone of the past was the most devastating obstacle to transcending the limits of humanity and becoming a superman. But one can overcome this obstacle in the mystical union with the eternal ring because it is situated beyond all causal chains.

In Heidegger's assessment, however, Zarathustra is destined not to be the superman, but only to be the teacher of two doctrines, the superman and the eternal recurrence. That is the answer to his momentous question, "Who is Nietzsche's Zarathustra?" This verdict on the ultimate destiny of Zarathustra is largely due to Heidegger's reading of Part III. In his view, the climax of Nietzsche's entire poem is reached in "On the Great Longing", and "A *divine* suffering is the content of Part Three of *Zarathustra*," as Nietzsche says in a posthumous note ("Who Is Nietzsche's Zarathustra?", 68). If a divine suffering is the content of Part III, it is fully articulated in the last four sections of Part III. In taking Part III as the culmination of the poem, Heidegger is safely within the conventional Nietzsche scholarship, although many commentators will place the climax in "The Seven Seals" rather than in "On the Great Longing." But this difference is of minor importance. "The Seven Seals" is no more than a poetic expression of the passionate longing for redemption, which has been building up in the three preceding sections. Longing without fulfillment is indeed intense suffering. As long as Zarathustra remains in this state of suffering, he cannot fully attain his redemption. Hence he cannot be the superman. As Heidegger says, Part III offers no possibility for the realization of superman.

Nietzsche, however, wants to demonstrate not only the possibility but the reality of superman, thereby fully living up to the claim he makes for Zarathustra in *Ecce Homo* (*Zarathustra* 6): "Here man is overcome every moment, the concept 'superman' here becomes the greatest reality." Who is this man that is overcome? He is the dwarf, the individual self alienated from the cosmic self. By their union, Zarathustra becomes the superman. This is the miracle of his self-overcoming, which has been achieved by the mystical union with Life. In this mystical event, the dwarf flies up like an eagle to the ring of eternity, thereby fulfilling Zarathustra's original ideal embodied in the flight of the eagle with the serpent coiled around its neck at the end of the Prologue. The serpent coiled around the eagle's neck is a poetic symbol for sexual union, and Zarathustra was lusting for such an erotic union in his passionate longing for the nuptial ring in "The Seven Seals". This is the erotic union of his individual self with his cosmic self, by which his will to power becomes one with the will of the entire universe. This is his sun-will. In chapter 1, we noted that the sun was his symbol of the superman. For a long time, he assumed that the superman was the hero of autonomous will. But his superhuman ideal has materialized as the hero of heteronomous will.

The sun-will of the superman is the will of a child. Like a child, the superman has no will of his own. In chapter 1, we noted the complaint that a child is an absurd terminus of the three metamorphoses. Although the child can create nothing significant with its feeble will, it alone is supposed to have the power of creation. This is an implausible view to many commentators. But the child can do nothing and everything because its will is identical with the will of the eternal ring. The child is a self-propelled wheel because it is one with the eternal ring, the only self-propelled wheel in the entire universe. By his mystical union with Life, Zarathustra becomes a divine child, who can say the sacred Yes. The superman is this divine child. This completes the final metamorphosis, which was prefigured by the childish behavior of the higher men in the

Ass Festival. This is the fourth and final stage in the Ladder of Redemption, which I discussed in chapter 4.

From Darkness into Sunlight (Part IV.20)

The mystical event has finally solved the problem of happiness, which was set as the central problem for Part IV. There can be no greater bliss than the rapture in the eternal ring. But no one can live in such rapture forever. The night will be succeeded by another day, and Zarathustra and his higher men have to come back from the night of intoxication to the sober world of daylight. What sort of significance can the midnight rapture have for the life in the world of daylight? The answer is obvious if the mystical experience is taken in the traditional sense. Tyler Roberts says that Nietzsche was introduced to mysticism by Schopenhauer's *The World as Will and Representation* and that he turned away from mysticism when he rejected Schopenhauer's pessimism ("Ecstatic Philosophy", 202). In *On the Genealogy of Morals* III.17, Nietzsche indeed gives a scathing critique of mysticism. He diagnoses it as an escape mechanism, which was devised by the ascetic priests to cope with the problem of suffering. Their common tactic is to numb the nerves and excite voluptuous ecstasies of sensuality, thereby producing the illusion of mystical union with God or Brahman. But this escape mechanism cannot overcome the problem of suffering. It can only create the illusion of finding the supernatural bliss.

This is a critique of traditional mysticism, which presupposes the demarcation between the natural and the supernatural worlds. For the vision of supernatural reality, the traditional mysticism requires the dulling or numbing of the normal awareness of the natural world. But Zarathustra's mystical experience takes place in the full awareness of natural reality, because there is no other reality than the natural world. Whereas the traditional mysticism is an ascetic event, Zarathustra's mysticism is a festive event, which takes place in the revelry of drinking and feasting. His mysticism celebrates natural reality, whereas the traditional mysticism repudiates it. Hence Nietzsche's critique of traditional mysticism does not apply to Zarathustra's mystical experience. Even so, his mysticism may turn out to be a temporary escape from harsh reality. Regarding the impact of Zarathustra's mysticism on the future, we can imagine two scenarios, one positive and one negative. On the negative scenario, the mystical experience is only a brief narcotic indulgence and a momentary escape from the temporal world to eternity. When Zarathustra comes back to the temporal world, he will find it much more unbearable than before. That is usually the negative effect of a narcotic escape. This is the negative impact thesis. On the positive scenario, the mystical experience will transform his entire existence and make him into a much stronger human being when he comes back to the temporal world. This is the positive impact thesis.

"The Sign" can be read to support either of these two views. Let us first note what happens in this section. Zarathustra emerges from his cave, glowing and strong like the rising sun, while all the higher men are still asleep. He wants to go to work. But he is not going to wait for them because they are not strong enough to be his companions. Then he suddenly hears the sharp cry of his eagle. Although he is glad to see that his eagle is already awake, he says, he still does not have the right men. At that moment, a vast swarm of doves descend and flutter around him, expressing their love. It is a cloud of love. Astonished at this miraculous event, he thinks, "What is happening to me?" He asked this question in "At Noon" in response to the marvelous dream beyond his control and power. Such marvelous happenings display the operation of accidents. When he sits down on a big stone, he encounters something even more startling. He is caressed by a gentle lion. A world of love is engulfing his entire existence. The lion and the birds not only show their love to him, but greet one another with love. Tears of joy well up in his eyes and fall on his hands, and the lion affectionately licks up those tears and growls bashfully.

When Zarathustra touches the gentle lion, he says, *"The sign is at hand."* This is a momentous announcement. He has been waiting for this sign for a long time. In "On Old and New Tablets" of Part III, he predicted that his sign would be "the laughing lion with the flock of doves". He is now surrounded by the laughing lion and the flock of doves. The long awaited sign has finally arrived; it is the sign for the arrival of his children. So he says, *"My children are near, my children."* Just then, the higher men come out of the cave to greet him, but they are frightened away by the roaring lion. Still dazed, he stands up from the stone and questions his heart: "What happened to me just now?" This question is the restatement in the past tense of "What is happening to me?", with which he responded to mystical events. His memory begins to return and he sees the stone, on which he sat the morning before and received the Soothsayer. He now realizes that he had succumbed to his ultimate sin of pity under the Soothsayer's seduction. But he dismisses it as a momentary lapse ("That had its time"). He is concerned not with happiness, but only with his work. Before getting on his work like the glowing sun, he makes his final statement, "Well then! The lion came, my children are near. Zarathustra has ripened, my hour has come: this is *my* morning, *my* day is breaking: *rise now, rise, thou great noon!*" (Z, 327).

By stressing the importance of work and disparaging happiness, Zarathustra appears to write off his mystical experience of the night before as a momentary lapse from his life of work. He seems to say that to be concerned with happiness and suffering is a sign of weakness and that this weakness reflected his ultimate sin. Having recovered from this weakness and the evening of intoxication, he is now rededicating himself to his work. In that case, he will be taking himself back to the end of Part III, and all the things that happened in Part IV will be only a series of foolish diversions. He will again be haunted by the problem of the unfulfilled longing, the absence of bliss, which troubled him prior to his Dionysian intoxication. This is a strong reason for opposing the addition of Part IV after Part III. This reason should become especially stronger if "The Drunken Song" is taken as the mystical culmination of Part IV. This is the negative impact thesis for the mystical reading of "The Drunken Song".

Let us now consider the positive impact thesis, taking *The Golden Ass* for our model. Lucius's mystical experience produces four positive effects: (1) the religious rebirth of a new devotee, (2) the transfiguration of his world, (3) his experience of divine love, and (4) the dedication of his life to the service of Isis. Lucius's mystical experience begins in a dream, in which Isis appears and assures him her grace and his salvation. The following morning, he experiences a dramatic change in the texture of his world. He finds himself in "a general atmosphere of joy, which is so pervasive that I sensed that every kind of domestic beast, and entire households, and the very weather seemed to present a smiling face to the world" (Apuleius, *The Golden Ass*, 222). The frosty previous day has been succeeded by a sunny day. The birds burst into sweet harmonies, and the trees smile with the budding of their foliage and whisper sweetly with the gentle motion of their branches (bk. 11.7). Lucius, who has gone through the act of initiation as a rite of voluntary death, is reborn by the providence of Isis. He now experiences the renewed sense of health and vitality (bk. 11.21). Lucius pours his revitalized energy into becoming an enthusiastic worker in the service of the Goddess (bk. 11.26). Finally, he rejoices in his love of the Goddess (bk. 11.24). His new strength and work confirm what he achieved in his mystical experience.

These four positive effects may also arise from Zarathustra's mystical experience. It all began in his love with Life, which was revealed in "The Dancing Song" and was reaffirmed in "The Other Dancing Song", and which was passionately expressed in "The Seven Seals". In the mystical experience of "The Drunken Song", he was fully initiated into the mystery of divine love and bliss. His mystical experience is none other than this ecstatic experience of divine love, which dramatically transforms the nature of his work and his world. The world that greets him the morning after his mystical experience is a world of love and bliss; he is greeted by countless doves and an affectionate lion. This is a dramatic transformation of his world, which is unaccountable without his mystical experience. His everyday world itself becomes mystical: "All this lasted for a long time, or a short time: for properly speaking, there is *no* time on earth for such things" (Z, 326). His world has been transformed from the world of revenge and despair to the world of love and bliss. This transformation loosens his heart and tears of joy well up in his eyes. Never before has he shed tears of joy in his entire life.

The most important transformation, however, has taken place in Zarathustra himself. Like Lucius, he has been reborn. As we noted earlier, he died from the temporal world and was reborn as a heavenly child in the eternal world. To be sure, there is no mention of either death or rebirth in "The Sign". But the title of this section is concerned with the sign that his children are near. The advent of his children is the central theme of this section. Zarathustra states it three times in "The Sign". When he touches the lion, he says, "*The sign is at hand*". When the lion laughs with joy over the affectionate birds, he says, "*My children are near, my children.*" Who are these children? Since they cannot be his literal descendants, many commentators have taken them to be his future followers.[4] But such followers would be his heirs. In "The Drunken Song", he said that the longing for heirs was the desperate wish of those who suffer and do not want themselves. Hence we cannot take "his children" as his followers. In fact, he equates the advent of his children with his own ripening: "Well then! The Lion came, my children are near, Zarathustra has ripened." This equation can come out right if the advent of his children is taken for the advent of his new self that has emerged from his mystical union with Life. His new self is born out of his old self in the eternal domain. One's children cannot belong to the next generation in the eternal world because it admits no temporal distinctions such as generations. In the eternal domain, therefore, one's child must be one's new-born self. The new-born self is the child that he passionately longed to have from the woman of Eternity in "The Seven Seals" of Part III. This fruition is the ultimate consummation of his love of Eternity.

The gentle lion stands for Zarathustra's new self. It is acting like a dog that has found its old master again. The beast is bashful even when it roars and growls. It has been transformed from a fierce beast to a gentle animal. This transformation represents Zarathustra's transformation from a lion to a child. Prior to the mystical event, he had roared like a fierce

---

4. Lampert, *Nietzsche's Teaching,* 311; Higgins, *Nietzsche's Zarathustra*, 311; Pippin, "Irony and Affirmation", 63.

lion throughout his long career except for a few occasions when he was terrified by his abysmal thought. But he has now become like the gentle lion. In the Ass Festival, the ass served as the symbol of a child for the cosmic self and as the model for the higher men to emulate in becoming children. Now the gentle lion serves as the symbol of a child for the individual self, which has become a child of Mother Nature. Thus the two beasts represent the two different sides of Zarathustra's innocent self, cosmic and individual. If the new lion stands for the new Zarathustra, the mystical event produces not only a brief span of intoxication in the well of eternity, but endows him with new power and energy in the temporal world. No wonder, he emerges from his cave, glowing and strong like the fresh morning sun. He is as strong as the roaring lion. This is in a vivid contrast with his condition at the opening scene of Part IV, where his melancholy made him look more like an old tired lion. But the old weary lion is now reborn as a fresh laughing lion. This completes the last of the three metamorphoses in his spiritual development. Gooding-Williams says that the passions of the earth are reborn within Zarathustra and achieve the third metamorphosis of the spirit in "The Sign" (*Zarathustra's Dionysian Modernism,* 294). But the third metamorphosis does not take place in "The Sign". It only displays and confirms the metamorphosis that has taken place in "The Drunken Song".

A Drama of the Soul (Part IV)

If Zarathustra's new children stand for his new self, why does he not call it his new child? Why does he use the plural "children" to refer to his singular individual "self"? It is my thesis that he uses the plural because he believes that one individual self is composed of many elements. In "On the Way of the Creator" of Part I, he said, "Lonely one, you are going the way of the creator: you would create a god for yourself out of your seven devils" (*Z,* 64f). The seven devils are the seven passions that are harbored in his earthly self, the dwarf, whom Zarathustra repeatedly called his devil and archenemy. He has created a god out of these seven

devils in the eternal ring. Now I propose that the seven devils are represented by the higher men. There are nine higher men altogether, but only
seven of them function as his shadows or alter egos. As we noted earlier,
the two kings are the exceptions to this stage function. In "On Those
Who Are Sublime" of Part II, he said that the sublime one "must redeem
his own monsters and riddles, changing them into heavenly children" (Z,
118). In that case, the arrival of his children should be none other than
the transformation of his wild monsters into gentle beasts. The laughing
lion and the flock of doves are those gentle creatures. They represent his
new-born passions, his new children. The fierce lion is only one of the
many monsters or wild dogs that can be reborn as lovely children. The
gentle lion is only a sign. Because one soul harbors many passions and
monsters, the rebirth of one soul can be the birth of many heavenly children. There is an implied symmetry between the old and new individual
self. Just as the old individual self was represented by many shadows and
alter egos, so the new individual self will be represented by many children. They are the right and strong men Zarathustra has been waiting for.

The representation of one soul by many monsters or children reflects
Zarathustra's view that the soul is not a simple, but a complex entity. Using his favorite metaphor, the soul can be described as a ball of snakes or
a cellar of wild dogs. The idea that the soul is a complex entity is a Platonic legacy. In the *Republic*, Plato compares the soul to a state composed of three classes. Zarathustra's great Hazar should be understood as
a kingdom that represents the composite structure of his soul or self. It is
a kingdom within the soul as much as Plato's ideal state can be a state
within the soul. Zarathustra's psychological kingdom begins with the assembly of his higher men, who represent his old self, and ends with the
birth of his new children, who represent his new self. The two kings'
tribute to Zarathustra represents the transfer of power from the old to the
new dynasty, whose mission is to reign over the tidal waves of despair
rising from the abyss. The entire Part IV is a continuous battle against
those tidal waves, which belong to Zarathustra's psychological landscape.
Part IV opened with him sitting on the highest peak and looking over the
abysses of the sea. This cosmic landscape is psychological. He called

those abysses his own abysses, that is, the abysses in his soul. The center of his future kingdom, from which he cast his fishing rod to all the seas, also belongs to his psychological landscape. So do the higher men who arise from the abyss to his bait.

Equally psychological is the scenery in "The Sign", in which Zarathustra is engulfed under the exploding flood of heavenly love. The laughing lion and the flock of affectionate birds can never be found in the real world. The entire Part IV is a psychological drama. The poetic device of psychological landscapes was introduced long before Part IV. Zarathustra's wandering over the mountains and oceans in Part III took place in a psychological landscape. The highest peak and the deepest abyss in his journey also belong to his psychological landscape. His climbing the highest peak with the dwarf on his shoulder was a drama as psychological as the drama of finding the Ugliest Man in the valley of serpent-death. The distinction between the day-wisdom and the night-wisdom in Part II was also psychological. The day-wisdom belongs to consciousness, and the night-wisdom to subconsciousness. In the course of its thematic development, *Thus Spoke Zarathustra* turns almost imperceptibly into a great psychological drama. In chapter 2, I said that Zarathustra's mission changed from teaching to learning and that the object of his learning was the nature of his own self. He has devised his psychological drama for this task of learning about his own psychological state. Robert Pippin calls his learning mission his politics of self-knowledge (*"Irony and Affirmation"*, 58). Zarathustra situates his enterprise of seeking self-knowledge in a political arena by staging it as a psychodrama with the higher men as its cast. This drama is as psychological as it is political, just like Plato's ideal state.

Let us now consider the entire Part IV as a psychodrama. It is my thesis that the function of this psychodrama is to exhibit the hidden nature of Zarathustra's ordeal with the abysmal thought. There is something truly mysterious about his recounting of the ordeal to his animals in "The Convalescent" of Part III. Although his encounter with the monster is alleged to be the most shattering experience in his life, he says amazingly little about what has really expired in that event. When he is clobbered by the monster, he simply collapses. When he recovers, he screams about the monster that crawled into his throat, but gives no indication of what sort of monster it was. Consequently, we cannot even tell with certainty whether the monster was the dwarf or the snake. Because Zarathustra's description of the monster alludes to both the dwarf and the snake, we called it the dwarf-snake monster in chapter 4. He opened his talk with the outburst of his great disgust with man and followed it with a modified quotation of the Soothsayer's words and his oblique reference to the cave of human decay. But he never explains the point of his quotation and reference, thereby making his entire utterance oracular. He does not even describe the monster and his terrible blow. As we noted in chapter 4, he never openly admits the recognition of the monster as his own animal self, as Oedipus admitted his tragic discovery that he was the criminal he was seeking. Instead he plays his favorite sphinx game and keeps his tragic secret to himself. He justifies this secretive behavior by his elaborate discourse on the impossibility of real communication.

How should we understand this secretive behavior? In my view, Zarathustra's difficulty really lies in communicating not only with his animals, but also with his own deep self. The abysmal thought is the heartworm burrowing in his own heart. When this monster wakes up in response to his summons, he says, "Hail to me! You are coming, I hear you. My abyss speaks, I have turned my ultimate depth inside out into the light" (Z, 216). The abyss is his own ultimate depth that he is trying to turn inside out. He is trying to expose his deepest hidden thought to make it visible. This is his attempt to understand his deepest self, the dwarf-snake monster, in a direct encounter. But this confrontational approach ends only in his getting clobbered by the monster and leaves him with no clear understanding of his monstrous self in "The Convalescent". In assembling the higher men, he is deploying a drastically different method to understand his deepest self. This is to externalize it, personify its various features, and project them on the stage for all to see. The baffling comedy of his higher men reflects the complex character of his soul. It is the drama of his soul.

We have already noted that the higher men are Zarathustra's shadows and alter egos. In the last chapter, we also noted that he established his identity with these shadows by solving the riddle of identity. This is the method that he had used in identifying the dwarf as his own self in "The Convalescent" of Part III. But he never openly declared this identification. Instead he kept it hidden under the cover of his sphinx game. This hidden secret was getting revealed when he identified himself with his shadows by solving the riddles of their identity in Part IV. Some of the shadows are more closely related to his inmost self than others. But all of them have come up from the abyss just as his most abysmal thought did in "The Convalescent". All of them suffer from their shattered ambition to achieve greatness and feel nothing but nausea at their fate of being dwarfed for eternity, as he did in "The Convalescent". All of them are trying to recover from this mortal sickness of nausea with the aid of his animals, as he did in "The Convalescent". They are reenacting what he experienced in "The Convalescent".

I do not mean to say that the higher men are reproducing exactly what Zarathustra went through in his seven-day ordeal. Their reenactment is not for reproduction, but for revelation. It is designed to reveal the secret that has been deeply buried in Zarathustra's own heart ever since his seven-day ordeal in "The Convalescent". In the last chapter, we noted the divergence of the higher men's reenactment from Zarathustra's original showdown with the monster from the abyss. After his speech on the creation of values in "On Old and New Tablets", he was clobbered by the spirit of gravity in "The Convalescent". After his speech in "On the Higher Men", his cave is assaulted by the spirit of melancholy. Unlike the first assault, the second assault is not real but only poetic. But the poetic reenactment provides a deeper insight into Zarathustra's great disgust with his own dwarfism. As we noted at the end of the last chapter, his seven-day ordeal gives only the external diagnosis of dwarfism, which we labeled as only one half of the story. This partial understanding is enriched by the internal diagnosis in the reenactment, which locates the cause of dwarfism in the shriveled condition of sensuality. This is the function of a psychodrama. It produces a deeper and clearer understanding of what goes on in the inner recesses of the soul by taking it out into the open.

Paul S. Loeb notes that the events of Part IV appear to have a close connection with "The Convalescent" of Part III. He tries to account for this peculiarity by his hypothesis that they have taken place prior to the conclusion of Part III, although Part IV is compositionally placed after Part III. He reads Part IV as a supplemental account of the events leading up to the climax in "The Seven Seals". With this, he wants to resolve the dispute between the tripartite and the quadripartite readings. The former takes only the first three Parts of *Zarathustra* as essential and treat Part IV as a gratuitous addition. The latter usually tries to save Part IV by claiming that it performs the critical function of deflating the overblown seriousness of the first three Parts. Loeb offers his account as an alternative to these two contending views. Since Part IV is only a supplement to Part III, there is no need to reject it for the integrity of *Zarathustra*. Loeb's real ambition is to maintain the tripartite reading without jettisoning Part IV. He gives the following reasons for relocating the events of Part IV between "On Old and New Tablets" and "The Convalescent" of Part III. "The Sign" presents the sign that Zarathustra's children are near and this is the sign that he was waiting for in "On Old and New Tablets". Therefore, the events of Part IV should have taken place after "On Old and New Tablets". But they must precede his encounter with the abysmal thought, because he could not have done it unless he had received the sign. Loeb makes this point by using "The Stillest Hour" of Part II: "the lion aspect of Zarathustra's sign announces his attainment of the lion's strength and voice required to command and awake the most abysmal thought" ("The Conclusion of Nietzsche's *Zarathustra*", 142).

Unfortunately, Loeb has misread what expires between Zarathustra and the awesome lady of "The Stillest Hour". When the lady commands him to speak "it" and break, he replies, "I lack the lion's voice for commanding" (Z, 146). Then the lady says to him that the lion's voice is not the requirement but the impediment for the frightful task. She advises him to become like a child instead of becoming a lion. There is one more defective link in Loeb's reasoning. If the long awaited sign is already realized and Zarathustra's children are coming before "Convalescent", we must assume that he has a short memory. In "The Seven Seals", he still expresses his passionate longing to have children from Eternity. Nevertheless, Loeb is clearly right in stressing the affinity of the higher men's nausea to Zarathustra's in "The Convalescent". But it is simpler to account for this affinity by postulating that the higher men are reenacting his ordeal in "The Convalescent". This reenactment does not extend to the end of Part IV, but it is hard to pinpoint its termination. We can only be certain that "The Awakening" clearly begins a new show. Thus the transition from the reenactment to the new show is subtle and gradual.

The seven higher men, who have functioned as the shadows from his past, represent the children of his old self. When they come out of the cave the next morning to join him, the new lion jumps toward them and roars savagely. At this scary moment, "they all cried out as with a single mouth, and they fled back and disappeared in a flash" (Z, 326). They cry out with a single mouth because they are the shadows of one single soul, just as the cry of distress was their collective cry. Then they all vanish like ghosts because they are the ghosts of his past self. This is the exorcism of Zarathustra's old ghosts. It works like psychoanalytic therapy, which brings out the hidden repressions from the depth of the soul to expose and understand their haunting presence. This is also the way the psychodrama is used as a therapeutic device. The hidden emotions and complexes are staged as concrete persons and agents. The roaring lion shows the most important feature of Zarathustrian therapy. The exposure and analysis of those ghost-like shadows are not enough for gaining psychological health. Those psychological moves can become effective only when they can generate a new strong self like the roaring lion.

By the time the higher men are driven back into the cave by the lion, they appear to be buried in the cave. This cave looks much like the cave of human decay Zarathustra saw in "The Convalescent" of Part III, when he exploded with his great disgust and nausea at humanity. Later, he saw the decay of this same cave dramatized in the valley of serpent-death, where he found the Ugliest Man dying his slow death. In "The Drunken Song", he referred to those rotting and dying in the valley of serpent-death as corpses and tombs to be awakened. Now we can see that Zarathustra's own cave has been the cave of human decay for the higher men. He has played the game of masks to conceal the decadent people in this cave. The most important function of Part IV as a psychological drama is to remove those masks and expose the pitiful condition of his alter egos. All the higher men have revealed themselves by telling their personal histories and exposed their game of dissemblance for greatness. They were all suffering from the neurosis that may be called the Faustian complex. Because they were neurotic, they looked so pathetic and ridiculous as many commentators have noted. Zarathustra had every reason to hide these alter egos behind his masks. But the merciless exposure of their condition finally terminates the game of masks. The higher men are now awakened and reborn as Zarathustra's new children, that is, his new self, which is represented by the new lion. His old self and their ghosts just vanish when the lion approaches and roars, that is, when the new self displays its power. The roaring lion is his new self chasing away the whining ghosts of his old self and drives them back to the cave for their internment. This is the Spinozan spiritual remedy for the Faustian malady. The gentle lion is the individual self in union with the cosmic self.

The higher men play two different roles before and after the mystical event. Before this event, they played the role of his old devils, who were struggling to recover from their despair and nausea just the way Zarathustra had done in "The Convalescent". When the Ugliest Man shouted to death, "Was *that* life? Well then! Once more!", he was feeling the revitalization of his dying self. His feeling of revitalization was shared by all other higher men. Thus revitalized, they played the rogues in concocting the Ass Festival and Zarathustra was amazed by their roguish defense of the festival. In his lexicon, a rogue is a lively devil. The higher men were beginning their transformation from his old shriveled devils to his new vibrant children. After the mystical event, however, they are no longer the roguish devils. They do not even share his vitality to get up fresh and strong in the morning. They are reduced to the old husks of his new-born children. These two roles of higher men can explain the drastic change in his handling of them. In the evening before, he was their solicitous host, who looked after their safety and comfort. The next morning, he suddenly becomes callous to their feeling and shows no concern whatsoever for their well-being, even when they are frightened by his lion. This abrupt change of his attitude toward the higher men is inexplicable if they are assumed to retain the same identity before and after the mystical event. On the other hand, if they are no longer his old devils in convalescence, but only the old husks of his new-born children, there would be no point in Zarathustra's continued concern with them. He must make a clean break with them for the integrity of his new children. So his lion drives them back to the cave to be buried there. This is his final settlement with his old ghosts.

We have considered the relation of Zarathustra's old and new self in his psychodrama. But that is only one half of the story because he has a twofold self. The higher men represent his individual self. In chapter 4, we noted that the cosmic self is represented by animals. But I should qualify this description because we have seen that the cosmic self can exist in two different modes, eternal and temporal. The animals represent the cosmic self in the temporal mode. This representational function is important for understanding the role of the cosmic self in the psychodrama of Part IV. Zarathustra's talk with his animals marks the opening of this drama. This is the sign of communion between his individual self and his cosmic self, which began in "The Convalescence". Thereafter, his animals are entrusted with the task of receiving and instructing the higher men, representatives of the individual self. This is the second sign of communion between the two selves. But his animals are not the only animals to make their presence felt in the psychodrama. The Voluntary Beggar learns the art of rumination from the cows. This is the third sign of communion of the individual self with the cosmic self. These three communions prepare for the Ass Festival in which the higher men as representatives of the individual self worship the ass as the symbol of the cosmic self. The worship of the cosmic self leads to Zarathustra's mystical union with the eternal ring, the cosmic self in its eternal mode.

The animals return with greater vitality in the morning after the mystical communion. While the higher men are still asleep in the cave,

Zarathustra comes outside and hears the cry of his eagle. He says to his animals, "You are the right animals for me; I love you. But I still lack the right men" (Z, 325). This is an astonishing statement. For the first time in his life, he says that he loves his animals. This is the expression of his love for his cosmic self in its temporal mode. Then suddenly he is submerged under countless swarming birds. These birds are affectionate doves. In Christian iconography, as Robert Gooding-Williams points out, the doves represent the outpouring of the Holy Spirit and its grace (*Zarathustra's Dionysian Modernism,* 294). The descent of affectionate doves on Zarathustra is the descent of love from his cosmic self to his individual self. In his amazement at this dramatic scene, he reaches out and touches the gentle lion. This is the birth of his new self from the flock of loving birds. This new self is born with the love of the cosmic self, just as Christ was born with love of the Holy Spirit. I have closely associated the cosmic self with animals, but here is an animal that represents his new individual self. But the lion is a special case. The fierce lion has been the symbol of the Faustian self. But it is now reborn as a gentle lion. Its loving relation with the flock of birds represents the union of love between Zarathustra's new individual self with his cosmic self.

The function of Zarathustra's psychodrama is similar to the function of purgation in Dante's scheme of salvation. At the end of chapter 4, I said that the three ladies in charge of Zarathustra's epic journey correspond in their roles roughly to Dante's three guides for his epic journey. Wisdom governs Zarathustra's journey as the Faustian hero. The Faustian phase of his journey corresponds to Dante's travel to Hell, which climaxes in the defiant assertion of Satan's will against his Creator in Cocytus. This phase of Dante's travel is governed by Virgil, the epitome of human wisdom. When Life takes over Zarathustra's journey from Wisdom, he goes through a long process of suffering and purgation, which corresponds to Dante's journey on the Purgatory. But Dante goes through this phase of his journey under the tutelage of Virgil. If he were replaced by Beatrice for this phase, there would be a perfect correspondence between the two epic courses. Eternity replaces Life for the consummation of Zarathustra's journey, just as St. Bernard of Clairveaux replaces Beatrice for the consummation of Dante's journey. Prior to his flight to the heavenly world, Dante's soul is made pure by the purgation of his sins. On his flight to the eternal domain, Zarathustra's soul has also become pure. He says to the higher men, "Leave me! Leave me! I am too pure for you" (*Z*, 321). His purity was achieved by a long process of purgation. But what is the sin that is purged in this process? It is the sin of pity. When he started receiving the higher men in "The Cry of Distress", he called pity his final sin. When he gets rid of all the higher men in "The Sign", he says that he is finally released from his pity for them. His pity of the higher men is his self-pity because they are the shadows and ghosts of his own self. Now I propose that self-pity is the necessary step in the conversion of self-hatred to self-love. That is, self-hatred is first converted to self-pity, which is then converted to self-love. Even in Dante's Purgatory, purgation is a conversion process: Sinful dispositions are converted to virtues.

With Zarathustra, self-hatred was his first sin because it was the root of all his sins. His first sin governed the life of his Faustian individual self, who projected his self-hatred as the hatred of others, especially the spirit of gravity. His self-hatred was converted to his self-pity when he realized that the dwarf was not really his enemy but his animal self. Instead of hatred, he felt compassion for the pitiful condition of the dwarf, which was expressed as his compassion for his soul in "On the Great Longing" of Part III. In Part IV, he feels the same compassion for the higher men. But his self-pity is the beginning of his self-love because it expresses his concern with the well-being of his animal self. His self-love is still stunted because his animal self is too ugly and too paltry to be worthy of his love. Self-pity is this stunted form of self-love. But self-pity is the last sin because it must be overcome for the perfection of self-love, the first virtue or the root of all virtues. But the conversion of self-pity to self-love is not any easier than the conversion of self-hatred to self-pity. The final conversion is accomplished in "The Drunken Song", where the ugly dwarf turns into a beautiful cosmic giant and the Faustian self achieves an ecstatic union with the Spinozan self. By this series of conversions, Zarathustra becomes free of self-pity. This point is demon-

strated when the lion roars and scares away the higher men. The gentle
lion is the symbol of Zarathustra's new self that shows no pity and no
mercy for the ghosts of his old self.

Let us now try to correlate the sequence of self-hatred, self-pity, and
self-love with the sequence of four stages in the Ladder of Redemption
that I presented in chapter 4. The Ladder of Redemption consists of the
following four stages: (1) the recognition of the dwarf as the animal self,
(2) the recognition of its cosmic dimension, (3) the activation of the
cosmic self by cosmic force, and (4) the reconciliation of the individual
self with the cosmic self in their ecstatic union. The first stage of his redemption takes a long time. It begins with Zarathustra's announcement
of the superman in the Prologue and continues in his recognition of the
identity of the body and the soul in Part I. Then, it goes through a long
process of generating and nurturing his self-hatred and finally explodes
in the outburst of his great disgust with man in "The Convalescent" of
Part III. It ends with his recognition of the dwarf as his animal self. The
cosmic dimension of the animal self is recognized "On the Great Longing". This is in the second stage of his redemption that ends with the discovery of his soul as his cosmic self. But he feels pity for his soul. This is
his self-pity, which is dissolved by the activation of his cosmic self in
"The Other Dancing Song". But the activation of the cosmic self leaves
his individual self in a perpetual frustration, which generates the pity for
his individual self in "The Seven Seals". This is the third stage of his redemption. His self-pity is finally converted to his self-love in "The
Drunken Song", and this conversion is fully displayed and announced in
"The Sign". This is the fourth and final stage of his redemption.

The New Dionysian Self

Because the birth of his children is the birth of his new self, as we noted
earlier, Zarathustra associates the coming of his children with his own
fruition: "The lion came, my children are near, Zarathustra has ripened,
my hour has come: this is my morning, *my* day is breaking: *rise now, rise,*

thou great noon!" (*Z*, 327). He has often associated the advent of the superman with the great noon. His new-born self is the superman. Robert Pippin observes that the great noon is the timeless present, which has no shadows stretching backward or forward ("Irony and Affirmation," pp. 55f). A human being can only be an ugly dwarf under the shadows from the past because they overpower his autonomous will. The superman should be free from those shadows. To our surprise, however, Zarathustra realized the superhuman ideal at midnight and emerges to greet the rising sun. But the great noon can also be marked by the rising sun. Every moment is high noon from the perspective of the sun. The shadows stretching forward or backward can affect only the worms crawling over the surface of the earth. Even midnight is high noon from the cosmic perspective of the superman, who has identified himself with the eternal ring. At the height of his mystical experience in "The Drunken Song", Zarathustra said, "Midnight too is noon" (*Z*, 323). Hence the superman of midnight is also the superman of great noon. This is confirmed by the new Zarathustra, who radiates his overflowing energy like the morning sun. This is the final confirmation of what was achieved in the Dionysian mystery of midnight.

Since the superman of great noon is fully realized in the Dionysian intoxication, he may be called a Dionysian hero. He is the hero of Dionysian naturalism because Dionysius stands for Mother Nature. Goethe is well known as Nietzsche's hero of naturalism. He says that Goethe embodied the naturalness of the Renaissance. The following is his description of Goethe's naturalness:

> He bore within him its strongest natural instincts. . . . he did not sever himself from life, he placed himself within it; nothing could discourage him and he took as much as possible upon himself, above himself, within himself. What he aspired to was *totality*. . . . Goethe was, in an epoch disposed to the unreal, a convinced realist. (*TI*, Expeditions 49)

In Nietzsche's philosophy, naturalism and realism go together. He says, "Napoleon was a piece of 'return to nature'" (*TI*, Expeditions 48). Hence

Goethe the great naturalist is a convinced realist. In Nietzsche's hall of fame, however, even the greatest artists are not the realists of the highest rank because they deal with fictions rather than with reality. He says, "A Homer would have created no Achilles, a Goethe no Faust, if Homer had been an Achilles and Goethe a Faust" (*GM* III.4). Homer would not have bothered to write an epic of Achilles if the poet had himself been the hero. The epic was an "unreal" substitute for being a real hero. The same is true of Goethe and his epic of Faust.

Nietzsche names Napoleon Bonaparte as the greatest naturalist and realist. He portrays the impressive stature of this Dionysian hero by using Goethe's encounter with him:

> Goethe . . . had no greater experience than that *ens realismum* called Napoleon. Goethe conceived of a strong, highly cultured human being . . . who . . . dares to allow himself the whole compass and wealth of naturalness, who is strong enough for this freedom . . . a man to whom nothing is forbidden, except it be *weakness,* whether that weakness be called vice or virtue. (*TI,* Expeditions 49)

The Latin phrase *ens realissimum*, which means "the most real being", is Kant's description of God as the ultimate reality (*Critique of Pure Reason,* A605/B633-A608/B636). Napoleon has become the most real being because he is one with Mother Nature. Nothing can be more real than Mother Nature in the world of Zarathustra or Spinoza. By virtue of his union with this ultimate reality, Napoleon Bonaparte stands as a Dionysian hero par excellence:

> A spirit thus *emancipated* stands in the midst of the universe with a joyful and trusting fatalism, in the *faith* that only what is separate and individual may be rejected, that in totality everything is redeemed and affirmed. . . . But such a faith is the highest of all possible faiths: I have baptized it with the name *Dionysos*. (*TI,* Expeditions 49)

For his Dionysian faith, Nietzsche singles out Napoleon as the only one to be called the superman without any qualifications in all his writings

(*GM*, I.16). Only Cesare Borgia comes close to this awesome title in Nietzsche's ranking. He refers to Borgia as "a kind of superman" (*TI*, Expeditions 37). Like Napoleon, he is not a creator of artful fictions, but an active agent in the real world.

When Zarathustra wakes up in the morning after the midnight intoxication, he also stands on his Dionysian faith. He is no longer "separate and individual". He has finally fulfilled his destiny in the loving union with his cosmic self. This cosmic union overcomes the cause of all his sufferings, namely, the strife between his individual and his cosmic self. This union also realizes the great *Hazar*, in which everything is redeemed and affirmed in totality, as indicated by the flock of loving birds. As we noted earlier, the descent of the loving birds stands for the cascading love from his cosmic self. This cosmic love is the foundation for the great *Hazar*, just as divine love is meant to be the foundation for the kingdom of Christ. He can still truly love his cosmic self even after his mystical intoxication. This is the enduring spillover effect from his mystical communion with the eternal ring. It is the ultimate outcome of his struggle against himself and the whole world. The union of the individual self with the cosmic self is the hardest task for any human beings. The individual self instinctively feels fear and horror in the face of the cosmic self, because the former cannot avoid the crushing weight of the latter. It is this instinctive fear and horror that Zarathustra called his most abysmal thought in "The Convalescent" of Part III. He talked about the same dreadful horror to the higher men when he said, "Do your hearts become giddy? Does the abyss yawn before you? Does the hellhound howl at you?" (*Z*, 286f). The cosmic self looks like a howling hellhound because it assails the individual self with countless slings and arrows. There is no way to be in love with such a monstrous entity.

The union of the individual self with the cosmic self endows Zarathustra with the superhuman power even in the world of daylight, because the cosmic self is the fountain of all power. Zarathustra's new individual self faces the world with Dionysian dynamism and activism. After announcing the sign for the advent of his children, he says, "Am I concerned with *happiness?* I am concerned with *work*" (*Z*, 327). He is

setting out on a journey of active work. This is the basic difference between his Dionysian mysticism and the traditional mysticism. Rapture is
the ultimate end for traditional mystical vision, but it is not for Zarathustra's. It gives him the new beginning and new power for active work. In
this regard, he is very much like Shiva. In chapter 4, we noted that Shiva
feels neither pleasure nor pain in his meditation, but experiences great
bliss only when he wakes out of his meditative mood and moves into his
cosmic dance. This is Shiva's activism and dynamism, which is diametrically opposed to the Buddhist quietism. For the Buddhists, meditation
is to withdraw from the turbulent world of *samsara* for the peace and
quiet of *nirvana*. But peace and quiet cannot be the end for Shiva. Like
Shiva, we noted in chapter 4, Zarathustra's cosmic self could not be
happy in its inactive state, as shown in "On the Great Longing" of Part
III. It had to become the active dancer in "The Other Dancing Song" of
Part III. His individual self is now going through the same transformation
in the last two sections of Part IV. He is meditative in "The Drunken
Song", but he becomes active in "The Sign". With his overflowing Dio-
nysian energy, he is ready to engage in the dance with the cosmic self.

In the last chapter, we noted that the Voluntary Beggar was a naturalized Buddha-figure and Zarathustra's alter ego. He claimed to have
conquered nausea by the art of rumination, which we interpreted as the
art of meditation. But he showed no sign of activism and dynamism. On
the contrary, he embodied the Buddhist quietism. Although his quietism
may be a perfect end point for the Buddhists, it cannot be for Zarathustra's alter ego. So we have to assume that the conquest of nausea cannot
be his ultimate end, but must be the new beginning for his active en-
gagement in the world. He must go through the same Dionysian transformation as Zarathustra's. His Buddhism should be Dionysian. Although Dionysian Buddhism may sound self-contradictory, it is the spirit
of Zen Buddhism, as it has been manifested in the Zen story of ox-
herding, which I recounted in the last chapter. At the end of this story,
the distinction between the ox and the ox-herd disappears. So does the
distinction between *samsara* and *nirvana*. When the ox-herd returns to
town, he is indistinguishable from all other folk. Instead of withdrawing

from the world to his meditation, the Zen master is now fully engaged in the world. The ox-herd stands for the individual mind, and the ox for the Buddha Mind, the cosmic self. In the moment of enlightenment, the individual mind becomes one with the Buddha Mind. This union provides the power for the Zen master's activism and dynamism. A similar union also takes place in the mind of a Taoist sage when he becomes a baby in tune with the flow of Tao. The Taoist's cosmic self is the flow of Tao. The morning after his mystical experience, Zarathustra looks like a Taoist sage and a Zen master. Their common ground is the union of the individual self with the cosmic self.

When the individual self embodies the inexhaustible power of the cosmic self, it can become an object of reverence because it is no longer a puny individual. It is divine because it is coextensive with Mother Nature, the Goddess of the whole world. Nietzsche says that the Dionysian hero Napoleon has reverence for himself (*TI*, Expeditions 49). The idea of self-reverence is highly puzzling. We encountered this puzzling idea in "On Self-Overcoming" of Part II, where Zarathustra said, "You still want to create the world before which you can kneel: that is your ultimate hope and intoxication" (*Z*, 113). In chapter 2, I raised the question of why you should ever feel reverence for the things you could create. Whatever you can create only manifests your power, and there is no reason for you to feel any reverence for your own power. The concept of self-reverence is much stronger than the concept of self-respect. Respect can obtain in the relation of equals, but reverence is limited to the relation between two entities glaringly unequal. The idea of self-respect is understandable because one can face oneself as one's equal. But the idea of self-reverence is incomprehensible because it makes no sense to face oneself as vastly superior to oneself. Therefore the Nietzschean ideal of self-reverence makes no sense in the standard conception of self-relation. It must be understood in the context of two selves. When the individual self understands its relation to the cosmic self, the former should feel reverence for the latter because the cosmic self is far greater than the individual self. This is the Dionysian conception of self-relation. Probably because Napoleon was conscious of his cosmic self, he not only had reverence for himself, but also called himself the man of destiny. The cosmic self is the ground of destiny or fate.

In Zarathustra's world, all existential problems have their roots in the matrix of self-relation, that is, in the relation of his individual self to his cosmic self. But he can find his cosmic self only through a long detour of the whole world, because the cosmic self is coextensive with the world. This long detour is the epic journey of discovering his ultimate selfhood, and this journey of self-discovery goes through a series of metamorphoses as Lucius does in *The Golden Ass*. The stone has become the dwarf. The black filthy snake has become the golden eternal ring. The ugly dwarf has been changed from a monstrous devil to a tender baby and then to a beautiful god in the eternal ring. The tidal waves of despair and melancholy that have emanated from the spirit of gravity and the abyss have been transformed to the whirling flocks of loving birds. By the power of love, the ugly dwarf is reborn as the gentile lion. By this series of miraculous transformations, Zarathustra has achieved the loving union of his individual self with his cosmic self. This self-love is his *amor fati* because the cosmic self is none other than all the things that happen to the self by fate. His self-love is also his self-reverence. The notion of self-reverence that makes no sense in the context of an individual to himself can gain profound significance in the relation of the individual to the cosmic self, which can be as holy as any deity.

The cosmic self is the Goddess of Nature that can fulfill Zarathustra's youthful dream: "All beings shall be divine to me." By recognizing her power of sanctification, he has completed his campaign of spiritualizing his natural existence. He initiated this campaign in The Motley Cow and concluded it by setting up the great Hazar. It has gone through three stages. The Faustian stage was conducted under the governance of Wisdom. It was transformed into the Spinozan campaign under the tutelage of Life. But the Spinozan campaign was elevated from the temporal to the eternal level for the love of Eternity. On this final stage, Zarathustra's love of Life took the mystical turn and eventuated in the Dionysian religion of Mother Nature. This religion of nature is the religion above all religions. It is not the simpleminded reversion to the primitive natural religion, which tries to reinstate the worship of the spirits of fields and forests, rivers, and mountains. Neither is it a complacent repudiation of the anti-natural religions, which have been devised as an escape from the natural world. On the contrary, it fully realizes the original love and reverence for Mother Nature that was expressed as the superstitious worship of local deities in primitive religions and that was misdirected toward the supernatural beings by the anti-natural religions. The Dionysian religion is the global religion for the worship of Mother Nature as the cosmic principle of Life and the goddess of all creation. The Dionysian faith we talked about earlier is the heart of this Dionysian religion. This is the ultimate outcome for Zarathustra's campaign for the spiritualization of secular culture. This hazardous campaign has been his long epic journey.

Zarathustra's epic career is the story of how easy it is to hate one's fate and how hard it is to overcome this hatred and turn it into *amor fati*. I will try to illustrate this point by using Kierkegaard's notion of despair, as articulated in *The Sickness unto Death*. Suppose that you hate yourself for being poor and ugly. You will soon realize that your poverty is determined by your social fate and your ugliness by your genetic fate. So your hatred of yourself quickly turns into your hatred of fate. In Kierkegaardian terms, this hatred is your despair over the necessity that has determined your finite self. If you are blessed with great fortunes, on the other hand, you may love your fate. But your fate never guarantees the security of those great fortunes. As soon as you realize your helplessness at the mercy of your fate, you are again in despair. Thus, the hatred of fate can be generated not only by misfortunes, but also by great fortunes. Your hatred of fate is at the same time your hatred of your self. You hate your self for being so helpless under the crushing power of fate.

The hatred of fate is the most natural response of the individual will to the world because it is bound to clash with the unlimited power of fate. As long as the individual self defiantly asserts its will against the world, it has no chance of coming to love the cosmic self. The individual self may even try to love the cosmic self in desperation, but such a desperate effort can at most turn self-hatred into self-pity. Although the acceptance of the cosmic self is the first step for the redemption from self-hatred, it does not automatically lead to love of this cosmic self. As we noted earlier, love of the cosmic self can never be achieved by the individual effort. It can come only from the power that transcends the individual will. Thus, *amor fati* is secured not locally in the relation of an individual self to itself. It is situated globally in the relation of an individual to his cosmic self. This global self-relation is equivalent to Kierkegaard's claim that the self-relation of a human being inevitably involves the relation to God. The cosmic self is the totality of Nature, which Spinoza calls God. Hence the relation of an individual self to his cosmic self is equivalent to the Kierkegaardian relation of an individual to God. This is no coincidence. Kierkegaard and Nietzsche, both of whom have come out of the Lutheran tradition, are working out the existential implication of Martin Luther's teaching on the mystery of faith as the vehicle of redemption. Whereas Kierkegaard retains the Lutheran orthodoxy, Nietzsche follows the Spinozan heterodoxy of naturalizing God. Just as Kierkegaard says that despair can be overcome only by grounding oneself in God, so Nietzsche says that nausea can be overcome only by the union of the individual self with the cosmic self.

We should notice not only that Zarathustra's account of nausea is closely linked to Kierkegaard's Christian analysis of despair in *The Sickness unto Death*, but also that Zarathustra's psychological epic journey reflects the Christian literary tradition. Dante's *Divina Commedia* is a great psychological epic. His three worlds of Hell, Purgatory, and Paradise are not physical but psychological. His epic journey is psychological. So are his three guides and travails. Milton's *Paradise Lost* is another great psychological epic because the mythological events such as Adam's encounter with God and his temptation by Satan should be read as psychological allegories rather than literal stories. Bunyan's *Pilgrim's Progress* is equally psychological. The epic journey of Christian takes place in the land of dream, that is, in a psychological world. Richard Schacht says that *Zarathustra* is Nietzsche's version of this psychological epic ("Zarathustra/*Zarathustra*", 232). All these Christian psychological epics are sustained by the invisible power of God. Nietzsche has constructed his psychological epic by naturalizing these Christian epics.

But his psychological epic is sustained by the visible power of God, Mother Nature. This makes his epic clearly a secular offshoot of the long venerable tradition of Christian sacred epics. In this secular form, Nietzsche's psychological epic reads more like the Zen fable of ox-herding on enlightenment than the Christian psychological epics, because this fable is a highly secular story of redemption. As Graham Parkes notes, there are deep resonances between Nietzsche's ideas and the Zen ideas on the nature of human existence and the mystery of the world ("The Orientation of the Nietzschean Text", 14).

The Zarathustrian Epic Cycle

As some commentators have noted, "The Sign" is remarkably similar to the conclusion of Plato's *Symposium*, which records one long evening of drinking and talking. The following morning, Socrates alone can wake up sober and face the rising sun, while the rest of the party are still drunk or asleep. They had talked on love and their talk reached its culmination in Diotima's story of love as told by Socrates. Her story describes the ladder of love, which begins with the love of body at the lowest rung, ascends to the love of soul, and finally reaches the love of Platonic Forms (*Symposium* 210a-212b). At the summit of this ascent, love is fulfilled in the mystical vision of Beauty itself (or the Form of Beauty). This Platonic ascent of love to the eternal world of Forms became the basic model for mystical experience in the West. Even *The Golden Ass* is supposed to have been written under its influence. Nietzsche was also fascinated by the Platonic model. The Ladder of Redemption, which I constructed and discussed in chapter 4, is Zarathustra's ladder of love. Its function is to redeem his love from his hatred.

According to Diotima, the highest virtue arises from the vision and love of Beauty itself, the Platonic Form of Beauty. Amazingly, the highest virtue is produced by love. This is an unusual view of virtue. Traditionally, virtue is linked to character, not to love. To understand her claim, we have to distinguish between two types of virtue, erotic and

ethical. The erotic virtues are virtues of love; the ethical virtues are virtues of character. The ethical virtue is virtue in our normal understanding. The erotic virtue is the super-normal one, which arises from love just
like a labor of love. The medieval Christians distinguished such an extraordinary virtue from the standard virtue by calling it the infused virtue.
Unlike the standard virtue, Aquinas says, the infused virtue cannot be
acquired by human effort. It can be achieved only by the infusion of divine love (*ST*, pt. 1-2, q. 65, a. 2). The ethical virtue is human; the erotic
virtue is divine. The former is an expression of human character and its
effort; the latter is an effortless expression of divine love and its power.

After Diotima's story is given by Socrates in the *Symposium*, Alcibiades barges into the party and describes what sort of person Socrates is
(*Symposium* 215a-222c). His praise of Socrates' virtues is extraordinary;
they go beyond his wildest dreams, he says. With his superlatives, Alcibiades is lauding the erotic virtues of Socrates rather than his ethical virtues. The erotic Socrates is different from the ethical Socrates, although
they may be engaged outwardly in the same virtuous act. There is nothing extraordinary about ethical virtues, however excellent they may be,
because they are achievable by human effort. But the erotic virtues are
extraordinary; they transcend normal human powers. Socrates could not
have developed his extraordinary virtue from his own power and character alone. The Socrates that wakes up early in the morning after a long
night of drinking and talking on love confirms what was said in praise of
his erotic virtues. Whereas the other participants can hardly wake up, he
is as strong and as fresh as if he had a sound sleep for the whole night.
This confirms Alcibiades' superlative praise of Socrates. But we will
miss the point of his praise unless we take it as the praise of his erotic
virtues. After all, his praise is meant to be the capstone of the long symposium in praise of the goddess of love and her power. Zarathustra's
morning after the night of his Dionysian intoxication performs the same
function as Socrates' morning after the night of the symposium. They at-
test to the extraordinary power of love and confirm the extraordinary virtues that have been born from that erotic power.

Just as the mystical Socrates is the erotic Socrates, so the mystical Zarathustra is the erotic Zarathustra. We should not forget that his mystical experience came in a chain of erotic events. The Shadow's erotic song on sensuality led to the worship of an ass, the symbol of erotic power, which in turn led to his erotic union with Life in the eternal ring. In "The Sign", he greets his animals with a message of love ("I love you"). The immense flock of birds whirling around him is "a cloud of love." Even the roaring lion is a creature of tender love. The lion and the birds rejoice in their mutual love. In the morning after his mystical experience, his entire world has turned into a vast ring of love. As I have said more than once, love and sensuality are the best remedy for melancholy. Hence the cosmic bond of love gives Zarathustra his final triumph over the spirit of gravity and his ultimate redemption. In such a state of love, he has the right to say that he has indeed ripened and that his hour has finally come. His work in such a state is bound to be the work of love. If his mystical experience were to be contained solely within the brief span of midnight, it would be no more than a momentary escape from the world of suffering. But his experience of love and joy overflows into his everyday world and transforms its entire texture. This is the working of Dionysian dynamism.

Zarathustra ends his epic journey by greeting the sun. He began his journey by greeting the same sun in the Prologue. He concludes his long journey by returning to its original point, thereby forming the ring of Zarathustria's epic journey. This sense of closure would be impossible if the book were to end with Part III. This again attests to the indispensability of Part IV for the integrity of the whole book. But the sun that marks the end of his journey does not have the same significance that the sun had at its beginning. In his first greeting to the sun, he treated the great star as a symbolic projection of his own Wisdom and his Faustian ideal of superman. When the Faustian ideal was shattered, he recognized the sun as a symbol of the sun-will, the cosmic necessity of Life. The symbolic transformation of the sun marked the substantive transformation of his spiritual campaign from the Faustian to the Spinozan mode. In his last greeting to the sun, he says: "You great star, you deep eye of happiness, what would your happiness be had you not those for whom you shine?" (Z, 324). This is the same as his first salutation to the sun except for the phrase, "you deep eye of happiness." The word "eye" has a special meaning in this phrase like "the eye of a cyclone." The sun stands not simply for happiness, but for the ultimate center of exploding happiness. By the end of his epic journey, the great star has been elevated from the symbol of the cosmic necessity of Life to the symbol of her exploding happiness. This elevation was secured by his flight to Eternity and his mystical vision of the eternal ring. He can now see the ring of eternal recurrence as the ring of exploding happiness. It radiates happiness just as the sun radiates its light. The sun has become the symbol for the eye of happiness in the eternal ring. The radiant wave of cosmic happiness is now shining upon his existence. By sharing this wave of happiness with the sun, he participates in the sun's own happiness. This is the closure for his cosmic partnership with the eternal ring.

In Christianity, the sun used to be the symbol of God. But Zarathustra's sun is not a supernatural entity. It is made of the same physical elements as the earth is. The great star is just a huge stone. In Zarathustra's world, the stone stands for the ultimate elements for the composition of all objects. The dwarf came up from the abyss and became the philosopher's stone in "On the Vision and the Riddle" of Part III. Like a stone, he was hard and heavy in enunciating the heavy thought of eternal recurrence and then in clobbering Zarathustra in "The Convalescent". Now that the dwarf is reborn as his new Dionysian self, he is not only strong but glows like the sun. The stone was the point of origination for his flight to Eternity and the point of his return. It is again at the stone ("Here is the stone") that he recollects his mystical flight in "The Sign". He is now sitting on a big stone on the ground and looking at a radiant stone in the sky. His epic cycle is the cycle of stones, which descend to the abyss and ascend to the eternal ring. His stones are the stones of love and hate. The stone of self-hatred is hung around the neck of the Faustian superman like a millstone. It is the immovable stone of the past and the stone of fate. But the Faustian superman recognizes this stone as the fate of his cosmic self and becomes the Spinozan superman. This Spinozan enlightenment is the first step for converting the stone of self-hatred to the eagle of self-love. Then the stone can fly like the sun. Hence the Zarathustrian epic cycle is the cycle of self-love. It begins and ends with self-love. The Faustian and the Spinozan supermen are the two pillars of this epic cycle that display the will to power of the eternal ring.

The ending of Zarathustra's epic cycle has one baffling feature. It appears to have all the signs of starting a new cycle. In the morning after the mystical conclusion, he is setting out on another mission of work. Even his gentle lion is behaving like a ferocious beast when it chases the higher men back into the cave. It appears to have all the potential to turn into a Faustian creature and assert its autonomous will. In chapter 4, I stressed the irrepressibility and ineliminability of the Faustian self. It is like Hydra's head. No sooner it is cut off, it grows right back. I have also pointed out that the Spinozan self is equally irrepressible and in-eliminable. Therefore, the Nietzschean dialectic of these two selves is an interminable process because it is the process of life. It is as eternal as the eternal recurrence, which is Life. It can have no beginning and no ending. This interminable process may turn Zarathustra's epic into an endless repetition of cycles. Therefore, there may be no final closure for his epic journey, either. The ending of the present cycle may well be the beginning of a new cycle. But it cannot be the repetition of the same. At the end of Part IV, Zarathustra is quite differently situated than he was at the Prologue. Whereas he was alone in the Prologue, he is now sur-rounded by the laughing lion and a flock of loving birds. He is now much stronger and happier. He has buried all the ghosts of his old self in the cave. Therefore, if he is destined to go through another cycle, he should begin it on a higher level than the previous cycle. The trajectory of his epic cycle should be a soaring spiral rather than a repetitious circle.

Selected Bibliography

Abrams, M. H. *Natural Supernaturalism: Tradition and Revolution in Romantic Literature*. New York: W. W. Norton, 1971.

Alderman, Harold. *Nietzsche's Gift*. Athens: Ohio University Press, 1977.

Allison, David. *Reading the New Nietzsche*. Lanham: Rowman and Littlefield Publishers, 2001.

Apuleius. *The Golden Ass*. Trans. P. G. Walsh. Oxford: Clarendon Press, 1994.

Babich, Babette. *Nietzsche's Philosophy of Science: Reflecting on the Ground of Art and Life*. Albany: SUNY Press, 1994.

Bauer, Bruno. *The Trumpet of the Last Judgement against Hegel the Atheist and Antichrist: An Ultimatum*. Lewiston, NY: Edwin Mellen, 1989.

Berdyaev, Nikolai. *The Meaning of the Creative Act*. New York: Collier Books, 1962.

Berkowitz, Peter. *Nietzsche: The Ethics of an Immoralist*. Cambridge, MA: Harvard University Press, 1995.

Bonaventure, Saint. *The Tree of Life*. In *The Works of Bonaventure* 1:95-144. Trans. Jose de Vinck. Paterson, NJ: St. Anthony Guild, 1960.

Borgeaud, Philippe. *The Cult of Pan in Ancient Greece*. Trans. Kathleen Atlas and James Redfield. Chicago: University of Chicago Press, 1988.

Campbell, Joseph. *The Masks of God: Primitive Mythology*. New York: Viking, 1959.

Carrithers, Michael. *The Buddha*. Oxford: Oxford University Press, 1983.

Clark, Maudemarie. *Nietzsche on Truth and Philosophy*. Cambridge: Cambridge University Press, 1990.

Conway, Daniel. "A Moral Ideal for Everyone and No One." *International Studies in Philosophy* 22 (1990): 17-29.

————. *Nietzsche's Dangerous Game.* Cambridge: Cambridge University Press, 1997.

Conze, Edward. *Buddhist Scriptures.* London: Penguin Books, 1959.

Dannhauser, Werner. *Nietzsche's View of Socrates.* Ithaca, NY: Cornell University Press, 1974.

Deleuze, Gilles. *Nietzsche and Philosophy.* Trans. H. Tomlinson. London: Athlone Press, 1983.

Detwiler, Bruce. *Nietzsche and the Politics of Aristocratic Radicalism.* Chicago: University of Chicago Press, 1990.

Donington, Robert. *Wagner's 'Ring' and its Symbols.* London: Faber and Faber, 1963.

Erigena, Scotus. *Periphysion: On the Division of Nature.* Trans. Myra Uhlfelder. Indianapolis: Bobbs-Merrill, 1976.

Feuerbach, Ludwig. *The Essence of Christianity.* Trans. George Eliot. New York: Harper and Row, 1957.

————. *The Essence of Faith according to Luther.* Trans. Melvin Cherno. New York: Harper and Row, 1967.

————. *Principles of the Philosophy of the Future.* Trans. Manfred Vogel. Indianapolis: Bobbs-Merrill, 1966.

Fletcher, Tenshin, and Scott David. *Way of Zen.* New York: St. Martin's, 2001.

Gilhus, Ingvild. "Carnival in Religion: The Feast of Fools in France." *Numen* 37 (1990): 24-52.

Goethe. *Faust.* Trans. Charles E. Passage. Indianapolis: Bobbs-Merrill, 1965.

Gooding-Williams, Robert. *Zarathustra's Dionysian Modernism.* Stanford: Stanford University Press, 2001.

Grimm, Jacob, and Wilhelm Grimm. *Deutsches Wörterbuch.* Munich: Deutsches Taschenbuch Verlag, 1984.

Handelman, Don, and David Shulman. *God Inside Out: Siva's Game of Dice.* Oxford: Oxford University Press, 1997.

Hartshorne, Charles. *Insights and Oversights of Great Thinkers: An Evaluation of Western Philosophy.* Albany: SUNY Press, 1983.

Heidegger, Martin. *Nietsche.* 4 vols. Ed. and trans. David Krell et al. San Francisco: HarperCollins, 1979-1982.

———. "Who Is Nietzsche's Zarathustra?" Trans. Bernd Magnus. In David Allison, ed., *The New Nietzsche*, 64-79. New York: Dell, 1977.

Herodotus. *The Persian Wars.* Trans. George Rawlinson. New York: Modern Library, 1947.

Higgins, Kathleen. *Nietzsche's* Zarathustra. Philadelphia: Temple University Press, 1987.

Hollingdale, R. J. *Nietzsche.* Baton Rouge: Louisiana State University Press, 1965.

Hollinrake, Roger. *Nietzsche, Wagner, and the Philosophy of Pessimism.* London: Allen and Unwin, 1982.

Houser, Caroline. *Dionysos and His Circle.* Cambridge, MA: Harvard University Hogg Art Museum, 1979.

Hoyle, Fred. *The Intelligent Universe.* London: Michael Joseph, 1983.

Jacobsen, Thorkild. *The Treasures of Darkness: A History of Mesopotamian Religion.* New Haven, CT: Yale University Press, 1976.

Jung, Carl. *Nietzsche's* Zarathustra: *Notes of the Seminar Given in 1934-1939.* Ed. James L. Jarrett. 2 vols. Princeton, NJ: Princeton University Press, 1988.

Kant, Immanuel. *Critique of Practical Reason.* Trans. Mary Gregor. Cambridge: Cambridge University Press, 1997.

———. *Critique of Pure Reason.* Trans. Werner Pluhar. Indianapolis: Hackett, 1996.

———. *Groundwork of the Metaphysics of Morals.* Trans. Mary Gregor. Cambridge: Cambridge University Press, 1997.

Kapleau, Philip. *The Three Pillars of Zen: Teaching, Practice, and Enlightenment.* Boston: Beacon, 1967.

Kaufmann, Walter. *Nietzsche.* 4th ed. Princeton, NJ: Princeton University Press, 1974.

Kierkegaard, Søren. *The Sickness unto Death.* Trans. Alastair Hannay. London: Penguin Books, 1989.

Krell, David. *Postponements: Woman, Sensuality, and Death in Nietzsche.* Bloomington, IN: Indiana University Press, 1986.

Lampert, Laurence. *Nietzsche's Teaching: An Interpretation of* Thus Spoke Zarathustra. New Haven, CT: Yale University Press, 1986.

Lea, F. A. *The Tragic Philosopher: A Study of Friedrich Nietzsche.* London: Methuen, 1957.

Leiter, Brian. "The Paradox of Fatalism and Self-Creation in Nietzsche." In John Richardson and Brian Leiter, eds., *Nietzsche,* 281-321. Oxford: Oxford University Press, 2001.

Lesses, Glenn. "Austere Friends: The Stoics and Friendship." *Apeiron* 26 (1993): 57-75.

Lippitt, John, and Jim Urpeth, eds., *Nietzsche and the Divine.* Manchester: Clinamen Press, 2000.

Loeb, Paul S. "The Conclusion of Nietzsche's *Zarathustra.*" *International Studies in Philosophy* 32/3 (2000): 137-52.

———. "The Dwarf, the Dragon, and the Ring of Eternal Recurrence: A Wagnerian Key to the Riddle of Nietzsche's *Zarathustra.*" *Nietzsche-Studien* 31 (2002): 91-113.

Long, A. A. *Hellenistic Philosophy: Stoics, Epicureans, Sceptics.* London: Duckworth, 1974.

Magnus, Bernd. *Nietzsche's Existential Imperative.* Bloomington, IN: Indiana University Press, 1978.

———, Stanley Stewart, and Jean-Pierre Mileur. *Nietzsche's Case: Philosophy as/and Literature.* New York: Routledge, 1993.

Miller, C. A. "Nietzsche's 'Daughters of the Desert': A Reconsideration." *Nietzsche-Studien* 2 (1973): 157-95.

Mistry, Freny. *Nietzsche and Buddhism: Prolegomenon to a Comprehensive Study.* Berlin: Walter de Gruyter, 1981.

Mitsis, Phillip. *Epicurus' Ethical Theory: The Pleasures of Invulnerability.* Ithaca, NY: Cornell University Press, 1988.

Morrison, Robert. *Nietzsche and Buddhism: A Study in Nihilism and Ironic Affinities.* Oxford: Oxford University Press, 1997.

Naumann, Gustav. *Zarathustra-Commentar,* 4 vols. Leipzig: Heffel Verlag, 1899-1901.

Nehamas, Alexander. "For Whom the Sun Shines: A Reading of *Also sprach Zarathustra.*" In Volker Gerhard, ed., *Friedrich Nietzsche: Also sprach Zarathustra*, 165-89. Berlin: Akademie Verlag, 2000.

———. *Nietzsche: Life as Literature.* Cambridge, MA: Harvard University Press, 1985.

Nishitani, Keiji. *The Self-Overcoming of Nihilism.* Trans. Graham Parkes and Setsuko Aihara. Albany: SUNY Press, 1990.

Parkes, Graham. "Nature and the Human 'Redivinized': Mahayana Buddhist Themes in *Thus Spoke Zarathustra.*" In John Lippitt and Jim Urpeth, eds., *Nietzsche and the Divine*, 181-99. Manchester: Clinamen Press, 2000.

———, ed. *Nietzsche and Asian Thought.* Chicago: University of Chicago Press, 1991.

———. "Nietzsche and Nishitani." *International Studies in Philosophy* 25 (1993): 51-60.

Paterson, R. W. K. *Nihilistic Egoist: Max Stirner.* Oxford: Oxford University Press, 1971.

Pfeffer, Rose. *Nietzsche: Disciple of Dionysus.* Lewisburg, PA: Bucknell University Press, 1972.

Pippin, Robert. "Irony and Affirmation in Nietzsche's *Thus Spoke Zarathustra.*" In Michael Gillespie and Tracy Strong, eds., *Nietzsche's New Seas*, 45-71. Chicago: University of Chicago Press, 1988.

———. *Modernism as a Philosophical Problem.* Oxford: Blackwell, 1991.

Platt, Michael. "What Does Zarathustra Whisper in Life's Ear?" *Nietzsche-Studien* 17 (1988): 179-94.

Plotinus. *The Enneads.* Trans. Stephen MacKenna. New York: Pantheon Books, 1969.

Plutarch. *Moralia.* Vol. 1. Trans. Frank Babbit. New York: G. P. Putnam's Sons, 1927.

Pseudo Dionysius the Areopagite. *The Divine Names and Mystical Theology.* Trans. John Jones. Milwaukee: Marquette University Press, 1980.

Richardson, John. *Nietzsche's System*. Oxford: Oxford University Press, 1996.

Roberts, Tyler. "Ecstatic Philosophy." In John Lippitt and Jim Urpeth, eds., *Nietzsche and the Divine*, 200-225. Manchester: Clinamen Press, 2000.

Rorty, Richard. *Contingency, Irony, and Solidarity*. Cambridge: Cambridge University Press, 1989.

Rosen, Stanley. *The Mask of Enlightenment: Nietzsche's Zarathustra*. Cambridge: Cambridge University Press, 1995.

Schacht, Richard. *Making Sense of Nietzsche: Reflections Timely and Untimely*. Urbana, IL: University of Illinois Press, 1995.

———. *Nietzsche*. London: Routledge, 1983.

———."Zarathustra/*Zarathustra* as Educator." In Peter Sedgwick, ed., *Nietzsche: A Critical Reader,* 222-49. Oxford: Blackwell, 1995.

Scheier, Claus-Artur. *Nietzsches Labyrinth: Das Ursprüngliche Denken und die Seele*. Freiburg: Alber, 1985.

Schelling, Friedrich. *Ideas for a Philosophy of Nature*. Trans. Errol Harris and Peter Heath. Cambridge: Cambridge University Press, 1988.

Schopenhauer, Arthur. *The World as Will and Representation*. Trans. E. F. J. Payne. 2 vols. New York: Dover, 1969.

Shapiro, Gary. *Nietzschean Narratives*. Bloomington, IN: Indiana University Press, 1989.

Smith, David. *Dance of Siva: Religion, Art and Poetry in South India*. Cambridge: Cambridge University Press, 1996.

Solomon, Robert. *Living with Nietzsche*. Oxford: Oxford University Press, 2003.

Sophocles. *Oedipus Tyrannus*. Trans. Peter Meineck and Paul Woodruff. Indianapolis: Hackett Publishing, 2000.

Spinoza. *Ethics*. Ed. James Gutmann. New York: Hafner, 1955.

Stambaugh, Joan. *The Other Nietzsche*. Albany: SUNY Press, 1994.

———. *Nietzsche's Thought of Eternal Return*. Baltimore: Johns Hopkins University Press, 1972.

Staten, Henry. *Nietzsche's Voice*. Ithaca, NY: Cornell University Press, 1990.

Stirner, Max. *The Ego and Its Own.* Ed. David Leopold. Cambridge: Cambridge University Press, 1995.

Strauss, David. *The Life of Jesus, Critically Examined.* Trans. George Eliot. Philadelphia: Fortress Press, 1973.

———. *The Old Faith and the New.* Trans. Mathilde Blind. Amherst, NY: Prometheus Books, 1997.

Strong, Tracy. *Friedrich Nietzsche and the Politics of Transfiguration.* Berke-ley: University of California Press, 1975.

Tanner, Michael. *Wagner.* London: HarperCollins, 1996.

Walsh, P. G. *The Roman Novel.* Cambridge: Cambridge University Press, 1970.

Weber, Max. *The Protestant Ethic and the Spirit of Capitalism and Other Writings.* Trans. Peter Baehr and Gordon Wells. New York: Penguin Books, 2002.

White, Alan. *Within Nietzsche's Labyrinth.* New York: Routledge, 1990.

Whitlock, Greg. *Returning to Sils-Maria: A Commentary to Nietzsche's Also sprach Zarathustra.* New York: Peter Lang, 1990.

Young, Julian. *Nietzsche's Philosophy of Art.* Cambridge: Cambridge University Press, 1992.

Yovel, Yirmiyahu. "Nietzsche and Spinoza: *amor fati* and *amor dei.*" In Y. Yovel, ed., *Nietzsche as Affirmative Thinker,* 183-203. Dordrecht: Martinus Nijhoff, 1986.

Zimmer, Heinrich. *Myths and Symbols in Indian Art and Civilization.* New York, Pantheon Books, 1946.

Index

About the Author

T. K. Seung was born in North Korea in 1930. That was long before the tragic division of Korea at the end of World War II, which led to the internecine war between two Koreas in 1950. Three years before this war, the author had escaped to South Korea and studied in Seoul High School and Yonsei University in Seoul. When the Korean War broke out, he joined the South Korean Army and served three years in the combat zone. After the war, he came to Yale University and studied philosophy and law. He taught at Yale, Fordham University, and Scripps College. He is currently the Jesse H. Jones Regents Professor in Liberal Arts, Professor of Philosophy, Professor of East Asian Studies, Professor of Government, and Professor of Law at the University of Texas at Austin.

The author of this book has taught and written in many different fields. His writings include *The Fragile Leaves of the Sibyl: Dante's Master Plan* (1962), *Kant's Transcendental Logic* (1969), *Cultural Thematics: The Formation of the Faustian Ethos* (1976), *Structuralism and Hermeneutics* (1982), *Semiotics and Thematics* (1982), *Intuition and Construction: The Foundation of Normative Theory* (1993), *Kant's Platonic Revolution in Moral and Political Philosophy* (1994), and *Plato Rediscovered: Human Value and Social Order* (1996).

The author takes a complex interdisciplinary approach in unraveling Nietzsche's most baffling work by engaging philosophy, psychology, religious studies, literary analysis, and cultural history. As a sequel to this volume, he is now writing *Nietzsche, Wagner, and Goethe: Their Spinozan Epics of Love and Power*. In this book, he proposes the thesis that Goethe's *Faust* started a new epic tradition under the inspiration of Spinoza's pantheistic naturalism and that this new tradition was further developed in Wagner's *Ring* cycle and Nietzsche's *Zarathustra*. These Spinozan epics are meant to succeed the Christian epics and to explore the destiny of humanity as the children of Mother Nature.